International Arbitration: Three Salient Problems

Second Edition

The vitality or, alternatively, vitiation of the international arbitral process remains a pressing subject. The explosion of inter-State, investor-State, and international commercial arbitration in recent years magnifies the importance of the subject.

This second edition combines the historical analysis of the first edition with a survey of the continued salience and contemporary developments for each of the three problems identified: (i) the severability of the arbitration agreement; (ii) denial of justice (and now other possible breaches of international law) by governmental negation of arbitration; and (iii) the authority of truncated international arbitral tribunals. The international arbitral process continues to be fortified against unilateral attempts to derail it and, to that end, this book will be a valuable guide for practitioners and scholars alike.

STEPHEN M. SCHWEBEL has been a student and practitioner of international arbitration since 1954 when he was a member of Aramco's legal team in the Onassis Arbitration. He served as a judge of the International Court of Justice 1981–2000 and as Court president 1997–2000.

LUKE SOBOTA is a founding partner of Three Crowns, a firm dedicated to international arbitration. He has extensive experience in investor-State, commercial, and inter-State arbitrations. He is co-author of the monograph *General Principles of Law and International Due Process* and is a lecturer on law at Harvard Law School.

RYAN MANTON is an associate at Three Crowns. He has appeared as counsel before a range of international tribunals in inter-State, investor-State, and international commercial arbitrations and other disputes. He previously taught public international law at Oxford, from where he also graduated with a DPhil in Law.

Recent Books in the Hersch Lauterpacht Memorial Lecture Series

International Arbitration
Three Salient Problems
Second Edition

STEPHEN M. SCHWEBEL
former President, International Court of Justice

LUKE SOBOTA
Three Crowns LLP, Washington, DC

RYAN MANTON
Three Crowns LLP, Paris

CAMBRIDGE
UNIVERSITY PRESS

CAMBRIDGE
UNIVERSITY PRESS

University Printing House, Cambridge CB2 8BS, United Kingdom

One Liberty Plaza, 20th Floor, New York, NY 10006, USA

477 Williamstown Road, Port Melbourne, VIC 3207, Australia

314–321, 3rd Floor, Plot 3, Splendor Forum, Jasola District Centre, New Delhi – 110025, India

79 Anson Road, #06–04/06, Singapore 079906

Cambridge University Press is part of the University of Cambridge.

It furthers the University's mission by disseminating knowledge in the pursuit of education, learning, and research at the highest international levels of excellence.

www.cambridge.org
Information on this title: www.cambridge.org/9780521768023
DOI: 10.1017/9781139015691

© Cambridge University Press 1987
© Stephen M. Schwebel, Luke Sobota, and Ryan Manton 2020

First published 1987
Second edition 2020

Printed in the United Kingdom by TJ International Ltd, Padstow Cornwall

A catalogue record for this publication is available from the British Library.

Library of Congress Cataloging-in-Publication Data
Names: Schwebel, Stephen M. (Stephen Myron), 1929- author. | Sobota, Luke A., author. | Manton, Ryan, 1987- author.
Title: International arbitration : three salient problems / Stephen M. Schwebel, Luke Sobota, Ryan Manton.
Description: Second edition. | New York : Cambridge University Press, 2019. | Series: Hersch lauterpacht memorial lectures | Includes bibliographical references and index.
Identifiers: LCCN 2019038345 (print) | LCCN 2019038346 (ebook) | ISBN 9780521768023 (hardback) | ISBN 9781139015691 (epub)
Subjects: LCSH: International commercial arbitration. | Conflict of laws–Arbitration and award. | Arbitration (International law)
Classification: LCC K2400 .S39 2019 (print) | LCC K2400 (ebook) | DDC 347/.09–dc23
LC record available at https://lccn.loc.gov/2019038345
LC ebook record available at https://lccn.loc.gov/2019038346

ISBN 978-0-521-76802-3 Hardback

Contents

Contents

Preface to the Second Edition

Some thirty years have passed since I was privileged to give the first in the continuing series of Hersch Lauterpacht Lectures at Cambridge University. The topics of my lectures were subsequently published in "International Arbitration: Three Salient Problems," which in 1988 was awarded by the American Society of International Law a Certificate of Merit as "a work of great distinction." As I wrote in the preface to the first edition:

Judge Lauterpacht devoted his professional life to international legal scholarship, and to invigorating the body of international law through that scholarship and his many other activities, among them, as a teacher of and adviser on international law, a member of the International Law Commission of the United Nations, and a Judge of the International Court of Justice. His attainments are unsurpassed by any international lawyer of this century. There could be no more suitable memorial to Lauterpacht than lectures on diverse problems of international law, delivered at the University where he taught and wrote with unmatched distinction and to which he was so attached.

The common thread that was explored in the first edition – the vitality or, alternatively, vitiation of the international arbitral process – is no less pressing a subject today than it was three decades ago. Much progress has been made in enhancing the vitality of arbitration, to which the explosion of inter-State, investor-State, and international commercial arbitration bears witness. Yet three issues identified in 1987 continue to persist.

The severability of the arbitration agreement, a cornerstone principle of international arbitration that is considered in the first chapter of this book, is more firmly established now than it was three decades ago. Yet respondents still from time to time call that principle into question by attempting to vitiate the arbitral process through invocation of a (supposed) defect in the underlying contract or treaty, while difficult issues also remain concerning the precise scope and limits of the principle.

These issues underscore the merit in analyzing and revisiting what remains a jurisprudentially subtle and practically important question.

One of the most striking features of arbitral practice over the past three decades has been how old problems have continued to arise in new guises. This is particularly apparent with the problem of States' various attempts to negate arbitration, and whether denial of justice may be invoked to confront that practice. This issue is considered in the second chapter of this book. The practice since the time of the first edition of this book underscores that governmental evasion and negation of arbitration can take a number of forms. Arbitral tribunals, and in particular those constituted under bilateral investment treaties, have responded to new attempts at governmental negation of arbitration. The question today is not only whether a State's refusal to arbitrate may constitute a denial of justice, but whether a State's attempt to negate arbitration – by, for example, improperly setting aside an international award in its domestic courts – may constitute a compensable expropriation of property rights, a breach of fair and equitable treatment, or another breach of an investment treaty.

The final question addressed in the third chapter is one that continues to arise in practice and to engender debate: the authority of a truncated tribunal to proceed to issue a final award. The issue comes to the fore when a party-appointed arbitrator resigns or otherwise refuses to participate in panel deliberations, whether unilaterally or at the behest of his or her appointing party. The jurisprudence on this topic has developed significantly with the trend toward judicial (rather than diplomatic) arbitration, in large measure as a result of a series of decisions by the Iran-United States Claims Tribunal and the confrontation of this problem in arbitral rules. There is a discernible preference among tribunals, institutions, and scholars to replace the obstructionist arbitrator and obviate the need for a truncated tribunal. Where this is not in the circumstances feasible, the authority of the remaining two members to proceed to a final determination is widely accepted. Either way, the trend has been to continue to fortify international arbitration against unilateral attempts to derail the proceedings.

Luke Sobota and Ryan Manton have researched and written this second edition. Their work is searching, perceptive, and meticulous. I am grateful to them for their efforts to critically assess the continued salience of the topics I first addressed back in 1987. My appreciation further extends to Devashish Krishan and Julia Sherman for their important contributions to this second edition. I would also like to thank Cambridge University Press for its publication of the second edition, and for its patience and understanding in indulging its completion.

Stephen M. Schwebel
South Woodstock, Vermont, 2019

Cases

Table of Cases

Table of Cases

I

The Severability of the Arbitration Agreement

A. The Question

The question that the first edition asked was this: where a contract or a treaty provides for arbitration of disputes that arise thereunder, does the invalidity, termination, nullification, or suspension of the contract or treaty vitiate the arbitral obligations of the parties? The answer to that question was that the trend of legal principle and practice was predominantly in one direction: an arbitration agreement is severable from the underlying agreement in which it is contained and therefore a defect in the underlying agreement does not necessarily vitiate the arbitration agreement itself. It was even suggested then that this classic question of the arbitral process may have been settled. The trend of legal principle and practice since then has only confirmed that position, as this update will seek to bear out.

Yet the question remains a salient one. It remains a salient question in theory because the severability of the arbitration agreement is a cornerstone of an effective arbitral process, yet its conceptual basis is not always well understood. It remains a salient question in practice because recalcitrant respondents continue to attempt to frustrate the arbitral process by invoking a (supposed) defect in the underlying agreement. A sound understanding of the conceptual basis of the principle of severability thus contributes significantly to appreciating its precise scope and limits. These issues underscore the merit in analyzing and revisiting what remains both a jurisprudentially nuanced and practically important question.

The question will be considered in public international law and in international commercial arbitration. International commercial arbitration cannot be discussed without reference to national arbitration law, and thus there will be some reference to national law, particularly the law of countries in which international commercial arbitration is frequently held. Wherever the question of severability arises, however, it will be seen that the trend has been toward the establishment of a principle of general application.

B. The Theory

It may be argued that if an agreement contains an obligation to arbitrate disputes arising under it, but the agreement is invalid or no longer in force, the obligation to arbitrate disappears with the agreement of which it is a part. If the agreement was never entered into at all, its arbitration clause never came into force. If the agreement was not validly entered into, then, prima facie, it is invalid as a whole, as must be all of its parts, including its arbitration clause. And if the agreement has been nullified or terminated – or, arguably, suspended – presumably it follows that the obligation to arbitrate disputes arising under the agreement is nullified, terminated, or suspended. Now if, in these various contingencies, there is no initial or sustained obligation to arbitrate under an agreement that either never came into force or is no longer in force, then the arbitral tribunal that may be or is constituted pursuant to the arbitration clause of the void or voided agreement has no standing to do anything; it cannot pass upon the validity of the agreement or upon the effect of the tribunal's establishment or upon its jurisdiction or upon the merits of the case because it cannot have a legal status that derives from a vacuum. "Nothing?" said King Lear: "Nothing will come of nothing."[1]

---

[1] William Shakespeare, *King Lear*, Act 1, Scene 1, line 92. Cf., "Nil posse creari de nilo." Lucretius, *De Rerum Natura*, line 155. Lord Macmillan in *Heyman* v. *Darwins Ltd.*, [1942] AC 356, 371, held: "If there has never been a contract at all, there has never been as part of it an agreement to arbitrate. The greater includes the less." See also the dissenting opinion of Sir Alastair Blair-Kerr in *Sojuznefteexport (SNE)* v. *Joc Oil Ltd.*, Court of Appeal of Bermuda, July 7, 1989, in XV *Yearbook Commercial Arbitration* (1990), pp. 431, 434: "If the November 1976 contract was 'non-existent' – that is to say it never came into existence – as it seems to me, it is quite ridiculous to suggest that the arbitration clause which formed part of that 'non-existent' contract would nevertheless, somehow, be deemed to have come into existence."

In logic, the foregoing line of argument is plausible. But in law it has been overcome by presumptions arising from principle and practice. If it is inherent in the arbitral (and judicial) process that a tribunal is the judge of its own jurisdiction, that it has *compétence de la compétence*,[2] it is no less inherent in that process that an arbitral tribunal shall have the competence to pass upon disputes arising out of the underlying agreement in which the arbitration agreement is contained, even where those disputes engage the initial or continuing validity of that underlying agreement. This essential doctrine of modern arbitration is called that of the severability, separability, or autonomy of the arbitration agreement. (In this discussion, in which these terms are employed interchangeably, "severability" will mainly be used.) The rationale of the doctrine of the severability of the arbitration agreement has four foundations. All of these foundations are emanations of the presumed will of the parties to achieve an effective arbitral process.

First, when two parties enter into a contract or a treaty providing for arbitration of disputes arising thereunder, and do so as they typically do in comprehensive terms – "any dispute arising out of or relating to this agreement" – they intend to require arbitration of *any* dispute not otherwise settled, including disputes over the validity of the contract or treaty. Had the parties, when concluding the agreement, been asked: "Do you mean, in providing that 'any dispute arising out of or relating to this agreement' shall be

---

[2] "Paragraph 6 of Article 36 [of the Statute of the International Court of Justice] merely adopted, in respect of the Court, a rule consistently accepted by general international law in the matter of international arbitration. Since the *Alabama* case, it has been generally recognized, following earlier precedents, that, in the absence of any agreement to the contrary, an international tribunal has the right to decide as to its own jurisdiction and has the power to interpret for this purpose the instruments which govern that jurisdiction. This principle was expressly recognized in ... the Hague Conventions ... The Rapporteur of the Convention of 1899 had emphasized the necessity of this principle, presented by him as being 'of the very essence of the arbitral function and one of the inherent requirements for the exercise of this function.' This principle has been frequently applied and at times expressly stated." *Nottebohm Case (Liechtenstein v. Guatemala) (Preliminary Objections), Judgment of 18 November 1953, I.C.J. Reports 1953*, p. 119. See also James Crawford, "Continuity and Discontinuity in International Dispute Settlement," 1 *Journal of International Dispute Settlement* (2010), pp. 3, 15–20 and, in the context of international commercial arbitration, William Park, "The Arbitrator's Power to Determine Jurisdiction," 13 *ICCA Congress Series* 55 (2006); and Jan Paulsson, *The Idea of Arbitration* (2013), pp. 54–58.

submitted to arbitration, to exclude disputes over the validity of the agreement?," surely they would have replied that they did not mean to exclude such disputes.[3] The will of the parties, actual or presumed, should be given effect.

Second, if one party could deny arbitration to the other party by the allegation that the agreement lacked initial or continuing validity, and if by such an allegation it could deprive an arbitral tribunal of the competence to rule upon that allegation, upon its constitution and jurisdiction and upon the merits of the dispute, then it would always be open to a party to an agreement containing an arbitration clause to vitiate its arbitral obligation by the simple expedient of declaring the agreement void.

In the ordinary run of national commercial intercourse, to accord each party the facility of evading its arbitral obligation in this fashion would be serious enough, for the cure would presumably require recourse to a national court, which would determine the validity or invalidity of the agreement between the parties and, if it upheld it, remit the parties to obligatory arbitration. That of itself would prejudice a key object of the agreement's provision for arbitration: namely, speed and simplicity of settlement of disputes, without the time-consuming trouble and expense of recourse to the courts. And it would involve the courts in the substantive determination of an otherwise arbitrable question in a fashion that they generally and rightly eschew. But in the less ordinary run of inter-State transactions, the result could be far more serious still: destruction of the arbitral remedy.[4] For normally there is no international

---

[3] See, in support of this construction of the intentions of the parties to an arbitration agreement, Pieter Sanders, "L'autonomie de la clause compromissoire," in ICC, *Hommage à Frederic Eisemann, Liber Amicorum* (1978), p. 33. See further Georges R. Delaume, *Transnational Contracts: Applicable Law and Settlement of Disputes* (1985), XIII, Section 13.08, pp. 59–61. The presumed intention of rational commercial actors to resolve all their disputes before one tribunal was central to the House of Lords' unanimous decision upholding the doctrine of severability in *Fiona Trust & Holding Corporation* v. *Privalov* [2007] 4 All ER 951. As for previous case law in which courts had drawn distinctions based on the scope of the language used in the arbitration agreements (e.g., a distinction between "arising under the agreement" and the apparently broader "in relation to the agreement"), Lord Hoffmann was dismissive: "the distinctions which they make reflect no credit upon English commercial law" (para. 12).

[4] Jan Paulsson, "International Arbitration Is Not Arbitration," 2 *Stockholm Arbitration Review* (2008), pp. 1, 2: "In the transnational environment, international arbitration is the only game. It is a de facto monopoly."

court with compulsory jurisdiction to determine and enforce the validity of the international agreement. And even in the sphere of international commercial contracts, which are legion, the procedure of requiring a party to have recourse to a national court to enforce the arbitral remedy against the other party would in many cases be, at best, prejudicial to the purposes of the arbitral process.[5] In other cases, in which the agreement runs not between two persons or companies of different nationality but between a foreign contractor and a government, not only would the contractor be loath to seek enforcement of his arbitral remedy in national courts; national courts may lack the de jure or de facto authority to require the executive branch to arbitrate contrary to its will, its executive order, or national legislation.

Thus the intention of the parties and the requirements of effective arbitration combine to give rise to the concept of severability. That concept is strengthened by – indeed, it is widely said, is essentially composed of – a third element as well. In reality, or, if not in reality, then in the contemplation of the law and as a matter of legal presumption, the parties to an agreement containing an arbitration clause conclude not one agreement but two: first, the substantive or principal agreement that provides for a certain course of action; second, an additional, separable agreement that provides for arbitration of disputes arising out of the principal agreement. Even if it be argued, or even if it be authoritatively decided, that the principal agreement is invalid, or voided, nullified, terminated, or suspended, nevertheless the arbitral agreement is separable and separated, and, so separated, survives to furnish a viable basis for the arbitral tribunal to rule upon such arguments or arrive at those or other determinations. Historically, in some legal systems, provision for arbitration of disputes arising under a contract was actually contained in (and had to be contained in) a separate piece of paper in order to meet the legal necessity of a clearly identifiable agreement to refer a dispute to arbitration and thereby oust the jurisdiction of the courts. Its severability and

---

[5] *Fiona Trust & Holding Corporation* v. *Privalov* [2007] 4 All ER 951, para. 6: "Particularly in the case of international contracts, [the parties] want a quick and efficient adjudication and do not want to take the risks of delay and, in too many cases, partiality, in proceedings before a national jurisdiction" (Lord Hoffmann).

survival accordingly were the more plausible. Indeed, even if the arbitration agreement were found not in a separate piece of paper but as a clause of a principal agreement, nevertheless the very concept and phrase "arbitration agreement" itself imports the existence of a separate or at any rate separable agreement, which is or can be divorced from the body of the principal agreement if needs be. Thus when the parties to an agreement containing an arbitration clause enter into that agreement, they conclude not one but two agreements, the arbitral one of which survives any initial or acquired invalidity of the principal agreement.

In the case of an arbitral tribunal whose procedure is governed by the national law of the place of arbitration, national courts to which appeal is made may uphold or exceptionally strike down the arbitration award that the arbitral tribunal has given in the exercise of its separable capacity.[6] But the courts of most countries will not review the holdings of the arbitrator on the substance of the case and accordingly will not challenge his or her holding with respect to the validity of the principal agreement that contains the arbitral clause.[7]

---

[6] In the case of an international arbitral tribunal whose proceedings are subject only to public international law, it is rare that a national court, including that of the territory in which the arbitral award is rendered, has the authority to annul the arbitral award. As for the International Court of Justice, subject to the characteristic qualifications upon its compulsory jurisdiction, the States concerned can agree to submit the validity of an arbitral award to its judgment, and did so by special agreement in the *Case concerning the Arbitral Award made by the King of Spain on 23 December 1906 (Honduras v. Nicaragua)* and by virtue of unilateral declarations accepting the Court's jurisdiction in *Arbitral Award of 31 July 1989 (Guinea-Bissau v. Senegal), Judgment of 12 November 1991, I.C.J. Reports 1991*, pp. 53, 197. (The former case is not unrelated to the topic of this chapter, for one of the contentions of Nicaragua was that the award was invalid because the treaty that was the basis for appointment of the King of Spain as arbitrator had lapsed before he agreed to act as arbitrator.) See also *Case concerning the Arbitral Award made by the King of Spain on 23 December 1906, Pleadings*, vol. I, pp. 175–180, 521–525, 755–764. There were also cases before the Permanent Court of International Justice and the Permanent Court of Arbitration concerning the review of the validity of international arbitral awards. Cf., the *Orinoco Steamship Company* (1910), James Brown Scott, *The Hague Court Reports* (1916), p. 226.

[7] Ten awards of the Iran-United States Claims Tribunal were appealed by Iran to Dutch courts, on the theory that they have authority over the proceedings of that Tribunal. See David P. Stewart, "The Iran-United States Claims Tribunal: A Review of Developments 1983–1984," *Law and Policy in International Business* (1984), pp. 750–752. See also William T. Lake and Jane Tucker Dana, "Judicial Review of Awards of the Iran-United States Claims Tribunal: Are the Tribunal's Awards Dutch?," ibid., p. 755, and J. C. Schultsz and S. L. Buruma, *Legislation in*

That most distinguished authority on international commercial arbitration, Professor Pieter Sanders, pointed out that this is still another – that is, a fourth – consideration that militates in favor of the rule of the severability of the arbitral clause because, if severability were not the rule, the courts would, contrary to the norm, be drawn into passing upon the substance of the dispute submitted to arbitration.[8]

It is not suggested that the four foregoing theoretical foundations of the doctrine of severability are unassailable. As experienced and acute an observer of the international arbitral process, public and private, as Dr. J. Gillis Wetter, had his doubts. He suggested that the notion of "arbitration agreement" implies "an assumption to the effect that each time when two parties enter into any sort of business contract that contains an arbitration clause they conclude not one but two contracts. In my experience such a conception is almost always very far from their minds as well as from those of their legal advisers." Yet, he continued, this same perception has prompted the creation of the doctrine of severability of the arbitration clause from the rest of the contract, a doctrine that he characterizes as "one of the main elements of what we conceive of as a modern and liberal law of arbitration, as opposed to an archaic or restrictive system." In his view, the doctrine "contains a large

---

the Netherlands and International Arbitration (1986), pp. 32–34. The Netherlands government responsively introduced legislation, which, if enacted, would restrict, but nevertheless within defined limits sustain, the jurisdiction of Dutch courts on appeal from awards of the Tribunal. Iran protested that that legislation was prejudicial to Iranian interests. Confronted with the fact that the draft legislation had been stimulated by its own decision to file actions in Dutch courts to set aside ten awards of the Tribunal, Iran withdrew all its suits in 1984. The proposed legislation has not been enacted.

[8] Sanders, *supra* note 3, pp. 33–34. See also Paulsson, *supra* note 2, p. 60: "A naked assertion of invalidity could easily frustrate the arbitration. More fundamentally, a vital part of the merits of the parties' dispute – the validity of their contract – would not be decided in their chosen forum." A fifth reason in support of the severability of the arbitration agreement is sometimes raised: one law governs the validity of the arbitral clause, whereas the law applicable to the substance of the dispute may be another law. It is believed that, on analysis, the fact that the law applicable to the arbitral clause is not necessarily the same as the law applicable to the substance of the dispute is not a reason for the severability of the arbitration agreement but rather a result of it. It is a consequence of the autonomy of the arbitral clause rather than a cause of that autonomy. See, in support of this reasoning, Sanders, *supra* note 3, p. 34, and Albert Jan van den Berg, *The New York Arbitration Convention of 1958* (1981), p. 146 (and note 20, *infra*); Gary B. Born, *International Commercial Arbitration* (2nd edition, 2014), pp. 464–466, 472 ff.

element of legal fiction" and despite it, "[i]t is – it still is – very difficult to explain how an arbitral tribunal whose jurisdiction derives from an instrument alleged to be invalid on that ground can be the sole judge of its own competence in such a situation. While most developed jurisdictions have come to accept the thesis as an axiom, because failing it the arbitral process would be ineffective, the doctrine militates against strict reason, assuming the existence of an alternative remedy."[9] (Dr. Wetter added that such an alternative remedy does not normally exist in contracts between States and aliens, where there is not an acceptable alternative forum for resolving disputes arising out of claims based on unilateral abrogation, repudiation, or breach.) Some commentators continue to share Dr. Wetter's sentiment that the principle of severability rests more on a necessary fiction than on sound legal principle.[10]

While Dr. Wetter's points are well taken, it is nevertheless believed that the doctrine of the severability of the arbitration agreement may be sustained on theoretical grounds and that, contrary to the suggestions of Dr. Wetter and others, the doctrine of severability is neither illogical nor fictional. It is no less logical than the doctrine that an arbitral or judicial tribunal is the judge of its own competence. One could argue that, as a matter of "strict reason," a tribunal whose incompetence is alleged cannot be the judge of its competence, and that for a tribunal that may lack the competence to judge a case to judge whether it is competent to judge a case is no less

---

[9] J. Gillis Wetter, "Salient Features of Swedish Arbitration Clauses," Address to the International Commercial Arbitration Symposium, Stockholm, March 5, 1982, published in *Yearbook of the Arbitration Institute of the Stockholm Chamber of Commerce 1983*, pp. 33, 35. For another able analysis of the rationale of severability at the same Symposium, see Kaj Hobér, "The Doctrine of Separability under Swedish Arbitration Law (Including Comments on the Position of American and Soviet Law)," published in *Svensk Junsttidning* 1983, pp. 257–271. See also Stockholm Chamber of Commerce, *Arbitration in Sweden* (1984), second revised edition, pp. 24–29. Pierre Lalive, like Wetter, supports severability but at the same time recognizes that the notion of the independence of the arbitral clause may not correspond with the facts or the true intention of the parties. P. A. Lalive, "Problèmes Relatifs a l'Arbitrage International Commercial," 120 *Recueil des Cours* (1967), vol. I.

[10] Adam Samuel, "Book Review – International Arbitration: Three Salient Problems," 5 *Journal of International Arbitration* (1988), pp. 119, 120. See also Mark McNeill and Ben Juratowitch, "The Doctrine of Separability and Consent to Arbtirate," 24 *Arbitration International* (2008), pp. 475, 477, describing that "[w]hatever that doctrine may lack in terms of logic, it recoups in practical desirability."

(indeed, is more) a "bootstrapping" operation than it is for a tribunal to treat its arbitral competence as severable from that of the principal agreement that contains a clause providing for arbitration. But in theory and practice, in law and in fact, the doctrine of *compétence de la compétence* is accepted as axiomatic in international law and as dominant in domestic law because it reflects the will of the parties to achieve an effective arbitral process.

Furthermore, while Dr. Wetter is doubtless right in suggesting that the parties to a contract do not mean to conclude two separate agreements, it does not follow that, if confronted with the question of whether the arbitration clause covers disputes over validity of the principal agreement, they would answer that question negatively. On the contrary, as Lord Hoffmann has expounded in a House of Lords decision unanimously upholding the doctrine of severability, "[i]f, as appears to be generally accepted, there is no rational basis upon which businessmen would be likely to wish to have questions of the validity or enforceability of the contract decided by one tribunal and questions about its performance decided by another, one would need to find very clear language before deciding that they must have had such an intention."[11] In any event, if the life of the law is not logic but experience, then experience has established and entrenched the doctrine of severability. It is now to this body of experience, of practice, that we turn.

Before doing so, however, two caveats to our general conclusion should be entered. It is in respect of these two caveats that the most relevant and interesting issues concerning severability now arise, and the issues arising out of these caveats are explored throughout this chapter.

First, where the question is not whether the principal agreement was or is valid, but whether it was actually concluded, there may be room to challenge the authority of the arbitral tribunal to determine that question on the basis that the parties never agreed to anything, including arbitration; while the tribunal may pass upon it (in the exercise of its *compétence de la compétence*), its conclusion may be subject to judicial control.[12] There is a distinction between the nullity of a contract – *ab initio* or, certainly, *ex post facto* – and its

---

[11] *Fiona Trust & Holding Corporation* v. *Privalov* [2007] 4 All ER 951, para. 7.
[12] See Sir Michael J. Mustill and Stewart G. Boyd, *The Law and Practice of Commercial Arbitration in England* (2nd edition, 1989), pp. 108–110 and, in particular, p. 109:

never having existed at all.[13] At the same time, even if the principal agreement were never entered into, this does not necessarily mean that there can be no arbitration agreement. The principle of severability also means that, independently of the principal agreement, parties may consent to an arbitration agreement.[14]

Second, where the question is not simply whether the principal agreement was or is valid, but whether the agreement to arbitrate as such was valid – whether, for example, it conformed to the then existing requirements for conclusion of a valid arbitration agreement under the law governing that agreement, or whether there is any other issue concerning the "direct impeachment of the arbitration agreement,"[15] – then, as above, while the arbitral tribunal is competent to pass upon that question (in the exercise of its *compétence de la compétence*), it is, as a rule, not competent to pass upon it with definitive effect.

The question in these cases becomes what amounts to a "direct impeachment of the arbitration agreement." An allegation of bribery, for instance, is unlikely to involve a direct impeachment of the arbitration agreement.[16] Attempts have sometimes been made at listing categories of vitiating circumstances that may necessarily bring down the arbitration agreement with the principal agreement, including where the principal agreement "is found to be void because of (i) *non est factum*, (ii) forgery, (iii) threat, (iv) mistake about the identity of the other party, or (v) signature by

"If the arbitration agreement is contained in article 17 of a contract composed of 20 articles, what kind of vitiating circumstance could it be which would cause articles 1–16 and 18–20 to be regarded as if the contract had never been signed, and yet leave article 17 to stand untouched among the ruins" (and compare, more recently, *Fiona Trust & Holding Corporation* v. *Privalov* [2007] 4 All ER 951, para. 18). See also Delaume, *supra* note 3, pp. 51–52 and footnotes thereto at p. 30; Carl Svernlöv, "What Isn't, Ain't," 8(4) *Journal of International Arbitration* (1991), p. 37; McNeill and Juratowitch, *supra* note 10, p. 475.

[13] Professor (as he then was) Jennings rightly distinguishes among nonexistent acts, acts that are null and void *ab initio*, and voidable acts. See R. Y. Jennings, "Nullity and Effectiveness in International Law," in *Cambridge Essays in International Law* (1965), pp. 66–67.

[14] Paulsson, *supra* note 2, p. 66: "Not much benefit is derived from labelling the contract as non-existent. The question is rather whether the clause, in context, evinces an intent to submit to arbitral jurisdiction disputes arising from the parties' relationship as it emerged in the course of the pre-contractual stage."

[15] *Fiona Trust & Holding Corporation* v. *Privalov* [2007] 4 All ER 951, para. 35, per Lord Hope.

[16] Ibid.

someone lacking authority to agree on behalf of the party alleged to be bound."[17] But no such list can ever be decisive. In every instance the question will remain, as above, whether the parties have consented to arbitrate.

Wherever a party challenges the arbitral tribunal's jurisdiction based on the alleged invalidity of the arbitration agreement, the ultimate decision will be for the relevant domestic court (at least in those cases where such domestic review is available). Thus the UNCITRAL Model Law, for example, first confirms the principles of *compétence de la compétence* and severability in Article 16(1):

The arbitral tribunal may rule on its own jurisdiction, including any objections with respect to the existence or validity of the arbitration agreement. For that purpose, an arbitration clause which forms part of a contract shall be treated as an agreement independent of the other terms of the contract. A decision by the arbitral tribunal that the contract is null and void shall not entail ipso jure the invalidity of the arbitration clause.

But then Article 16(3) provides that:

The arbitral tribunal may rule on a plea [that it does not have jurisdiction] either as a preliminary question or in an award on the merits. If the arbitral tribunal rules as a preliminary question that it has jurisdiction, any party may request, within thirty days after having received notice of that ruling, the [relevant domestic court] to decide the matter, which decision shall be subject to no appeal; while such a request is pending, the arbitral tribunal may continue the arbitral proceedings and make an award.

These provisions, which have been widely adopted in domestic legislation, seek to strike a balance between recognizing that an arbitral tribunal cannot have the ultimate authority to determine the validity of the arbitration agreement by which it is itself purporting to derive the authority to determine its jurisdiction, while preventing unmeritorious challenges to the validity of the arbitration agreement from derailing the arbitral process.[18]

---

[17] McNeill and Juratowitch, *supra* note 10, pp. 486–487.

[18] As the Explanatory Note to the Model Law explains in para. 26: "In those cases where the arbitral tribunal decides to combine its decision on jurisdiction with an award on the merits, judicial review on the question of jurisdiction is available in setting aside proceedings under article 34 or in enforcement proceedings under article 36." UNCITRAL Model Law on International Commercial Arbitration (1985), Article 16. See also in respect of enforcement proceedings, Article V(1)(a) of the New York Convention on the Recognition

C. The Practice

We turn now to an analysis of how codifications of arbitral procedure and the holdings of particular cases have established the doctrine of severability in positive law. This analysis demonstrates that the leading arbitral conventions and rules unanimously provide for or contemplate the severability of the arbitration agreement. It also demonstrates that the decisions of international tribunals are similarly consistent, albeit tribunals are still confronted from time to time by firm challenges to severability from respondents.

1. Arbitration Conventions and Rules

The proliferation of international arbitral rules since the publication of the first edition has resulted in a number of new or updated institutional rules that were not in force in 1987. This section considers how the doctrine of severability has been codified first in arbitral conventions and second in the rules of arbitral institutions.

(A) ARBITRATION CONVENTIONS

(i) New York Convention

The New York Convention on the Recognition and Enforcement of Arbitral Awards of 1958 has no provision that is directly in point.[19]

and Enforcement of Foreign Arbitral Awards. Where the tribunal sits as an international arbitral tribunal governed by public international law, then its decision on this seminal aspect of its competence is embraced by its pervasive power to judge its own jurisdiction. Where the arbitral tribunal sits pursuant to an agreement between a State or State enterprise and an alien, public international law normally will not govern its procedure. Whether the parties to an arbitration agreement between a State and an alien or to an arbitration agreement contained in an international commercial contract between private parties have the freedom to agree upon an arbitration "unbound" by any elements of national arbitration law was, and remains, a contentious question beyond the scope of this discussion. But it is pertinent to note that there is some evidence of a trend towards choosing as the place of arbitration in such cases countries whose arbitration law accords the arbitrators the widest freedom to decide upon questions of procedure and of governing law or rules of arbitration. Yet even in such countries, the arbitrators may not be empowered to determine definitively a question of the validity of the agreement to arbitrate.

[19] The rules of international arbitral law accord the arbitration tribunal the fundamental authority to determine its jurisdiction. Articles 48 of the 1899 Hague Convention and 73 of the 1907 Convention do not directly engage the question

However, Article V is inferentially relevant, in that it lists, in five subparagraphs, various grounds "only" on which the court of a Contracting State may refuse recognition and enforcement of a foreign arbitral award, among them, that the arbitration agreement is not valid under its governing law, that the party against whom the award was invoked was not given proper notice of the arbitration proceedings, that the award is *ultra vires*, that the arbitral procedure was faulty, and that the award has been set aside by a competent authority of the country in which it was made. None of these and the other exclusive grounds stated on which recognition and enforcement may be refused include the claim or conclusion that the principal agreement that contains the arbitration agreement is invalid. Thus, by implication, the New York Convention may be said to sustain severability.[20]

of the severability of the arbitration agreement. But they imply not the slightest derogation from it; indeed their implications support severability. The structure of the 1953 Draft Convention on Arbitral Procedure of the International Law Commission of the United Nations equally is not such as squarely to pose the question of severability. Article 35 of the Model Rules on Arbitral procedure subsequently adopted by the International law Commission in 1958 is more directly in point. It sets out four grounds on which the validity of an award may be challenged, among them, that "the understanding to arbitrate or the *compromis* is a nullity." But the ground that the principal agreement which contains the *compromis* is a nullity is not given; accordingly, the inference is that that is not a tenable ground for challenging the validity of an arbitral award or, correspondingly, the competence of the tribunal to render it. While these codifications of the international law of international arbitration do not directly deal with the distinct question of severability, the last is relevant on the foregoing count and all are relevant insofar as the logic of the principle of *compétence de la compétence* bears on that of severability.

[20] In his able study of the Convention, Albert Jan van den Berg does not reach this conclusion and contends that the New York Convention does not imply severability just because the arbitration agreement may be governed by a law other than the law that governs the principal agreement. *Supra* note 8, pp. 145–146. However, there is room for questioning his conclusion that it must be presumed that the Convention is "indifferent" as to the severability of the arbitral clause. For Article V specifies that recognition and enforcement of the award may be refused "only if" the party concerned furnishes proof that the parties to the arbitration agreement were "under the law applicable to them," under some incapacity, "or the said [arbitration] agreement is not valid under the law to which the parties have subjected it or, failing any indication thereon, under the law of the country where the award was made . . ." (J. Gillis Wetter, *The International Arbitral Process, Public and Private* (1979), vol. V, p. 310). And the other exclusive grounds for refusal illustrated in the body of this book are also listed. Now none of these directly suggest that among the grounds on which recognition and enforcement can be refused is invalidity of the principal agreement, because Article V refers (by reference back

(ii) European Convention on International Commercial Arbitration

The European Convention on International Commercial Arbitration of 1961 provides, in Article V, paragraph 3:

> Subject to any subsequent judicial control provided for under the *lex fori*, the arbitrator whose jurisdiction is called in question shall be entitled to proceed with the arbitration, to rule on his own jurisdiction and to decide upon the existence or the validity of the arbitration agreement or of the contract of which the agreement forms part.[21]

Article V is thus supportive of severability, for it affirms the authority of the arbitrators to decide upon the existence or validity of the principal agreement and implies – note the use of the disjunctive "or" – that the arbitrators' decision upon the existence or validity of the principal agreement does not govern their decision on the existence or validity of the arbitration agreement. However,

---

to article II of the Convention) not to the principal agreement but to the arbitration agreement. However, it might in support of van den Berg's analysis be maintained that Article V(1)(a) refers to the question of whether the arbitration agreement is valid "under the law to which the parties have subjected it. . . ." etc., and that, under that law, the doctrine of severability might or possibly might not apply; hence the Convention is "indifferent" to severability. That is to say, the arbitration agreement might be invalid only for the reason that it is part of a principal agreement that is itself invalid, by application of the governing law. That is a possible interpretation of the New York Convention but not a compelling one. Practically speaking, it is the less compelling in view of van den Berg's analysis of what would be the governing law; if that law is that of the forum, it is unlikely to counter severability, since the law of fora where international arbitrations tend to take place sustains severability. See also Born, *supra* note 8, p. 357: "In reality, the New York Convention neither 'adopts' nor is 'indifferent to' the separability doctrine. Rather, Articles II and V(1)(a) of the Convention rest on the premise that arbitration agreements can, and will ordinarily, be separate agreements and that these agreements therefore will often be treated differently from, and subject to different rules of validity and different choice-of-law rules than, the parties' underlying contracts."; *Balkan Energy (Ghana) Limited* v. *Ghana*, PCA Case No. 2010-7, Interim Award, 22 December 2010, para. 114: "The New York Convention does not expressly treat competence-competence (or separability). Nothing in the Convention expressly requires (or debars) application of those established doctrines. But, as Born points out, Articles II(3) and V(1) of the Convention recognize that both arbitral tribunals and courts may consider and decide disputes about the arbitrators' jurisdiction. Articles V(1)(a) and V(1)(c) of the Convention contemplate that an arbitral tribunal may have made an award notwithstanding jurisdictional objections and will have addressed issues of the validity of the arbitration agreement. The fact that such determinations are subject to judicial review, as at the stage of enforcement, has as its premise that arbitral tribunals are entitled to pass upon their jurisdiction without prior judicial determination."

[21] Wetter, *supra* note 20, vol. V, p. 319.

decisions on both questions are subject to any control provided under the law applicable to the arbitral proceedings – a provision that may not be fully consistent with severability.[22]

(iii) ICSID Convention

The Convention on the Settlement of International Investment Disputes between States and Nationals of Other States (the ICSID Convention) of 1965 provides, in Article 41, that: "The Tribunal shall be the judge of its own competence."[23] Article 25 provides that jurisdiction of the ICSID Center under whose auspices arbitral tribunals are formed embraces any legal dispute arising directly out of an investment between a Contracting State and a national of another Contracting State which the parties consent to submit.[24] "When the parties have given their consent, no party may withdraw its consent unilaterally."[25] This provision has been authoritatively construed to mean that a State's attempted unilateral rescission of an agreement to submit disputes for resolution by an ICSID tribunal does not impair the tribunal's jurisdiction.[26] It may be argued – quite reasonably, it is believed – that what a State or party cannot do directly it cannot do indirectly; that, if it is not entitled to vitiate the arbitral process by withdrawing its agreement to arbitrate, it is not entitled to vitiate the arbitral process by maintaining that the principal agreement containing the arbitral obligation is void or voided.[27]

---

[22] Professor Sanders interprets this provision as recognizing the severability of the arbitration agreement. But he criticizes the introductory phrase of Article V, paragraph 3, of the Convention, "Subsequent to any judicial control provided for under the *lex fori*," because while he views it as correct insofar as it covers the existence or validity of the arbitration agreement, it is not correct insofar as it relates to the validity of the contract of which the arbitral clause forms a part. If a contract was not concluded, the contract's arbitral provision is equally defective. But the question of validity is distinguishable from the contract's existence and is one to which judicial recourse should not apply. Sanders, *supra* note 3, p. 35.

[23] Wetter, *supra* note 20, vol. V, p. 445.   [24] Ibid., p. 446.   [25] Ibid., p. 439.

[26] Georges R. Delaume, "State Contracts and Transnational Arbitration," 75 *American Journal of International Law* (1981), pp. 785, 788–789. The *travaux préparatoires* of the ICSID Convention emphasize the irrevocability of consent to arbitration. Convention on the Settlement of Investment Disputes between States and Nationals of Other States, *Analysis of Documents Concerning the Origin and Formulation of the Convention)*, vol. I, citations to Article 25, paragraph 1, "consent." See also Christoph H. Schreuer et al. (ed.), *The ICSID Convention: A Commentary* (2nd edition, 2009), pp. 254–263.

[27] Schreuer, *supra* note 26, pp. 260–261.

The basis of consent to arbitration in most ICSID arbitrations is not a single arbitration agreement, but rather a standing offer of arbitration made by a State in a bilateral investment treaty (BIT) combined with the later acceptance of that offer by a qualifying investor when filing the arbitration.[28] But once the consent of the parties to arbitration becomes perfected by the investor's acceptance of the State's standing offer to arbitration, then it must be the case that a State can neither withdraw its consent unilaterally, nor vitiate that consent by maintaining that the underlying treaty containing that consent is void or voided.

The Arbitration (Additional Facility) Rules of ICSID explicitly provide, in Article 45, paragraph 1:

Objections to Competence
(1) The Tribunal shall have the power to rule on its competence. For the purposes of this Article, an agreement providing for arbitration under the Additional Facility shall be separable from the other terms of the contract in which it may have been included.[29]

Thus the ICSID Additional Facility Rules expressly embody the doctrine of severability.

(B) ARBITRATION RULES

(i) UNCITRAL Rules and Model Law

The Arbitration Rules of the United Nations Commission on International Trade Law, as revised in 2010 (the UNCITRAL Arbitration Rules), are squarely on point. It should be noted that the original 1976 Rules were commended by the United Nations General Assembly in a resolution that characterized them as "acceptable in countries with different legal, social and economic systems" and that recalled that they "have been prepared after extensive consultation with arbitral institutions and centres of international commercial arbitration." The revised 2010 Rules were similarly commended. Article 23(1) of the revised 2010 Rules provides:

---

[28] See Jan Paulsson, "Arbitration Without Privity, " 10 *ICSID Review* (1995), p. 232.
[29] Wetter, *supra* note 20, vol. V, pp. 38–39.

16

The arbitral tribunal shall have the power to rule on its own jurisdiction, including any objections with respect to the existence or validity of the arbitration agreement. For that purpose, an arbitration clause that forms part of a contract shall be treated as an agreement independent of the other terms of the contract. A decision by the arbitral tribunal that the contract is null shall not entail automatically the invalidity of the arbitration clause.

This again upholds the principles of *compétence de la compétence* and severability in simple terms, while also contemplating situations where the nullity of the contract may entail the invalidity of the arbitration clause.

The United Nations Commission on International Trade Law further adopted, in 1985, the UNCITRAL Model Law on International Commercial Arbitration. Article 16, entitled "Competence of arbitral tribunal to rule on its jurisdiction," provides, in paragraph 1:

The arbitral tribunal may rule on its own jurisdiction, including any objections with respect to the existence or validity of the arbitration agreement. For that purpose, an arbitration clause which forms part of the contract shall be treated as an agreement independent of the other terms of the contract. A decision by the arbitral tribunal that the contract is null and void shall not entail *ipso jure* the invalidity of the arbitration clause.[30]

It will be observed that, not only does this Model Law for international commercial arbitration specify severability; it also, and rightly, links that provision with the competence of the arbitral tribunal to rule on its jurisdiction. The UNCITRAL Model Law has since been widely adopted, in whole or in part, in a number of domestic jurisdictions, thus further contributing to the widespread acceptance of the principle of severability.[31]

(ii) PCA Rules
The 2012 Permanent Court of Arbitration Rules affirm both *compétence de la compétence* and severability, in Article 23:

The arbitral tribunal shall have the power to rule on its own jurisdiction, including any objections with respect to the existence or validity of the arbitration agreement. For that purpose, an arbitration clause that forms

---

[30] XI *Yearbook Commercial Arbitration* (1986), p. 385.   [31] See Section C.3, *infra.*

part of a contract, treaty, or other agreement shall be treated as an agreement independent of the other terms of the contract, treaty, or other agreement. A decision by the arbitral tribunal that the contract, treaty, or other agreement is null, void, or invalid shall not entail automatically the invalidity of the arbitration clause.[32]

These Rules recognize that a defect in the underlying contract or treaty will not "automatically" entail the invalidity of the arbitration clause, thus recognizing that there may be cases where the arbitration clause will be deemed valid notwithstanding the defect in the underlying contract or treaty.

(iii) ICC Rules
The Rules of Arbitration of the International Chamber of Commerce, the latest version of which are the 2017 ICC Rules, also embrace severability. Article 6, paragraph 9, prescribes:

Unless otherwise agreed, the arbitral tribunal shall not cease to have jurisdiction by reason of any allegation that the contract is non-existent or null and void, provided that the arbitral tribunal upholds the validity of the arbitration agreement. The arbitral tribunal shall continue to have jurisdiction to determine the parties' respective rights and to decide their claims and pleas even though the contract itself may be non-existent or null and void.

This provision asserts the principle of severability in categorical and comprehensive terms. The provision even anticipates that an arbitration agreement may be upheld even where the underlying contract is "non-existent," although this is "provided that the arbitral tribunal upholds the validity of the arbitration agreement."

(iv) London Court of International Arbitration Rules
The Arbitration Rules of the London Court of International Arbitration, the latest version of which are the 2014 Rules, provide, in Article 23, paragraphs 1 and 2:

[32] Compare, as cited in the first edition, Article 4 of the Permanent Court of Arbitration Rules of Arbitration and Conciliation for the Settlement of International Disputes between Two Parties of Which Only One State is a State of 1962, which did not explicitly embrace severability ("The arbitral Tribunal, which shall be the judge of its own competence, shall have the power to interpret the instruments on which that competence is based" [Wetter, *supra* note 20, vol. V, p. 54]).

23.1 The Arbitral Tribunal shall have the power to rule upon its own jurisdiction and authority, including any objection to the initial or continuing existence, validity, effectiveness or scope of the Arbitration Agreement.

23.2 For that purpose, an arbitration clause which forms or was intended to form part of another agreement shall be treated as an arbitration agreement independent of that other agreement. A decision by the Arbitral Tribunal that such other agreement is non-existent, invalid or ineffective shall not entail (of itself) the non-existence, invalidity or ineffectiveness of the arbitration clause.

Like the ICC Rules, the LCIA Rules thus assert the principle of severability in categorical and comprehensive terms. They even provide that the nonexistence of the underlying contract does not "of itself" mean the nonexistence of the arbitration clause, which can be presumed to mean that the nonexistence of the underlying contract will not mean the nonexistence of the arbitration clause provided that it can be established that the parties have otherwise consented to the arbitration clause.

(v) Singapore International Arbitration Centre Rules

The 2016 Arbitration Rules of the Singapore International Arbitration Centre provide in Article 28(2) that:

The Tribunal shall have the power to rule on its own jurisdiction, including any objections with respect to the existence, validity or scope of the arbitration agreement. An arbitration agreement which forms part of a contract shall be treated as an agreement independent of the other terms of the contract. A decision by the Tribunal that the contract is null and void shall not entail ipso jure the invalidity of the arbitration agreement, and the Tribunal shall not cease to have jurisdiction by reason of any allegation that the contract is non-existent or null and void.

The SIAC Rules thus clearly embrace severability in similar terms to in the UNCITRAL Rules and Model Law.

(vi) Hong Kong International Arbitration Centre Rules

The 2018 Administered Arbitration Rules of the Hong Kong International Arbitration Centre provide in Article 19 that:

(1) The arbitral tribunal may rule on its own jurisdiction under these Rules, including any objections with respect to the existence, validity or scope of the arbitration agreement(s).

(2) The arbitral tribunal shall have the power to determine the existence or the validity of any contract of which an arbitration agreement forms a part. For the purposes of Article 19, an arbitration agreement which forms part of a contract, and which provides for arbitration under these Rules, shall be treated as an agreement independent of the other terms of the contract. A decision by the arbitral tribunal that the contract is null and void shall not necessarily entail the invalidity of the arbitration agreement.

The HKIAC Rules therefore also clearly embrace severability in similar terms to in the UNCITRAL Rules and Model Law.

2. *The International Cases*

(A) *THE DELAGOA BAY RAILWAY CASE*

The issue of severability was early raised in the course of a notable international law case, the *Delagoa Bay Railway* arbitration. The *Delagoa Bay Railway* arbitration of 1900 between the United States and Great Britain, as claimants, and Portugal, as defendant, was an inter-State arbitration that concerned the question of what compensation was due from Portugal for its rescission of a railway concession and seizure of a railroad.[33] In determining compensation, the arbitral tribunal held that Portugal had acted unlawfully, and concluded that Portugal either should have accorded the concessionaire more time for extension of the railway or referred the matter to arbitration under the contract. But there was no clear ruling as to whether or not the contractual arbitral remedy survived Portugal's annulment of the concession.[34]

While the *Delagoa Bay Railway* arbitration itself is not in point, what is of interest is that there was a rescission by the Portuguese Government of a concession contract that contained a provision for arbitration; that the United States apparently was of the view that arbitral recourse under the contract by the concessionaire disappeared with the contract's rescission; but, that this view was based

---

[33] The award is summarized in M. Whiteman, III *Damages in International Law* (1943), pp. 1695–1703. The award is briefly summarized and evaluated by R. Dolzer, "Delagoa Bay Railway Arbitration," in Bernhardt (ed.) *Encyclopedia of Public International Law* (1981), pp. 74–75. The text of the *compromis* and of the award is published in La Fontaine, *Pasicrisie Internationale* (1902), pp. 397–410.

[34] La Fontaine, *supra* note 33, p. 401, and Whiteman, *supra* note 33, p. 1697.

on the fact that the Company had "practically ceased to exist" as well as on the legal thesis that, if Portugal wished to have recourse under the contract to arbitration, it should rescind its rescission of it. Portugal, on the other hand, appears to have maintained that arbitral recourse under the contract did survive its annulment or rescission of it. In the event, Portugal acceded to US and British diplomatic pressure to arbitrate on an inter-State level the amount of compensation due. The difference between the Portuguese and US viewpoints on the separability of the arbitration clause of the contract was not resolved, nor, indeed, as far as the documentation available reveals, was it at any stage even thoroughly argued. Nevertheless the *Delagoa Bay Railway* case does indicate that, when these diplomatic exchanges took place in 1889, there was not agreement between the United States and Portugal on the question now under analysis.

(B) *THE ANGLO-IRANIAN OIL COMPANY CASE*

Another case in which governments took differing positions on the question at issue that were unresolved in the proceedings was the *Anglo-Iranian Oil Company* case (1952).[35] It will be recalled that the Iranian Government in 1951 adopted the principle of the nationalization of the oil industry in Iran and dispossessed the Anglo-Iranian Oil Company, despite various provisions of the concession contract between the Government and the Company, among them the provision that: "Any differences between the parties of any nature whatever and in particular any differences arising out of the interpretation of this Agreement and the rights and obligations therein contained . . . shall be settled by arbitration."[36] The contract contained detailed provisions for the constitution and competence of the arbitration tribunal. When nationalization took place, the Company invoked arbitration in accordance with the terms of the contract.[37] Iran replied that "the fact of nationalization of the petroleum industry . . . is not referable to arbitration . . . ."[38] The

---

[35] See *Anglo-Iranian Oil Co. Case (Jurisdiction), Judgment of July 22nd, 1952, I.C.J. Reports 1952*, p. 93; and *Anglo-Iranian Oil Co. Case (United Kingdom* v. *Iran), Pleadings.*
[36] *Anglo-Iranian Oil Co. Case, Pleadings, supra* note 35, p. 30. [37] Ibid., p. 38.
[38] Ibid., p. 40.

British Government brought proceedings in the International Court of Justice, and among the points it urged was that, despite the nationalization and refusal of Iran to arbitrate, the obligation to arbitrate pursuant to the contract's arbitration clause remained in force. It maintained in its memorial that:

43. The Government of the United Kingdom has submitted ... that the Government of Iran is not entitled to terminate by legislative action a Convention which it expressly undertook not to terminate by legislative action ... However, assuming – though the Government of the United Kingdom denies the validity of any such assumption – that the Government of Iran was entitled, notwithstanding the circumstances in which the Convention was concluded and its express provision to the contrary, to terminate it unilaterally, it is submitted that such right of unilateral termination did not – or did not necessarily – extend to Article 22 of the Convention. That Article provides for the arbitration of all disputes relating to the interpretation of the Convention. ...

It is arguable – and the argument is not devoid of apparent logic – that, if the Convention is denounced, such denunciation must include the whole of it and cannot stop short of any particular article. The Government of the United Kingdom submits that this is not necessarily so, in particular, in relation to the present case, for the following reason: Even if it were possible for the Government of Iran to assert that the unilateral denunciation of the Convention for the purpose of nationalization was dictated by the vital interests of the State, it does not follow that these vital interests of the State demanded that the termination of the Convention be combined with the cancellation of the clause which is the proper instrument for providing a remedy – in the form of adequate compensation determined in accordance with law as applied by the arbitrators – for what is undeniably a breach of the contract. Even assuming that unilateral termination was admissible, it would still have been possible – and proper – for the Iranian Government to approach the Anglo-Iranian Oil Company and say: 'We find ourselves under a necessity, for inescapable reasons of State, to put an end to the Convention. We cannot, therefore, admit that under Article 22 of the Convention the arbitrators or the sole arbitrator have the right to pass upon the legality of the measure taken and, in particular, to decree the restitution of the concession.' However, as a matter of law, and, in the words of Article 21 of the Convention, 'on principles of mutual goodwill and good faith' as well as on a 'reasonable interpretation of this Agreement,' we are prepared to abide by an award of arbitrators as to the compensation due to the Company for the breach of the Convention.' Instead the Iranian Government has refused to submit the dispute, even within the limited compass as suggested, to arbitration and has provided that compensation is to be determined by the Iranian Parliament.[39]

Iran replied that it considered the concession contract null and void, and thus obviously refused to name an arbitrator and to accept the mode of settlement provided for in the contract.[40] In oral argument, Iran's advocate, Professor Henri Rolin, contended that the arbitral clause of the concession "followed the fate of the concession contract. Article 22 of the concession contract has been annulled by the nationalization law."[41]

The International Court of Justice, which found that it lacked jurisdiction to pass upon the merits of the case, did not rule upon the question at issue. However, in his dissenting opinion, Judge Levi Carneiro stated the following:

The argument has been taken even further: it has been said and repeated ... that the Iranian Government always considered the 1933 Concession to be "null and void." It has been contended that "the invalid Concession of 1933 and all its Articles disappeared automatically." As a result, it is said, Articles 21 and 22 of the "so-called Concession" have become non-existent. It would seem, however, that ... Article 22 provides mandatorily and in the widest terms, that any differences between the Parties of any nature whatever, and in particular any differences arising out of the interpretation of this Agreement and of the rights and obligations therein contained ... shall be settled by arbitration. The same Article lays down detailed rules governing the constitution of the arbitration tribunal.

The Iranian Government states expressly that it refuses to appoint an arbitrator and to accept the procedure laid down in Article 22. It justifies this decision by the contention that the Concession granted to the Anglo-Iranian Oil Company is null and void. This contention would appear to be ill-founded because neither the Iranian laws of March 15th and 20th, 1951, nor that of May 1st of the same year, provided for the dissolution of the Anglo-Iranian Oil Company or the annulment of its contract, nor could they, in fact, do so. Even if the annulment of the contract could have been decreed, for the purpose of nationalizing the oil industry, by the unilateral act of one of the parties to the contract – the Iranian Government – it would not follow that this act would exclude the jurisdiction of the arbitral tribunal provided for in Article 26 of this contract. It could be argued that that tribunal would retain jurisdiction to decide as to the

---

[39] *Anglo-Iranian Oil Co. Case, supra* note 35, pp. 118–119.   [40] Ibid., p. 305.
[41] Ibid., p. 501 (translation supplied).

effects and the questions resulting from this act and to assess the compensation payable, and also to decide whether it considers such compensation to be legitimate.[42]

Thus the *Anglo-Iranian Oil Company* case furnishes a dramatic but indecisive evocation of the question under analysis.

(C) THE ICAO COUNCIL CASE

However, the essential principle of severability was – in effect if not in terms – addressed and upheld by the International Court of Justice in its judgment upon the *Appeal Relating to the Jurisdiction of the ICAO Council* (1972). In that case, India took the position that the Council of the International Civil Aviation Organization (ICAO) lacked jurisdiction to deal with complaints of Pakistan against India for prohibiting the flight of Pakistani civil aircraft over Indian territory. Those complaints were based on the 1944 Chicago International Civil Aviation Convention and on a Transit Agreement that India maintained had been terminated or suspended as between India and Pakistan; thus, India contended, those international agreements could not furnish the ICAO Council with jurisdiction over complaints concerning their breach. The ICAO Council had, however, assumed jurisdiction, and its so assuming was the cause for India's appeal to the International Court of Justice. India based the jurisdiction of the Court over its appeal on the terms of the Chicago Convention and Transit Agreement, which provided not only for resort to the ICAO Council but for appeal from the decision of the Council to the Court. Pakistan, for its part, while maintaining that the ICAO Council had jurisdiction over its complaints against India, denied that the Court had jurisdiction over an appeal from the Council's finding of its jurisdiction. Pakistan argued that India was debarred from affirming the competence of the Court because India herself claimed that the relevant treaties were not in force with the result, Pakistan maintained, that their jurisdictional clauses were inapplicable.

The Court declined to accept both the arguments of India and of Pakistan on these points. In denying Pakistan's argument about the jurisdiction of the Court, the Court held:

---

[42] *Anglo-Iranian Oil Co. Case, supra* note 35, p. 164.

It will be convenient to deal first with the contention that India is precluded from affirming the competence of the Court because she herself maintains ... that the Treaties are not in force between the Parties, which contention, if correct, would entail that their jurisdictional clauses were inapplicable .... The Court however holds that this contention of Pakistan's is not well-founded for the following reasons ...

(a) What India has affirmed is that the Treaties – which are multilateral ones – are suspended (or that their operation is suspended) as between herself and Pakistan. This is not the same thing as saying that they are not in force in the definitive sense, or even that they have wholly ceased to be in force as between the two Parties concerned.

(b) Nor in any case could a merely unilateral suspension *per se* render jurisdictional clauses inoperative, since one of their purposes might be, precisely, to enable the validity of the suspension to be tested. If a mere allegation, as yet unestablished, that a treaty was no longer operative could be used to defeat its jurisdictional clauses, all such clauses would become potentially a dead letter, even in cases like the present, where one of the very questions at issue on the merits, and as yet undecided, is whether or not the treaty is operative – i.e., whether it has been validly terminated or suspended. The result would be that means of defeating jurisdictional clauses would never be wanting.[43]

In rejecting India's argument about the jurisdiction of the ICAO Council, the Court held that:

... it involves a point of principle of great general importance for the jurisdictional aspects of this – or of any – case. This contention is to the effect that since India, in suspending overflights in February 1971, was not invoking any right that might be afforded by the Treaties, but was acting outside them on the basis of a general principle of international law, 'therefore' the Council, whose jurisdiction was derived from the Treaties, and which was entitled to deal only with matters arising under them, must be incompetent. Exactly the same attitude has been evinced in regard to the contention that the Treaties were suspended in 1965 and never revived, or were replaced by a special regime. The Court considers however, that for precisely the same order of reason as has already been noticed in the case of its own jurisdiction in the present case, a mere unilateral affirmation of these contentions – contested by the other party –

---

[43] *Appeal Relating to the Jurisdiction of the ICAO Council, Judgment, I.C.J. Reports 1972,* pp. 46, 53–54.

cannot be utilized so as to negative the Council's jurisdiction. The point is not that these contentions are necessarily wrong but that their validity has not yet been determined. Since therefore the Parties are in disagreement as to whether the Treaties ever were (validly) suspended or replaced by something else; as to whether they are in force between the Parties or not; and as to whether India's action in relation to Pakistan overflights was such as not to involve the Treaties, but to be justifiable *aliter et aliunde*, – these very questions are in issue before the Council, and no conclusions as to jurisdiction can be drawn from them, at least at this stage, so as to exclude *ipso facto* and *a priori* the competence of the Council.

To put the matter in another way, these contentions are essentially in the nature of replies to the charge that India is in breach of the Treaties: the Treaties were at the material times suspended or not operative, or replaced, – hence they cannot have been infringed. India has not of course claimed that, in consequence, such a matter can never be tested by any form of judicial recourse. This contention, if it were put forward, would be equivalent to saying that questions that prima facie may involve a given treaty, and if so would be within the scope of its jurisdictional clause, could be removed therefrom at a stroke by a unilateral declaration that the treaty was no longer operative. The acceptance of such a proposition would be tantamount to opening the way to a wholesale nullification of the practical value of jurisdictional clauses by allowing a party first to purport to terminate, or suspend the operation of a treaty, and then to declare that the treaty being now terminated or suspended, its jurisdictional clauses were in consequence void, and could not be invoked for the purpose of contesting the validity of the termination or suspension, – whereas of course it may be precisely one of the objects of such a clause to enable that matter to be adjudicated upon. Such a result, destructive of the whole object of adjudicability, – would be unacceptable.[44]

Thus the International Court of Justice held that a party to a treaty cannot defeat the provision for adjudication or arbitration that the treaty contains by maintaining that it has terminated the treaty. "Such a result, destructive of the whole object of adjudicability, would be unacceptable." Acceptance of such a contention would make all arbitral clauses "potentially a dead letter."[45]

---

[44] Ibid., pp. 64–65.
[45] See, citing this case, International Law Commission, *Draft articles on Responsibility of States for Internationally Wrongful Acts, with commentaries* (2001), Article 50, Comment 13, p. 133: "It is a well-established principle that dispute settlement provisions must be upheld notwithstanding that they are contained in a treaty

The late Judge Sir Gerald Fitzmaurice drove this fundamental point home with his characteristic cogency in the Court's *Fisheries Jurisdiction* case. In his Separate Opinion, he recalled:

> This contention seems however to belong basically to the same order of argument as was put forward before the Court in the recent case of the *Jurisdiction of the ICAO Council* . . ., and by both the then Parties, though with different objects, – on the one side to contest the jurisdiction of the ICAO Council to deal with a certain matter and, on the other side, to contest the competence of the Court to determine the question of the Council's jurisdiction in that matter. Reduced to its simplest terms, the process is to argue that a jurisdictional clause, even if it is otherwise duly applicable on its own language, can be *ipso facto* nullified or rendered inapplicable by purporting (unilaterally) to terminate or suspend the instrument containing it, or (as in the present case) to declare it to have become inoperative or to be spent, and the jurisdictional clause with it
>
> It is always legitimate to seek to maintain (whether correctly or not) that a jurisdictional clause is, *according to its own terms*, inapplicable to the dispute, or has lapsed; – and in that event it is for the tribunal concerned to decide the matter, in the exercise of the admitted right or function of the *compétence de la compétence* – . . . But this must equally be so where the alleged cause of inapplicability or inoperativeness of the jurisdictional clause lies not in that clause itself but in the language of, or in considerations pertaining to, the instrument containing it, – for otherwise there would be no way of testing (in so far as it affected the jurisdictional clause) the validity of the grounds of inapplicability or inoperativeness put forward; and the *compétence de la compétence* would be nullified or would be nullifiable *a priori*, – in short, as the Court said in the *Council of ICAO* case . . . "means of defeating jurisdictional clauses would never be wanting" – since;
>
> > "If a mere allegation, as yet unestablished, that a treaty was no longer operative could be used to defeat its jurisdictional clauses, all such clauses would become potentially a dead letter."[46]

The relevance of this holding to the question of severability is plain. As Professor Prosper Weil, in maintaining that arbitral clauses are independent and survive termination of the contracts that contain them, points out:

---

which is at the heart of the dispute and the continued validity or effect of which is challenged."

[46] *Fisheries Jurisdiction (United Kingdom v. Iceland), Jurisdiction of the Court, Judgment, I.C.J. Reports 1973*, p. 31.

La Cour internationale de Justice vient de consacrer avec éclat une solution analogue en ce qui concerne les clauses juridictionelles insérées dans les traités internationaux … et l'on ne voit pas de motif pour ne pas l'étendre aux clauses compromissoires insérées dans les contrats.[47]

(D) THE LOSINGER & CO. CASE

The Losinger & Co. case was an involved litigation that comprised two arbitral awards as well as proceedings between Switzerland and Yugoslavia before the Permanent Court of International Justice that were concluded by a settlement before judgment was rendered. In arbitral proceedings before a former President of the Swiss Federal Tribunal, Henri Thélin, who served as umpire, the Kingdom of Yugoslavia challenged the competence of the umpire on four grounds, one of which was:

The arbitration clause has become null and void as a result of the annulment of the contract.[48]

In response, the umpire held:

… Yugoslavia contested the umpire's competence … on the sole ground that "the contract … which lays down the arbitral procedure for the contracting parties, is without effect, in view of the repudiation of the contract by Decision of the Council of Ministers … so that in reality the provisions regarding arbitration as well as the contract itself are now inexistent". … At the hearing … the representatives of the Respondent reiterated this ground in the following terms: "The annulment of the contract resulted in the annulment of the arbitral clause contained in it and therefore brought to an end the possibility of recourse to arbitration."

This argument does not withstand examination. If it were well-founded, it would allow a party to escape from the jurisdiction of an arbitral tribunal simply by enacting a unilateral measure in a dispute precisely for which arbitration had been provided (i.e., a dispute concerning "the execution and interpretation of clauses and conditions of the … agreement"). The question of the legality of the termination of the contract … and of

---

[47] P. Weil, "Les Clauses de Stabilisation ou d'Intangibilité Insérées dans les Accords de Développement Economique," *Mélanges offerts à Charles Rousseau* (1974), p. 325. Accord: F.A. Mann, "The Consequences of an International Wrong in International and National Law," XLVIII *British Year Book of International Law* (1976–1977), p. 60, note 3.

[48] The award of 30 October 1935 is published in *The Losinger & Co. Case, P.C.I.J.*, Series C, No. 78 (1936), p. 105; see p. 109 (translation supplied).

the refusal of Yugoslavia to execute it in the future, certainly relates to the interpretation of the agreement . . .

Inasmuch as Article XVI [the arbitration clause] is not affected [by annulment of the agreement], it must, . . . govern the present dispute, which is one of "disagreements" or "disputes" for which the arbitral jurisdiction was adopted by the parties.

The grounds for the annulment put forward do not affect in any way the intention of the parties to provide for arbitration to decide whether the annulment of the contract was justified or not. Indeed, there is consistent case-law that "the unilateral annulment of a contract has no effect on the arbitration clause, which remains in force, at least until the legal position has been established regarding the grounds of annulment" and the consequences of an unjustified annulment.

The case-law confirms this approach. The most recent decision of the Swiss Federal Tribunal in this matter (*Tobler* v. *Blaser*, 7 October 1933, *Recueil officiel des arrêts*, vol. 59, 1, p. 177 et seq.) includes, amongst other considerations, the following:

> "Even if it is included in the contract to which it relates in the same written act and therefore forms an integral part of that contract, it does not simply become one of the ordinary provisions of the contract, but rather an independent clause of a special nature, with the result that rescission of the contract cannot entrain automatically the annulment of the arbitral clause. The arbitral clause would only become void if the reasons for rescission of the contract affected, at the same time, the arbitration clause (where, for example, one of the parties had signed the contract whilst incapable of understanding or under duress)."

In other words, when a contract provides for the difficulties to which its interpretation or execution could give rise to be submitted to arbitration, this clause remains in force even where the contract has been rescinded for reasons having nothing to do with the actual intention of the parties to refer the matter to an arbitrator. This is, in fact, the situation in the present case.

The annulment of the contract of 2 March 1929 is therefore without effect on the arbitration clause."[49]

In the proceedings that followed before the Permanent Court of International Justice, Yugoslavia did not raise again the argument that cancellation of the contract of itself vitiated the arbitral remedy.

---

[49] Ibid., pp. 110–111 (translation supplied).

(E) *LENA GOLDFIELDS ARBITRATION*

A concession agreement was made in 1925 between the Lena Goldfields Company, a British corporation, and the Government of the Union of Soviet Socialist Republics, granting the Company extensive mining rights. Article 90(1) of the agreement provided:

All disputes and misunderstandings in regard to the construing or fulfillment of this Agreement . . . on the declaration of either of the parties, are examined and settled by the Court of Arbitration.[50]

By 1929, the Company, which initially operated at a profit, claimed that the Government rendered performance of the concession agreement impossible. Citing what it saw as manifest violations of the concession agreement, the Company invoked arbitration.

In its award, the Court of Arbitration ruled that it had been duly constituted. It so held despite the fact that, after the Soviet Government and the Company had requested the super-arbitrator upon whom they had agreed to set a date for convening the tribunal but before it met, the Soviet Government telegraphed that Lena had "dissolved the Concession Agreement" by its stating that it took no further responsibilities, by refusing further financing, and by withdrawing the power of attorney of its representatives.[51] The Soviet Government "further said that in these circumstances the Arbitration Court had ceased to function."[52] The Company responded that the Arbitration Court was properly and completely constituted. The Court of Arbitration noted that, when the Government had advanced its defenses and counterclaims, it had not mentioned Article 86 of the agreement, which authorized dissolution of the concession agreement by the Court upon proof that Lena, "by its own fault," had failed to perform essential undertakings.[53] At the Court's first session, Lena argued that the concession agreement necessarily continued to exist until formally dissolved by the Court under Article 86; and Lena

---

[50] The above quotation is from a report of the case in *The Times* (London) of 3 September 1930, p. 7. That report is largely reprinted in 36 *Cornell Law Quarterly* (1950), p. 44 (hereinafter "Award"). For extensive analyses of the award, see A. Nussbaum, "The Arbitration between the Lena Goldfields, Ltd., and the Soviet Government," ibid., p. 31 and V. V. Veeder, "The *Lena Goldfields* Arbitration: The Historical Roots of Three Ideas" 47 *International and Comparative Law Quarterly* (2004), p. 747.

[51] See Award, para. 10.   [52] Ibid., para. 10.   [53] Ibid., para. 8.

maintained that, if it succeeded in establishing its claims of the Government's non-performance, it would then be time for the Court to declare the agreement dissolved. The report continues:

The Court decided that the Concession Agreement was still operative and that according to the plain language of Article 90, paragraph 6, the jurisdiction of the Court remained unaffected . . .[54]

Nevertheless, the Soviet Government maintained its decision not to attend the arbitration, and wholly repudiated "the Court and all the arbitration proceedings."[55] The Court subsequently held:

Although the Government has thus refused its assistance to the Court, it remains bound by its obligations under the Concession Agreement and in particular by the terms of Article 90, the arbitration clause of the contract.[56]

With regard to the Government's contention that Lena had dissolved the concession agreement, the Court of Arbitration ruled that it was "the Government which was the cause of Lena's financial difficulties."[57] The Court decided in favor of Lena, awarding it damages plus interest, and then resolved: " . . . that the concession agreement is dissolved."[58]

In this case, which remains of contemporary interest for more than one reason, the Government, as the Court of Arbitration recalled,[59] claimed that the Company had by its actions rescinded the contract with the result that the arbitral process was vitiated; the Company maintained that fault lay with the Government, that the Company had not rescinded and that any rescission could only be

---

[54] Ibid., para. 11.   [55] Ibid., para. 14.   [56] Ibid., para. 15.
[57] Ibid., para. 21.   [58] Ibid., para. 33.
[59] V. V. Veeder has, following further research, contended that the basis of the Soviet Government's challenge to the jurisdiction of the Court of Arbitration was not that the underlying contract had been dissolved but rather that Lena, by making a claim for the termination of the concession after the Court of Arbitration had been constituted, had advanced "a new claim which raises a dispute which is not within the scope of the original dispute in respect of which the members of that tribunal have been appointed as arbitrators" (Veeder, *supra* note 50, p. 782). But that is not how the Court of Arbitration appears to have treated the Soviet Government's argument given its notation in the Award that the Government had "contended that . . . [Lena] had dissolved the Concession Agreement; and the Government further said that in these circumstances the Arbitration Court had ceased to function" (*Lena Goldfields*, Award, para. 10).

effected by the Court of Arbitration; and the Court of Arbitration agreed with the Company and dissolved the agreement only after rendering jurisdictional awards and a judgment on the merits on the assumption that the agreement remained in force. Accordingly, the judgment of the Court of Arbitration in the *Lena Goldfields* case is authority for the holding that, where a party claims that the jurisdiction of an arbitral tribunal has been vitiated by dissolution of the contract that provides for arbitration, the tribunal retains the capacity to render a valid arbitral award.[60]

---

[60] In his analysis of the case, Professor Nussbaum interpreted the position of the Soviet Government on the issue of the court's constitution to be that, by its actions, Lena had rescinded the contract, with the result that the jurisdiction of the arbitral court had lapsed. Of this position, Professor Nussbaum wrote:

" ... it can be stated that neither in cases nor in legal writing has it ever been asserted – much less proved – that an arbitration agreement loses its force if one of the parties (as alleged was done by Lena) rescinds the underlying contract. What has been asserted is only that if the underlying contract is void *ab initio*, then the attached arbitration agreement likewise breaks down so as to leave no legal basis for an arbitral procedure. The latter proposition, which is questionable, we need not discuss. Breach of contract, whether it amounts to rescission or not, is manifestly the proper and main object of arbitration. Had Lena committed a breach, it was for the Government to sue Lena before the arbitral tribunal for damages or other reparations. Far from destroying the competence of the tribunal, Lena's alleged one-sided act of rescission would have created another ground of competence." Nussbaum, *supra* note 50, pp. 37–38; footnotes omitted. For exposition of arguments that the Soviet Government is said to have advanced before the Court of Arbitration, see Rashba, "The Settlement of Disputes in Commercial Dealings with the Soviet Union," 45 *Columbia Law Review* 530, 539–540 (1945); those arguments are refuted by Nussbaum, *supra* note 50, pp. 38–41.

For an international arbitral award – and a national judgment annulling it – concerning whether a governmental party to a contract with an alien can escape its arbitral obligations not by dissolving the principal agreement containing the arbitration clause but by dissolving the national enterprise that has entered into the principal agreement see *Société des Grands Travaux de Marseille* v. *East Pakistan Industrial Corporation* in V *Yearbook Commercial Arbitration* (1980), pp. 177–185 and *Société des Grands Travaux de Marseille* v. *People's Republic of Bangladesh and Bangladesh Industrial Development Corporation*, Judgment of May 5, 1976, an extract of which is printed in *Arrêts du Tribunal Federal Suisse rendus en 1976, Recueil Officiel*, vol. 102 (I), pp. 574–583. An English translation of passages of the judgment is found in V *Yearbook Commercial Arbitration* (1980), pp. 217–220.

(F) *BP V. LIBYA*

The question of the severability of an arbitration agreement was tersely treated in the award of Judge Gunnar Lagergren in *BP Exploration Company (Libya) Limited* v. *The Government of the Libyan Arab Republic* (1973).[61] Judge Lagergren had been designated as sole arbitrator by the President of the International Court of Justice pursuant to an arbitration clause of a 1966 Concession Agreement that comprehensively provided: "If at any time during or after the currency of this Concession any difference or dispute shall arise between the Government and the Company concerning the interpretation or performance hereof, or anything herein contained or in connection herewith ...,"[62] etc. It also prescribed that " ... the sole Arbitrator shall determine the applicability of this Clause and the procedure to be followed in the Arbitration."[63] Libya requested the President of the International Court of Justice not to appoint an arbitrator in this and allied cases, maintaining, *inter alia,* that the Company no longer had any status as a concession holder, and was no longer legally authorized, under the law of Libya, to exercise any right in relation to the concession. Libya so maintained in a dispute that arose out of the nationalization of "the activities of BP Exploration Company (Libya) Limited" and the vesting of "all ... rights" of the Company.[64] In replying to Libya, the President of the Court considered that this objection to constitution of the arbitration was for the sole arbitrator to settle.[65]

Judge Lagergren inferentially disposed of the question of severability in these terms:

1. *The Jurisdiction of the Tribunal*

The Jurisdiction of the Tribunal derives from Clause 28 which is cited in Part I above and which provides, in particular, that the Tribunal shall determine the applicability of the said Clause and the procedure to be followed in the arbitration ...

---

[61] 53 *International Law Reports* 297.   [62] Ibid., p. 302.   [63] Ibid., p. 303.
[64] Ibid.
[65] The position of Libya and of the President of the International Court of Justice is related in *Texaco Overseas Petroleum Company (TOPCO) and California Asiatic Oil Company* v. *the Government of the Libyan Arab Republic*, Preliminary Award of 27 November 1975, 53 *International Law Reports*, at pp. 389, 390–391, 406–407.

The Tribunal holds the said Clause 28 to be applicable to the present arbitration proceedings, and to vest the Tribunal with the required jurisdiction.[66]

Judge Lagergren held: "The BP Concession can be said to remain in force and effect as a contractual instrument only in the sense that it forms the basis of the jurisdiction of the Tribunal and of the right of the Claimant to claim damages from the Respondent before the Tribunal."[67] He reiterated: "The BP Nationalisation Law was effective to terminate the BP Concession except in the sense that the BP Concession forms the basis of jurisdiction of the Tribunal and of the right of the Claimant to claim damages from the Respondent before the Tribunal."[68]

Judge Lagergren's award accordingly constitutes authority for the conclusion that, where a State has terminated – in law as well as in fact – a contract containing an obligation to arbitrate disputes arising under that contract, the arbitral agreement survives and provides the basis for the establishment and jurisdiction of the arbitral tribunal.

(G) *TOPCO* V. *LIBYA*

The sole arbitrator, Professor René-Jean Dupuy (also appointed by the President of the International Court of Justice), dealt fully and decisively with the question of severability in his Preliminary Award of 1975 in *TOPCO* v. *Libya*. His award[69] merits extensive quotation:

14. As for the solution of the problem which creates the question of the jurisdiction of the Sole Arbitrator in the present case, that solution is linked to the answer to be given to the two following questions:

A. Supposing that the measures of nationalization could have had the effect of voiding the Deeds of Concession themselves, can this effect extend to the provisions of these Deeds relating to arbitration and, more specifically, to Clause 28?

. . .

16. The principle to which it is appropriate to refer in this matter is that of the autonomy or the independence of the arbitration clause. This principle, which has the consequence of permitting the arbitration clause

---

[66] 55 *International Law Reports*, at p. 308.   [67] Ibid., p. 354.   [68] Ibid., p. 356.
[69] Ibid., pp. 407–412. Some of Professor Dupuy's footnotes are omitted.

to escape the fate of the contract which contains it, has been upheld by several decisions of international case law. More particularly, in this connection, two decisions should be cited:

– On the one hand, the award given in the *Lena Goldfields* case ...
– On the other hand, the award in the *Losinger* case ...

17. It is not only international case law but also municipal case law which uphold the autonomy or the independence of the arbitration clause whenever the local courts are called upon to decide questions of private international law relating to international commercial arbitration. Particularly significant in this context is the case law of the French Court of Cassation: indeed, according to old case law which goes back to the year 1843, the arbitration clause is, in principle, null and void in French law. Thus, French law, rightly or wrongly, takes a position which, as a general rule, is unfavourable to arbitration. Nevertheless, in a famous decision of 7 May 1963,[12] [n. 12: [1963] *D. Jur.* 545, note Robert; [1963] *J.C.P.* II No. 13405, note Goldman; *Rev. Arb.* 60 (1963); 52 *Rev Crit. D. Int'l Privé* 615 (1963), note Motulsky] the Court of Cassation held that:

"In matters of international arbitration, the arbitration agreement, concluded separately or included in the juridical act to which it is related, always has, except in exceptional circumstances, a complete juridical autonomy excluding it from being affected by an eventual invalidity of that act."

The principle of the autonomy of the arbitration clause has since then been confirmed by several decisions;[13] [n. 13: See three decisions rendered on 18 May 1971 ([1972] *D. Jur.* 37, note Alexandre; *Rev. Arb.* 2 (1972), note Kahn; 61 *Rev. Crit. D. Int'l Privé* 124 (1972), note Mezger; 99 *Journal du Droit International* ("Clunet") 62 (1972), note Oppetit) and the *Hecht* decision of 4 July 1972 (99 Clunet 843 (1972), note Oppetit, and *Rev. Arb.* 89 (1974)). See also on the *Hecht* decision: Francescakis, "Le principe jurisprudentiel de l'autonomie de l'accord compromissoire après l'arrêt Hecht de la Cour de Cassation", *Rev. Arb.* 67 (1974)] and one can say that it is now solidly established in French private international law.

18. The writings of legal scholars also recognize the full autonomy of the arbitral clause or the arbitration agreement. Thus, a Uruguayan jurist, Professor Jiménez de Aréchega[14] [n. 14: "L'Arbitrage entre les Etats et les Sociétés Privées Etrangères", *in Mélanges en l'Honneur de Gilbert Gidel* 367 (1961), at 375] writes:

"The existing precedents demonstrate, on the contrary, that a government bound by an arbitration clause cannot validly free itself of this obligation by an act of its own will such as, for example, by changing its internal law, or by a unilateral cancellation, of the contract or of the concession."

The same principle is confirmed by an Italian jurist, Mr. Kojanec,[15] [n. 15: "The Legal Nature of Agreements Concluded by Private Entities with Foreign States", in *Colloquium on International Commercial Agreements Organized in 1968 by the Hague Academy of International Law* 299 *et seq.* (1969), at 330] in the following terms:

"But we think, on the contrary, that the arbitration clause has a separate life in relation to the contract to which it refers. This must be considered a fundamental principle in arbitration, otherwise the very possibility of ascertaining and declaring the nullity of the contract would be denied and the arbitration clause would lose its content and its legal effect... We must therefore conclude that the obligation to have recourse to arbitration continues to subsist even in the context of the legal order of the State purporting, by a legislative act, to annul or modify unilaterally the contract to which it is a party and which provides for this procedure. Indeed, if such legislation constitutes the exercise of sovereign powers, it must be observed that, in this case, the purpose of arbitral proceedings consists in ascertaining the legitimacy of the use of such powers and this scope may not be nullified by one of the parties."

Professor Weil is of the same opinion[17] [n. 17: Weil, "Problèmes Relatifs aux Contrats Passés entre un Etat et un Particulier", 128 *Recueil des Cours de l'Académie de Droit International de la Haye (R. C A.D.I.)* 95 (1969), at 222]:

"The mechanism established by the parties with the view of settling their eventual disputes should be capable of being put in motion precisely in order to judge the legality and the consequences of a measure which the State may have been led to take in the exercise of its sovereign power; to permit the State to free itself from the obligations it freely undertook for the settlement of disputes, which may arise between it and its contracting party, would be tantamount to depriving this essential clause of the contract of any effectiveness. Consequently, the State cannot modify unilaterally the mechanism established for the settlement of disputes in a direct way by dictating through its authority a change in the arbitration clauses, or in an indirect way through refusing to accept the arbitral procedure as it is provided in the contract, or by putting obstacles in the way of its operation; by such actions, the State would be committing an unlawful act. Furthermore, it would be less acceptable for a State to revoke the contract in its entirety in order to claim that the arbitration clause has become inoperative and thus to evade its effects by such a device. Indeed, it is unanimously recognized that arbitration clauses are autonomous in relation to the other provisions of the contract and that the invalidity or the termination of the contract remains without influence on them."

In one of his other works,[18] [n. 18: Weil, "Les Clauses de Stabilisation ou d'Intangibilité Insérées dans les Accords de Développement Economique", in *Mélanges Offerts à Charles Rousseau* 301 (1974), at 325] the same author emphasizes the reason for this solution by pointing out that:

> "... it is indispensable, if these clauses are to make sense, that they should escape the fate of the rest of the contract: What use would it be to provide that any difficulty resulting from the implementation of the contract would be submitted to arbitration if when the first difficulty occurs the contracting State is able to free itself from the arbitration clause by taking refuge behind its prerogatives in contractual matters?"

Finally, the same view is held by Swiss specialists in international law. Thus, Pierre Lalive writes[19] [n. 19: P. Lalive, "Problèmes Relatifs à l'Arbitrage International Commercial", 120 *R.C.A.D.I.* 569 (1967), at 593]:

> "Whatever the nature which municipal laws attribute to the arbitration clause, the majority of these laws recognizes its independent character, or at least, they make a presumption in this sense, with the consequence that the arbitration clause does not necessarily follow the fate of the principal contract in the event that the contract is null and void ... The same solution is justified in a way *a fortiori* in *international* arbitration where the necessity is still more critical to prevent or respond to dilatory tactics."

The Preliminary Award in *TOPCO* v. *Libya* constitutes, in itself and in the authorities it quotes, direct and substantial authority for the principle that an arbitration agreement contained in a principal agreement between a State and an alien survives termination of the principal agreement. This is the case despite the fact that, in his subsequent award on the merits, Professor Dupuy did not find the principal agreement to be terminated in law, and despite the fact that the arbitration clause in question provided that it encompassed disputes arising "after the currency of this Concession...." The holdings of Professor Dupuy, because of their terms, cannot be distinguished on these grounds.

(H) *LIAMCO* V. *LIBYA*

The 1977 Award of Dr. Sobhi Mahmassani, who was appointed by the President of the International Court of Justice as sole arbitrator in the case brought by the *Libyan American Oil Company (LIAMCO)* v. *The Government of the Libyan Arab Republic,*[70] provides another illustration of this principle of international arbitration. In a case whose facts were like those at bar in the *TOPCO* case, Dr. Mahmassani held as follows on the question of severability:

It is widely accepted in international law and practice that an arbitration clause survives the unilateral termination by the State of the contract in which it is inserted and continues in force even after that termination. This is a logical consequence of the interpretation of the intention of the contracting parties, and appears to be one of the basic conditions for creating a favorable climate for foreign investment.

This rule was adopted by decisions of the International Court of Justice (ex. in *Ambatielos Case* in 1952 and 1953), and of many Arbitral Tribunals (ex. in *Losinger and Co.* v. *State of Yugoslavia*). Such decisions have confirmed the obligation of the State to arbitrate with a private party according to the terms of the contract despite the protest or default of the State and despite arguments that the agreement containing the arbitration clause had been terminated or come to an end.

It has been contended by the Libyan Government ... that it rejects arbitration as contrary to the heart of its sovereignty. Such argument cannot be retained against said international practice, which was also confirmed in many international conventions and resolutions. For instance, the Convention of 1966 on the Settlement of Investment Disputes between States and Nationals of other States provides, in its Article 25, that whenever the parties have agreed to arbitrate no party may withdraw its consent unilaterally. More generally, Resolution No. 1803 (XVII) of the United Nations General Assembly, dated 21 December 1962, while proclaiming the permanent sovereignty of peoples and nations over their natural resources, confirms the obligation of the State to respect arbitration agreements (Section I, paras. 1 and 4).

Therefore, a State may always validly waive its so-called sovereign rights by signing an arbitration agreement and then by staying bound by it.

Moreover, that ruling is in harmony with Islamic law and practice. ...

***

As the arbitration clause and the procedure outlined therein are binding upon the contracting parties, and the procedure outlined therein being imperative, the Arbitral Tribunal constituted in accordance with such

---

[70] 62 *International Law Reports*, p. 140.

clause and procedure should have exclusive jurisdiction over the issues of the dispute. No other tribunal or authority, local or otherwise, has competence in the matter.[71]

(1) ELF AQUITAINE IRAN V. NATIONAL IRANIAN OIL COMPANY

In a Preliminary Award rendered in 1982, Professor Bernhard Gomard dealt with questions of competence and severability in the following context. The National Iranian Oil Company (NIOC) in 1966 concluded an exploration and production agreement with French State and private interests, duly ratified by Iran, which contained a comprehensive arbitration clause. It included the provision that the sole arbitrator, "in arriving at the award, shall in no way be restricted by any specific rule of law, but shall have the power to base his award on considerations of equity and generally recognized principles of law and in particular International Law."[72] Two oil fields were discovered, and their commercial exploitation began in 1978. A dispute arose over the claimed failure of NIOC to meet its contractual obligations to repay investments advanced by Elf and to sell oil at the preferential price provided for in the agreement. On January 8, 1980, the Revolutionary Council of the Islamic Republic of Iran adopted a Single Article Act, providing:

All the Oil Agreements, which at the discretion of the Special Committee to be convened by the Ministry of Oil, may be found to be at variance with the provisions of the Act on Nationalization of the Oil Industry of Iran, shall be declared null and void, and all the claims arising from entering into and performance of such agreements, shall be settled

---

[71] Ibid., p. 178. It will have been noted that Dr. Mahmassani referred to the *Ambatielos Case* before the International Court of Justice as supporting the autonomy of the arbitration clause. A review of the Court's judgments in that case does not reveal the relevant elements which Dr. Mahmassani found in them. Cf., *Ambatielos Case, (Jurisdiction), Judgment of July 1st, 1952, I.C.J. Reports 1952*, p. 28; *Ambatielos Case (Merits: Obligation to Arbitrate), Judgment of May 19th, 1953, I.C.J. Reports 1953*, p. 10. Nor is the arbitral award of 1955 in the *Ambatielos Claim* relevant; see XII *U.N. Reports of International Arbitral Awards* 87(*U.N.R.I.A.A.*).

[72] The award is published in part in XI *Yearbook Commercial Arbitration* (1986), at p. 97; the governing law clause is found at p. 99. For an analysis of the award, see Philippe Fouchard, "L'Arbitrage *Elf Aquitaine Iran c. National Iranian Oil Company*: Une Nouvelle Contribution au Droit International de l'Arbitrage," *Revue de l'Arbitrage* (1984, No. 3), p. 333.

according to the resolution of such Committee. Such Committee shall be held with participation of the Representative of the Ministry of Foreign Affairs.[73]

By letter of August 11, 1980, Elf was informed by NIOC that the Special Committee had declared the 1966 agreement null and void *ab initio*. Elf invoked arbitration in pursuance of the arbitration clause contained in the 1966 agreement, which accorded a residual authority to the President of the Danish Supreme Court to appoint a sole arbitrator. He appointed Professor Gomard. NIOC objected on various grounds to the arbitrator's competence. The arbitrator described two of the resultant questions as follows:

(A) Does an arbitrator designated in accordance with an arbitral clause contained in a contract between the parties have competence to rule on his own competence to act as arbitrator?
(B) Does an arbitral clause form an integrated part of the contract in which it is inserted with the consequence that the clause is subject to all exceptions raised against the contract; *or* does an arbitral clause enjoy the autonomy (or independence or separability) that it can form the basis of an arbitration between the parties even after objections against the validity of the contract have been raised by one of the parties?[74]

On the question of the competence of the arbitrator to rule upon his own competence, Professor Gomard held:

The parties are in agreement that the Sole Arbitrator has competence to decide whether or not he is competent to act as arbitrator in accordance with Art. 41 of the Agreement. NIOC, however, has added that NIOC is an Iranian Company and is bound by Iranian law alone. Under Iranian law NIOC cannot be bound by nor take part in an arbitration purportedly instituted under an agreement declared void under Iranian law.

It is a fundamental principle in international arbitration recognized in treaties dealing with arbitration, in several arbitral awards, and by writers on the law of arbitration that an arbitrator has "competence over the competence."

The rationale behind the principle of the arbitrator's competence over the competence is a widely recognized need to establish a system of law providing enterprises engaged in activities in other countries under contract with the government of that country or with an institution or

---

[73] XI *Yearbook Commercial Arbitration* (1986), p. 98.   [74] Ibid.

company under the control of that government with access to a tribunal or other organ completely independent of the parties and of their respective governments, in the event that disputes that cannot be settled by negotiation should arise.[75]

He observed that the principle of *compétence de la compétence* had been accepted in treaties, by leading legal scholars, the International Court of Justice, and in arbitral awards, and concluded:

The Sole Arbitrator has, therefore, reached the conclusion that even in the absence of the agreement between the parties on his competence to decide on his competence to act as arbitrator in the present case, he has – in accordance with considerations of equity and by virtue of principles of international law – such competence.[76]

On the question of the autonomy of the arbitration clause, the arbitrator concluded:

In this Preliminary Award the Sole Arbitrator cannot and has not attempted to reach a decision on the merits of the objection made by NIOC that the Agreement, as a consequence of the decision made by the Special Committee, is null and void *ab initio*. This Preliminary Award, however, must determine whether the arbitration clause contained in Art. 41 of the Agreement enjoys an autonomy or independence in the sense that the nullity of the Agreement alleged by one of the parties, *in casu* NIOC, cannot affect the validity of the arbitration clause, *or* whether the arbitration clause as part of the Agreement is of no force and effect if the Agreement is to be regarded as a nullity.

It is a generally recognized principle of the law of international arbitration that arbitration clauses continue to be operative, even though an objection is raised by one of the parties that the contract containing the arbitration clause is null and void. The jurisdiction of an arbitrator or arbitration board designated in accordance with an arbitration clause is unimpaired, even though the contract containing the arbitration clause is alleged to be null and void.

The rational strength of this principle is apparent. In the absence of access to international courts, arbitration under an international rule of law presents a workable and qualified system for the settlement of disputes independent of both parties involved. This is evidenced *inter alia* by the wide acceptance of the various international conventions on arbitration. Arbitration offers the parties the possibility of adjusting in their agreement the general law of arbitration in a way that makes their submission to

---

[75] Ibid., p. 101.   [76] Ibid., p. 102.

arbitration acceptable from the point of view of their different nationalities.

An arbitration clause may not always be operative in cases where it is clearly indicated by the facts and circumstances that there never existed a valid contract between the parties. The facts and circumstances that have been made known to the Sole Arbitrator concerning the agreement in the present case do not so indicate. The autonomy of an arbitration clause is a principle of international law that has been consistently applied in decisions rendered in international arbitrations, in the writings of the most qualified publicists on international arbitration, in arbitration regulations adopted by international organisations and in treaties. Also, in many countries the principle forms part of national arbitration law.[77]

He accordingly held that:

The Sole Arbitrator has, by the weight of the authority cited and of the rationale of the principle of the autonomy of arbitration clauses, been led to the conclusion, that the arbitration clause binds the parties and is operative unimpaired by the allegation by NIOC that the Agreement as a whole is null and void *ab initio*. This conclusion does not in any way prejudice the outcome of a later decision as to whether the Agreement is null and void as alleged by NIOC. NIOC is completely free if they so wish to develop further in their pleadings at a later stage the justifications for the allegation of nullity and the consequences of the nullity of the Agreement, if established, for the claims raised by ELF.[78]

In reaching these conclusions, the arbitrator referred to several other authorities on severability.[79] The award in the *Elf Aquitaine*

---

[77] XI *Yearbook Commercial Arbitration*, pp. 102–103.   [78] Ibid., p. 103.

[79] See, e.g., *Sapphire International Petroleums Ltd.* v. *National Iranian Oil Company (NIOC)* (1963). The text of the arbitral award of March 15, 1963 of Judge Pierre Cavin, as sole arbitrator, is printed at 35 *International Law Reports*, p. 137. The *Sapphire* case involved a government-owned corporation, NIOC, in a dispute with a foreign company over a contract containing an arbitration agreement. NIOC declared the contract terminated and at the same time recognized that termination of the contract did not foreclose recourse to arbitration under the contract. This is indicated by the fact that, when it declared the contract terminated, NIOC reserved the remedies to which it was entitled under the provisions of the Agreement. The arbitral award further affirms that: "The validity and extent of this arbitration clause, as well as the fact that it is an arbitration clause, are neither open to question nor in dispute." Ibid., p. 166. NIOC did not dispute the continuing validity of the arbitration agreement, but rather maintained that the appointment of the sole arbitrator was null because the arbitral remedy had been invoked initially by Sapphire

v. *NIOC* case constitutes still another arbitral authority that
unequivocally sustains and develops the severability principle of
international arbitration.

(J) *SOJUZNEFTEEXPORT V. JOC OIL LIMITED*

The award in this arbitration, as well as the decisions of the
Supreme Court and Court of Appeal of Bermuda concerning the
enforcement of the award, provide another application of severability, while also shedding light on its scope.[80]

The case arose out of a contract for the sale of oil entered into
between the All-Union Foreign Trade Association, or Sojuznefteexport (incorporated in the Soviet Union with a legal personality
separate from the State), and Joc Oil Limited (a company incorporated in Bermuda). The contract included an arbitration agreement
providing for arbitration at the Foreign Trade Arbitration Commission of the USSR Chamber of Commerce and Industry (FTAC), in
Moscow, in accordance with FTAC's rules of procedure. A dispute
arose concerning Joc Oil's refusal to pay for certain supplies of oil
that Sojuznefteexport had supplied to it. Sojuznefteexport claimed
damages for that non-payment and Joc Oil made several counterclaims, including for late delivery.

Joc Oil objected to the FTAC's jurisdiction on the basis that the
contract was invalid *ab initio* because of noncompliance with
requirements under Soviet law for approval of foreign trade transactions. Joc Oil submitted that the arbitration agreement was therefore also invalid and that the principle of severability did not apply
under Soviet law, with the result that the tribunal was not competent to hear the dispute.

The tribunal, after reviewing Soviet law, upheld the severability of
the arbitration agreement in these terms:

Petroleums Ltd. rather than Sapphire International Petroleums Ltd. (to
whom the former was said to have assigned its rights). Accordingly, while
the award as such does not treat severability, the proceedings as a whole
provide support for that principle.

[80] The award is published in part in XVIII *Yearbook Commercial Arbitration* (1993), at
p. 92. The decision of the Bermudan Supreme Court is summarized in the
decision of the Bermudan Court of Appeal, which is published in XV *Yearbook
Commercial Arbitration* (1990), at p. 384.

Proceeding from the above analysis of the Soviet material and procedural legislation applicable to the dispute in question, the Commission has recognised that an arbitration agreement (arbitration clause) is a procedural contract, independent from the material-legal contract and that therefore the question as to the validity or invalidity of this contract does not affect the agreement of the parties about the submission of the existing dispute to the jurisdiction of the FTAC. The Commission has come to the conclusion that the arbitration clause contained in the contract is valid and therefore in accordance with the right assigned to it has recognised itself as competent to hear the dispute as to its essence and to rule upon it.[81]

The tribunal, exercising that competence, held that Sojuznefteexport could not claim the contractual price of the goods because the sale contract was indeed invalid for failure to comply with the signing formalities under Soviet law, but that it was entitled to restitution in a sum equal to the value of the amount of the shipments delivered and unpaid. Joc Oil's counterclaims were all rejected.

Sojuznefteexport's attempts to enforce this award in Bermuda were initially unsuccessful. The judge in the Supreme Court of Bermuda, following a review of Soviet law, concluded that, "[a]ll in all I am not satisfied that the doctrine of separability or whatever it is called was, at the relevant time of this contract, or even now is part of Soviet law."[82] It followed for the judge that, if there were no valid contract, there was no valid arbitration agreement, and therefore the arbitral tribunal had no competence to determine the dispute. The judge then went further and explained that, "[e]ven if he were wrong and there was some degree of separability in Soviet law, any such separability would not assist [Sojuznefteexport] in the case of voidness ab initio of the underlying contract."[83]

The Court of Appeal, by majority, reversed the Supreme Court's decision. The majority's opinion explained that "practically all systems admit some degree of separability of the arbitration clause from the main contract and the real question to be canvassed is to what extent is the doctrine of separability permitted."[84] It found that the Soviet system was one such system. It also derived support

---

[81] XVIII *Yearbook Commercial Arbitration* (1993), at p. 99.
[82] XV *Yearbook Commercial Arbitration, supra* note 80, at p. 394.   [83] Ibid.
[84] Ibid., p. 402.

from general doctrine and cited the conclusion to the first edition of this book,[85] as well as the conclusion of Professor Pieter Sanders: "Separability has become, like the competence of the arbitrator to rule upon his competence, a truly international rule of law."[86]

The Court of Appeal acknowledged the two qualifications on severability noted above (namely "where the existence of the contract itself is contested" and "when the attack is not upon the principal agreement but upon the validity of the arbitration clause itself").[87] With respect to the first qualification, the majority concluded that this was not a case of a nonexistent contract, but rather one of invalidity. The majority explained that "[Sojuznefteexport] and Joc Oil had entered into a contract which turned out to be an invalid transaction solely for lack of two authorized signatures by one of the parties."[88] There was an important distinction between an invalid and a nonexistent contract, the majority pointed out, with reference to civil law, common law, and the first edition of this book. With respect to the second qualification, the majority confirmed that the Soviet law requirements for approval of foreign trade transactions did not apply to the arbitration agreement itself.[89]

The President of the Bermudan Court of Appeal dissented because he considered that the contract was invalid in a way that rendered it nonexistent. As he put it: "If the actions of the unauthorized person do not create any civil law rights and duties until ratification, is not this another way of saying that until ratification the purported 'contract' does not come into being, is nonexistent?"[90] He reasoned in turn that:

If the November 1976 contract was 'non-existent' – that is to say it never came into existence – as it seems to me, it is quite ridiculous to suggest that the arbitration clause which formed part of that 'non-existent' contract would nevertheless, somehow, be deemed to have come into existence. The authorities appear to be all against the suggestion that the so-called doctrine of separation should apply in such circumstances.[91]

The majority responded in a "Post Scripture regarding the Dissenting Opinion." In its view, nothing in the President's dissenting opinion cast doubt on the majority's holding that the contract in this case was

---

[85] Ibid., p. 414. [86] Ibid. [87] Ibid., pp. 408–409. [88] Ibid., p. 421.
[89] Ibid., p. 406. [90] Ibid., p. 433. [91] Ibid., p. 434.

invalid rather than nonexistent. The majority recalled again the legal authorities it had cited, including the first edition of this book, and added that "[t]he Shorter Oxford English Dictionary defines 'invalidate' as meaning (1) to render invalid; (2) to render of no force or effect, esp. to deprive of legal efficacy. One cannot deprive a non-existent contract of legal efficacy because it never possessed any."[92]

The split within the Court thus turned not on the soundness of the principle of severability, nor on its proper scope – given both the majority and dissenting opinions appeared to recognize that there may be difficulties applying severability in the case of nonexistent contracts – but rather on the more particular question of what is meant by a nonexistent contract.

(K) WORLD DUTY FREE CO. LTD V. KENYA

The principle of severability was applied in an ICSID-administered arbitration brought under an arbitration agreement contained in a contract between a British company, World Duty Free Co. Ltd., and the Kenyan Airports Authority, acting on behalf of the Government of Kenya.[93] World Duty Free alleged that Kenya had, among other

---

[92] Ibid., p. 431.

[93] *World Duty Free Company Limited* v. *The Republic of Kenya*, ICSID Case No. ARB/ 00/7, Award, October 4, 2006. The principle of severability has also been recognized in passing in other ICSID cases (*Plama Consortium Limited* v. *Bulgaria*, ICSID Case No. ARB/03/24, Decision on Jurisdiction, February 8, 2005, paras. 130, 212, rejecting that any allegations of misrepresentation concerning an investment contract could affect Bulgaria's consent to arbitrate under the Energy Charter Treaty, and also relying on the principle of severability as a reason for not applying a most-favored nation clause to a dispute settlement provision; and *Malicorp Limited* v. *Egypt*, ICSID Case No. ARB/08/18, Award, February 7, 2011, para. 119(a), relying on the principle of severability when deciding to consider allegations of misrepresentation and corruption in respect of the underlying contract as a matter going to the merits of the case rather than the tribunal's jurisdiction to determine the merits). See also *CCL* v. *Kazakhstan*, SCC Case No. 122/2001, 1 *Stockholm International Arbitration Review* (2005), pp. 123, 135–137. A case brought under a bilateral investment treaty and administered by the Stockholm Chamber of Commerce, rejecting Kazakhstan's submission that the termination of the underlying contract by the Kazakh courts affected the arbitration agreement. In those cases where the consent to arbitrate comprises the standing offer to arbitrate contained in a bilateral investment treaty, combined with the investor's acceptance of that offer by launching arbitration, it is particularly clear that no defect in any investment contract between the investor and the host State could infect that consent to arbitrate.

things, unlawfully expropriated its duty free businesses at two Kenyan airports. But Kenya responded that the underlying contract between the claimant and Kenya was unenforceable because it had been procured by the payment of a bribe from the claimant to the then President of Kenya – a fact that the claimant admitted and even described in its first submission. It was on this basis that the tribunal dismissed the claim as being contrary to international public policy as well as the public policy of the United Kingdom and Kenya (which were the relevant laws applicable to the contract).[94] But the tribunal emphasized that the bribery infected the underlying agreement only and not the arbitration agreement specifically:

> Lastly, the Tribunal notes that no evidence was adduced or argument submitted by either of the Parties to the effect that the bribe specifically procured Article 9 of the Agreement, containing the Parties' agreement to arbitration under the ICSID Convention. Accordingly, in accordance with well-established legal principles under English and Kenyan law, the Tribunal operates on the assumption that the Parties' arbitration agreement remains subsisting valid and effective for the purpose of this proceeding and Award.[95]

The principle of severability therefore allowed the tribunal to exercise its jurisdiction to dismiss the claim because of the bribery. Without the principle of severability, the mere allegation of bribery in respect of the underlying contract may have deprived the tribunal of jurisdiction at the outset.

(L) *STRAN GREEK REFINERIES V. GREECE*

The extent to which severability has become such a widespread and fundamental principle of general application in international law and arbitration is underscored by its application by the European Court of Human Rights.[96] In this case, a Greek company, Stran Greek Refineries (the applicant before the European Court), entered into a contract with the Greek State in 1972, then ruled by a military junta, for the construction of an oil refinery. After this company had spent considerable sums toward the construction of

---

[94] *World Duty Free, supra* note 93, paras. 137–188.   [95] Ibid., para. 187.
[96] *Stran Greek Refineries* v. *Greece* (1994) 19 EHRR 293.

that refinery, the democratic government that had replaced the junta decided, in 1977, that the contract was not in the national interest and terminated it.

The path from there to the European Court of Human Rights was a long and winding one. The company first sought a remedy before the Greek courts, but the Greek State challenged the jurisdiction of the Greek courts on the basis that the parties had agreed to arbitration in their contract. The Athens Court of First Instance rejected that objection, including because, as the European Court described, "the ministerial committee on the economy had terminated the contract in issue in its entirety ... which had the effect of rendering the arbitration clause void as it was not an autonomous provision."[97] Yet the Greek State proceeded with the arbitration anyway, in which the tribunal awarded Stran Greek Refineries a significant award of damages against the Greek State. The Greek State, contradicting its earlier position, challenged this award before the Greek courts on the basis that the arbitral tribunal lacked jurisdiction given the termination of the contract. This was rejected by the Court of First Instance and the Court of Appeal. The Court of Appeal held that:

In modern Greek legislation the principle of the autonomy of an arbitration clause in relation to the contract prevails. The termination of the contract, for whatever reason, does not bring an end to the power of the arbitrators designated to hear disputes which have arisen during the period of validity of the contract.... The decision of the ministerial committee on the economy did not annul the arbitration clause contained in Article 27 of the contract and, accordingly, it does not preclude the arbitrators from examining the merits of the dispute.[98]

The Greek State, however, appealed to the Court of Cassation and, while that appeal was pending, the Greek Parliament specifically rejected the application of the severability principle with respect to Stran Greek Refineries' contract:

The true and lawful meaning of the provisions of [the legislation] concerning the termination of contracts entered into between 21 April 1967 and 24 July 1974 is that, upon the termination of these contracts, all their

---

[97] Ibid., para. 11.   [98] Ibid., para. 18.

terms, conditions and clauses, including the arbitration clause, are ipso
jure repealed and the arbitration tribunal no longer has jurisdiction.[99]

The Court of Cassation upheld the constitutionality of this "clarifi-
cation," holding that:

... the main issue is the acceptance or rejection of the principle of the
autonomous character of the arbitration clause and of its scope. For a long
time this matter has been the subject of significant differences of opinion
in international case-law and among legal writers. In some countries the
principle of the survival of the clause to resolve disputes arising prior to
the termination of contracts ... prevails. In other countries the dominant
view is that termination of the contract entails the annulment of the clause
and therefore the referral of all the disputes to the ordinary courts. In
other countries again, the accepted view is that the autonomous character
of the arbitration clause operates only in respect of certain types of
dispute. It was therefore necessary to provide an interpretation of Law
no. 141/1975 and that interpretation resolved the problem for the purposes of Greek law by opting for the annulment of arbitration clauses ...
and the removal of jurisdiction from the arbitration court.[100]

The company and its shareholder subsequently brought a claim to
the European Court of Human Rights alleging that by virtue of its
whipsawing tactics "the State had effectively removed jurisdiction
from the courts called upon to determine the validity of the arbitration award and prevented any proper judicial investigation of the
subject of the dispute." The Court agreed and concluded that "the
State infringed the applicants' rights under Article 6 para. 1 (art.
6-1) by intervening in a manner which was decisive to ensure that
the – imminent – outcome of proceedings in which it was a party
was favourable to it."[101]

---

[99] Ibid., para. 22.   [100] Ibid.

[101] Ibid., para. 50. Article 6(1) of the European Convention provides: "In the
determination of his civil rights and obligations or of any criminal charge
against him, everyone is entitled to a fair and public hearing within a reasonable time by an independent and impartial tribunal established by law. Judgment shall be pronounced publicly but the press and public may be excluded
from all or part of the trial in the interests of morals, public order or national
security in a democratic society, where the interests of juveniles or the protection of the private life of the parties so require, or to the extent strictly
necessary in the opinion of the court in special circumstances where publicity
would prejudice the interests of justice." Convention for the Protection of
Human Rights and Fundamental Freedoms, Rome, 4.XI.1950 (European
Convention).

The Court also held that the Greek State had breached Article 1 of Protocol 1 of the Convention.[102] The Court accepted the applicant's submission that the legislation interfered with the applicants' property right by cancelling the debt arising out of a final and binding arbitral award. The Court held this to be unjustified in the sense that the conduct did not strike a fair balance between the demands of the general interest of the community and the requirements of the protection of the individual's fundamental rights:

> The Court does not doubt that it was necessary for the democratic Greek State to terminate a contract which it considered to be prejudicial to its economic interests. Indeed according to the case-law of international courts and of arbitration tribunals any State has a sovereign power to amend or even terminate a contract concluded with private individuals, provided it pays compensation (Shufeldt arbitration award of 24 July 1930, Reports of International Arbitral Awards, League of Nations, vol. II, p. 1095). This both reflects recognition that the superior interests of the State take precedence over contractual obligations and takes account of the need to preserve a fair balance in a contractual relationship. However, the unilateral termination of a contract does not take effect in relation to certain essential clauses of the contract, such as the arbitration clause. To alter the machinery set up by enacting an authoritative amendment to such a clause would make it possible for one of the parties to evade jurisdiction in a dispute in respect of which specific provision was made for arbitration.[103]

The Court cited in support of this reasoning several of the cases described earlier in this chapter. This clear recognition of the principle of severability by the European Court of Human Rights, to the point of condemning the Greek State for flouting it, illustrates how widespread the acceptance of this principle has become.

---

[102] Article 1 of Protocol 1 of the European Convention provides: "Every natural or legal person is entitled to the peaceful enjoyment of his possessions. No one shall be deprived of his possessions except in the public interest and subject to the conditions provided for by law and by the general principles of international law. The preceding provisions shall not, however, in any way impair the right of a State to enforce such laws as it deems necessary to control the use of property in accordance with the general interest or to secure the payment of taxes or other contributions or penalties."

[103] *Stran Greek Refineries* v. *Greece, supra* note 96, para. 72.

(M) *BALKAN ENERGY V. GHANA; WATERVILLE HOLDINGS V. GHANA*

These two cases provide further examples of international tribunals supporting the principle of severability, although they also again indicate that respondent States may continue to challenge – and their home courts may still sometimes reject – the principle.

Balkan Energy v. *Ghana* (of which Judge Schwebel was a member of the tribunal appointed by Balkan Energy) involved a Power Purchase Agreement (PPA) entered into between the Ghanaian subsidiary of a British energy company (Balkan Energy) and Ghana.[104] That PPA provided for Ghanaian law as the governing law and contained an arbitration agreement providing for arbitration seated in The Hague in accordance with the UNCITRAL Rules.

Balkan Energy launched an arbitration alleging that Ghana had failed to perform the contract. Ghana objected to the tribunal's jurisdiction based on Article 181(5) of the Ghanaian Constitution, which requires parliamentary approval for any "international business or economic transaction to which the Government is a party." No such approval had been given in this case. Although Ghana acknowledged the principle of severability, it still objected to the tribunal's jurisdiction on the basis that, as the tribunal summarized, "the same law that applies to the validity of the underlying contract may also apply to the arbitration agreement and may independently render the arbitration agreement invalid."[105] Ghana further contended that the question of the validity of the arbitration agreement in light of this constitutional provision was non-arbitrable because, under Ghanaian law, only the Ghanaian courts were competent to interpret the Constitution.

The arbitral tribunal rejected Ghana's jurisdictional objection. It started by recalling that "[t]wo bedrock principles of international arbitration bear on the issues before the Tribunal, namely, the principle of competence-competence, and the principle of separability of the arbitration clause from the contract of which it is part."[106] These "two bedrock principles" were also set out in Article 21 of the 1976 UNCITRAL Rules, as well as under Ghanaian law and the law of the seat (Dutch law). The tribunal considered that

---

[104] *Balkan Energy (Ghana) Limited* v. *Ghana*, PCA Case No. 2010-7, Interim Award, December 22, 2010.
[105] Ibid., para. 109. [106] Ibid., para. 99.

these principles could not be undermined by Ghana's jurisdictional objection, which wrongly assumed that Ghanaian law determined the validity of the arbitration agreement.

The tribunal instead applied the law of the seat (Dutch law) as the applicable law of the arbitration agreement. The tribunal did so on the basis of the "validation principle," according to which it should be presumed that "the Parties opted for an approach that would validate rather than render invalid the arbitration agreement."[107] The tribunal then determined that the arbitration agreement was valid under Dutch law, finding that under Dutch law the constitutional provisions of a foreign law could not invalidate an otherwise valid arbitration agreement. The tribunal buttressed its conclusion by reference to the principle that a State could not rely on its own law to invalidate an arbitration agreement into which it had entered and the principle of estoppel given that competent Ghanaian officials had previously held out that the arbitration agreement was valid under Ghanaian law when entering into the PPA. The tribunal concluded that the arbitration agreement "is both valid and enforceable independently from the issue of the validity of the PPA, and that the Parties are bound by this commitment to international arbitration."[108]

The tribunal finally addressed the fact that Ghana had also launched proceedings before the Ghanaian High Court and obtained an injunction restraining Balkan Energy from proceeding with the arbitration until the Ghanaian courts determined whether the PPA and arbitration agreement were (in)valid. Balkan Energy in turn sought an anti-suit injunction from the tribunal in respect of the Ghanaian proceedings, which the tribunal declined to grant, though the tribunal itself decided that it should not defer to the Ghanaian courts in respect of its jurisdiction. As the tribunal explained:

The request by [Ghana] for a postponement of the proceedings puts this Tribunal in the invidious position of having to decide between, on the one hand, upholding the validity of the principles of competence-competence and separability and, on the other hand, accepting the consequences arising from an injunction against proceedings in an arbitration which the Parties have previously accepted in a formal and written arbitration

---

[107] Ibid., para. 149.   [108] Ibid., para. 167.

agreement. The Tribunal is not only convinced that it has acted correctly in finding in favour of its jurisdiction in the arbitration but it also believes, as the Claimant has argued, that it has an obligation to give effect to the commitment of the Parties to arbitration.[109]

The tribunal nevertheless decided to set down a procedural calendar that would allow it to take into account the Ghanaian courts' decisions at the merits stage of the arbitration.

The Ghanaian Supreme Court proceeded to hold that the PPA was an "international business or economic transaction to which the Government is a party" within the meaning of Article 181(5) of the Ghanaian Constitution and remitted the matter to the High Court to determine the PPA's consequent (in)validity. The Supreme Court held that the arbitration agreement itself was not such a transaction, but its subsequent reasoning appeared to reject the principle of severability:

An international commercial arbitration draws its life from the transaction whose dispute resolution it deals with. We therefore have difficulty in conceiving of it as a transaction separate and independent from the transaction that has generated the dispute it is required to resolve.[110]

The arbitral tribunal, in its decision on the merits, did not revisit the question of severability, but it disagreed with the Supreme Court's characterization of the PPA as an "international business or economic transaction to which the Government is a party" within the meaning of Article 181(5), including because it was entered into by Ghana and a company incorporated in Ghana, and accordingly upheld the validity of the PPA under Ghanaian law.[111]

Balkan Energy successfully applied for the recognition of the final award in the US District Court for the District of Columbia, which upheld the validity of the arbitration agreement and the arbitral tribunal's jurisdiction to determine that validity.[112]

*

Waterville Holdings Ltd v. *Ghana* concerned similar issues about the effect of Article 181(5) of the Ghanaian Constitution on the validity of

---

[109] Ibid., para. 190.
[110] Cited in Award on the Merits. See *Balkan Energy (Ghana) Limited* v. *Ghana*, PCA Case No. 2010-7, Award on the Merits, April 1, 2014, para. 332.
[111] Ibid., paras. 374–397.
[112] See *Balkan Energy Limited* v. *Ghana*, 302 F. Supp. 3d 144 (D.D.C. 2018).

an arbitration agreement.[113] Waterville Holdings Ltd, a company incorporated in the British Virgin Islands, entered into two contracts with Ghana for the renovation of three football stadiums in advance of the African Cup of Nations football tournament (the Stadia Contracts). Ghana terminated these contracts on the basis that Waterville failed to obtain the necessary funding required under the contracts. Ghana paid some money to Waterville for work done and also later paid further sums as part of a settlement agreement. But a former Attorney-General of Ghana, acting as a private citizen, then brought a "public interest action" claiming that the sums paid under the contracts and settlement agreement were unlawfully paid because these contracts were "international economic or business transactions" that had not obtained the required approvals from the Ghanaian Parliament in accordance with Article 181(5) of the Ghanaian Constitution. The Supreme Court upheld this claim and declared that the contracts and settlement agreement were void and ordered all the money paid thereunder to be repaid to Ghana.

Ghana subsequently launched enforcement proceedings in the Ghanaian High Court in order to recover these sums. Waterville sought a stay of those proceedings on the basis of the arbitration agreements contained in the contracts. The High Court rejected that application and in so doing issued a flat rejection of the principle of severability:

The contract[s] [Waterville] is relying on in seeking for a referral to arbitration do not exist. They have been declared null and void as not having been approved by Parliament. The requirement for arbitration is not separate and separable from the main contract as Defense Counsel has contended but essentially part and parcel of it. If the contracts are declared null and void, so are the provisions in it relating to arbitration.[114]

The Ghanaian Court of Appeal dismissed Waterville's appeal against that decision. It was at this point that the claimant launched arbitration under the arbitration agreements contained within the Stadia Contracts seeking, among other things, orders that the contracts and settlement agreement were valid and enforceable, and that Ghana was not entitled to recover the sums it had paid to

---

[113] *Waterville Holdings (BVI) Limited* v. *Ghana*, ICC Case No. 20561/TO, Partial Award on Jurisdiction, March 20, 2017.
[114] Ibid., para. 72.

Waterville. The arbitration agreement provided for arbitration seated in London under the ICC Rules and the Stadia Contracts provided that Ghanaian law was the applicable law of those contracts.

Ghana objected to the tribunal's jurisdiction. At the heart of Ghana's objections was the argument that "the Stadia Contracts having been declared void ... as a matter of Ghanaian law so too must be the Arbitration Agreements therein."[115] Ghana acknowledged that Ghanaian legislation provided for the principle of severability,[116] but it submitted that Article 181(5) of the Ghanaian constitution prevailed, and it relied on the Ghanaian Supreme Court's decision concerning Balkan Energy (described above) for this proposition. Ghana also contended that the Claimants' claims were non-arbitrable because they involved the interpretation of the Ghanaian Constitution, which law fell within the exclusive jurisdiction of the Ghanaian courts.

The tribunal rejected Ghana's arguments on severability, but upheld much of Ghana's position on non-arbitrability. It first reasoned that, under English conflict of laws rules that presume the applicable law of the arbitration agreement is the same as the applicable law of the underlying contract, the applicable law of the arbitration agreement was Ghanaian law. It accordingly decided the question of severability from the perspective of Ghanaian law, although it recognized that Ghanaian law was virtually the same as English law on this point. The tribunal's reasoning was short and simply involved a rejection that the Ghanaian authorities relied on by Ghana stood for the proposition that the principle of severability must "yield to the constitutional order."[117] The tribunal distinguished the Supreme Court's decision concerning Balkan Energy as being only concerned with holding that an arbitration agreement was not an "international business transaction" within the meaning of the Article 181(5) of the Ghanaian Constitution.

---

[115] Ibid., para. 84.

[116] Section 3(1) of the Alternative Dispute Resolution Act 2010 provides that: "Unless otherwise agreed by the parties, an arbitration agreement which forms or is intended to form part of another agreement, shall not be regarded as invalid, non existent or ineffective because that other agreement is invalid or did not come into existence or has become ineffective and shall for that purpose be treated as a distinct agreement."

[117] *Waterville Holdings (BVI) Limited* v. *Ghana, supra* note 113, para. 101.

But the tribunal went on to hold, contrary to the tribunal in the *Balkan Energy* case, that the claimant's key claims (for declarations that the Stadia Contracts and settlement agreement were valid and enforceable, and that it was not required to repay money to Ghana) were non-arbitrable because these claims concerned matters that fell within the exclusive jurisdiction of the Ghanaian courts to interpret and apply Article 181 (5) of the Constitution. The tribunal did reason that, "to the extent there are matters not within the jurisdiction of the Supreme Court, the Arbitration Agreements remain valid and binding,"[118] but it upheld its jurisdiction under those arbitration agreements only in respect of the quantum of money to be repaid.

*

These two cases underscore how firmly established the principle of severability now is in international arbitration. But the same may not be said of the courts of respondent States, which may insist, as the Ghanaian courts did in these cases, upon the primacy of domestic law when resisting arbitration.

(N) OTHER ICC ARBITRATIONS

In his valuable article on "L'Autonomie de la Clause Compromissoire," Professor Pieter Sanders briefly summarizes passages of several ICC arbitrations, in which the parties are not named, and in which the principle of the severability of the arbitration agreement was dealt with and generally sustained.[119] While he interprets Case No. 1007 (1959) as failing to recognize the autonomy of the arbitral clause, he notes that the arbitrator in Case No. 1024 (1959) based his judgment on the ICC Rule that the claimed invalidity or non-existence of the principal agreement does not render the arbitrator incompetent.[120] He reports that in Case No. 1526 (1968), which concerned a concession contract between a private party and a developing State, the principle of the severability of the arbitration agreement was explicitly accepted: " ... the arbitration agreement, whether concluded separately or included in the legal instrument to which it applies, always manifests, apart from exceptional circumstances, a complete legal autonomy, preventing its being prejudiced

---

[118] Ibid., para. 113.   [119] Sanders, *supra* note 3, pp. 39–41.   [120] Ibid., p. 39.

by an eventual invalidity of that instrument."[121] In Case No. 1507 (1970), the arbitrator held that the arbitration agreement is autonomous and thus may be governed by a law other than that which applies to the principal agreement.[122] In Case No. 2091 (1972), which concerned a lease between an international organization and a French company, the arbitrator relied upon the autonomy of the arbitration clause to apply a law to it which was not applicable to the principal agreement and to sustain the arbitration agreement.[123] In Case No. 1955 (1973), the arbitral tribunal, noting that French law regularly affirmed in international commercial cases the entire independence of the arbitral clause from the validity of the contract containing it, found itself competent to judge the case.[124]

Numerous ICC arbitrations from the last three decades have continued to sustain the general principle of severability, while also shedding light on the contours of the principle. In ICC Case No. 8938, for example, the tribunal approved the principle in extremely broad terms:

[By] virtue of the independent rule of international arbitration law, embodied in Art. 8(4) of the Rules, the arbitral clause is autonomous and juridically independent from the main contract in which it is contained either directly or by reference, and its existence and validity are to be ascertained, taking into account the mandatory rules of national law and international public policy, in the light of the common intention of the parties, without necessarily referring to a state law.[125]

---

[121] Ibid., p. 40; translation supplied. The award is published, with a note by Yves Derains, in Clunet, *Journal du droit international* (1974), p. 915.
[122] Sanders, *supra* note 3, pp. 40–41.   [123] Ibid., p. 41.
[124] Ibid. Another ICC award, Case No. 2694 (1977), upholding severability of the arbitration agreement, is noted in Clunet, *Journal du droit international* (1978), at pp. 985–989; see also Case No. 2476 (1976), Clunet, *Journal du droit international* (1977), pp. 936–939. Still another international arbitral award (ad hoc) of interest is summarized as *Company Z and others (Republic of Xanadu)* v. *State Organization ABC (Republic of Utopia)* (1982), VIII *Yearbook Commercial Arbitration* (1983), pp. 94, 103, 105, 111. That award on jurisdiction of April 30, 1982 was published under its true name, *Framatome S.A. et al. v. Atomic Energy Organization of Iran*, in Clunet, *Journal du droit international* (1984), p. 58, prefaced by an analysis by Bruno Oppetit, "Arbitrage et Contrats d'Etat, l'Arbitrage *Framatome et autres* c. *Atomic Energy Organization of Iran*," ibid., p. 37.
[125] *Exclusive Agent* v. *Manufacturer*, Final Award, ICC Case No. 8938, XXIV *Yearbook Commercial Arbitration* (1999), p. 176.

Other tribunals have clarified that an arbitration agreement will not necessarily be severable, but may suffer the same fate as the underlying contract where, for example, the defect in the underlying contract directly affects the arbitration agreement. Thus, in *Westinghouse* v. *National Power Corporation (Philippines)*, the tribunal explained that "[t]here may be instances where a defect going to the root of an agreement between the parties affects both the main contract and the arbitration clause."[126] By "a defect going to the root of the agreement," the tribunal appears to have meant a defect that vitiates the parties' consent both to the underlying contract and to the arbitration agreement. The tribunal gave the "obvious example" of "a contract obtained by a threat."[127] The *Westinghouse* case itself concerned allegations of bribery in respect of which the tribunal considered that "it would remain to be seen whether bribery, if proved, affects both the main contract and the arbitration clause and renders both null and invalid."[128] In the event, the bribery allegations were unproven and so the question did not need to be determined.[129]

3. National Arbitral Jurisprudence

It would exceed the scope of this book if more than summary reference to national arbitral jurisprudence were to be given, although some recent jurisprudence, from the UK in particular, sheds valuable light on the foundations, scope, and limits of the principle of severability.

---

[126] ICC Case No. 6401/BGD, Preliminary Award on Issues of Jurisdiction and Contract Validity, 7–1 *Mealey's International Arbitration Report* B-1 (1992), p. 20.

[127] Ibid. But see, with more caution, Paulsson, *supra* note 2, p. 69, emphasizing that, in practice, cases of duress are rare, especially in commercial settings, and tend to emerge in the context of amending an existing contract. In such cases one must be careful to distinguish situations where "[d]uress relates to the bargain and not the arbitration clause."

[128] ICC Case No. 6401/BGD, Preliminary Award on Issues of Jurisdiction and Contract Validity, *supra* note 126.

[129] However, the question of the effect of bribery in respect of the underlying contract on the validity of the arbitration agreement would arise again, and would need to be determined, in both the *World Duty Free* case, discussed above, and the *Fiona Trust* case, discussed below.

The award of sole arbitrator Dupuy in the *TOPCO* v. *Libya* case quoted above gives a sense of the French law, where the autonomy of the arbitral clause is accepted in both domestic and international commercial arbitration.[130] The severability of the arbitration agreement is now enshrined in Article 1447 of the Code of Civil Procedure, which provides that "La convention d'arbitrage est indépendante du contrat auquel elle se rapporte. Elle n'est pas affectée par l'inefficacité de celui-ci."[131] Despite the breadth with which French cases and commentators sometimes state the principle of severability, the principle may not save the arbitration agreement in cases where the underlying agreement was never concluded.[132]

---

[130] Sanders, *supra* note 3, pp. 42–43 and the authorities cited by Dupuy (55 *International Law Reports, supra* note 66, pp. 407–412). See also *Menicucci c. Mahieux* (1975), 65 *Revue critique de droit international privé* (1976), pp. 508–510, noted by P. Fouchard in *Revue de l'Arbitrage* (1977), pp. 146–150; the *Gosset Case* (1963), *Revue de l'Arbitrage* (1963), p. 60, and *Dalloz* (1963), p. 545 with note by Jean Robert; the *Hecht* case (1972), *Revue de l'Arbitrage* (1974) p. 89 and Ph. Francescakis, "Le principe jurisprudentiel de l'autonomie de l'accord compromissoire après l'arrêt Hecht de la Cour de Cassation," ibid., p. 67; VI *Yearbook Commercial Arbitration* (1981), pp. 7–8; P. Fouchard, *L'Arbitrage Commercial International* (1965), vol. II, pp. 148–150; and J. Rubellin-Devichi, *L'Arbitrage* (1965), pp. 109–111; E. Gaillard and J. Savage (eds), *Fouchard, Gaillard, Goldman on International Commercial Arbitration* (1999), pp. 198ff; *Municipalité de Khoms El Mergeb c. Société Dalico*, Cour de Cassation (1 Ch. clv.), December 20, 1993, *Revue de l'Arbitrage* (1994), pp. 116–117 ("la clause compromissoire est indépendante juridiquement du contrat principal qui la contient directement ou par référence et que son existence et son efficacité s'apprécient, sous réserve des règles impératives du droit français et de l'ordre public international, d'après la commune volonté des parties").

[131] Article 1506 confirms that Article 1447 (which is contained in the chapter of the Code of Civil Procedure concerning domestic arbitration) applies to international arbitration. Note that the application of severability to domestic arbitration marks a change from the state of French law at the time of the first edition, which further reinforces the vitality of the principle.

[132] Pierre Mayer, "The Limits of Severability of the Arbitration Clause," in A. J. Van den Berg (ed.), *Improving the Efficiency of Arbitration Agreements and Awards: 40 Years of Application of the New York Convention* (1999), pp. 261, 264: "The scenario in which an arbitration clause most clearly would not be severed, and hence would be invalid, is where the assent of one of the parties is lacking. If the person to whom the offer is made does not accept it, then no contract has been formed, and the arbitration clause contained in the offer has not been agreed to any more than any of the other clauses, for there was no specific mutual agreement with respect to that clause." As Mark S. McNeill and Ben Juratowich point out, although some French court judgments speak of

The position in Switzerland, meanwhile, was illustrated in the *Losinger & Co.* arbitral award's quotation of Swiss authority and the principle of severability is now confirmed by Article 178(3) of the Swiss Law on Private International Law, which provides that "[t]he validity of an arbitration agreement cannot be contested on the ground that the main contract may not be valid."[133]

In the United States, the Supreme Court, in the leading case of *Prima Paint* v. *Flood & Conklin Mfg. Co.*, in applying a clause providing for arbitration under the rules of the American Arbitration Association, interpreted the Arbitration Act of 1925 to mean that "arbitration clauses as a matter of federal law are 'separable' from the contracts in which they are imbedded, and that where no claim is made that fraud was directed to the arbitration clause itself, a broad arbitration clause will be held to encompass arbitration of the claim that the contract itself was induced by fraud."[134] That position was reaffirmed by the Supreme Court in *Buckeye Check Cashing, Inc.* v. *Cardegna*.[135] In that case, which concerned a challenge to the legality of the underlying contract, the Court held that "because respondents challenge the Agreement, but not specifically its arbitration provisions, those provisions are enforceable apart from the remainder of the contract." The Court did note that "[t]he issue of the contract's validity is different from the issue of whether any agreement between the alleged obligor and obligee was ever concluded," but it left open the question of whether and how severability may apply in that latter category of cases.[136]

---

severability applying despite the "inexistence" of the underlying contract, this tends to involve situations not where the underlying contract was never entered into, but rather situations where, because of some legal defect in the underlying contract, it is thereby considered nonexistent. See McNeill and Juratowitch, *supra* note 10, pp. 481–482.

[133] See discussion of the *Losinger & Co. Case*, *supra*.

[134] *Prima Paint* v. *Flood & Conklin Mfg. Co.*, 388 U.S. 395, 402 (1967). See Gerald Aksen, "*Prima Paint* v. *Flood & Conklin — What Does It Mean?*," 43 *St. John's Law Review* (1968), p. 1.

[135] *Buckeye Check Cashing, Inc.* v. *Cardegna*, 546 U.S. 440, 449 (2006). See Adam Samuel, "Separability and the US Supreme Court Decision in Buckeye v. Cardegna," 22 *Arbitration International* (2006), p. 477. See more generally on severability and related issues in US law, George Bermann, "The 'Gateway' Problem in International Commercial Arbitration," 37 *Yale Journal of International Law* (2012), p. 1.

[136] *Buckeye Check Cashing, Inc.* v. *Cardegna*, 546 U.S. at 444, fn. 1.

In England, the situation has been, at least historically, more complicated, but has now clearly developed in favor of the severability of the arbitration clause. As late as 1992, Steyn J held in *Harbour Assurance Co. Ltd.* v. *Kansa General International Insurance Co. Ltd* that existing authority did not allow him to find that an arbitration agreement survived an underlying contract that was deemed void *ab initio* for illegality.[137] The Court of Appeal, however, reversed that finding,[138] and the principle of severability was soon confirmed in broad terms by section 7 of the Arbitration Act 1996, which provides that:

Unless otherwise agreed by the parties, an arbitration agreement which forms or was intended to form part of another agreement (whether or not in writing) shall not be regarded as invalid, non-existent or ineffective because that other agreement is invalid, or did not come into existence or has become ineffective, and it shall for that purpose be treated as a distinct agreement.

The House of Lords has since set down one of the more lucid decisions available as to the attributes of severability, in *Premium Nafta Products Ltd* v. *Fili Shipping Co Ltd (the Fiona Trust).*[139] That case concerned allegations of bribery in respect of a number of standard-form charterparties. The allegations of bribery did not relate to the arbitration agreements themselves and, in these circumstances, the House of Lords unanimously held that there could be no question about the validity of those arbitration agreements. Both of the Law Lords who delivered judgments emphasized that this outcome was based on the presumed intention of the contracting parties. As Lord Hoffmann put it:

In approaching the question of construction, it is therefore necessary to inquire into the purpose of the arbitration clause. As to this, I think there can be no doubt. The parties have entered into a relationship, an agreement or what is alleged to be an agreement or what appears on its face to be an agreement, which may give rise to disputes. They want those disputes decided by a tribunal which they have chosen, commonly on the grounds of such matters as its neutrality, expertise and privacy, the availability of legal services at the seat of the arbitration and the unobtrusive efficiency of its supervisory law. Particularly in the case of international

---

[137] [1993] 1 Lloyd's Rep 81.   [138] [1993] 1 Lloyd's Rep 455.
[139] [2007] 1 All ER (Comm) 891.

contracts, they want a quick and efficient adjudication and do not want to take the risks of delay and, in too many cases, partiality, in proceedings before a national jurisdiction.

If one accepts that this is the purpose of an arbitration clause, its construction must be influenced by whether the parties, as rational businessmen, were likely to have intended that only some of the questions arising out of their relationship were to be submitted to arbitration and others were to be decided by national courts. Could they have intended that the question of whether the contract was repudiated should be decided by arbitration but the question of whether it was induced by misrepresentation should be decided by a court? If, as appears to be generally accepted, there is no rational basis upon which businessmen would be likely to wish to have questions of the validity or enforceability of the contract decided by one tribunal and questions about its performance decided by another, one would need to find very clear language before deciding that they must have had such an intention.[140]

Lord Hope expanded on this by outlining the unintended consequences of rejecting severability in a case such as this:

It is not just that the parties would be deprived of the benefit of having all their disputes decided in one forum. The jurisdiction clause does not say where disputes about the validity of the contract are to be determined, if this is not to be in the forum which is expressly mentioned. The default position is that such claims would have to be brought in the jurisdiction where their opponents were incorporated, wherever and however unreliable that might be, while claims for breach of contract have to be brought in England. But why, it may be asked, would any sensible businessmen have wished to agree to this? ... Why, having chosen their jurisdiction for one purpose, should they leave the question which court is to have jurisdiction for the other purpose unspoken, with all the risks that this may give rise to?[141]

The Law Lords nonetheless made it clear that the scope of severability had its limits, especially where there is a question as to whether the main contract was entered into at all. Lord Hoffmann explained that:

Of course there may be cases in which the ground upon which the main agreement is invalid is identical with the ground upon which the arbitration

---

[140] Ibid., para. 7.   [141] Ibid., para. 28.

agreement is invalid. For example, if the main agreement and the arbitration agreement are contained in the same document and one of the parties claims that he never agreed to anything in the document and that his signature was forged, that will be an attack on the validity of the arbitration agreement. But the ground of attack is not that the main agreement was invalid. It is that the signature to the arbitration agreement, as a 'distinct agreement,' was forged. Similarly, if a party alleges that someone who purported to sign as agent on his behalf had no authority whatever to conclude any agreement on his behalf, that is an attack on both the main agreement and the arbitration agreement.[142]

But Lord Hoffmann also recognized that "the allegation ... that there was no concluded agreement (for example, that terms of the main agreement remained to be agreed) is not necessarily an attack on the arbitration agreement."[143] His Lordship explained instead that, "[i]f the arbitration clause has been agreed, the parties will be presumed to have intended the question of whether there was a concluded main agreement to be decided by arbitration."[144]

This nuanced approach sheds light on the interpretation of section 7 of the Arbitration Act, which provides that "an arbitration agreement ... shall not be regarded as ... non-existent ... because that other agreement is invalid, or *did not come into existence*" (emphasis added). It is, in line with Lord Hoffmann's approach, better to read section 7 as meaning that an arbitration agreement should not be regarded as nonexistent *just* because the underlying contract did not come into existence (say, for want of agreement on a material term). As the Law Lords in *Fiona Trust* contemplated, there will be cases where the nonexistence of the underlying contract does necessitate the nonexistence of the arbitration agreement. But there will, as Lord Hoffmann also pointed out, be cases where the nonexistence of the main contract does *not* necessitate the nonexistence of an arbitration agreement. The question in every case reduces to whether the parties have consented to *arbitration*.

---

[142] Ibid., para. 17. Lord Hope similarly explained, at para. 34, that "[i]ssues as to whether the entire agreement was procured by impersonation or by forgery, for example, are unlikely to be severable from the arbitration clause."
[143] Ibid., para. 18.   [144] Ibid.

Severability is the rule in innumerable other States too, including Belgium,[145] China,[146] Germany,[147] Hong Kong,[148] the Netherlands,[149] Russia,[150] Singapore,[151] and Sweden.[152] It has been remarked that "it is virtually impossible to identify reported national court decisions rendered in the past several decades which reject or question the separability presumption" (although the Ghanaian cases described above counsel perhaps more caution).[153]

Thus the principle of the severability of the arbitration agreement that is supported by the weight of international arbitral codification and cases is substantially supported as well by the national arbitral jurisprudence of leading centers of national and international commercial arbitration. While not the rule in all countries or at all times, it clearly enjoys the predominant position.[154]

D. Conclusions

In the light of the analysis of this chapter, it is believed that the following conclusions from the first edition were, and remain, justified:

– As a matter of theory, and as widely recognized by the analyses of commentators, the principle of the severability of an arbitration clause from the principal agreement which contains it is sound.

– As a matter of practice, that principle has been sustained by the terms and implications of arbitration conventions and rules, and by the case law, whether of public international law, international commercial arbitration, or national arbitration.

---

[145] Judicial Code, Article 1690(1) (adopting the UNCITRAL Model Law).
[146] Arbitration Law, Article 19.   [147] Code of Civil Procedure, Article 1040(1).
[148] Arbitration Ordinance, Section 34(1) (adopting the UNCITRAL Model Law).
[149] Code of Civil Procedure, Article 1053.
[150] Law of International Commercial Arbitration, Article 16(1) (adopting the UNCITRAL Model Law).
[151] International Arbitration Act, First Schedule, Article 16(1) (adopting the UNCITRAL Model Law).
[152] Arbitration Act, Section 3.   [153] Born, *supra* note 8, p. 390.
[154] The *ICCA Handbook on International Commercial Arbitration*, first published in 1984 and regularly updated since, contains in its national reports from some eighty countries, including countries to which reference has not been made above, a number of entries on severability of the arbitration agreement, which invariably uphold the doctrine of severability.

II

Denial of Justice, and Other Breaches of International Law, by Governmental Negation of Arbitration

A. The Question

The second question asked in the first edition was this: where a State refuses to arbitrate pursuant to a clause in a contract between that State and an alien, which provides that arbitration between them shall be the exclusive remedy for settlement of disputes under that contract, does such refusal constitute a denial of justice under international law? Several related questions were also asked. Is it open to the contracting State to plead inability to arbitrate under its law, or failure to exhaust local remedies, or sovereign immunity, as a valid defense to the charge of a denial of justice flowing from negation of arbitration? Is the alien entitled to seek an arbitral ruling on the question of denial of justice, or is that question one which arises only on the plane of State-to-State relations?

The first edition recognized that, unlike the question of severability of the arbitration agreement examined in the first chapter, these questions were not as commonplace in the practice of international arbitration. But they were not so rare as to make their examination rarefied. Since that first edition, the remarkable growth in international arbitration, and of the importance of its role in international commerce, has increased the salience of how an alien, or a tribunal, may respond to a State's attempts to negate arbitration. That same growth has also resulted in State attempts to negate arbitration taking a number of different forms. The question is now not only whether a State's refusal to arbitrate under a contract may constitute a denial of justice, but whether a State's attempt to negate arbitration – by, for example, improperly setting aside a locally-made arbitral award – may constitute a compensable expropriation, a breach of fair and equitable treatment or another breach of an investment treaty.

B. The Theory

Denial of justice, as a cause of action in public international law, is now frequently pleaded by claimants in arbitrations between investors and States conducted under investment treaties entered into between States. It is generally accepted that a State's obligations under customary international law include an obligation not to deny justice to foreign nationals, and it is also generally accepted that the standard of fair and equitable treatment typically found in investment treaties encompasses the same obligation.[1]

So far as denials of justice in relation to domestic court conduct are concerned, the content of denial of justice has developed so as to channel a limited type of conduct to the level of an international delict. There are two key ways in which denial of justice does this. First, denial of justice does not arise merely upon the incorrect application of the local law in the local courts. The tribunal in *Mondev v. United States* instead explained that:

> In the end the question is whether, at an international level and having regard to generally accepted standards of the administration of justice, a tribunal can conclude in the light of all the available facts that the impugned decision was clearly improper and discreditable, with the result that the investment has been subjected to unfair and inequitable treatment.[2]

---

[1] See generally, Jan Paulsson, *Denial of Justice in International Law* (2005); Rudolf Dolzer and Christoph H. Schreuer, *Principles of International Investment Law* (2nd edition, 2012), pp. 178–182; Campbell McLachlan, Laurence Shore and Matthew Weiniger, *International Investment Arbitration: Substantive Principles* (2nd edition, 2017), pp. 296–308.

[2] *Mondev v. United States*, ICSID Case No. ARB(AF)/99/2, Award, October 11, 2002, para. 127. See also *Azinian v. United Mexican States*, NAFTA/ICSID Case No. ARB(AF)/97/1, Award, November 1, 1999, paras. 102–103: "A denial of justice could be pleaded if the relevant courts refuse to entertain a suit, if they subject it to undue delay, or if they administer justice in a seriously inadequate way, . . . There is a fourth type of denial of justice, namely the clear and malicious misapplication of the law."

Second, denial of justice does not arise merely upon the decision of a particular domestic court. There is rather a requirement, as a substantive element of denial of justice, that the investor makes reasonable attempts to exhaust effective local remedies.[3]

The alleged denial of justice typically concerns a State's failure to provide justice through its domestic courts, including by failing to accord foreign nationals access to its courts (what may be called domestic denials of justice). But the more particular question with which this chapter is first concerned – and a more controversial one – is whether this core concept embraces the failure of a State to afford an alien access to the *arbitral tribunal* to whose constitution that State has consented (what may be called international denials of justice).

At the time of the first edition, the most comprehensive treatment of this question had been provided by that noted scholar and practitioner, Dr. F.A. Mann. Writing in the *British Year Book of International Law* of 1967, Dr. Mann said, with respect to "Refusal of arbitration as a denial of justice," the following (and he is quoted at length because his analysis not only is germinal; it remains, still, one of the most extensive and searching published considerations of the question):

... there are many circumstances in which the attitude of one party to an arbitration clause and, in particular, of the contracting State results in the impossibility of setting up or operating the arbitration tribunal. Usually this is the direct responsibility of the State; as, for instance, when the State fails, and no other person or body is authorized, to appoint an arbitrator. Or the responsibility is indirect as, for instance, when an arbitrator withdraws from the proceedings, perhaps even at the request of the State, and there is no machinery for appointing a substitute. Can such or similar lack of co-operation on the part of the respondent State, which frustrates arbitration, be considered as a denial of justice so as to permit the State

---

[3] Paulsson, *supra* note 1, p. 7: "[I]nternational law does not impose a duty on states to treat foreigners fairly at every step of the legal process. The duty is to create and maintain a *system of justice* which ensures that unfairness to foreigners either does not happen, *or is corrected*"; James Crawford, *Brownlie's Principles of Public International Law* (8th ed., Oxford University Press, 2012), p. 620: "The existence of the rule of admissibility that the alien should first exhaust local remedies is a reflection of the special character of denial of justice claims"; *Loewen v. United States*, ICSID Case No. ARB(AF)/98/3, Award, June 26, 2003, para. 154: "No instance has been drawn to our attention in which an international tribunal has held a State responsible for a breach of international law constituted by a lower court decision when there was available an effective and adequate appeal within the State's legal system."

entitled to protect the interests of the contracting alien to invoke the rules of international responsibility? An affirmative answer has been given by Switzerland, the United Kingdom and France, though, not unnaturally, the opposite view has been taken by their opponents, namely Yugoslavia, Iran and Lebanon respectively . . . . [4]

Dr. Mann considered that, with the exception of one category of cases, an affirmative answer should be given. He explained that:

It would be wrong to fasten upon the fact that mere non-performance or breach of a contract made between a State and an alien does not necessarily constitute a tort within the meaning of the rules of State responsibility, and to conclude that the repudiation of an arbitration clause cannot, as such, be treated as a denial of justice. Whatever the position may be in regard to contractual obligations in general, the repudiation of an arbitration clause has a distinct and special character in that it involves the denial of access to the only tribunal which has jurisdiction and upon which the parties have agreed. The failure to afford access to tribunals has traditionally been treated as a peculiar and particularly grave instance of State responsibility. It is submitted, therefore, that it would be in line with the accepted tendency of international law, sound doctrine and the demands of justice to hold that a State which repudiates an arbitration clause denies justice. In the past, it is true, denial of justice in the strict and narrow sense of the term implied the failure to afford access to the tribunals of the respondent State itself. But there is no reason of logic or justice why the doctrine of denial of justice should not be so interpreted as to comprise the relatively modern case of the repudiation of an arbitration clause. The respondent State which, wilfully and as a result of its own initiative, has failed to implement an arbitration clause, can hardly allege that it has afforded justice in general or the agreed justice in particular, or complain that it is aggrieved by being held responsible for its own deliberate acts. Nor should it be argued that denial of justice presupposes the failure of the State as sovereign to provide proper access to its tribunals, while the State which simply disregards an arbitration clause acts, not as a sovereign, but in the same manner as any private person could do. This would be a somewhat conceptualist reasoning. In its practical effect the failure of a contracting State to implement an arbitration clause is tantamount to barring access to the tribunal which could, should, and is agreed to, be available. Obstruction by a State has a different quality from obstruction by a private person. [5]

---

[4] F.A. Mann, "State Contracts and International Arbitration," *XLII British Yearbook of International Law* (1967), pp. 1, 26–29.

[5] Ibid.

Dr. Mann went on to note that "[t]here are occasions when the failure to implement an arbitration clause results from specific legislation directed against the contracting alien." This, he explained, "is really an *a fortiori* case."[6] He considered that more difficult questions arose where the State's failure to arbitrate resulted "from general and in every respect unobjectionable legislation which it enacts."[7] He referred here to the *Losinger* case, where a Swiss firm had launched an arbitration against Yugoslavia, seated in Yugoslavia, and Yugoslavia had then introduced a general and facially nondiscriminatory law requiring all lawsuits against the State to be brought before Yugoslav courts. The sole arbitrator, surprisingly and wrongly, determined that he did not have jurisdiction to determine whether he could proceed and Switzerland ultimately espoused its national's claim before the Permanent Court of International Justice (but the claim was settled before decision). For Dr. Mann, there was no denial of justice. He explained that, in his view, "[e]ven if the umpire had not rendered a decision, but the Yugoslavian Government had kept aloof from the arbitration in reliance on the law of 1934, a denial of justice would not have occurred, for the failure to participate would have been sanctioned by a general law enacted by the *lex arbitri.*"[8]

It was argued in the first edition that Dr. Mann's conclusion that there is no reason of logic or doctrine why denial of justice should not be interpreted to comprise the case of repudiation of an arbitration clause is sound, for the reasons which he so well states. But it was also argued that the principle could have been extended more widely and that Dr. Mann was wrong to contend that there is no denial of justice where the State's refusal to arbitrate is based on a general law within the *lex arbitri*. What is decisive instead, it was suggested, is not the law governing the contract or arbitration under it, but the fact that there is a contract between a State and an alien. That fact suffices to bring the resultant relationship within the sphere of protection of international law. It does not render the contract an instrument of international law in the way a treaty is such an instrument, and it does not mean that every violation of the contract is a violation of international law. But it does mean that the rights that the contract provides cannot be

[6] Ibid.   [7] Ibid.   [8] Ibid.

taken by sovereign act without the responsibility that international law entails. States frequently act vis-à-vis aliens in accordance with their municipal law but that of itself does not dispose of all question of their responsibility under international law. An action of a State that as applied to an alien is arbitrary or tortious is not absolved of its wrongfulness by the mere reason that the contractual relationship affected is governed by its law. The right of an alien to arbitration of disputes arising under a contract is a valuable right, at times so valuable that the alien will contract only on condition of contractual assurance of that right. That right quite generally is to an international form of arbitration, but that is not the critical point. If the alien's right to arbitration is negated by the contracting State, a wrong under international law ensues, whatever the law governing the contract, the arbitration agreement, or the arbitral process—no less than a wrong under international law ensues if a State takes the property of an alien without just compensation whether or not the right to that property derives from its municipal law.

The situation may not be as clear-cut where the State has pleaded the nullity of its obligation to arbitrate based on a restriction on the authority of the State or its agencies to agree to arbitration that existed at the time of the arbitration agreement. The question in these cases is not one of the State concluding an arbitration agreement and thereafter enacting legislation or taking measures, general or particular, nullifying the arbitration agreement; the question rather is whether an agreement to arbitrate is effective if it does not comport with prior, outstanding restrictions upon the authority of the State to arbitrate.

Sometimes in practice the State or State entity may specifically represent in the underlying contract, or even in the arbitration agreement, that it, or those signing on its behalf, have the authority to enter into the contract or the arbitration agreement. But even in the absence of such representations, a State is generally not permitted to invoke its own law in order to defeat its promise to arbitrate. As Professor Paulsson observed in his analysis of the Preliminary Award in *Benteler* v. *Belgium,* a case that involved Belgium's unsuccessful attempt to rely on a Belgian law limiting the capacity of public-law entities to conclude arbitration agreements that existed at the time the State of Belgium concluded an arbitration agreement with German private parties:

The Theory

The prevailing view is that it would be contrary to fundamental principles of good faith for a State party to an international contract, having freely accepted an arbitration clause, later to invoke its own legislation as grounds for contesting the validity of its agreement to arbitrate. This principle of good faith has been applied by international arbitrators as an imperative norm perceived without reference to any specific national law. A leading precedent is an award rendered in 1971 under the Rules of Arbitration of the International Chamber of Commerce, in which the tribunal stated that:

"... international *ordre public* would vigorously reject the proposition that a State organ, dealing with foreigners, having openly, with knowledge and intent, concluded an arbitration clause that inspires the cocontractant's confidence, could thereafter, whether in the arbitration or in execution proceedings, invoke the nullity of its own promise."[9]

Professor Paulsson noted that the tribunal in the *Benteler* v. *Belgium* case (composed of Professor Claude Reymond, as President, and Messrs. Böckstiegel and Franchimont) recorded the following approaches used to confirm the principle that a State may not invoke its own law to contest the validity of its consent to arbitrate:

(i) Acknowledging a distinction between internal *ordre public* and a less constraining international *ordre public*, and then holding that a prohibition against the State or State entities' agreeing to arbitration is applicable only in domestic matters (the *Galakis* approach).

(ii) Applying a presumption that with respect to State or parastatal entities in international contracts, the capacity of the State or its subdivisions to conclude arbitration agreements is governed by the proper law of the contract rather than the internal law of the State.

---

[9] Jan Paulsson, "May a State Invoke Its Internal Law to Repudiate Consent to International Commercial Arbitration?," 2 *Arbitration International* (1986), p. 90. The Award of November 18, 1983 in *Benteler* v. *Belgium* is reproduced in English translation in 1 *Journal of International Arbitration* (1984), p. 184 and in *European Commercial Cases* (1985), p. 101, and a report is found in X *Yearbook Commercial Arbitration* (1985), p. 37. The original report in French is found in *Journal des Tribunaux* (Brussels, 1984), pp. 230–232. The quotation from an arbitral award is drawn by Professor Paulsson from ICC Case No. 1939, between an Italian company and an agency of an African State, an extract of which is found in Yves Derains, "Le statut des usages du commerce international devant les juridictions arbitrales," 1973 *Revue de l'Arbitrage*, pp. 122, 145.

(iii) Holding the prohibition of agreements to arbitrate to be contrary to international public order, in the sense that a State which has concluded an arbitration agreement would be held to act contrary to international *ordre public* if it later tried to affirm that its internal law was incompatible with the undertaking to arbitrate.

(iv) A more moderate variant of the last approach involves an analysis similar to that underlying the notion of estoppel or, as the *Benteler* Award puts it, allowing the international arbitrator to disregard the State's internal prohibition if "the circumstances of the case are such that the State would be acting *contra factum proprium* by raising it."[10]

The coexistence of these approaches, the *Benteler* tribunal inferred, indicates that "the present state of international arbitration law" is that a State may not use its national law to contest its own consent to arbitrate.[11]

It is believed that the foregoing analysis of which the *Benteler* award is an exemplar comports with the conclusion that what is a violation of international "ordre public" is in this instance a denial of justice under international law as well. But where a State relies not upon a preexisting statute to claim exemption from the obligation to arbitrate, but on legislation enacted or measures taken after the conclusion of the arbitration agreement, that is an *a fortiori case*; even if it be contended that reliance upon a preexisting statute may not constitute a denial of justice, surely invocation of an escape clause devised and applied after the entry into force of the arbitration agreement in order to evade it does constitute a denial of justice.

The same core principle was accepted in the *Elf Aquitaine Iran v. NIOC* Preliminary Award of 1982, where the sole arbitrator, Professor Gomard, observed that "[i]t is a recognized principle of international law that a state is bound by an arbitration clause... and cannot thereafter unilaterally set aside the access of the other party to the system envisaged by the parties in their agreement for the settlement of disputes."[12] This fundamental principle has only

---

[10] Paulsson, *supra* note 9, p. 96.

[11] *Benteler* v. *Belgium, supra* note 9, p. 190. The arbitral tribunal cited these factors as confirming the conclusion it reached on another, dispositive ground, namely, that Belgium's restriction on the authority of the State to engage in arbitration is subject to the exception of a treaty provision which allows it to resort to arbitration. The tribunal found such a treaty provision to be governing.

[12] XI *Yearbook Commercial Arbitration* (1986), pp. 98, 103.

become more readily accepted over the past three decades in a number of cases that will be discussed more fully below. As the tribunal in *Salini* v. *Ethiopia* stated: "There is a substantial body of law establishing that a state cannot rely on its own law to renege on an arbitration agreement."[13]

The conclusion that the first edition reached was thus a general one: a State commits a denial of justice whenever it refuses to arbitrate contrary to its earlier agreement to do so – whether by declaration, specific legislation, or general legislation enacted before or after the consent to arbitrate was given.

The question of whether a State that refuses to arbitrate commits a denial of justice had, at the time of the first edition of this book, attracted a measure of scholarly analysis beyond that of Dr. Mann. It was striking then that, while support for the view that such a refusal does constitute a denial of justice was substantial, there was little opinion to the contrary. More recent scholarly analysis offers instances of both support and critique of this proposition, albeit the focus of relevant analysis has shifted to the new forms of obstruction that have arisen in the context of modern investor-State arbitration.

Dr. F.V. García Amador, who wrote the following in his capacity as Special Rapporteur of the International Law Commission on State Responsibility, maintained that in the context of a contract that provides for an international type of arbitration though it does not stipulate that a particular substantive law other than the contracting State's law shall apply, "non-fulfilment of the arbitration clause would directly give rise to the international responsibility of the State":

The mere fact that a State agrees with an alien private individual to have recourse to an international mode of settlement automatically removes the contract, at least as regards relations between the parties, from the jurisdiction of municipal law. Unlike the *Calvo Clause* which reaffirms the exclusive jurisdiction of the local authorities, agreements of this type imply a 'renunciation' by the State of the jurisdiction of the local authorities. If an arbitration clause of this type were governed by municipal law, it could be amended or even rescinded by a subsequent unilateral act of the

---

[13] *Salini Costruttori SPA* v. *Ethiopia*, ICC Arbitration No 1063/AER/ACS, Award Regarding the Suspension of the Proceedings and Jurisdiction, December 7, 2001, para. 161.

State, which would be inconsistent with the essential purpose of stipulations of this type, whatever the purpose of the agreement or the character of the contracting parties. Accordingly, as the obligation in question is undeniably international in character, non-fulfilment of the arbitration clause would directly give rise to the international responsibility of the State.[14]

A Committee on Nationalization of Property of the American Branch of the International Law Association in 1957 found "an undeniable denial of justice" in the following circumstances:

Where the alien already enjoys the advantages of arbitration by the terms of his contract with the State, he is not bound to do more than exhaust the remedy arbitration provides. Should the State refuse to arbitrate, local remedies would thereby be exhausted and the diplomatic intervention of the alien's State would be in order. . . . If, as in the case of Iran, the State which purports lawfully to take the property of an alien refuses to submit its action to the adjudication of the arbitral tribunal whose competence it earlier accepted, its action constitutes an undeniable denial of justice.[15]

The American Law Institute's *Foreign Relations Law of the United States, Restatement of the Law Second*, holds:

Breach of agreement to arbitrate. If a contract between a state and an alien includes an arbitration clause, refusal of the state to submit a dispute to arbitration in compliance with the clause is a denial of procedural justice. . . .[16]

The American Law Institute's *Foreign Relations Law of the United States (Revised)*, as adopted in 1986, states that:

[A] state may be responsible for a denial of justice under international law . . . if, having committed itself to a special forum for dispute settlement, such as arbitration, it fails to honor such commitment. . . .[17]

---

[14] F.V. García Amador, "Responsibility of the State for Injuries Caused in Its Territory to the Person or Property of Aliens – Measures Affecting Acquired Rights," *Yearbook of the International Law Commission 1959*, vol. II, pp. 1, 32.

[15] *Proceedings and Committee Reports of the American Branch of the International Law Association*, 1957–1958, p. 75, notes 25, and p. 76 (reprinted in Southwestern Legal Foundation, *Selected Readings on Protection of Private Foreign Investments*, 1964, p. 37, note 25, and p. 38).

[16] American Law Institute, *Foreign Relations Law of the United States, Restatement of the Law Second*, 1965, p. 582.

[17] American Law Institute, *Restatement of the Law, Foreign Relations Law of the United States (Revised)*, 1986, Section 712, comment *h*.

Professor Alfred Verdross of the University of Vienna similarly concluded:

[I]f ... the defending State refuses to have recourse to arbitration, or if it delays the proceedings or refuses to execute the arbitral award, the private party may solicit the diplomatic *protection* of its government, since these acts or defaults constitute a denial of justice, which according to international law, gives the national State of the damaged party the right to intervene against the State guilty of the denial of justice.[18]

Charles de Visscher, the Belgian scholar who served as a judge of the International Court of Justice, expressed his support for the possibility of both domestic and international denials of justice in his *Theory and Reality in Public International Law:*

... the international responsibility of the nationalizing State is brought into play when it nationalizes a foreign enterprise in violation of an obligation freely and precisely assumed by it in an international agreement. This responsibility may also be involved, in connection with an undertaking contained in a contract under municipal law, if there is a denial of justice to the foreign concessionary through default of the ordinary courts or through a refusal to submit the dispute to any arbitral procedure that may have been substituted for internal jurisdiction.[19]

Numerous other leading authorities were cited in the first edition in support of the thesis being advanced.[20]

It was recalled by contrast that Ambassador Sompong Sucharitkul of Thailand had contended that there was:

... nothing sacrosanct, nothing final about arbitration, least of all the peremptory character, the impossibility of derogation from an obligation

---

[18] "The Status of Foreign Private Interests Stemming from Economic Development Agreements with Arbitration Clauses," printed in *Selected Readings, supra* note 15, pp. 117, 136.

[19] *Theory and Reality in International Law* (1957), translation by Percy E. Corbett, p. 194.

[20] Kenneth S. Carlston, "Concession Agreements and Nationalization," 52 *American Journal of International Law* (1958), p. 265; Prosper Weil, "Problèmes Relatifs aux Contrats Passés entre un Etat et un Particulier," 128 *Recueil des Cours* (1969), vol. III, p. 222; R.B. von Mehren and P.N. Kourides, "International Arbitrations between States and Foreign Private Parties: The Libyan Nationalization Cases," 25 *American Journal of International Law* (1981), p. 537; Riccardo Luzzato, "International Commercial Arbitration and the Municipal Law of States," 157 *Recueil des Cours* (1977-IV), pp. 17, 94; Hague Academy of International Law, *Colloquium on International Trade Agreements* (1969), pp. 330, 372 (Professor G. Kojanec), p. 345 (Professor George von Hecke).

to arbitrate. This would be more effective than international law, more powerful than supra-national law. It would be almost divine if once the State permits itself to submit to arbitration, it cannot allegedly derogate from this submission. However, it should be pointed out that the character of arbitration is itself voluntary, it is in itself extra-legal and conciliatory.[21]

Yet it was noted that other support had not been found in the literature for the position which Ambassador Sucharitkul may be viewed as taking that repudiation of the obligation to arbitrate contained in a contract with an alien is not a denial of justice.[22] This was by no means to suggest that there was virtual unanimity among international legal scholars in support of the thesis that a State's refusal to arbitrate is a denial of justice. The question had not been widely or profoundly addressed. But there was reason to conclude that support for the proposition was strikingly predominant among those who had considered the question.

Since the first edition, Professor Paulsson, in his leading treatment of denial of justice, clearly expressed his support for the proposition that a State's refusal to arbitrate may constitute a denial of justice.[23] Paulsson proceeds from the premise that "experience has shown, time and time again, that it is a crucial fact for the foreign victim of miscarriages of justice to achieve a neutral (i.e., international) adjudication of his grievance."[24] Proceeding from that premise, Paulsson quotes with approval from the leading decision in *Himpurna* v. *Indonesia* (discussed below, in which Paulsson himself chaired the tribunal): "it is a denial of justice for the courts of a State to prevent a foreign party from pursuing its remedies before a forum to the authority of which the State consented, and on the availability of which the foreigner relied in making investments explicitly envisaged by that State."[25]

---

[21] Hague Academy of International Law, *Colloquium on International Trade Agreements* (1969), p. 359.

[22] It was further noted that G. F. Amerasinghe, in *State Responsibility for Injuries to Aliens* (1967), p. 118, concluded that "refusal to make available the remedial rights afforded by the transnational system, i.e., by arbitration, would amount to a breach of international law. The local remedies are not relevant here."

[23] Paulsson, *supra* note 1, pp. 149–157.   [24] Ibid., p. 149.

[25] Ibid., p. 152 (emphasis added by Paulsson, in his book). This case is discussed more fully below. See also Richard Garnett, "National Court Intervention in Arbitration as an Investment Treaty Claim," 60 *International Comparative Law Quarterly* (2011), pp. 485, 488; and, more cautiously, Berk Demirkol, *Judicial Acts and Investment Treaty Arbitration* (2018), p. 176, fn. 102.

Among those who have cast doubt on the first edition's conclusion that a State's refusal to arbitrate may constitute a denial of justice, Martins Paparinskis has questioned it on the basis, first, that an arbitral tribunal "is not an organ the conduct of which is attributable to the State for the purposes of responsibility," and, second, that "unless the State commits a wrongful act by breaching the contract by public powers ... ,[26] its failure to participate in proceedings would *prima facie* not breach international law."[27]

Those observations are sensible from the general perspective of the law of State responsibility. But specific responses to both observations may be made.

So far as the attribution point is concerned, the proposition that a State's refusal to arbitrate may constitute a denial of justice takes aim not at the conduct of the tribunal, but at the conduct of the State in negating the arbitration. Switzerland's pleadings in the *Losinger* case, discussed in more detail below, provide a helpful illustration of this distinction. Yugoslavia had tried to shift the focus from its conduct in producing obstacles to the arbitration to which it had agreed with a Swiss company onto the arbitrator's decision in that case to reject his competence. But Switzerland, which had taken up the claim on behalf of its national before the PCIJ, made it clear that its complaint focused on Yugoslavia's legislation that, as Yugoslavia itself contended before the arbitrator, operated retrospectively so as to deprive the arbitrator of jurisdiction; this, Switzerland contended, was "an act directly perpetrated by the State which permitted it to deprive the arbitral clause of its content. There is the violation of the duty of a State to respect the rights of aliens."[28] More generally, it is well accepted that denial of justice covers a State's preventing a party from accessing a tribunal in the context of domestic denials of justice;[29] there is no reason of principle or policy why that denial of access cannot form the relevant conduct in the case of international denials of justice too.

---

[26] A proposition for which he quotes Stephen M. Schwebel, "On Whether a Breach by a State of a Contract with an Alien Is a Breach of International Law," in Stephen M. Schwebel (ed.), *Justice in International Law* (1994), p. 425.

[27] Martins Paparinskis, *The International Minimum Standard and Fair and Equitable Treatment* (2014), p. 210, fn. 267.

[28] The *Losinger & Co. Case*, P.C.I.J., Series C, No. 78, p. 26, at p. 367 (translation supplied).

[29] See, for example, Paulsson, *supra* note 1, pp. 44–53; Ch. 6.

As for the point that a State's breach of contract does not, *ipso facto*, create a breach of international law, it is possible both to accept that general principle and to acknowledge that a State's refusal to arbitrate is a special category of breach of contract that may, in principle, be set apart from the general run of contract breaches. This point is considered in more detail below.

In addition to those critiques, it is worth noting the practical observation made by Alan Redfern in his review of the first edition of this book. His view was that a party facing a State that refuses to arbitrate would be "best advised to press ahead with the arbitration if at all possible, so as to obtain a default award, rather than pin its hopes on receiving compensation for a 'denial of justice.'"[30] It is true that, as international arbitration procedures have developed, there are now greater possibilities of moving forward with an arbitration in the absence of a respondent's participation – including, as discussed in the third chapter, before a truncated tribunal. It may even be that the tribunal's determination to avoid a denial of justice may encourage a tribunal to move forward with an arbitration notwithstanding the respondent State's refusal to participate.[31] That itself serves to remedy the denial of justice. Moreover, as some of the new cases discussed below demonstrate, denial of justice by governmental negation of arbitration has continued to arise, including in some novel contexts.

Other recent cases have placed in sharp relief the unfortunate reality that, even where possible, pressing ahead in the face of a State's refusal to arbitrate and successfully obtaining a default award may be of little value to a claimant if the respondent State, or State-owned entity, is intent on its refusal to comply with the award. This is especially so if the respondent State is able to rely on its own complaisant courts to set the award aside or defeat enforcement without cause. The facts of the landmark *Saipem* v. *Bangladesh* case lay bare the salience of this problem.[32] The backdrop to that case was an earlier Bangladesh-seated arbitration brought by an Italian company, Saipem, against a Bangladeshi State-owned entity, Petrobangla.

---

[30] Alan Redfern, "Book Review – International Arbitration: Three Salient Problems," 4 *Journal of International Arbitration* (1987), pp. 165, 166.

[31] See Sections C.2(i), (j), and (m), *infra*.

[32] See *Saipem* v. *Bangladesh*, ICSID Case No. ARB/05/7, Decision on Jurisdiction, March 21, 2007; Award, June 30, 2009.

During that arbitration, Petrobangla successfully applied to the Bangladeshi courts to first enjoin the arbitration and then revoke the authority of the tribunal to hear the arbitration. The arbitral tribunal nevertheless proceeded, having determined that the decisions of the Bangladeshi courts could not affect it, and it delivered an award of damages in favor of Saipem for Petrobangla's breach of contract. But Petrobangla then applied to the Bangladeshi courts to set the award aside, to which those courts replied that there was nothing to set aside because the award was "a nullity." As Petrobangla had no assets outside of Bangladesh, it seemed to have "successfully" negated the arbitration.

That was until Saipem turned toward its direct right to launch an arbitration against Bangladesh under the Italy-Bangladesh Bilateral Investment Treaty. Saipem invoked and quoted the first edition of this text: "The contractual right of an alien to arbitration of disputes arising under a contract to which it is party is a valuable right, which often is of importance to the very conclusion of the contract."[33] The investment tribunal agreed. It reasoned that "the right to arbitrate and the rights determined by [an] Award are capable in theory of being expropriated."[34] The tribunal went on to hold that those rights, as part of Saipem's overall investment in Bangladesh, had been expropriated in this case, and ordered Bangladesh to pay damages in the amount that Petrobangla owed as damages from the earlier arbitration (plus interest).

The *Saipem* tribunal thereby triggered a line of cases that has markedly expanded the options available to an alien when faced with a State's attempts to negate arbitration – while at the same time grappling with the conceptual difficulties to which such a rapid and significant development of international law has inevitably given rise. These new cases represent the most notable development in this area of law since the time of the first edition and, on the basis that understanding these cases is indispensable to any treatment of the issue of the recourse available to an alien when faced with a State's attempted negation of arbitration, they are considered in detail below.

*

Before turning to consider in some detail the relevant practice, both in respect of denial of justice and other causes of action, four

---

[33] Ibid., Decision on Jurisdiction, *supra* note 32, para. 131.
[34] Ibid., Award, *supra* note 32, para. 122.

related issues that were examined in the first edition may be considered at this point.

The *first* related issue concerns the relevance of the general principle that a State's breach of a contract with an alien is not *ipso facto* a breach of international law. This general principle, as noted above, has been cited against the proposition that a denial of justice may arise from a State's repudiation of an arbitration agreement.

The starting point is that a contract between a State and an alien is not an instrument of international law; it therefore does not give rise to obligations under the law of treaties. On this, there is no dispute.[35] But there is considerable authority in support of the proposition that, while mere breach by a State of a contract with an alien governed by domestic law is not a violation of international law, a "non-commercial" act of a State contrary to such a contract may be. Thus in the classic *Shufeldt Claim*, the Guatemalan Legislative Assembly passed a decree that repudiated the American claimant's chicle concession, which was held to engage the international responsibility of Guatemala and render it liable for damages.[36] In more recent jurisprudence, the key question has been framed as whether the respondent State "stepped out of the contractual shoes" and, "in fact, acted in its sovereign capacity" when it committed the contractual breach in question.[37] From this perspective, then, there is nothing unprincipled about a State's repudiation of its contractual agreement to arbitrate through the exercise of sovereign capacity, for example, through the enactment of legislation preventing arbitration against the State, giving rise to international responsibility.

The point of principle becomes even clearer when one recalls that, in domestic denial of justice cases, a breach of contract for which no effective remedy is reasonably available in domestic courts could give rise to a denial of justice.[38] From this it

---

[35] See generally, Schwebel, *supra* note 26; more recently, see, for example, *Waste Management* v. *Mexico (No. 2)*, ICSID Case No. ARB(AF)/00/3, Award, para. 175; *Parkerings-Compagniet AS* v. *Lithuania*, ICSID Case No. ARB/05/8, Award, para. 448; *Suez Sociedad General de Aguas de Barcelona SA* v. *Argentina*, ICSID Case No. ARB/03/19, Decision on Liability, para. 153.

[36] *Shufeldt Claim (Guatemala, US)* (1930) II RIAA 1079.

[37] *Vigotop Ltd* v. *Hungary*, ICSID Case No. ARB/11/22, Award, October 1, 2014.

[38] See generally on the reasonableness qualification to the requirement to exhaust local remedies, Paulsson, *supra* note 1, pp. 112–120.

can also be contended that a State's repudiation of an arbitration agreement, for which no effective remedy is reasonably available, may give rise to a denial of justice. This line of reasoning is reflected in the American Law Institute's *Foreign Relations Law of the United States* (as revised in 1986). Section 712 provides:

Economic Injury to Nationals of Other States
A state is responsible under international law for injury resulting from:

(1) a taking by the state of the property of a national of another state that is (a) not for a public purpose, or (b) discriminatory, or (c) not accompanied by provision for just compensation...

(2) a repudiation or breach by the state of a contract with a national of another state
   (a) where the repudiation or breach is (i) discriminatory; or (ii) motivated by other non-commercial considerations and compensatory damages are not paid or
   (b) where the foreign national is not given an adequate forum to determine his claim of breach or is not compensated for any breach determined to have occurred;

(3) other arbitrary or discriminatory acts or omissions by the state that impair property or other economic interests of a national of another state.

Comment h to this section provides, in relevant part:

With respect to any repudiation or breach of a contract with a foreign national, a state may be responsible for a denial of justice under international law if it denies to an alien an effective domestic forum to resolve the dispute and has not agreed to any other forum; *or if, having committed itself to a special forum for dispute settlement, such as arbitration, it fails to honor such a commitment;* or if it fails to carry out a judgment or award rendered by such domestic or special forum.

(Emphasis added.)

All of this is a reflection of the reality that the right of an alien to arbitration of disputes under a contract is a valuable right, at times so valuable that the alien will contract only on condition of contractual assurance of that right. That, too, was the view of Dr. Mann: "[w]hatever the positon may be in regard to contractual obligations in general, the repudiation of an arbitration clause has a distinct and special character in that it involves the denial of access to the only tribunal which has jurisdiction and which upon the parties have agreed."[39]

The *second* related issue is whether an alien may properly assert a cause of action under international law like denial of justice before an arbitral tribunal constituted pursuant to a contract with a State. The question may, in practice, pose few difficulties. If the State is not in fact able to block the arbitration from proceeding altogether, then, as Redfern observed, the alien may be best advised simply to pursue the arbitration by making the same claims it would have made irrespective of the respondent State's default. Adding denial of justice as a claim may serve little practical benefit. In each of the three well-known arbitrations of *BP*,[40] *Texaco*[41] and *LIAMCO*[42] v. *Libya*, for example, wherein Libya refused to participate, none of the aliens considered it necessary to invoke denial of justice in addition to expropriation. If the alien decides to pursue a claim, however, it may be able to do so under an investment treaty which requires fair and equitable treatment and provides a means to resolve disputes in respect of that obligation.

There is also the situation where the alien, faced with a respondent State's attempt to negate the arbitration in some way, may wish to impress upon the tribunal that, were it to sustain the respondent State's refusal to arbitrate, this would give rise to a denial of justice contrary to international law. In this context tribunals have clearly rejected the proposition that, just because the applicable substantive law may be a domestic law, the arbitration should therefore be "insulated from the imperatives of international law."[43] On the contrary, the tribunal in *Construction Pioneers* v. *Ghana* explained "that there is today ample authority in international arbitral

---

[39] F.A. Mann, "State Contracts and International Arbitration," XLII *British Year Book of International Law* (1967), pp. 1, 26.

[40] *BP Exploration Company (Libya) Limited* v. *Government of the Libyan Arab Republic*, 53 *International Law Reports*, p. 297.

[41] *Texaco Overseas Petroleum Company (TOPCO) and California Asiatic Oil Company* v. *The Government of the Libyan Arab Republic*, 53 *International Law Reports*, p. 389.

[42] *Libyan American Oil Company (LIAMCO)* v. *Government of the Libyan Arab Republic*, 62 *International Law Reports*, p. 141.

[43] *Himpurna California Energy Ltd.* v. *Indonesia*, Interim Award and Final Award, September 26, 1999 and October 16, 1999, XXV *Yearbook Commercial Arbitration* (2000), p. 109, para. 175. *Construction Pioneers Baugesellschaft Anstalt* v. *Government of the Republic of Ghana, Ministry of Roads and Transport*, ICC Case No. 12078/DB/EC, Partial Award, December 22, 2003, para. 131.

jurisprudence for the proposition that the existence of a contract involving a State or State party, as in the present case, is 'suffic[ient] to bring the resultant relationship [with the foreign counter party] within the sphere of protection of international law.'"[44]

The *third* related issue is whether it is open to the contracting State to plead its sovereign immunity as a valid defense to the invocation of arbitration, and, hence, to the charge of denial of justice flowing from the negation of arbitration? The answer to this question is clearly not. A State is entitled, in certain circumstances, to plead immunity from suit against it, which is maintained in the courts of another State, on the principle *par in parem non habet imperium*. But the principle that one sovereign shall not judge another without the latter's consent cannot apply to proceedings before an arbitral tribunal, which is the instrument of the sovereignty of no State; one sovereign is not sitting in judgment upon another.[45] Since sovereign immunity cannot properly be pleaded before such an arbitral tribunal, a plea of sovereign immunity provides no defense to the claim – certainly if made before such a

---

[44] *Construction Pioneers Baugeselleschaft Anstalt, supra* note 43, para. 131 (quoting the first edition of this book).

[45] See, in support of this analysis, the arbitral award of an ICC-named sole arbitrator, sitting in Sweden, in ICC Case No. 2321, *Solel Boneh International Ltd. (Israel) and Water Resources Development International (Israel)* v. *The Republic of Uganda and National Housing and Construction Corporation of Uganda* (1974). Uganda sought to plead sovereign immunity. The arbitrator held: "As arbitrator, I am myself no representative or organ of any State. My authority as arbitrator rests upon an agreement between the parties to the dispute and by my activities I do not, as do State judges or other State representatives, engage the responsibility of the State of Sweden. Furthermore, the courts and other authorities of Sweden can in no way interfere in my activities as arbitrator, neither direct me to do anything I do nor to direct me to abstain from doing anything which I think I should do. . . . As I do not consider that the doctrine of sovereign immunity has any application whatsoever in arbitral proceedings which are, as in Sweden, conducted independently of local courts, it is not necessary to enter upon the question of a waiver of immunity. . . ." Clunet, *Journal du Droit International* (1975), pp. 938, 940. See also the note by Yves Derains that follows, especially at p. 944. A report is also found in I *Yearbook Commercial Arbitration* (1976), pp. 133–135 and in J. Gillis Wetter, "Pleas of Sovereign Immunity and Act of Sovereignty before International Arbitral Tribunals," 2 *Journal of International Arbitration* (1985), pp. 7, 9–10. For another award to similar effect which relies upon the *Solel Boneh* award, see *S.P.P. (Middle East) Limited et al. and the Arab Republic of Egypt et al.* (1983), XXII *International Legal Materials* (1983), pp. 752, 770–771, 774, 776 (annulled by the Paris Court of Appeal on another ground).

tribunal – that a State's refusal to arbitrate gives rise to a denial of justice. This is irrespective of any question of waiver of immunity, which is only relevant to the extent of any proceedings before a national court in connection with an arbitration.

The *fourth* related issue is whether it is open to the contracting State to plead failure to exhaust local remedies as a valid defense to the charge of denial of justice flowing from negation of arbitration. This, as will be seen from the study of practice below, was precisely the plea, which was the, or a, principal defense advanced by Yugoslavia in the *Losinger & Co.* case, by Iran in the *Anglo-Iranian Oil Company* case, and by Lebanon in the *Compagnie du Port de Beyrouth* case.

The International Court of Justice has stated the rule of the exhaustion of local remedies, in the context of diplomatic protection claims, in the following terms:

> The rule that local remedies must be exhausted before international proceedings may be instituted is a well-established rule of customary international law; the rule has been generally observed in cases in which a State has adopted the cause of its national whose rights are claimed to have been disregarded in another State in violation of international law. Before resort may be had to an international court in such a situation, it has been considered necessary that the State where the violation occurred should have an opportunity to redress it by its own means, within the framework of its own domestic legal system.[46]

In the context of denial of justice, Professor Paulsson has formulated the test as being qualified by whether there is a "reasonable possibility of an effective remedy."[47]

---

[46] *Interhandel Case (Switzerland v. United States), Judgment of March 27, 1959, I.C.J. Reports 1959*, pp. 6, 27.

[47] Paulsson, *supra* note 1, p. 118. See also *Chevron v. Ecuador*, UNCITRAL, PCA Case No. 2009-23, Second Partial Award on Track II, August 30, 2018, para. 7.117: "In the Tribunal's view, it is well settled that a claimant asserting a claim for denial of justice committed by a State's judicial system must satisfy, whether as a matter of jurisdiction or admissibility, a requirement as to the exhaustion of local remedies or, as now better expressed, a substantive rule of judicial finality. Even the grossest misconduct by a lower court or manifest unfairness in its procedures is not by itself sufficient to amount to a denial of justice by a State, unless the judicial remedies that exist in that State either do not correct the deficiencies in the lower court's judgment (once exhausted by the foreign national) or are such that none affords to the foreign national any reasonable prospect of correcting those deficiencies in a timely, fair and effective manner."

But the rule of exhaustion of local remedies has no application to the case of a refusal by a State to arbitrate pursuant to a contractual obligation with an alien to arbitrate, for at least three reasons.

In the first place, when a State undertakes an obligation in a contract with an alien to arbitrate disputes arising under that contract, and when it subsequently repudiates that obligation, it stands in breach of an obligation "of conduct" or "of means," rather than an obligation "of result."[48] A State can obligate itself to act in a particular way; or it can oblige itself to achieve a particular result. If its obligation is no more than the latter, it is free to achieve that result by a variety of means, and, as long as it ultimately does so, no breach of an international obligation arises. The rule of exhaustion of local remedies applies to such obligations of result; and a breach of an international obligation in such cases arises only if the alien concerned has exhausted the effective local remedies available without achieving the promised result. Where, however, the State has bound itself by an obligation of conduct to act in a particular way – for example, to arbitrate disputes with an alien – then it is in no position to say that it will enable justice to be done in another way; it has bound itself to providing the specified means of arbitration and where, by its conduct, it fails to do so, violation of its obligation arises. The requirement of exhaustion of local remedies does not come into play.

This approach may be countered by the contention that, when a State contracts with an alien, it does not conclude an instrument of international law; thus it undertakes no "international" obligations but only the obligations of the contract and those provided by the governing municipal law (normally, that of the contracting State). But this critique embodies an important *non sequitur.* As already discussed above, contractual obligations must still be exercised in a way that is consistent with a State's international obligations.

In the second place, when a contract between a State and an alien provides that the exclusive remedy for settlement of disputes under that contract is arbitration, arbitration is the sole remedy,

---

[48] See, generally, James Crawford, *State Responsibility: The General Part* (2013), pp. 220–223.

which is to be exhausted, standing in lieu of local remedies. It was so argued by Switzerland, the United Kingdom, and France when they espoused the claims of their nationals in the *Losinger, Anglo-Iranian,* and *Compagnie du Port de Beyrouth* cases.[49] Perhaps the most emphatic of the arguments advanced was that of the United Kingdom, which maintained that, since arbitration of disputes was prescribed, "... on any view, therefore, the Company was not obliged or even permitted to have recourse to Iranian municipal courts."[50] While the issue was not passed upon by the Permanent Court of International Justice or the International Court of Justice, it has been authoritatively addressed in terms supportive of this conclusion by the following authorities.

In his award in *LIAMCO* v. *Libya,* the sole arbitrator, Dr. Sobhi Mahmassani, held as follows:

As the arbitration clause and the procedure outlined therein are binding upon the contracting parties, and the procedure outlined therein being imperative, the Arbitral Tribunal constituted in accordance with such clause and procedure should have exclusive jurisdiction over the issues of the dispute. No other tribunal or authority, local or otherwise, has competence in the matter.

The exclusive and compulsory character of the arbitration process in such a case is widely admitted in international law. It has been affirmed by international arbitral precedents, such as the *British Petroleum Arbitration* referred to above, and has also been incorporated in the Convention of 1966 on the Settlement of Investment Disputes between States and Nationals of other States. Its Article 26 reads as follows:

"Consent of the parties to arbitration under this Convention shall, unless otherwise stated, be deemed consent to such arbitration to the exclusion of any other remedy ...."[51]

---

[49] See discussion in Section C.1, *infra.* The plaintiff States supplied considerable support for their position, some of which is referred to above.

[50] *Anglo-Iranian Oil Co. Case (United Kingdom v. Iran), Pleadings,* p. 365.

[51] *Libyan American Oil Company (LIAMCO) v. Government of the Libyan Arab Republic,* 62 *International Law Reports,* pp. 179–180. See, in respect of the relevant implications of Article 26 of the ICSID Convention and the *Losinger, Anglo-Iranian, Electricité de Beyrouth,* and *Compagnie du Port* cases, Stephen M. Schwebel and J. Gillis Wetter, "Arbitration and the Exhaustion of Local Remedies," 60 *American Journal of International Law* (1966), p. 484.

García Amador was more categoric. He concluded that where, in a contract or concession between a State and an alien, there should be recourse to international arbitration to settle any dispute which may arise thereunder:

the recourse to international jurisdiction . . . is not subject to the requirement that local remedies must be exhausted . . . for the said instruments
would be deemed to contain a tacit waiver, by the State making the
contract with an alien, of the right to require the exhaustion of local
remedies. Furthermore, if the essential purpose of the arbitration clause
in those instruments is precisely to empower the parties to present a claim
before an international tribunal whenever a dispute arises, what would be
the sense of requiring recourse to municipal jurisdiction? And, in strict
accuracy, is it not also the essential design of such instruments that all
disputes concerning their interpretation and application should be
removed from local jurisdiction?[52]

In his Preliminary Award in *Elf Aquitaine Iran* v. *National Iranian Oil Company*, the sole arbitrator, Professor Gomard, provided a comprehensive response to NIOC's contention that the alien's arbitration claim was precluded by unexhausted local remedies:

The International Court of Justice has declared that "The rule that local
remedies must be exhausted before international proceedings may be
instituted is a well-established rule of customary international law", *Interhandel* case (Switzerland v. United States of America) (1959) *I.C.J. Reports*,
at page 27. This rule of local remedies or redress that would require ELF
to present its claims to the [Iranian] Special Committee before turning to
an international remedy does, however, govern only complaints made by a
state in the exercise of its right of diplomatic protection of its nationals, cf.
e.g. *Manual of Public International Law*, 1958, edited by *Max Sorensen*, p. 582,
and not, as pointed out by *Maurice Bourquin* in an article in *The Business
Lawyer*, Volume XV (1960) p. 860 et seq., to a request from a party to an
agreement on arbitration to initiate arbitral proceedings under that agreement. The parties have by choosing arbitration established a procedure
for settlement of disputes which excludes the national legal remedies
provided for in national legislation. The established procedure also
implies that each party is entitled to have disputes settled by arbitration

---

[52] "International responsibility. Fifth Report by Dr. F.V. García Amador, Special Rapporteur," *Yearbook of the International Law Commission 1960*, vol. II, p. 57. See also Luzzato, cited *supra* note 20, at p. 94.

without evoking diplomatic protection and thus without fulfilling conditions to be met in order for their government to exercise diplomatic protection.[53]

In the third place, it is an established principle of international judicial and arbitral practice that the requirement of exhaustion of local remedies does not apply (in a case where it otherwise would apply) where there are no local remedies to exhaust. Thus the Permanent Court of International Justice in 1939 held that: "There can be no need to resort to the municipal courts if those courts have no jurisdiction to afford relief. . . ."[54] Moreover, local remedies must be exhausted only if they can be effective.[55] As discussed above, more recent doctrine and case law has framed the question as being whether there is a "reasonable possibility of an effective remedy."[56]

Where a State refuses to carry out the terms of an arbitral clause of a contract with an alien, there normally are no administrative or judicial remedies of that State that an alien could invoke which could oblige the State to arbitrate. Particularly where the State so refuses pursuant to legislation enacted subsequent to the conclusion of the contract, it would be most exceptional to find local remedies capable of overriding such legislation. If there are no effective remedies to which the alien contractor could resort to require the State to arbitrate, then, for this further reason, the rule of exhaustion of local remedies would not apply.

---

[53] XI *Yearbook Commercial Arbitration, supra* note 12, pp. 104–105.

[54] *The Panevezys-Saldutiskis Railway Case, P.C.I.J.*, Series A, No. 76, p. 18.

[55] As held, for example, by Dr. Algot Bagge in 1934 in the *Claim of Finnish Shipowners against Great Britain in Respect of the Use of Certain Finnish Vessels during the War*, III *U.N.R.I.A.A.*, pp. 1481, 1543. See also, for example, Paulsson, *supra* note 1, ch. 5. In his Separate Opinion in the *Norwegian Loans Case*, Judge Lauterpacht observed:

> For the requirement of exhaustion of local remedies is not a purely technical or rigid rule. It is a rule which international tribunals have applied with a considerable degree of elasticity. In particular, they have refused to act upon it in cases in which there are, in fact, no effective remedies available owing to the law of the State concerned or the conditions prevailing in it. (*I.C.J. Reports 1957*, pp. 34, 39.)

[56] Paulsson, *supra* note 1, p. 118. See also *Chevron v. Ecuador*, UNCITRAL, PCA Case No. 2009-23, Second Partial Award on Track II, August 30, 2018, para. 7.117.

The question is not whether there are remedies in lieu of arbitration, which if pursued might afford the alien contractor compensation for the wrong of which he complains. There may indeed be such remedies, which in some cases might be effective, but they do not remedy the wrong at issue: that of the failure to provide the arbitral recourse for which the contract provides. In respect of that failure, recourse to local remedies is not required or, it may be argued, as it was in the *Anglo-Iranian Oil Company* case, even permitted.

C. The Practice

The relevant practice consists both of the contentions of States before international tribunals and arbitral awards. Those arbitral awards consist not just of those awards wherein denial of justice is addressed, but also recent investment treaty awards that have considered how other standards of treatment may apply in the context of States' attempts to negate arbitration.

1. Contentions of States

The origins of denial of justice as a means of confronting a State's attempt to negate arbitration can be found in the contentions of States before international tribunals.[57]

---

[57] The I.C.J. has recognized that the pleadings of States before *national* courts can amount to State practice (*Jurisdictional Immunities (Germany v. Italy), Judgment, I.C.J. Reports 2012*, para. 55), and there is no obvious reason why the same cannot apply to the pleadings of States before *international* tribunals: Maurice Mendelson, "The Formation of Customary International Law," 272 *Recueil des Cours* (1998), pp. 155, 204; Ian Brownlie, "Some Problems in the Evaluation of the Practice of States as an Element of Custom," in *Studi di diritto internazionale in onore di Gaetano Arangio Ruiz*, vol. I (2004), pp. 313, 315: "it seems obvious that statements made by Agents and Counsel before international tribunals constitute State practice"; Schwebel, *supra* note 26, pp. 70–71; Paparinskis, *supra* note 27, Introduction to the Paperback Edition; Michael Wood, ILC Special Rapporteur on the Identification of Customary Law. "Second Report on Identification of Customary International Law" (May 22, 2014) U.N. doc. A/CN.4/672, para. 41.

(A) *THE LOSINGER & CO. CASE*

The Losinger & Co. case is the earliest of four cases before the Permanent Court of International Justice and the International Court of Justice in which the issue of a denial of justice for evasion of the arbitral remedy was argued. (The facts of this complex case most relevant to the question under discussion are summarized above.) Switzerland initially maintained that Yugoslavia, by invoking before an arbitrator a subsequently enacted law in order to vitiate a prior compromissory clause of a contract with an alien, had abused its rights;[58] violated the fundamental international legal norm of *pacta sunt servanda*;[59] and deprived Losinger of its acquired right to arbitration.[60] It sought the Court's "judgment to the effect that the Yugoslav Government cannot claim release from the terms of a clause of its contract with the *Société anonyme Losinger & Cie*, by adducing the Yugoslav law of July 19, 1934 concerning the conduct of State litigation, which came into force on October 19, 1934, and which is therefore of more recent date than that contract."[61]

Yugoslavia replied that it had breached no international obligation[62] and that, in any event, Losinger & Co. had failed to fulfil the precondition for Switzerland to advance an international claim: the exhaustion of local remedies.[63] It cited and adopted an arbitral award by Max Huber where he held that "a claim of an international character based on an alleged denial of justice can only be entertained if the judicial remedies afforded by the competent municipal courts have first been exhausted."[64] It maintained that the contract with Losinger, including the arbitration clause, was governed by Yugoslav law and that Losinger was obliged to resort to Yugoslav courts to challenge the retroactive application of Yugoslavia's 1934 law, a challenge that it contended Yugoslav courts could entertain.[65] Since the 1934 law on its face was not necessarily retroactive and since the Yugoslav courts had not upheld retroactive

---

[58] *The Losinger & Co. Case, P.C.I.J.*, Series C, No. 78, p. 26.   [59] Ibid., pp. 32–34.
[60] Ibid., pp. 35–38.   [61] Ibid., p. 9.   [62] Ibid., pp. 121–129.
[63] Ibid., pp. 129–135.
[64] Ibid., pp. 130–131. (While the Objection of the Yugoslav Government did not provide the source of this quotation, it appears to be *Affaire des biens britanniques au Maroc espagnol* (1925), II U.N.R.I.A.A., p. 617.)
[65] *The Losinger & Co. Case, P.C.I.J.*, Series C, No. 78, pp. 132–135, 254, 257.

application of the 1934 law to the arbitral clause, Yugoslavia had committed no act that could be construed as a violation of international law. It had adopted a law generally debarring arbitral action against the State, and, if the arbitrator in response to it had held that his competence was suspended, that was no fault of Yugoslavia's, and no denial of justice engaging its international responsibility.[66]

The Swiss Agent, Professor Georges Sauser-Hall, responded that the arbitral remedy under the Losinger contract was exclusive and that Losinger would not have signed the contract without it. He stated that Switzerland sought from the Court the declaratory judgment that Yugoslavia's objection to the arbitrator's jurisdiction founded on retroactive application of the 1934 law was contrary to international law.[67] He observed that Yugoslavia – which before the Court maintained that the Yugoslav courts had not found the 1934 law to have or not to have retroactive effect – had claimed retroactive application before the arbitrator and had never withdrawn that claim. It was now estopped by considerations of good faith from pleading uncertainty about retroactivity when it had pleaded preclusive certainty before the arbitrator.[68] Sauser-Hall made it clear that Switzerland saw a denial of justice in Yugoslavia's undermining of the exclusive arbitral remedy for which the contract with Losinger provided by its argument to the arbitrator that the retroactive application of the 1934 law vitiated Losinger's arbitral access. "The notion of denial of justice ... particularly comprehended obstruction of access to the competent tribunals."[69] The arbitral obstructions to which Losinger had been subjected were the responsibility of the Yugoslav State; not only its legislation, which it argued to the arbitrator was "ordre public," but its administration of that legislation were subject to criticism.[70] Sauser-Hall maintained that there was no effective recourse in Yugoslav courts against the 1934 law and set out what was the precise nature of the denial of justice of which Switzerland complained, in these terms:

---

[66] Ibid., pp. 191–193, 199–200.   [67] Ibid., p. 295.   [68] Ibid., pp. 307, 317.
[69] Ibid., p. 313 (translation supplied).
[70] Ibid., pp. 313–314, 315–317, 366–367.

Losinger & Co. had sought access to the arbitral tribunal established by the contract. It sought nothing more. The Yugoslav State had the obligation to accept that jurisdiction. It had contractually submitted to it. Now, it paralyzed the jurisdictional potency of the sole competent tribunal, that of the arbitrator. The proof was indubitably produced: one need only read the arbitrator's interlocutory decision and the demands made of him by the Yugoslav representatives. That is the complaint of Switzerland: ... Yugoslavia's having blocked access to the competent tribunal, the arbitral tribunal. ...[71]

Sauser-Hall concluded that:

It cannot be denied that breach of an obligation to arbitrate is a flagrant violation of law; and, when that obligation had been concluded between a State and an alien, that violation constitutes a disavowal of the status guaranteed to aliens by the rules of international law ....[72]

Yugoslavia had endeavored to place responsibility on the shoulders of the arbitrator, but the arbitrator had responded to a plea of the Yugoslav State – a plea that was "contrary to the arbitration clause. Yugoslavia was obliged to accept arbitration; its plea was the application of a posterior law to the contract and was contrary to its provisions ...."[73] This was not a simple procedural defense, it was "an act directly perpetrated by the State which permitted it to deprive the arbitral clause of its content. There is the violation of the duty of a State to respect the rights of aliens."[74] Whether or not the arbitrator was right to dismiss the arbitration, the fact remains that there was a governmental decision to renege upon its arbitration agreement.

A judgment of the Court did not ensue, since the Parties settled the case and requested that it be discontinued.[75]

While Switzerland's claims of violation of international law (denominated as a denial of justice or otherwise) by Yugoslavia's objecting to the arbitrator's jurisdiction on the ground of retroactive application of the 1934 law are clear, it is equally clear that Yugoslavia did not concede any violation of international law, by denial of justice or otherwise. It is striking, however, that apparently

---

[71] Ibid., p. 317 (translation supplied).   [72] Ibid., p. 365 (translation supplied).
[73] Ibid., p. 366 (translation supplied).   [74] Ibid., p. 367 (translation supplied).
[75] *The Losinger & Co. Case*, P.C.I.J., Series A/B, No. 69, Order of December 14, 1936.

nowhere did Yugoslavia contend that a definitive rupture by it of the arbitral agreement would not engage its international responsibility. Yugoslavia refrained from directly replying to this Swiss contention by arguing that the act of suspending the arbitration was the arbitrator's and that disavowal of the arbitral remedy by retroactive application of the 1934 law could not be imputed to the State of Yugoslavia until Yugoslav courts had ruled that it had such application. One might therefore deduce from the pleadings an implicit acknowledgement by Yugoslavia that definitive repudiation by it of the arbitral remedy contained in the contract would have constituted a denial of justice.

(B) *THE ANGLO-IRANIAN OIL COMPANY CASE*

In the *Anglo-Iranian Oil Company* case, the Iranian Government claimed to have annulled the concession of the company through enactment of the Iranian Oil Nationalization Act of 1 May 1951. Article 22 of the concession agreement concluded by Iran and the company in 1933 provided for arbitration of "[a]ny differences between the parties of any nature whatever...."[76] In its application instituting proceedings, the United Kingdom asked the Court, *inter alia:*

(a) To declare that the Imperial Government of Iran are under a duty to submit the dispute between themselves and the Anglo-Iranian Oil Company, Limited, to arbitration under the provisions of Article 22 ... and to accept and carry out any award issued as a result of such arbitration.
(b) Alternatively,
   (i) ...
   (ii) To declare that Article 22 ... continues to be legally binding on the Imperial Government of Iran and that, by denying to the Anglo-Iranian Oil Company, Limited, the exclusive legal remedy provided in Article 22 ... the Imperial Government have committed a denial of justice contrary to international law....

The refusal of the Imperial Government of Iran to have recourse to arbitration constitutes a denial of justice

45. This refusal of the Iranian Government to allow the clause of the Concession Convention providing for arbitration any effect whatever

---

[76] *Anglo-Iranian Oil Co. Case, Pleadings, supra* note 50, p. 31.

enhances the unlawfulness of the unilateral termination of the Convention and adds to it the element of another international delinquency, namely, denial of justice. For some such procedure of arbitration on compensation is essential if the principle of the nationalization of the oil industry in Iran is conceded. The Oil Nationalization Act of 1st May 1951 itself provides for the determination of compensation, but ... this provision is illusory and nominal since the Iranian Parliament is itself to adjudicate upon the claims of the Company. There is no principle of law more fundamental than that a party cannot be judge in its own cause ... It would have been possible for the Government of Iran, while insisting on its right to terminate the Convention of 1933 on account of the law nationalizing the oil industry in Iran, to leave the arbitration clause of Article 22 intact.

46. For the reasons set out in the two preceding paragraphs, the Government of the United Kingdom contends that, even if the Iranian Government was entitled to cancel unilaterally the Convention of 1933, such cancellation need not, necessarily or automatically, extend to the arbitration clause of the Convention so as to exclude the Arbitration Court (provided for in that clause) as the body to assess compensation. Reasons of legal principle, supported by precedent, and considerations of good faith require that that clause should be given effect in every possible case. The refusal of the Government of Iran to give any effect at all to the arbitration clause of the Convention and its determination to remain the sole judge in matters arising out of the unilateral cancellation of the Convention – in particular with regard to the compensation due to the Anglo-Iranian Oil Company – constitute tortious actions which engage the international responsibility of Iran.

47. There cannot in this case be any question of the responsibility of the Imperial Government of Iran being dependent upon any previous exhaustion of available local remedies, since it is an established principle of international judicial and arbitral practice that the requirement of exhaustion of local remedies does not apply in cases where there are no local remedies to exhaust. There are no local remedies under the law of Iran against a law passed by the Iranian legislature. Moreover, the legal remedies for a breach of the Convention of 1933 are the remedies provided for in Article 22 of the Convention, namely, recourse to the Arbitration Court provided for in that Article. That legal remedy the Government of Iran has repudiated expressly and repeatedly – a repudiation which in itself constitutes the international delinquency of denial of justice. Further, Iran has not only excluded arbitration as a remedy for the Company to use if the Company disputes, as it does, the legality of the expropriation. The expropriation has itself been justified in part by allegations of default or misconduct on the part of the Company, yet Iran has not called upon the Arbitration Court provided for in the Convention to examine these

allegations, although this Arbitration Court certainly had exclusive jurisdiction to pronounce upon allegations of default. Instead Iran has made
herself the judge in her own cause on this issue also.[77]

It is of interest to note, given this book's origins in the Lauterpacht
Lectures, that the quoted passages of the British Memorial in the
Anglo-Iranian Oil Company case are taken virtually verbatim from a
draft prepared by the then Professor Lauterpacht, who was one of
the British counsel in the case, and who had been retained by the
Company to prepare on its behalf the first draft of what became the
British Memorial.[78] The passages quoted characterizing the Iranian
Government's refusal to abide by the arbitration clause as "an
international delinquency consisting in denial of justice"[79] appear
in Lauterpacht's draft. He described that refusal as amounting "to a
tortious action which engages the international responsibility of
Iran."[80]

Iran replied that, apart from the fact that the "Iranian nation"
had always considered the 1933 concession to be null and void, the
concession had disappeared with the nationalization; accordingly
Article 21 (providing that: "This Concession shall not be
annulled ...."),[81] and Article 22, providing for arbitration, had also
become non-existent and were a "dead letter."[82] There was no
denial of justice because of the overthrow of Articles 21 and 22,
because the nationalization law was (allegedly) not discriminatory.[83] Moreover:

The charge of denial of justice may only be raised in conformity with
international law after the exhaustion of local remedies. To maintain that
the refusal to arbitrate, pursuant to Article 22, is of itself a denial of justice
is to fail to recognize that, even assuming the validity of the 1933 concession, Article 22 no longer exists and has not survived the nationalization
law. Furthermore, there is no denial of justice since the impossibility of
application of Article 22 of the concession has given rise to a transfer of
competence to Iranian jurisdiction. The nullification of Article 22 puts an
end to what in reality was a "privilege" ....[84]

---

[77] Ibid., pp. 120–122.
[78] See E. Lauterpacht, editor, *International Law Being the Collected Papers of Hersch
Lauterpacht*, vol. 4 (1978), p. 23.
[79] Ibid., p. 50. See also, p. 74.   [80] Ibid., p. 52.
[81] *Anglo-Iranian Oil Co. Case, Pleadings, supra* note 50, p. 31.
[82] Ibid., p. 288 (translation supplied).   [83] Ibid., p. 290.
[84] Ibid., p. 291 (translation supplied).

By a vote of nine to five, the International Court of Justice decided that it lacked jurisdiction in the case and thus it did not render judgment on the merits.[85] The pleadings in the *Anglo-Iranian Oil Company* case nevertheless constitute a classic confrontation of the question of denial of justice in circumstances that continue to have contemporary reverberations. Iran's refusal to arbitrate was pointedly denominated a denial of justice by the United Kingdom and was one of the principal counts[86] on which it advanced its case. Iran denied that it had committed a denial of justice, but its contentions were not convincing. Its claim that its arbitral obligations disappeared with the concession contract conflict with the rule of severability discussed in the first chapter. Its claim that there was no denial of justice because of the presence of local, Iranian, remedies was misconceived. Those remedies of appeal to a committee of the Majlis related to compensatory elements of the merits, not to requiring arbitration in accordance with the terms of the concession contract. Iran's reliance on such an appeal to respond to the claim of denial of justice did not meet the point, namely, that for a State to refuse the exclusive remedy that it had bound itself by a contract with an alien to accord is to deny justice by the very act of refusing that remedy.

Only one Judge of the Court dealt with the question of denial of justice, Judge Levi Carneiro. In his wide-ranging opinion that dissented on declining jurisdiction, Judge Levi Carneiro agreed with the British contention that the refusal of Iran to set up the arbitration tribunal provided for in the concession contract "constitutes a denial of justice on the part of the Iranian Government." He saw "in this a grave violation of international law."[87]

(c) *ELECTRICITÉ DE BEYROUTH COMPANY CASE*

In the *Electricité de Beyrouth Company* case, differences arose in 1953 between the Lebanese Government and the French concessionaire, turning on a level of charges for electricity. The Company requested arbitration pursuant to a clause of its concession, which provided that:

---

[85] *Anglo-Iranian Oil Co. Case (Jurisdiction), Judgment of July 22, 1952, I.C.J. Reports 1952*, p. 93.
[86] Ibid.   [87] Ibid., pp. 164–166. See also p. 171.

... disputes which arise between the concessionaire and the Government concerning the execution or interpretation of the clauses of this concession shall be brought before the competent administrative jurisdiction, unless the concessionaire makes use of the right which it nevertheless reserves to submit the dispute to an arbitral tribunal composed of three arbitrators, one named by the Government, the other by the concessionaire, and the third by the two arbitrators, or, failing their agreement, by the vice president of the Conseil d'Etat of the French Republic.[88]

The Lebanese Government did not positively respond to the demand for arbitration,[89] even though the Company proposed that the third arbitrator be appointed by the President of Lebanon, a proposal which apparently was accepted.[90] Rather, the Government sequestered the concessionary enterprises. The Company thereupon reiterated its demand for arbitration, chose its arbitrator, and expressed the hope that the Government would not place the Company "devant un véritable déni de justice."[91] This demand for arbitration was disregarded. After diplomatic representations which did not produce a satisfactory result, France instituted proceedings before the International Court of Justice.

The French Government maintained, among other contentions, that:

By refusing arbitration, the Lebanese Government was in breach of ... the Memorandum of Conditions and consequently of the Franco-Lebanese Treaty of January 24, 1948; this denial of justice would, moreover, by itself have constituted a wrongful act under international law, even if the Treaty had not existed. The refusal of arbitration by the Lebanese Government... thus constitutes at one and the same time a violation of a treaty and a denial of justice in the sense in which this term is used in the law relating to international responsibility.[92]

The case was settled by agreement between the French and Lebanese Governments after submission of the French Application and

---

[88] *Electricité de Beyrouth Company Case (France v. Lebanon), Pleadings*, p. 5; translation supplied.

[89] Ibid., p. 187.   [90] Ibid., pp. 191, 192.   [91] Ibid., p. 58.

[92] Ibid. See also the French Application Instituting Proceedings, ibid., p. 14, where, referring *inter alia* to "the denial of justice involved in the Lebanese Government's refusal to accept arbitration... ," France asked that "the rules of international law that are applicable to the situation of its national ... should be respected" and also asked "for adequate reparation for the failure to observe these rules."

Memorial, and before the Lebanese Government had put in a Counter-Memorial.[93] Thus there is no reply by Lebanon to the charge by the French Government of commission of a denial of justice. The explanation advanced by Lebanon for failure to arbitrate was through diplomatic channels, and it did not treat the claim of denial of justice.[94]

(D) CASE CONCERNING THE COMPAGNIE DU PORT, DES QUAIS ET DES ENTREPÔTS DE BEYROUTH AND THE SOCIÉTÉ RADIO-ORIENT

The Compagnie du Port in this dispute was a French concessionaire in a position like that in which the company in the *Electricité de Beyrouth Company* case found itself. It possessed certain tax immunities which the Lebanese Government was claimed to have infringed. Confronted with what it saw as a unilateral modification of its concession agreement, the company sought arbitration, invoking an arbitral clause whose terms were the same as those in the prior case.

The Lebanese Government gave no positive reply. France accordingly brought proceedings in the International Court of Justice. The French Application made it clear that its action against Lebanon was based on two causes: first, the imposition of taxes on the concessionaire from which it was exempt; second, in refusing recourse to arbitration.[95] On the second point, the French Memorial argued that there resulted a denial of justice, in these terms:

2. Since 1952, the Compagnie du Port, des Quais et des Entrepôts de Beyrouth has been requesting the Lebanese Government to settle outstanding disputes by the method open to it by its concessionary instruments. The Lebanese Government refuses and by so doing is guilty of a denial of justice involving its international responsibility.

---

[93] *Electricité de Beyrouth Company Case, Order of July 29, 1954, I.C.J. Reports 1954,* p. 107.

[94] *Electricité de Beyrouth Company Case, Pleadings, supra* note 88, p. 48.

[95] *Case Concerning the Compagnie du Port, des Quais et des Entrepôts de Beyrouth and the Société Radio-Orient (France v. Lebanon), Pleadings,* pp. 6–7. The French Application sought, *inter alia,* a declaration of the international responsibility of the Lebanese Government and a judgment that that Government was under an obligation to make good the damage suffered by the Company as a result of measures which prevented it from operating according to the rules which Lebanon was under an obligation to observe (ibid., pp. 9–10).

According to M. Charles de Visscher[96]...denial of justice may be defined as "any failure in the organization or exercise of the jurisdictional function involving an omission on the part of the State to discharge its international duty of according the judicial protection to foreigners." In the case of the Compagnie du Port de Beyrouth the denial of justice is seen in its simplest form: a denial pure and simple. The Compagnie du Port de Beyrouth has not been allowed to assert its rights before the judge to whom it was entitled by its contract to apply, the provisions of which contract had been guaranteed by the Franco-Lebanese Monetary Agreement of 1948. That denial of justice constitutes an unlawful international act...it violates...the obligation incumbent upon Lebanon to enable every foreigner to assert his rights effectively... The Lebanese Government cannot maintain that it was not required to ensure to the Company the remedy it had itself accepted against measures taken by the legislative authorities. When a State has granted a concession to a foreigner or has concluded with him a contract, it is bound to furnish him with the domestic remedies calculated to secure fulfilment of the contract, even against decisions by the higher authorities of the State. The Compagnie du Port, ... had an available remedy against the acts of those authorities. Access to that remedy was refused to it.

For the Lebanese Government expressly refused arbitration ... deciding the question in its own favour and refusing to allow its claims to be checked by the arbitrator whose jurisdiction it had recognized beforehand. Accordingly, the Government of the French Republic considers that, by the mere fact of not having between 1952 and 1959 replied to repeated requests of the Company to have recourse to arbitration, and later by its formal refusal, the Lebanese Government is guilty of a denial of justice.[97]

In its Preliminary Objections, Lebanon replied, *inter alia*, that it had not refused to go to arbitration;[98] that, if there had been a refusal, it would not have been an act within the ambit of Lebanese submission to the jurisdiction of the International Court of Justice;[99] and that the Company had failed to exhaust local remedies. It extensively developed this third defense contending that, in Lebanon, there is recourse in a case in which one of the contracting parties refuses to go to arbitration.[100] Lebanon nowhere challenged

---

[96] Citing his lectures in the *Recueil des Cours*, 1935, vol. II, p. 390.

[97] *Case Concerning the Compagnie du Port, des Quais et des Entrepôts de Beyrouth and the Société Radio-Orient, Pleadings, supra* note 95, pp. 39–40; translation supplied.

[98] Ibid., pp. 63–64.   [99] Ibid., pp. 60–61.   [100] Ibid., pp. 67–70.

directly the French contention that a refusal to arbitrate pursuant to the arbitration clause of the concession was a denial of justice under international law.

The Observations and Conclusions of the French Government on the foregoing Lebanese Preliminary Exceptions included the following analysis on local remedies:

The Lebanese Government invokes the rule of the exhaustion of local remedies and claims that the French Government's request is inadmissible because it is premature.

If we understand the reasoning of the Lebanese Government, it means that, following constant refusal of arbitration by that Government, ... the Compagnie du Port ... should have 'exhausted' local remedies which we are told exist and are effective in the matter. Thus the Compagnie du Port, failing to obtain arbitration, should have sued the Lebanese State in the civil courts ...

Now what does [the compromissory clause] really mean? Here, as in the *Losinger* case, ...is a State which has concluded a contract with a foreign concessionary company for the carrying out of important public works. The Losinger Company had had compulsory arbitration inserted as a term in its contract; the Compagnie du Port, too, reserved the right to choose between judicial proceedings and arbitration. The Lebanese Government accepted and appears still to accept the 1925 text, and therefore the principle of that choice. That being so, it is strange that, because the Company requested the arbitration to which it had an indisputable *right*, the Lebanese Government should claim ...that 'instead of pursuing the remedies available to it under Lebanese law, the Compagnie du Port chose, following its usual custom, to refuse to submit to the law.' The Court will appreciate this curious attitude towards a company which was only making use of rights specifically acknowledged in its favour by the Lebanese Government.

The Company had *reserved* to itself the right to submit to arbitration certain disputes of its own choosing. This betrayed no distrust of Lebanese jurisdiction. The Company, however, was able by arbitration to secure a speedy and entirely impartial decision, since the arbitration commission was to be composed of persons whose selection offered every possible safeguard.

The possibility of arbitration, common in questions of important works, was a basic feature of the contract; it had been agreed to by the Lebanese State and still is.

If the Company opted for arbitration in virtue of the right abovementioned, the result of that option was to withdraw finally from all Lebanese courts the dispute for which the option was exercised. By recognizing the

Company's right to that option, the Lebanese Government undertook in advance not to require the Company to apply to its courts. Otherwise, there was no option, no right was 'reserved' to the Company, since its remedy would, in every case, lie with the Lebanese court. No interpretation which makes a treaty clause useless or absurd can be upheld. As Mr. Sauser Hall, Agent for the Swiss Government, said in the *Losinger* case ... 'it is in the nature of every arbitration clause to withdraw a dispute from the jurisdiction of the ordinary courts; otherwise the insertion of an arbitration clause would have no meaning.'[101] From the moment that the Compagnie du Port has, even on a single occasion, requested arbitration concerning no matter what dispute, it has met the conditions required in order that the local remedies rule cannot be urged against it.

But, before all else, it must be repeated that, once the Company had opted for arbitration, the dispute could at no time, and under no pretext, be denied the way of arbitration and compulsorily submitted to the ordinary courts. The question, therefore, is not whether it is theoretically possible under Lebanese law for a State signing an arbitration clause to be obliged by a judicial decision to have recourse to arbitration against its will.

The effect of recourse to arbitration, which the Company had reserved to itself as a possibility was, as stated above, to withdraw the existing dispute from the jurisdiction of the Lebanese courts. It would be a modification of the Company's contractual rights to claim that, by way of an action for non-execution of the arbitration clause, the Lebanese courts could have been seised of disputes which the Company had not intended to submit to them.

Lastly, the Government of the French Republic would remind the Court that no State can plead that local remedies have not been exhausted when it has itself, in breach of its treaty obligations, prevented the foreigner who complains of loss from asserting his rights before the jurisdiction available to him. The Permanent Court stated in its Judgment No. 9.[102] ...: "It is, moreover, a principle generally accepted in the jurisprudence of international arbitration, as well as by municipal courts, that one Party cannot avail himself of the fact that the other has not fulfilled some obligation *or has not had recourse to some means of redress*, if the former Party has, by some illegal act, prevented the latter from fulfilling the obligation in question, *or from having recourse to the tribunal which would have been open to him.*"

The Lebanese Government prevented the Compagnie du Port from having recourse to the arbiters.

3. In order that an assertion by the Lebanese Government may not go unanswered, the Government of the French Republic must add that

---

[101] *The Losinger & Co. Case, P.C.I.J.*, Series C, No. 78, p. 269.
[102] *Case Concerning the Factory at Chorzów, P.C.I.J.*, Series A, No. 9, p. 31.

recourse to the Lebanese courts would not, in its opinion, have been effective . . . .[103]

The case was settled before the Court gave judgment.[104] But not only are the positions in the case of the States concerned significant; the fact that Lebanon pleaded local remedies, but did not argue that a denial of justice would not arise if those remedies did not oblige it to arbitrate, perhaps suggests its acquiescence in the French claim that a definitive refusal to arbitrate would be tantamount to a denial of justice.

(E) UNITED STATES CLAIMS OF LIBYAN DENIALS OF JUSTICE

In response to the decrees of Libya affecting interests of the companies which later were at issue in the Texaco[105] and LIAMCO[106] arbitrations, the United States Embassy in Tripoli, on September 14, 1973, delivered a note of protest to Libya which contained this passage:

The concession agreements governing the operations of the oil companies specifically provide that: 'The contractual rights expressly created by this concession shall not be altered except by mutual consent of the parties.' They further provide for arbitration of disputes not otherwise settled. Accordingly, failing further negotiations between the parties on the basis of respect for their contractual rights, the proper remedy for the current disputes between the companies and the Libyan Government is clearly arbitration. The United States Government understands that the companies in question have requested arbitration; it expects that the Government of the Libyan Arab Republic will respond positively to their request since failure to do so would constitute a denial of justice and an additional breach of international law.[107]

---

[103] As cited in *Case Concerning the Compagnie du Port, des Quais et des Entrepôts de Beyrouth and the Société Radio-Orient, Pleadings, supra* note 95, at pp. 87–96; translation supplied.

[104] *Case Concerning the Compagnie du Port, des Quais et des Entrepôts de Beyrouth and the Société Radio-Orient (France v. Lebanon), Order of 31 August 1960, I.C.J. Reports 1960*, p. 186.

[105] *Texaco Overseas Petroleum Company (TOPCO) and California Asiatic Oil Company v. The Government of the Libyan Arab Republic, 53 International Law Reports*, p. 389.

[106] *Libyan American Oil Company (LIAMCO) v. Government of the Libyan Arab Republic, 62 International Law Reports*, p. 141.

[107] Department of State, *Digest of United States Practice in International Law, 1975* (1976), p. 490.

Libya, in the event, did not respond to the requests for arbitration, but the American companies were able to proceed with those arbitrations notwithstanding Libya's default.

On April 18, 1979, awards having been handed down in the those arbitrations, the US government restated its position on denial of justice in a note to the *Tribunal de grande instance, Paris*, in support of LIAMCO's attempt to obtain an exequatur of the LIAMCO award in France. The note stated in part:

It is the position of the United States Government that contracts validly concluded between foreign governments and nationals of other states should be performed by the parties to those contracts in accordance with their terms. ... Where the breach of such a contract by a foreign government is arbitrary or tortious or gives rise to a denial of justice, a violation of international law ensues. ... [T]he failure of a government to respect a contract with an alien to arbitrate disputes arising under that contract constitutes a denial of justice under international law.[108]

The *Tribunal de grande instance* granted an exequatur.

It is of interest to recall that the arbitral clauses at issue in these cases provided for appointment of a sole arbitrator by the President of the International Court of Justice in case a party failed to appoint its arbitrator. In the event, sole arbitrators were so appointed. Nevertheless, the United States took the position that a failure by Libya to "respond positively" to the companies' demands for arbitration – its failure "to respect a contract with an alien to arbitrate disputes" – would "constitute a denial of justice." For the reasons explained at the outset of this chapter, it is believed that this broad concept of denial of justice (which is reflected as well in the *Turriff* v. *Sudan* case to which we next turn) is correct.

2. Arbitral Awards: Negation of Arbitration as Denial of Justice

The position that refusal by a State to afford the arbitral remedy for which its contract with an alien provides constitutes a denial of justice finds support in a number of arbitral awards which appear to bear on the question.

---

[108] Diplomatic note 139 of the United States Embassy in Paris, quoted in R.B. von Mehren and P.N. Kourides, *supra* note 20, pp. 487–488, note 44.

(A) *TURRIFF CONSTRUCTION (SUDAN) LIMITED V. THE SUDAN*

An arbitral tribunal, applying the Permanent Court of Arbitration's Rules of Arbitration and Conciliation for Settlement of International Disputes between Two Parties of Which Only One is a State, rendered an arbitral award in 1970 in a case between Turriff Construction (Sudan) Ltd., a British company, and the Government of the Republic of the Sudan, which concerned a construction contract which the Company claimed the Government had wrongfully repudiated. The Government and the Company agreed to submit the case to arbitration at The Hague. The arbitration agreement provided that the Tribunal would be the judge of its competence and could issue an award notwithstanding any absence of one of the parties.[109] After the proceedings were well advanced, the Sudanese Government withdrew, on the claim that a non-commercial consideration beyond the competence of the Tribunal had come to light. The Tribunal held:

> The position is clear. The Government made a deliberate choice. Instead of admitting the contract and fighting the claim on its merits it decided to advance as the first line of defence that the contract was void from the beginning or voidable and avoided and that it would be against good conscience to enforce it against it. Until the 8th May it was willing and indeed anxious to have these matters debated before and decided by the Tribunal. It extended the Submission to enable this to happen. At a very late stage it had a change of opinion and decided that it did not want these matters debated. The Tribunal accordingly concluded that no good reason for withdrawal or absence had been shown. They also concluded that, the withdrawal not being justified, it would have been a denial of justice had they refused to exercise the power to proceed in the absence of the Government. It would have been a denial even if no charge of fraud had been made. The charge having been made and no justification for absence having been shown to the Tribunal, they considered it imperative to proceed and give Turriff the opportunity of clearing itself of such charge and proving their claims against the Government if they could.[110]

This seems to be a holding by an international arbitral tribunal that, where a Government without good cause withdraws from an arbitral

---

[109] The award is unpublished, but an extensive report of the case by one of the arbitrators, L. Erades, "The Sudan Arbitration," 17 *Nederlands Tijdschrift voor International Recht* (1970), p. 200, contains substantial passages of the award.
[110] Ibid., p. 218.

proceeding to which it is bound, the arbitral tribunal itself would be a party to, or at least would have permitted, "a denial of justice" if it declined to proceed in the absence of the Government. Whether the Tribunal referred to a denial of justice in a technical sense, as that term is customarily used in international law – that is, in this case, to a denial of justice by the Government of the Sudan – is not clear. Perhaps it used the term in another sense, simply to mean that a failure to proceed would be an injustice.[111] Yet the award is open to the construction that to give effect to Sudan's attempt to frustrate the arbitral process would give rise to a denial of justice. The *Turriff* award, however summary on this point, thus arguably is authority for the position that, if a State by its unjustified absence from arbitral proceedings causes an international arbitral tribunal not to proceed, a denial of justice under international law results.

(B) THE DELAGOA BAY RAILWAY CASE

The *Delagoa Bay Railway* arbitration of 1900 between the United States and Great Britain, as claimants, and Portugal, as defendant, has been described in the first chapter. The concession for whose annulment compensation was sought provided that all questions which might arise between the concessionaire and the Portuguese Government concerning the execution of the contract were to be submitted to arbitration. But when a dispute arose over a time limit laid down by the Government during which the concessionaire was required to extend the railway line, the Government rescinded the contract and seized the line, at that time not being prepared to go to arbitration with the Company. The arbitrators, who were three Swiss jurists named by the President of the Swiss Federal Council, held that Portugal committed a wrong by going beyond the bounds of the concession contract in either not affording more time to extend the railway line "or, failing that, requesting a decision on this point by arbitrators as foreseen by ... the contract."[112] While on this point the Tribunal's award is terse, it accordingly seems to support

---

[111] That was the interpretation given, for example, by Alan Redfern in his review of the first edition of this book, *supra* note 30, pp. 166, 167.

[112] La Fontaine, *Pasicrisie Internationale* (1902), p. 401.

the position that failure by a State to carry out an undertaking in a contract with an alien to submit disputes arising thereunder to arbitration is an unlawful act in international law, that is, in this context, a denial of justice.

That in substance is the conclusion reached by Professor Gillian White in her book, *Nationalisation of Foreign Property*, where she maintains:

Breach of arbitration provisions

For there is considerable authority in support of the proposition that the cancellation of a concession in breach of an undertaking to submit the matter to arbitration is an unlawful act entitling the alien's national State to intervene. It constitutes a wrong in itself and quite distinct from the question of compensation.

. . .

The celebrated case of the *Delagoa Bay Railroad* also illustrates this principle. A concession for the construction of a railway was granted by the Portuguese Government to an American national. The construction proceeded in accordance with the agreed plans until the Government requested an extension of nine kilometres to be laid in eight months. This proved to be impossible, and at the expiration of the eight month period, the Government annulled the concession and seized the railway. . . . The action . . . was in breach of Article 53 which provided that all questions which might arise between the Company . . . and the Government touching the execution of the contract were to be submitted to arbitration. The United States took up the claim presented by the concessionaire's widow, and the British Government intervened on behalf of the British company which held the majority of the stock of the Portuguese operating company. The case finally went to arbitration on the issue of the amount of compensation, Portugal having admitted her liability, but the arbitrators' statement of the reasons for their award is illuminating. Compensation was assessed on the basis of reparation for injury done unlawfully, which basis was selected from three possibilities for the reason that the decree rescinding the concession and the act of taking possession of the railway went beyond the bounds of the concession. It was stated that there should have been either an additional agreement as to the time for laying the final section, or the matter should have been referred to arbitration under Article 53.[113]

---

[113] *Nationalisation of Foreign Property* (1961), pp. 169–171.

The Practice

(C) THE CASE OF BEALE, NOBLES AND GARRISON

This case turned upon Venezuela's disavowal of contracts for the establishment of a steamship line and a colonization scheme. Of this case, Professor White writes:

The State's liability for cancellation in these circumstances has been based on denial of justice, understood in the broad sense of an unjustified, arbitrary act causing injury to the rights of an alien. In the case of *Beale, Nobles and Garrison* the United States/Venezuelan Commission found that the contracts suffered from an initial invalidity because of lack of authority of the Government agent concerned; but that if they had been valid and the concessionaires had requested a reference to arbitration in accordance with the contracts and had met with the refusal of the Venezuelan Government, "then a question might have arisen whether there was not such a denial of justice on the part of that government as would have warranted the interposition of the good offices of the United States on behalf of the injured parties." The arbitration clause in this contract covered doubts, differences, difficulties or misunderstandings of any class or nature arising from or having connection with the contract. The Commission stated that if language had any meaning, the attempt to revoke was clearly a "difficulty" of the sort contemplated by the clause.[114]

The passages in question in the original report merit quotation:

But, passing this, it is further to be observed that the clause in both of the contracts providing for arbitration at Caracas clearly shows that neither of them, on any pretext, was ever to be made cause for an international claim. It is true that it has been urged in answer to this, that both contracts were struck down by the decrees annulling them, and that the arbitral clause fell with them. But that argument is more specious than real. It is conceded, of course, that one party to a contract cannot break it at his pleasure and without the consent of the other, but when both parties agree, as in this case, that any doubts, differences, difficulties, or misunderstandings of any class or nature whatever that may arise from, or have any connection with, or in any manner relate to the contract shall be referred to arbitration, and one of the parties declares that he is not bound by the contract and attempts to annul it, then the attempt to revoke, of necessity, if language has any meaning, being a "difficulty" relative to the contract, must be one of the questions agreed to be submitted. If these contracts had been good and valid in other respects, and the Messrs. Beales and Nobles had demanded that the "difficulty"

[114] Ibid., p. 171.

growing out of their annulment should be referred to arbitration as provided, and the government at Caracas had refused its assent to the submission, then a question might have arisen whether there was not such a denial of justice on the part of that government as would have warranted the interposition of the good offices of the United States on behalf of the injured parties. No such demand appears to have been made, but the case was submitted to the old commission under the convention of 1866, and was decided by the umpire upon the assumption just stated, that the decrees annulled the provision as to arbitration, and thus produced the very result of converting into cause for an international claim a difficulty relating to the contract which by its terms expressed in the most solemn manner was never to be made such on any pretext whatever. A distinction was made in argument between a reference of differences or misunderstandings arising out of the construction of the contracts, and a difficulty as to the existence of the contract itself, it being admitted that a controversy of the first kind was legitimate matter for arbitration, but the second was not, or rather could not be made so, because when the contract was annulled there was no longer any provision for arbitration. But that assumes the right to annul without making the revocation a subject of arbitral decision, and such assumption cannot be made without the further assumption that a difficulty *relative* to the contract does not and was not intended to include a question as to whether there was such a contract. The case seems to us too clear for doubt, and on this ground alone, if there was no other, we should reject the claim.[115]

Since the contracts in question were found in this award between the United States and Venezuela to be invalid, the quoted passage would seem to be *obiter dicta*. But it is of interest both in its statement about a denial of justice and the "specious" claim that annulment of a contract containing an arbitration clause vitiates the arbitral obligation.

(D) *NORTH AND SOUTH AMERICAN CONSTRUCTION CO. V. CHILE*

A Kentucky corporation, the North and South American Construction Company, in 1888 entered into a contract with the Government of Chile for the building of railroad lines. The Chilean Government abrogated the contract in 1890. The Company complained, demanding damages. The case was referred to a United States-Chilean Claims Commission. There the Chilean Government

---

[115] J.B. Moore, IV *International Arbitrations*, pp. 3562–3563.

demurred to the claimant's memorial on the grounds appearing in the passage about to be quoted. The Commission's majority delivered this opinion:

The legal relations between the Government of Chile on the one hand, and the North and South American Construction Company on the other hand, have been regulated by articles 18 ... and 49 of the general conditions for the construction of railways ... which are as follows:

"ARTICLE 18. The contractor or contractors will be considered for the ends of the contract as Chilean citizens. In consequence they renounce the protection which they might ask of their respective governments, or which these might officiously lend them in support of their pretensions."

"ARTICLE 49. The difficulties or disputes of any nature which may arise in the interpretation and extension of the contract will be decided summarily and without other appeal by the arbitrating arbitrators named, one by the ministry of industry and public works, another by the Supreme Court of Justice, and the third by the contractor."

This contract obtained the sanction of a law in Chile by an act of the two houses of the Chilean Congress and has been signed by the President of the Republic of Chile.

... We are of the opinion that these articles when construed together mean the same thing; they mean that all questions arising out of the contract itself, such as the proper construction to be placed on any of its provisions, the amount of payment due, the annihilation of the contract in the case provided for by the contract itself, shall be decided summarily and without appeal by the tribunal of arbitrators, ... In regard to all these purposes of the contract, the contractor agrees to be considered as a Chilean citizen and to be treated in all respects as a Chilean citizen who might enter into a similar contract for similar purposes. To this extent, and to this extent only, has the claimant agreed to renounce the protection which as a citizen of the United States it had a right to demand from its own government.

It is further to be asserted that the different provisions aforesaid must be considered as being in co-relation, giving to the memorialist, in lieu of its agreement to be considered for the ends of the contracts as a Chilean citizen and of its renunciation of the protection of its government, the assurance that "the difficulties or disagreements of every nature which may arise in the interpretation or execution of the contract will be decided summarily and without appeal by three arbitrating arbitrators." This last provision must be looked upon as one of the considerations of the contract; it should have the effect to exempt the memorialist from the jurisdiction of the regular courts of Chile and to subject it to the competence and to the decision of the tribunal of arbitration ... .

This tribunal of arbitration would have been competent, ... to decide the question of the taking possession of the company's property by the Chilean Government, ...

By the decree of September 11, 1891, suppressing the tribunal of arbitration ... the rights of the memorialist ... have been suppressed without having been since re-established. It is not to be doubted that in view of the suppression of one of the principal considerations of the contract, concerning jurisdiction by the Chilean Government, the memorialist cannot be further considered bound by the corresponding obligation concerning jurisdiction, according to which it renounces the protection of its government; seeing that by renouncing this protection for the ends of the contract it has placed itself under the protection of that tribunal of arbitration provided for ... .

By the suppression of this tribunal of arbitration the memorialist has recovered its entire right to invoke or accept the mediation or protection of the Government of the United States.

Finally, it is to be noted that the first article of the convention of Santiago, of August 7, 1892, provides that all claims on the part of corporations, companies, or private individual citizens of the United States upon the Government of Chile ... shall be referred to this arbitration commission; ... that the memorialist is a company, which ... has neither relinquished nor lost its quality of American citizenship. ... It is further undeniable that a wrong has been done to the memorialist by the suppression of that court of arbitration which had been competent to decide about the taking possession of the property and the bonds of the claimant. ...

The demurrer, therefore, should be overruled and the respondent government required to answer.[116]

This international arbitral award appears to support these conclusions:

(i)   abrogation by a State of a contract providing for the exclusive settlement of disputes by arbitration does not nullify the obligation to arbitrate;

(ii) such an arbitral clause withdraws the dispute from the local courts and local remedies need not be exhausted;

(iii) of most immediate interest, "... a wrong has been done ... by the suppression of that court of arbitration which had been competent to decide about the taking of possession of the

---

[116] Ibid., vol. III, pp. 2318–2322.

property and the bonds of the claimant" – i.e., an international wrong tantamount to a denial of justice. That is in substance the interpretation which the late Professor D.P. O'Connell placed on the case:

> To take the extreme example of unilateral abrogation of the contract by the State itself, as occurred in the *North and South American Construction Co.* case, where Chile suppressed the body which under the terms of the contract was to arbitrate differences; this is itself an international wrong ... and hence a claim will lie.[117]

(E) *SOCIÉTÉ DES GRANDS TRAVAUX DE MARSEILLE V. PEOPLE'S REPUBLIC OF BANGLADESH AND BANGLADESH INDUSTRIAL DEVELOPMENT CORPORATION*

The East Pakistan Industrial Development Corporation (EPIDC), a corporation wholly owned by the Pakistan Government, in 1965 concluded a contract with a French company, *Société des Grands Travaux de Marseille* (SGTM), for construction of a gas pipeline in East Pakistan, which became, in 1971, the People's Republic of Bangladesh. The contract provided for arbitration in Geneva under the Rules of the International Chamber of Commerce. The contract declared Pakistani law to govern the contract.

In 1969, SGTM brought a claim under the contract and invoked arbitration. The parties jointly agreed upon a sole arbitrator (Mr. Andrew Martin, Q.C.), and agreed that the arbitration would take place in Geneva under its arbitration law. In accordance with ICC procedure, terms of reference submitted by the arbitrator so stating were signed by the parties on 7 May 1972.

Two days later, the President of Bangladesh issued Order No. 39, which provided for the immediate establishment of the Bangladesh Industrial Development Corporation (BIDC), and established its identity with EPIDC, transferring to BIDC the shares, board, officers, and assets of EPIDC, and its debts and liabilities "unless the Bangladesh Government otherwise directed."[118] Order No. 39 decreed that:

---

[117] D.P. O'Connell, *International Law* (1970), vol. II, p. 1064.

[118] The arbitral award in ICC Case No. 1803 (1972), in *Société des Grands Travaux de Marseilles (France)* v. *East Pakistan Industrial Development Corporation,* is published in part in V *Yearbook Commercial Arbitration* (1980), pp. 177–185. The quotation is found at p. 178.

All arbitration proceedings to which, immediately before the commencement of this Order, the East Pakistan Development Corporation was a party shall be deemed to have abated and no award or decision made or given in such proceedings shall have any effect or be binding on, or enforceable against, the East Pakistan Development Corporation or the Bangladesh Industrial Development Corporation, and all power or authority to act on behalf of the East Pakistan Development Corporation in any such proceedings shall be deemed to be revoked and cancelled with effect from the 26th day of March, 1971, and any provision in the contract or agreement providing for the settlement by arbitration of the disputes in respect of which such proceedings were instituted, shall be deemed to be of no legal effect .....[119]

By subsequent decrees, the President of Bangladesh dissolved EPIDC, and issued a Disputed Debts Order, providing that any contractual debt of the "erstwhile" EPIDC shall be deemed not to have been incurred if such debt or contract "was the subject matter of any dispute."[120] Days before the arbitral hearings, still another order was decreed, in turn dissolving BIDC, vesting its assets in the Bangladesh Government, and providing that any representations made by creditors of BIDC or any predecessor in title shall be considered by the Government which shall have the power to pay *ex gratia* compensation.[121]

In condemning the Bangladeshi Government's dissolution of a Bangladeshi corporation in order to vitiate an arbitration in progress, and Bangladesh's vesting of the corporation's assets but not its liabilities in the Government, the arbitrator held that both the public order of Switzerland, the place of arbitration, and international law, were violated on more than one count. The violations of international law assigned were extraterritorial extensions of the jurisdiction of Bangladesh to affect an arbitration in progress in Switzerland; and a taking of the assets of the Bangladesh corporation on terms, which, as they affected the interests of its French creditor, were discriminatory and confiscatory. The arbitrator did not expressly hold that the action of Bangladesh in repudiating arbitration constituted a denial of justice, nor did he speak in more general terms of a violation of State responsibility. There is no indication in the arbitrator's award that counsel for the plaintiff presented argument to the arbitrator in this vein.

[119] Ibid.   [120] Ibid., p. 179.   [121] Ibid.

In annulment proceedings, the Swiss Federal Tribunal approached the case, as did the Geneva court from which appeal was made, in terms of Swiss "ordre public." It held that the actions of Bangladesh, not being directed against citizens of Switzerland, did not offend Swiss public order. As for considerations of international public order, the Swiss Federal Tribunal held:

> *International Public Order*
> The appellant has relied on, in addition to Swiss public order, 'ordre public international,' which would also preclude the application of the Orders of Bangladesh in the present case. This notion seems never to have been used by the Federal Supreme Court. . . . It concerns rather a formula proposed by certain authors, who do not, however, give it a precise and unambiguous meaning. It cannot be ascertained how this 'ordre public international' would limit the application of foreign law more, or in another manner, than Swiss public order does. Since the appellant does not give any indication in this respect, this question cannot be examined in more detail.[122]

Professor Lalive is sharp in his criticism of that holding:

> As for international public order – truly international – the judgment reveals the perplexity of the judges . . . who admit to not seeing "how this international public order would limit the application of foreign law more, or in another manner, than Swiss public order does." Without entering into details, it suffices to indicate that, in this case and in the *Losinger* case, the unilateral repudiation of an arbitral obligation is illicit in international law, and is a deliberate violation of the principle of good faith, and it would have been perfectly possible in this case to consider that there had been a violation of "international public order" and consequently to renounce posing any question whatever of territorial attachment.[123]

It is plain, from the tenor of this passage, his invocation of the *Losinger* case at greater length elsewhere in his critique, and his attack on Swiss courts in this case for their "ratification of what one must denominate as a denial of justice,"[124] that Professor Lalive saw

---

[122] V *Yearbook Commercial Arbitration* (1980), pp. 217, 220.
[123] Pierre Lalive, "Droit International Privé," XXXIV *Annuaire suisse de droit international* (1978), p. 400.
[124] Pierre Lalive, "Arbitrage international et ordre public suisse, une surprenante décision du Tribunal fédéral: l'arrêt SGTM/Bangladesh," 97 *Revue du droit suisse* (1978), at p. 549 (translation supplied). See also p. 533, where Lalive reads the arbitrator's award in this case as in accord with the position taken by

what the Swiss Federal Tribunal most decidedly did not see: that the actions of Bangladesh constituted a denial of justice under international law. The fact remains that this case, as Swiss courts treated it, weighs – if only inferentially – against and not in support of construing a repudiation of an arbitration agreement with an alien as a denial of justice. That conclusion may be mitigated somewhat by the impression, which the judgment of the Swiss Federal Tribunal gives, that the argument of denial of justice was not made to, or, if made to, was not sufficiently understood by it.

(F) *FRAMATOME ET AL.* V. *ATOMIC ENERGY ORGANIZATION OF IRAN*

In the *Framatome* case,[125] the Atomic Energy Organization of Iran (a public corporation) had concluded with a foreign company, Framatome, and others, a contract governed by Iranian law containing an arbitration clause. After several months during which the contract was performed by both parties, a dispute arose, and the Atomic Energy Organization terminated the contract. Framatome initiated arbitration, appointing an arbitrator. The Atomic Energy Organization, while contesting the validity of the arbitration clause, also appointed an arbitrator while reserving its rights. It maintained that the contract was not valid, that it had been irregularly applied, and

the Swiss Government in the *Losinger & Co. Case* to the effect that a State's unilateral repudiation of an arbitral agreement is contrary to public international law and to Swiss public policy. See also pp. 540, 541–542, 546–547.
For his part, Professor Karl-Heinz Böckstiegel has written:
...when a state makes use of its powers of controlling a corporation and legislating to change its legal form to evade obligations of that state controlled corporation in a contract and an arbitration clause, this must be considered an abuse of rights. An example is the case Société des Grands Travaux de Marseille...the arbitration award...holding the defendants severally liable seems convincing, while the decision of the Swiss Federal Tribunal...with a contrary result is most objectionable as has been pointed out by Pierre Lalive. ("The Legal Rules Applicable in International Commercial Arbitration Involving States or State-Controlled Enterprises," in ICC, *60 Years of ICC Arbitration* (1984), p. 138.)
[125] As noted above, the award was initially published under the title *Company Z and Others (Republic of Xanadu)* v. *State Organization ABC (Republic of Utopia)*, VIII *Yearbook Commercial Arbitration* (1983), p. 94. The quotations are essentially drawn from that report. The award was published under its true name and in its original French in Clunet, *Journal du Droit International*, (1984), p. 58, prefaced by an analysis by Oppetit. The arbitrators were Professor Pierre Lalive, Professor Berthold Goldman, and Professor Jacques Robert.

that the dispute could not, under the law of Iran, be submitted to international arbitration. Among the grounds it advanced to challenge the validity of the arbitration clause and the Tribunal's jurisdiction was that, subsequent to the conclusion of the contract containing the arbitral clause, a new Constitution of Iran had been adopted by the Islamic Republic of Iran; and that, since the contract was governed by the law of Iran, it was governed by Iranian law as amended and adopted under that Constitution, with the result that that law could and did nullify the undertaking to arbitrate. On the question of whether the parties wished "to submit their contractual relations, and in particular the validity of the undertaking to arbitrate, to Iranian law, purely and simply, or to Iranian law 'in its evolution,' in other words including future legislative or constitutional provisions which could nullify or paralyze the undertaking to arbitrate," the Tribunal held:

Such a demonstration [of the latter thesis] has not been made, or even attempted, and this is not by chance. Such an interpretation of the choice of law clause would not only be contrary to the principle of interpretation, generally recognized and constantly applied by international case law, known as the principle of effectiveness, giving a worthwhile meaning to the terms used; as noted for example by the Permanent Court of International Justice in the case concerning acquisition of Polish nationality, an interpretation which would deprive the treaty (or the contract) of a large part of its practical value cannot be accepted. As this particular case concerns contractual undertakings between a private party and a foreign State or foreign public organization, such a joint intention of the parties cannot be supposed in the absence of express and unequivocal indications: it cannot be accepted that the parties wished or simply accepted that the validity and effectiveness of a contractual clause as fundamental as an arbitration clause should be subject to a sort of condition entirely within the power of one party, the occurrence of which would depend solely on the will of the State of which the public organization party to the said contract and to the undertaking to arbitrate is an instrumentality.

It is superfluous to add that a general principle, universally recognized nowadays in both inter-State relations and international private relations (whether this principle is considered as international public policy, as appertaining to international commercial usages or to recognized principles of public international law and the law of international arbitration or *lex mercatoria*) would in any case prohibit the Iranian State – even if it had the intention, which is not the case – to repudiate the undertaking to arbitrate which it made itself or which a public organization such as the

Atomic Energy Organization would have made previously. The position of contemporary positive law of international relations is well summed up by Judge Jiménez de Aréchaga, who wrote (in a study in *Mélanges Gidel*, 1961, p. 367 et seq.) that a Government bound by an arbitration clause – and the observation is equally true for undertakings made directly as for those made by the intermediary of a public organization, as in this case – "cannot validly free itself of this obligation by an act of its own will, such as for example a change in its internal law or by unilateral termination of the contract."

The above observations may seem marginal, as it has not been shown that the Iranian authorities had the intention to apply the new Constitution to free themselves of undertakings to arbitrate previously concluded by the State of Iran itself or by its public organizations. These observations are, however, pertinent to the extent that they can throw light upon the true meaning of the Article of the Constitution. Indeed, where doubt arises concerning the exact scope of this text, as when doubt arises on the scope of any act of a State, *there is always a presumption that the State in question wished to act in conformity with the principles or rules of public international law, and not in breach of them.* This generally recognized principle of interpretation confirms, if indeed this were necessary, the conclusion already reached by the Arbitral Tribunal, according to which the Article of the new Constitution quoted *cannot* be invoked in the present case to put in question the validity of the undertaking to arbitrate, provided that the undertaking was validly made beforehand.[126]

Since Iran had not definitively renounced its arbitral obligations but submitted its challenge of their viability to arbitration, it may be said that the quoted passage is *obiter dicta*. It is nevertheless of high interest in more than one respect. It runs counter to the argument of Dr. Mann recounted at the outset of this chapter that, if the *lex arbitri* is that of the litigant State, that State may lawfully and retroactively extinguish its arbitral obligations by enactment of a general law affecting actions against the State. Such a law was very much in point in this case, but the Tribunal held to the contrary of Dr. Mann's thesis, and did so, it is believed, on persuasive grounds. Moreover, the award squarely states that a repudiation by a State of an undertaking to arbitrate which it or its public corporation had made with an alien would conflict with recognized principles of public international law and with the law of international arbitration. It does not expressly refer to the resultant denial of justice, but

---

[126] VIII *Yearbook Commercial Arbitration* (1983), pp. 108–109.

the award can reasonably be read as so meaning. That conclusion is reinforced by the award's affirmation of "the fundamental principle of the binding force of undertakings freely concluded (*pacta sunt servanda*) which applies both to the contract in dispute and the inter-State agreements concluded"[127] by Iran. Finally, the award is significant in another respect as well, in its reference to the presumption that a State must be presumed to wish to act in conformity with international law. That important presumption is applied below.

(G) *ELF AQUITAINE IRAN V. NATIONAL IRANIAN OIL COMPANY*

Professor Gomard's Preliminary Award of 1982 in the *Elf Aquitaine* case was introduced in the first chapter. In his award, the sole arbitrator recounted that NIOC challenged the admissibility of the arbitration proceedings on the ground that the Special Committee established pursuant to Iran's Single Article Act of 1980 had declared the 1966 petroleum agreement in question to be null and void *ab initio*. Accordingly, in NIOC's view, arbitration based on a clause of that agreement was not possible. The award records NIOC's reservation maintaining that "NIOC's appearance at the meeting in Copenhagen was in no way to be construed as an acceptance of the arbitration proceedings":[128] NIOC maintained that Iran was entitled to nullify NIOC's obligation to arbitrate, by means of a holding of a governmental committee established pursuant to a law enacted years after the agreement containing the arbitration clause was concluded, ratified by Iran, and implemented – a committee holding that the agreement was void *ab initio*.

Among the grounds on which the sole arbitrator rejected the foregoing position of NIOC was that a State "is bound by its obligations under international agreements or concessions,"[129] in accordance with the principle of *pacta sunt servanda*. He supported this holding with references to the *Lena Goldfields* case[130] and *Saudi*

---

[127] Ibid., p. 114.
[128] XI *Yearbook Commercial Arbitration, supra* note 12, p. 98. (See also Philippe Fouchard, "L'Arbitrage *Elf Aquitaine Iran c. National Iranian Oil Company*: Une Nouvelle Contribution au Droit International de l'Arbitrage," *Revue de l'Arbitrage* (1994), p. 333.)
[129] XI *Yearbook Commercial Arbitration, supra* note 12, p. 101.
[130] Ch. I, *supra* note 50.

Arabia v. *Aramco.*[131] Thus, on this ground as well as that of the principle of the autonomy of the arbitration clause, the sole arbitrator concluded that "the arbitration clause binds the parties and is operative unimpaired by the allegation by NIOC that the Agreement as a whole is null and void *ab initio.*"[132] He further affirmed "the principle of international law that provides that States are bound by arbitral clauses in their international contracts . . ." and held that that principle comprises contracts made not only by the State itself but by a company controlled by the State (as he found NIOC to be).[133] He affirmed "the obligation under international law to respect agreements on arbitration,"[134] and repeated that: "It is a recognized principle of international law that a state is bound by an arbitration clause contained in an agreement entered into by the state itself or by a company owned by the state and cannot thereafter unilaterally set aside the access of the other party to the system envisaged by the parties in their agreement for the settlement of disputes."[135] Professor Gomard invoked the conclusion of Judge Jiménez de Aréchaga that: "The existing precedents demonstrate . . . that a government bound by an arbitration clause cannot validly free itself of this obligation by an act of its own will such as, for example, by changing its internal law, or by a unilateral cancellation of the contract or of the concession."[136] The sole arbitrator quoted Professor Prosper Weil's conclusion that:

. . . the State cannot modify unilaterally the mechanism established for the settlement of disputes in a direct way by dictating through its authority a change in the arbitration clauses, or in an indirect way through refusing to accept the arbitral procedure as it is provided in the contract, or by putting obstacles in the way of its operation; by such actions, the State would be committing an unlawful act. Furthermore, it would be less acceptable for a State to revoke the contract in its entirety in order to

---

[131] 27 *International Law Reports* (1963), p. 117. Professor Gomard also referred to the analyses of Professor Prosper Weil, "Problèmes Relatifs aux Contrats Passés entre un Etat et un Particulier," 128 *Recueil des Cours* (1969-III), p. 101, and "Les clauses de stabilisation ou d'intangibilité insérées dans les accords de développement économique," in *Mélanges offerts à Charles Rousseau,* (1974), p. 301.

[132] XI *Yearbook Commercial Arbitration, supra* note 12, p. 103. [133] Ibid.
[134] Ibid., p. 104. [135] Ibid.
[136] The quotation, drawn from "L'arbitrage entre les Etats and les Sociétés Privées Etrangères," *Mélanges en l'Honneur de Gilbert Gidel* (1961), pp. 367, 375, is found in 96 *International Law Reports* (1994), pp. 275–276.

claim that the arbitration clause has become inoperative and thus to evade its effect by such a device.[137]

The sole arbitrator also quoted Ahmed Sadek El-Kosheri's conclusion that: "The State ... is bound to respect all contractual commitments, above all the arbitration clause ..." and cited Dr. El-Kosheri's adoption of the holding of the *Aramco* award that: "'No one may derogate from his own grant' is a legal maxim which is universally accepted ... it applies to all legal relationships, whether in private law or in public law."[138]

These holdings and quotations by Professor Gomard are, it is believed, eminently sound. While they do not in terms declare that a State's repudiation of its arbitral obligations under a contract with an alien constitutes a denial of justice, Professor Gomard held that a State "is bound by its obligations under international agreements or concessions" in accordance with the principle of *pacta sunt servanda*, a conclusion that he specifically applies to the arbitral obligation. Moreover, he affirms "the principle of international law" that "States are bound by arbitral clauses in their international contracts," and adopts the conclusion that a State which repudiates the arbitral procedure prescribed in a contract with an alien commits "an unlawful act." Thus repudiation of that binding arbitral provision is in breach of international law; such a repudiation, of itself, is an independent violation of international law, tantamount, it is submitted, to a denial of justice.

(H) AN UNPUBLISHED AND UNNAMED AWARD

That exceptionally experienced and distinguished international arbitrator, Claude Reymond, in 1985 revealed that an unpublished arbitral award held that, for a State to refuse to participate in an arbitration arising out of an arbitral clause to which it has subscribed constitutes a case of "déni de justice entrainant sa responsabilité internationale."[139] The unpublished and unnamed

---

[137] 96 *International Law Reports, supra* note 136, p. 276. The reference is to the former study of Professor Weil referred to in note 131, *supra*.

[138] 96 *International Law Reports, supra* note 136, pp. 276–277. The reference is to Dr. El-Kosheri's lectures, "Le régime juridique créé par les accords de participation dans le domaine pétrolier," 147 *Recueil des Cours* (1975-IV), p. 221.

[139] Claude Reymond, "Souveraineté de l'Etat et Participation à l'Arbitrage," *Revue de l'Arbitrage* (1985), pp. 517, 523.

award thus directly sustains the thesis advanced in this chapter that such a refusal by a State gives rise to a denial of justice under international law.

(1) *HIMPURNA V. INDONESIA; PATUHA V. INDONESIA*

These two landmark arbitrations together represent one of the most well-known instances of a respondent State attempting to derail an arbitration.[140] They proceeded in parallel and produced materially identical awards, and so the following discussion will for the sake of simplicity refer only to *Himpurna v. Indonesia*.[141] This arbitration, brought by Himpurna California Energy Ltd (Bermuda), a Bermuda-incorporated subsidiary of a US company, against the Republic of Indonesia, arose in connection with another arbitration that Himpurna had brought against the Indonesian State Electricity Corporation, PT. (Persero) Perusahaan Listruik Negara (*PLN*). Himpurna brought its arbitration against PLN under long-term contracts for the sale and purchase of electricity generated by Himpurna in Java and which PLN had committed to purchase in defined quantities for a period of thirty years and, critically, in US dollars. That obligation to purchase electricity in US dollars became especially onerous to PLN in the wake of the Asian financial crisis and the collapse of the Indonesian currency, and PLN stopped purchasing the electricity from Himpurna. The tribunal, seated in Jakarta and operating under the 1976 UNCITRAL Rules and Indonesian law, held that this was a breach of contract – rejecting PLN's defenses, including hardship – and awarded Himpurna US$390 million in damages.

The arbitration that Himpurna brought against Indonesia was based on a letter sent by Indonesia's Minister of Finance to Himpurna (before the arbitration against PLN) in which the Minister stated that, as long as Himpurna's material obligations under the

---

[140] These arbitrations were previously discussed in Stephen M. Schwebel, "Injunction of International Arbitral Proceedings and Truncation of the Tribunal," 18–4 *Mealey's International Arbitration Report* (2003), p. 33. Further aspects of these arbitrations concerning the kidnapping of an arbitrator, and the resulting truncated tribunal, are discussed in the third chapter.

[141] *Himpurna California Energy Ltd.* v. *Indonesia*, UNCITRAL, Interim Award and Final Award, September 26, 1999 and October 16, 1999, XXV *Yearbook Commercial Arbitration* (2000), p. 109.

energy sale contracts were fulfilled, the Government of the Republic of Indonesia "will cause Pertamina and PLN … to honor and perform their obligations as due in the [energy sale contract]." The letter also provided for arbitration under the UNCITRAL Rules in Jakarta, but it did not prescribe the applicable law. Following the conclusion of Himpurna's arbitration against PLN, Himpurna proceeded with its arbitration under the Minister's letter, claiming that Indonesia was liable for the award rendered in Himpurna's favor, which PLN had not paid.

The tribunal comprised Professor Jan Paulsson as chair, Mr Albert de Fina of Australia and Professor Pryatna Abdurrasyid of Indonesia. Himpurna and Indonesia signed Terms of Appointment, and Himpurna filed its Statement of Claim. But then both Himpurna and Indonesia, as well as PLN, found themselves subject to proceedings before the Jakarta Central District Court. The claimant in those proceedings was Pertamina, an Indonesia State-owned energy company that was not a party to Himpurna's arbitration against Indonesia, but that nonetheless sought a declaration that the Minister's letter did not create enforceable rights, together with an injunction restraining Himpurna and Indonesia from participating in the arbitration until the court had decided the matter. The Jakarta court granted that injunction, which it clarified was subject to a fine of US$1 million per day in the event of breach.

The injunction was a strange one in several respects. Compounding the obscurity of Pertamina's interest in the arbitration and the striking *per diem* penalty, no statutory authority for the Indonesian court's power to make such an anti-suit injunction was ever provided to the tribunal, nor any example of such an injunction ever having been made before by an Indonesian court. Such was the evident novelty of the injunction that some of its details, including when it would become binding, were communicated *ex parte* to one of the parties, Indonesia. But there was little doubt as to the seriousness of the injunction's implications. On top of the fine, Indonesia itself had reserved before the Jakarta court its right to apply, in the event of Himpurna's breach of any injunction, for an order declaring contempt of court and even imprisonment (although of whom, exactly, it was unclear). More broadly, the proceedings before the Jakarta court appeared to represent a naked attempt by the respondent State in an arbitration to unilaterally rely on the

conduct of a State-owned corporation and its own courts in order to
derail a pending arbitration.

The procedural skirmishes between the parties – and between
Indonesia and the tribunal – were many and are recorded at length
in the report of the tribunal's awards. They culminated, as will be
described more fully in the next chapter, in what Professor Pryatna
would later refer to as his kidnapping by Indonesian officials on his
way to the hearing in The Hague, following which he ceased to
participate in the arbitration.[142] But the key points for this chapter
emerge from the tribunal's interim order determining that the
arbitration should proceed notwithstanding the Jakarta court's
injunction and Indonesia's decision not to participate in the arbitration on that basis. Article 28(2) of the UNCITRAL Rules permitted the tribunal to continue with proceedings unless the defaulting
party could show "sufficient cause" for its failure to appear at the
hearing. The tribunal held that Indonesia could not show such
cause.

The tribunal first approached the matter from the premise that
Indonesia had contractually agreed to take part in arbitration
under the Minister's letter and by signing the Terms of Appointment. The question was therefore whether there was any contractual basis on which Indonesia could plead that it was no longer
bound by that contractual commitment. There was not. In particular, the tribunal held that Indonesia had not established that it was
powerless to prevent State-owned Pertamina from instituting and
maintaining this action, and so any plea of *force majeure*, which
would require at the very least that the impediment be beyond
the invoking party's control, was unavailable.

But the tribunal also found, on "an alternative basis," that Indonesia's conduct constituted "a violation of international law."[143]
The tribunal rejected the notion that the arbitration was "insulated
from the imperatives of international law,"[144] observing that international law was itself a part of Indonesian law and that allowing
a State to "paralyse" the arbitral process by relying on its own court
decision would amount to an "evisceration of the arbitral

---

[142] The tribunal having decided to hold the hearing in The Hague rather than
Jakarta in accordance with Article 16 of the UNCITRAL Rules.
[143] Interim Award, *supra* note 141, paras. 150, 152.   [144] Ibid., para. 175.

process."[145] The tribunal in this context quoted a passage from the writings of F.V. García Amador, as quoted in the first edition of this book:

> The mere fact that a State agrees with an alien private individual to have recourse to an international mode of settlement automatically removes the contract, at least as regards relations between the parties, from the jurisdiction of municipal law ... [A]greements of this type imply a "renunciation" by the State of the jurisdiction of the local authorities. If an arbitration clause of this type were governed by municipal law, it could be amended or even rescinded by a subsequent unilateral act of the State, which would be inconsistent with the essential purpose of stipulations of this type, whatever the purpose of the agreement or the character of the contracting parties. Accordingly, as the obligation in question is undeniably international in character, non-fulfillment of the arbitration clause would directly give rise to the international responsibility of the State.[146]

The tribunal, in the face of the opinion of Indonesia's expert that "[i]t is in the highest degree offensive to the Indonesian court to seek to identify the court as one with the State,"[147] had little trouble responding by reference to basic principles of State responsibility. It thus adopted the holding of the Iran-United States Claims Tribunal, sitting in plenary session (with a full bench of nine judges), that "[i]t is a well-settled principle of international law that any international wrongful act of the judiciary of a state is attributable to that state."[148] The tribunal then went on to describe the internationally wrongful act in question:

> it is a denial of justice for the courts of a State to prevent a foreign party from pursuing its remedies before a forum to the authority of which the State consented, and on the availability of which the foreigner relied in making investments explicitly envisaged by that State. ... [A] state is responsible for the actions of its courts, and one of the areas of state liability in this connection is precisely that of denial of justice.[149]

---

[145] Ibid., paras. 177–178.

[146] Ibid., para. 179 (quoting F.V. García Amador, *Responsibility of the State for Injuries Caused in Its Territory to the Person or Property of Aliens – Measures Affecting Acquired Rights*, 1959).

[147] Ibid., para. 173.

[148] Ibid., para. 172 (quoting *Islamic Republic of Iran v. United States of America*, Award No. 586-A27-FT of 5 June 1998).

[149] Ibid., at para. 184.

The tribunal held that the Jakarta Court's exercise of its "purported injunctive powers," for which no statutory authority had been provided, amounted to a denial of justice.[150] The tribunal accordingly held that Indonesia was in default under the Terms of Appointment of the tribunal to which it had agreed, and that Indonesia had failed to show sufficient cause for such failure.[151]

In its final award, produced just several weeks later, the (truncated) Tribunal held that the Minister's letter was binding under Indonesian law, Indonesia was obliged under that letter to cause PLN to pay the sum for which it was liable following the first arbitration, and, given PLN's failure to pay that sum, Indonesia was now liable to pay that sum.

The holding of the *Himpurna* tribunal that a State commits a denial of justice under international law when its courts lend themselves to interdiction and frustration of international arbitral processes is a significant addition to the existing practice. But it is not only that. The more concrete effect of the case is as a demonstration that denial of justice may not only furnish a cause of action in a proceeding subsequent to a negated arbitration, as was the case with much of the practice considered in the first edition of the book. Denial of justice may also provide the inspiration and legal basis for the tribunal to prevent that negation from happening in the first place.

(J) *SALINI COSTRUTTORI SPA V. FEDERAL DEMOCRATIC REPUBLIC OF ETHIOPIA, ADDIS ABABA WATER AND SEWAGE AUTHORITY (ETHIOPIA)*

This case involved a similar attempt by a respondent State to rely on an injunction issued by its courts in order to halt a locally-seated arbitration – and a similarly strong response from the tribunal.[152] The arbitration was based on an arbitration agreement contained

---

[150] Ibid., para. 187. The tribunal noted, as a further ground for proceeding with the arbitration, that the injunction was not even directed at the tribunal, and therefore could not constrain it, but rather had been directed solely at the parties (at paras. 189–197).
[151] Ibid., para. 198.
[152] *Salini Costruttori SPA v. Ethiopia*, ICC Arbitration No 1063/AER/ACS, Award Regarding the Suspension of the Proceedings and Jurisdiction, December 7, 2001.

in a contract between Salini, an Italian company, and the Addis Ababa Water and Sewage Authority,[153] relating to a project for the construction of water treatment facilities in Ethiopia. The arbitration agreement provided for arbitration (although the parties disputed whether it provided for arbitration under the ICC Rules or rules in the Ethiopian Civil Code), seated in Ethiopia, and with Ethiopian law as the applicable substantive law. Salini commenced arbitration following various disagreements with Ethiopia concerning the performance of the contract and a tribunal was constituted with Professor Emmanuel Gaillard as chair, together with Professor Piero Bernadini and Dr. Nael Bunni.

Following extensive communications between the parties and the tribunal concerning the place of the hearing, the tribunal decided for reasons of convenience that this should be Paris rather than Addis Ababa, as Ethiopia had requested. Ethiopia then applied to the ICC Court for the disqualification of all three arbitrators on several grounds, including by "improperly" and "abusively" deciding to hold the hearing in Paris. The tribunal itself responded that the parties had agreed in the Terms of Reference to the possibility of holding hearings other than in Ethiopia, and there was no basis for any allegation of bias arising from this ordinary procedural decision. The ICC Court rejected Ethiopia's challenge, a decision that was final according to the ICC Rules. Yet Ethiopia then launched an "appeal" against the ICC Court's decision with the Ethiopian Supreme Court, which in turn issued an injunction against the tribunal restraining it from proceeding with the arbitration pending resolution of the appeal. Ethiopia also commenced an action in the Federal First Instance Court of Ethiopia requesting a declaration that the arbitral tribunal did not have jurisdiction. That court issued another injunction in an attempt to prevent the tribunal from proceeding with the arbitration.

Ethiopia further warned that a court could attach the property of, or even sentence for contempt of court, any person who breached that injunction. Ethiopia later clarified that threat: "the arbitrators

---

[153] There was a dispute between the parties as to whether the proper respondent was the Addis Ababa Water and Sewage Authority, or the Federal Democratic Republic of Ethiopia, but the parties ultimately agreed that the tribunal did not need to address this issue, which could be addressed at the enforcement stage instead (see ibid., para. 116). The respondent is referred to herein as "Ethiopia" for convenience.

would be in contempt of court and would then be unwilling to travel to Ethiopia, preventing them from fulfilling their functions under the ICC Rules and necessitating their replacement."[154] Ethiopia extended that threat to Salini in the event that its representatives attended the hearing that the tribunal had scheduled to hear the parties' submissions on how the tribunal should respond to the Ethiopian injunctions. That hearing went ahead, in Salini's presence and Ethiopia's absence, and Salini later noted to the tribunal that it understood contempt proceedings had indeed been initiated in Ethiopia against its representatives who attended the hearing.

The tribunal held that it would not suspend the arbitration because of the Ethiopian injunctions. The tribunal explained that an arbitration agreement is not "anchored exclusively in the legal order of the seat of the arbitration," but is instead "validated by a range of international sources and norms extending beyond the domestic seat itself."[155] Those sources included the obligation of a State under Article II(1) of the New York Convention to recognize arbitration agreements and which, despite the Convention not having been ratified by Ethiopia, existed as a matter of Ethiopian law anyway. The tribunal acknowledged that proceeding with the arbitration did create some risk for the enforceability of the award given that Ethiopia's courts, as the courts of the seat, had the power to set aside the tribunal's award. But the tribunal responded that other considerations, including the duty it owed to the parties and the imperative of avoiding a denial of justice, took priority:[156]

This [duty to render an enforceable award] does not mean, however, that the arbitral tribunal should simply abdicate to the courts of the seat the tribunal's own judgment about what is fair and right in the arbitral proceedings. In the event that the arbitral tribunal considers that to follow a decision of a court would conflict fundamentally with the tribunal's understanding of its duty to the parties, derived from the parties' arbitration agreement, the tribunal must follow its own judgment, even if that requires non-compliance with a court order.

To conclude otherwise would entail a denial of justice and fairness to the parties and conflict with the legitimate expectations they created by entering into an arbitration agreement. It would allow the courts of the seat to convert an international arbitration agreement into a dead letter,

---

[154] Ibid., para. 81.   [155] Ibid., para. 129.   [156] Ibid., paras. 142–143.

with intolerable consequences for the practice of international arbitration more generally.[157]

The tribunal fortified its position by referring to a number of classic precedents for the proposition that a State, having agreed to arbitration, could not then invoke its own law to renege on that arbitration agreement.[158] The tribunal recognized that, although this was widely established in situations where the State had relied on its own law as a basis to withdraw from arbitration, there were fewer cases where the State had relied on its own courts as a basis to withdraw from an arbitration. But it had no doubt that the principle was the same. The tribunal recognized that, as a matter of public international law, the courts of a State were an organ of the State, whether or not they may in fact act independently of other organs of a State.[159] "The Respondent," the tribunal explained, "should not be permitted to renege upon an agreement to submit disputes to international arbitration by the device of resorting illegitimately to its own courts, just as it should not be permitted to do so by resorting to its own law."[160] The tribunal, having refused to suspend the arbitration, proceeded to reject Ethiopia's jurisdictional objections, leaving the merits to be determined at a later date. The case settled instead.[161]

The tribunal's reasoning is a firm affirmation of general principle and a confirmation of its application to a respondent State's reliance on its own courts in an attempt to derail an arbitration, although determining the dividing line between "legitimate" and "illegitimate resorts" by a respondent State to its own courts may

---

[157] The tribunal cited, in this connection, the decision of a distinguished tribunal chaired by Jiménez de Aréchaga in ICC Case No. 4695, where the tribunal, confronted with the argument that the arbitration agreement was invalid under the law of the country of the respondent company, held that "if the tribunal finds, as it does, that it has jurisdiction, it cannot fail to exercise it. Otherwise, it would be concurring in a failure to exercise jurisdiction and could even be accused of a denial of justice."

[158] Referring, for example, to the *Framatome* and *Elf Aquitaine* cases already discussed in this chapter.

[159] *Salini, supra* note 152, paras. 165–176.   [160] Ibid., para. 174.

[161] R. Mohtashami, "In Defense of Injunctions Issued by the Courts of the Place of Arbitration: A Brief Reply to Professor Bachand's Commentary on *Salini Costruttori S.p.A. v. Ethiopia*," 20-5 *Mealey's International Arbitration Report* (2005), p. 21.

present difficulties in some cases.[162] Those difficulties could be mitigated by focusing more closely on the traditional elements of denial of justice. Eric Schwartz, who appeared as counsel for Ethiopia in this case, made precisely this point in some reflections offered after the tribunal's award.[163] Schwartz recognized that, "[i]n modern international law, a State denies justice no less when it refuses or fails to arbitrate with a foreign national when it is legally bound to do so, or when it, whether by executive, legislative or judicial action, frustrates or endeavors to frustrate international arbitral processes in which it is bound to participate."[164] Based on a summary of several classic authorities on denial of justice, Schwartz went on to explain that "the denial must ordinarily be 'manifest' or 'flagrant.' It must be 'clearly improper and discreditable' insofar as it is 'arbitrary' and 'shocks, or at least surprises, a sense of judicial propriety.'"[165] From this, Schwartz considered that "[i]t can be argued that an international arbitral tribunal would, for its part, consecrate a denial of justice, contrary to the legitimate expectations of the parties when entering into their arbitration agreement, if, without being constrained to do so, it were to acquiesce in a judicial order that failed to comport with minimum international standards."[166] The test, according to Schwarz, is that "[i]t is not the blocking of an arbitration that in and of itself constitutes a 'denial of justice,' but rather the blocking of an arbitration in a manner that is manifestly arbitrary and improper."[167] Whether such manifest arbitrariness and impropriety exists in any case would depend, as in all denial of justice cases, on a close examination of the facts.

(K) *NIOC V. ISRAEL*

This exceptional case warrants mention, if only as an interesting illustration of the variety of circumstances in which denial of justice

---

[162] Ibid. (offering a critical view of the tribunal's reasoning, albeit from the perspective of respondent's counsel). See similarly, both in terms of view and perspective, E. Schwartz, "Do International Arbitrators Have a Duty to Obey the Orders of Courts at the Place of Arbitration? Reflections on the Role of the Lex Loci Arbitri in the Light of a Recent ICC Award," in *Liber Amicorum in Honour of Robert Briner* (2005), p. 795.

[163] Schwartz, *supra* note 162, p. 795.

[164] Ibid., p. 810 (quoting Schwebel, *supra* note 140, p. 38).   [165] Ibid.

[166] Ibid.   [167] Ibid., p. 811.

may arise in the context of a State's attempts to negate arbitration.[168] In 1968, at a time when relations between Iran and Israel were less tense than they would become following Iran's 1979 revolution, the National Iranian Oil Company (NIOC) entered into a contract with Israel for the construction of an oil pipeline running across Israeli territory from the Mediterranean port of Ashkelon to the Red Sea port of Eilat. This was part of a wider project to transport Iranian oil through Israel on its way to European customers. A dispute later arose and in 1994 NIOC commenced arbitration under the contract's arbitration agreement. The contract provided for *ad hoc* arbitration, without providing for a seat.

NIOC nominated its arbitrator, but Israel refused to do the same. This was more problematic than it typically is given the relevant wording of the arbitration agreement:

Each Party shall appoint one arbitrator. If such arbitrators fail to settle the dispute by mutual agreement or to agree upon a Third Arbitrator, the President of the International Chamber of Commerce in Paris shall be requested to appoint such Third Arbitrator.[169]

Unlike with respect to the appointment of the Third Arbitrator, this arbitration clause did not provide any mechanism for the appointment of a party-nominated arbitrator in the event of a party's failure to make a nomination (and did not identify any institutional rules, which might have provided an answer). NIOC turned to the French courts for assistance. In 1995 it first requested the President of the *Tribunal de grande instance, Paris* to appoint an arbitrator, as it was entitled to do under Article 1493 of the New Code of Civil Procedure in cases where France is the seat of the arbitration, or French procedural law is otherwise applicable. But neither of those two conditions existed and so the French judge refused. The French judge also noted that Israeli law provided a mechanism to appoint an arbitrator upon a party's default and so there could be no "denial of justice."

---

[168] 2002 *Revue de l'Arbitrage* 427; aff 'd *Cour de cassation*, February 1, 2005, Gazette du Palais, April 27–28, 2005 at p. 34. See also, for an English translation of the decision of the *Cour de cassation*, XXX *Yearbook Commercial Arbitration* (2005), p. 125.

[169] Quoted in *State X v. Company Z, Judgment of the Swiss Federal Tribunal*, Case No. 4A_146/2012, January 10, 2013 (concerning Israel's challenge to a Partial Award of the tribunal dealing with certain arguments as to its composition).

Following the continued failure to resolve the dispute, in 1999 NIOC returned to the *Tribunal de grande instance* with the submission that relief from the Israeli courts was not possible because the Israeli courts, considering Iran an "enemy state," would not follow the usual procedure. But the French judge maintained his rejection of NIOC's application and held that, even if there were a sufficient link to France, there would still be no denial of justice because the judge was not satisfied that it was impossible for NIOC to seek relief from either an Israeli court (since the prior judicial refusal to hear Iranian parties might be overturned) or an Iranian court. But NIOC successfully reversed that decision on appeal to the Paris Court of Appeal. The Court held that there would be a denial of justice because it assumed that effective relief could not be obtained in Israel or Iran. Notwithstanding the defective arbitration agreement that the parties had made, the Court held that "the right for a party to an arbitration agreement to have its claims submitted to an arbitral tribunal is a rule of public policy." Most expansively, the Court held that, even though the arbitration was not seated in France and French procedural law was not applicable, the French courts could act in order to prevent a denial of justice abroad if there were a sufficient link to France – which it held to exist because of the arbitration agreement's reference to the ICC, which was a French legal entity with its headquarters in Paris.[170] The *Cour de cassation* upheld the Court of Appeal's decision on appeal in 2005.

It must first be observed that the case was decided on the basis of French law. Professor Paulsson describes the French law providing for the court to intervene in cases of denial of justice as a "singular use of the expression; it does not denote breach of a duty on the part of any court or indeed legal order, but rather commands the French judge to step in if no one else will."[171] Yet the case remains instructive as a matter of public international law because, as Paulsson explains, the decision of the Court of Appeal could have been justified by virtue of denial of justice as a delict under international law. "The denial of justice in *NIOC* v. *Israel*," he explains, "did not require inaction of the Israeli courts; it was consummated when the

---

[170] See the amended French Code of Civil Procedure, Article 1505(4), which now expressly provides for this possibility.

[171] Paulsson, *supra* note 1, p. 12, fn. 7.

government refused to name an arbitrator."[172] Paulsson further explains that:

This was a denial of justice not because all parties have a right to the implementation of their arbitration agreement, but because the government had made a promise to a foreign party that the justice it would vouchsafe was that of arbitration. The failure to respect this promise ... is an international delict. Applying international law as a part of French law, the French courts (assuming once more that they had jurisdiction) would be entitled to find that there had been a denial of justice.[173]

The tribunal, once constituted, decided that the seat of the arbitration would be Geneva.[174] The ultimate outcome of the arbitration is unclear.

(L) BANK OF AMERICA, OPIC CLAIM DETERMINATION

This case was not an arbitration, but rather a determination by the United States' Overseas Private Investment Corporation (OPIC) in response to Bank of America's claim for loss arising out of its role in what OPIC described as "one of the world's largest power projects."[175]

The project involved several major US companies (Bechtel, Enron, and General Electric) investing in an Indian-incorporated company, Dabhol Power Company (DPC), for the purposes of developing, constructing and operating a power plant and associated facilities in India. Bank of America provided financing for this project. DPC had entered into a Power Purchase Agreement (PPA) with the Maharashtra State Electricity Board (MSEB), which was owned by the Indian State of Maharashtra. Both the Government of Maharashtra (GOM) and the Government of India (GOI) agreed in separate contracts to guarantee MSEB's obligations under the PPA, while the GOM entered into further obligations in State Support Agreements. MSEB defaulted on its purchase obligations under the PPA and rescinded it, and the GOM and GOI refused to pay under the guarantees. Each of the PPA, the State Support Agreements and the two guarantees provided for arbitration in

---

[172] Ibid., p. 157. [173] Ibid.
[174] *State X* v. *Company Z, Judgment of the Swiss Federal Tribunal, supra* note 169.
[175] Bank of America, OPIC Claim Determination, September 30, 2003, para. 6.

London under the UNCITRAL Arbitral Rules, although the PPA and GOI guarantee provided for Indian law as the applicable substantive law, while the State Support Agreements and GOM guarantee provided for English law. DPC commenced separate arbitrations under the PPA (against MSEB), the State Support Agreements (against GOM), and the GOM and GOI guarantees.

MSEB responded by bringing an action to the Maharashtra Electricity Regulatory Commission (MERC), seeking, among other things, a declaration that MSEB had validly rescinded the PPA and an injunction restraining DPC from pursuing arbitration against MSEB. MERC granted that injunction and determined that only it, and not any arbitral tribunal, had jurisdiction in respect of disputes arising out of the PPA. DPC unsuccessfully appealed this to the Bombay High Court, which held that it was for MERC to determine its own jurisdiction, but DPC then successfully appealed to the Indian Supreme Court, from which it obtained a decision ordering the Bombay High Court to determine whether MERC had properly exercised its jurisdiction. On remand, the Bombay High Court held that MERC was correct to determine that it had jurisdiction over the disputes, a decision that DPC again appealed to the Supreme Court. Injunctions were also granted by the Bombay High Court restraining DPC from pursuing arbitration under the GOM guarantee and by the Delhi High Court restraining DPC from pursuing arbitration under the GOI guarantee.

OPIC, for the purposes of determining whether Bank of America had a recoverable claim under its insurance contract with OPIC, considered whether the frustration of DPC's arbitration rights by GOI, GOM, and the Indian courts constituted a violation of international law. OPIC, acting when the second appeal to the Indian Supreme Court was still pending, held that the conduct of the Indian entities amounted to a denial of justice contrary to international law. It noted that the Restatement of Foreign Relations (Third), § 712, comment h provided that "a state may be responsible for a denial of justice under international law if ... having committed itself to a special forum for dispute settlement, such as arbitration, it fails to honor such commitment."[176] OPIC also noted the US Diplomatic Note made in connection with the Libyan expropriations:

---

[176] Ibid., para. 73.

It is the position of the United States Government that contracts validly concluded between foreign governments and nationals of other states should be performed by the parties to those contracts in accordance with their terms . . . . Where the breach of such a contract by a foreign government is arbitrary or tortious or gives rise to a denial of justice, a violation of international law ensues . . . . [and] the failure of a government to respect a contract with an alien to arbitration of disputes arising under that contract constitutes a denial of justice under international law.[177]

OPIC concluded that:

There is abundant evidence in this case that Indian foreign governing authorities (i) have denied DPC access to international arbitration of its disputes with MSEB, the GOM and the GOI, (ii) have obstructed DPC's efforts to appeal denial of those arbitration rights, and (iii) have failed to honor their own commitments regarding access to international arbitration. OPIC concurs with the Insured that the actions of these authorities in committing to international arbitration and then failing to honor that commitment constitute a denial of justice that satisfies the Section 4.01 requirement of a violation of international law.[178]

OPIC clarified that DPC had "made all reasonable efforts to pursue its rights through the local courts," including by litigating its rights before MERC, challenging MERC's decision before the Bombay High Court, and twice appealing to the Supreme Court of India. In those circumstances Bank of America was "not required to prove that DPC has exhausted *all* local remedies."[179]

It is also worth noting that, in related proceedings brought by Bechtel and others before an arbitral tribunal operating under the Rules of the American Arbitration Association, the tribunal held that the Indian courts and MERC, MSEB, and other Indian entities had "enjoined and otherwise taken away Claimants' international arbitration remedies ... in violation of established principles of international law, in disregard of India's commitments under the UN Convention as well as the Indian Arbitration Act."[180] The tribunal accordingly held that Bechtel and others were able to recover under an insurance policy covering expropriation.

---

[177] Ibid., para. 74.   [178] Ibid., para. 75.
[179] Ibid., paras. 76–77 (emphasis added).
[180] *Bechtel Enterprises International (Bermuda) Ltd et al.* v. *Overseas Private Investment Corporation*, Award, September 3, 2003, 16 *World Trade and Arbitration Materials* (2004), p. 417.

(M) *CONSTRUCTION PIONEERS V. GHANA*

This arbitration arose out of a contract between Construction Pioneers, a Liechtenstein-incorporated company, and Ghana's Ministry of Roads and Transport for the construction of a road in Ghana.[181] The contract was governed by Ghanaian law and contained an arbitration agreement providing for ICC arbitration seated in Ghana. Disputes arose under the contract, Construction Pioneers commenced arbitration, and the Ministry, after participating in the early stages of that arbitration (albeit objecting to the tribunal's jurisdiction), applied to the High Court of Justice of Accra to revoke the authority of the tribunal. This was on the basis that the arbitration concerned matters of criminal fraud that were within the exclusive jurisdiction of the Ghanaian courts. The Ghanaian court granted that application, and also made an order that the arbitration agreement itself ceased having effect in its entirety, following which the Ministry no longer participated in the arbitration.

A majority of the tribunal, including Eric Schwartz as presiding arbitrator, nevertheless confirmed that it should continue with the arbitration. It emphasized its "duty," notwithstanding the applicability of Ghanaian arbitration law as *lex arbitri*, "to ensure that the parties' arbitration agreement is not improperly subverted" and, thus, consecrate a "'denial of justice,' as that principle is understood in international law."[182] The majority, in this connection, explained "that there is today ample authority in international arbitral jurisprudence for the proposition that the existence of a contract involving a State or State party, as in the present case, is [quoting the first edition of this book] 'suffic[ient] to bring the resultant relationship [with the foreign counter party] within the sphere of protection of international law.'"[183] Even though the contract had specified the application of Ghanaian law, the majority cited the *Himpurna* tribunal for the proposition that the dispute could not be "insulated from the imperatives of international law" – which, the

---

[181] *Construction Pioneers Baugeselleschaft Anstalt* v. *Government of the Republic of Ghana, Ministry of Roads and Transport*, ICC Case No. 12078/DB/EC, Partial Award, December 22, 2003.
[182] Ibid., para. 130.   [183] Ibid., para. 131.

tribunal also added, formed part of Ghanaian common law in any event.[184]

The relevant obligations of international law included, the majority continued, the obligation to recognize arbitration agreements under Article II of the New York Convention, an obligation that should itself be applied in a way that comports with international law, including the obligation not to deny justice. The majority then recalled that:

> ... a State denies justice when its courts are closed to foreign nationals or render judgments against foreign nationals that are arbitrary. In modern international law, a State denies justice no less when it refuses or fails to arbitrate with a foreign national when it is legally bound to do so, or when it, whether by executive, legislative or judicial action, frustrates or endeavors to frustrate international arbitral processes in which it is bound to participate.[185]

The majority appeared to consider that both kinds of denial of justice – a potential domestic denial of justice by virtue of the Ghanaian court's treatment of Construction Pioneers in the domestic proceedings *and* a potential international denial of justice if the tribunal permitted those courts to negate the arbitration – were implicated by the facts here. The tribunal explained that "[a]n international arbitral tribunal, such as the present one, may itself,

---

[184] Compare, for example, the reasoning of the tribunal in *Duke Energy* v. *Ecuador*, ICSID Case No. ARB/04/19, Award, August 18, 2008, para. 396:

> The Claimants argue that it is widely accepted under international law that a State which refuses to respect its promise to arbitrate with a foreign party commits a denial of justice. Doing so, it fails to recognize that Ecuador's promise related to a domestic arbitration with a local company. The arbitration had its seat in the country, was governed by the local arbitration law, and conducted under local institutional rules. The alleged ground for nullity arose under the law governing the arbitration. This situation differs from that in which a State agrees to international arbitration with a foreign party and then raises a defense of lack of jurisdiction arising from an incapacity under its own law while the arbitration agreement is valid under the law governing the arbitration.

That reasoning could pose problems to a foreign investor who operates in a host State by way of a locally-incorporated company (and may be required by the host State to so operate). The reasoning appears inconsistent with other authorities, including *Construction Pioneers* v. *Ghana*, to the extent that it suggests the application of the local law as the law governing the arbitration should be determinative.

[185] Quoting from Schwebel, *supra* note 140, p. 38.

thus, consecrate a denial of justice by recognizing and giving effect to a State court decision purporting to revoke its authority where that decision does not comport with international standards."[186] The tribunal proceeded to hold that the Ghanaian court's decision purporting to revoke the tribunal's authority did not comport with international standards, and the Ministry's application to the court was itself improper, because they were both made without regard to the actual claims within the tribunal's jurisdiction, none of which concerned the issues of fraud that the Ministry and the Ghanaian court said were within the exclusive jurisdiction of the Ghanaian courts. The Ghanaian court's failure even to consider this fact rendered its judgment "completely arbitrary"[187] and its failure to explain how the arbitration agreement could cease having effect in its entirety was "manifestly arbitrary."[188] The tribunal accordingly proceeded with the arbitration and went on to deliver several awards on the merits.[189]

(N) *WASTE MANAGEMENT V. MEXICO*

This arbitration brought under NAFTA's Chapter Eleven and the Rules of the ICSID Additional Facility arose out of a concession contract entered into between a US company's Mexican subsidiary and the Mexican City of Acapulco for the provision of certain waste disposal services.[190] The claimant investor, as Professor Paulsson has described, "sought to extend" the case law described above by contending "that a denial of justice arises where the government simply makes it burdensome (not impossible) to use the arbitral mechanism."[191]

That attempt failed. The investor, before launching its ICSID arbitration, had launched arbitration in Mexico under the arbitration agreement in its concession contract, which provided for arbitration under the Rules of Mexico's National Chamber of Commerce (CANACO). The City of Acapulco objected to the tribunal's jurisdiction and, after CANACO had requested the parties to pay

---

[186] *Construction Pioneers Baugeselleschaft Anstalt, supra* note 43, para. 135.
[187] Ibid., paras. 140–141.   [188] Ibid., para. 143.
[189] As well as its Partial Award of December 22, 2003, the tribunal delivered an Interim Award of August 3, 2004 and a Final Award of October 2, 2006.
[190] *Waste Management v. Mexico (No 2)*, ICSID Case No. ARB(AF)/00/3.
[191] Paulsson, *supra* note 1, p. 153.

advances of costs, the City refused to pay its half share. The total sum requested was significant (about US$550,000) and the investor refused to pay the full sum itself. The arbitration was therefore discontinued. The investor instead launched ICSID arbitration alleging a number of breaches of international law, including denial of justice arising from the events before the CANACO tribunal. The ICSID tribunal declined to see any denial of justice in those events. It summarized that CANACO, itself not a State organ, "apparently behaved in a proper and impartial way," concluding that "the discontinuance of the arbitration, a decision made by the Claimant on financial grounds, did not implicate the Respondent in any internationally wrongful act." In response to the investor's argument that the "litigation strategy adopted by the City itself amounted to a denial of justice," the tribunal reasoned that "a litigant cannot commit a denial of justice unless its improper strategies are endorsed and acted on by the court, or unless the law gives it some extraordinary privilege which leads to a lack of due process. There is no evidence of either circumstance in the present case."[192]

(o) SWISSBOURGH V. LESOTHO

This arbitration, which involved a rare finding of State responsibility for a denial of justice based on a State's negation of arbitration, reveals the ongoing relevance of this form of denial of justice, albeit in a rather unexpected case. The underlying award remains confidential, but some of its aspects can be discerned from the decisions of the Singaporean courts in set-aside proceedings.

The arbitration arose out of a dispute between several Lesothoan and South African investors on the one hand, and Lesotho on the other hand. The dispute concerned mining leases granted to one of the investors that had been revoked by Lesotho following the decision to implement a major infrastructure project, the Lesotho Highlands Water Project, which necessitated the flooding of the land for which the licenses were granted.

---

[192] See Professor Paulsson approving the tribunal's reasoning and explaining that "there is no absolute international duty to finance arbitral proceedings," but noting that some arbitral rules provide for certain solutions of which a claimant facing a recalcitrant respondent may avail itself (ibid., p. 154).

In 2009, the investors, having failed to obtain redress in the Lesotho courts, launched a case against Lesotho under the dispute settlement provisions contained in the Southern African Development Community (SADC) Treaty – a treaty entered into by the fifteen member States of the SADC. That treaty provided for a judicial body charged with hearing disputes under the SADC Treaty. The investors claimed before the SADC Tribunal that Lesotho had expropriated their property but then, in 2010 – before the investors' claim could be decided – the member States of the SADC unanimously decided to suspend the operation of the SADC Tribunal following complaints about its operation by Zimbabwe in the wake of an unrelated case brought against it. The member States later dissolved the SADC Tribunal.

The shuttering of the SADC Tribunal during the investors' case against Lesotho prompted them in 2012 to launch arbitration against Lesotho under the arbitration agreement contained in another SADC instrument, the SADC's Finance and Investment Protocol (FIP). That arbitration was governed by the UNCITRAL Rules, administered by the Permanent Court of Arbitration and seated in Singapore. The investors contended that Lesotho's role in shuttering the SADC Tribunal without providing any alternative means for their claim to be heard, produced, among other breaches, a denial of justice contrary to the FIP's provision that "investments and investors shall enjoy fair and equitable treatment in the territory of any State Party."[193]

A majority of that tribunal (David Williams and Doak Bishop; Judge Petrus Nienaber dissenting) dismissed a range of jurisdictional objections (while upholding others in respect of certain claimants), and upheld the denial of justice claim and several other claims.[194] As the remedy for Lesotho's breaches, the tribunal directed the investors and Lesotho to constitute a new tribunal in order for the investors' original expropriation claim to be heard. Although the tribunal's reasoning on denial of justice is not

---

[193] The Singapore Court of Appeal summarized the essence of the investors' claim as alleging the "wrongful act of interfering with and displacing the means provided and existing at that time for vindicating grievances before the SADC Tribunal by shuttering that avenue" (*Swissbourgh Diamond Mines (Pty) Ltd v. Kingdom of Lesotho* [2018] SGCA 81, para. 4).

[194] *Kingdom of Lesotho v. Swissbourgh Diamond Mines (Pty) Ltd* [2017] SGHC 195, paras. 45(d) and 147(b).

available, the tribunal apparently accepted that a State may be responsible for a denial of justice where it frustrates an international arbitral process – or, in this case, a binding dispute settlement process under the SADC Treaty – in which it has agreed to participate.

Lesotho thereafter successfully applied to the Singapore High Court for the setting aside of the award on the ground that the award dealt with a dispute not contemplated by and not falling within the terms of the submission to arbitration.[195] This decision was upheld by the Court of Appeal with somewhat different reasoning.[196] But neither court disturbed the tribunal's reasoning on the merits of the arbitration, including its reasoning on denial of justice.[197]

3. Arbitral Awards: Negation of Arbitration as Other Breaches of International Law

The burgeoning case law of arbitral tribunals adjudicating disputes between investors and States under bilateral investment treaties continues to illustrate the range of possibilities for how aliens and arbitral tribunals may respond to a respondent State's attempts to negate arbitration.[198] It is in this context that arbitral tribunals have

---

[195] Within the meaning of Article 34(2)(a)(iii) of the UNCITRAL Model Law on International Commercial Arbitration, as incorporated into Singaporean law (*Kingdom of Lesotho* v. *Swissbourgh Diamond Mines (Pty) Ltd* [2017] SGHC 195).

[196] *Swissbourgh Diamond Mines*, supra note 193.

[197] The Court of Appeal did consider that the investors' failure to exhaust local remedies also constituted a ground depriving the arbitral tribunal of jurisdiction (ibid., paras. 205–224), however this was on the basis of a specific provision in the FIP that required the exhaustion of local remedies before claims thereunder could be pursued – rather than as a substantive element of a denial of justice claim.

[198] It may also be noted for completeness that the European Court of Human Rights may provide a remedy in certain circumstances. In *Stran Greek Refineries* v. *Greece* (1994) 19 EHRR 293 (discussed in Chapter 1), Greece had passed a law terminating the contract, and the Greek Parliament "clarified" that this included the termination of the arbitration agreement, while proceedings were pending before the Greek courts for the enforcement of an arbitral award under that arbitration agreement. The Court held that the award was a "possession" under Article 1 of Protocol 1 of the European Convention on Human Rights, and that "[b]y choosing to intervene at that stage of the proceedings in the Court of Cassation by a law which invoked the termination of the contract in question in order to declare void the arbitration clause and to annul the arbitration award of 27 February 1984, the legislature upset, to the detriment of the applicants, the

developed a line of authority whereby a party's right to arbitrate, as well as an arbitral award, may be considered important elements of a protected investment under a BIT, the expropriation or other mistreatment of which investment may trigger international responsibility.[199]

(A) SAIPEM V. BANGLADESH

This landmark case arose out of a contract between an Italian company, Saipem, and a Bangladeshi State-owned entity, the Bangladesh Oil Gas and Mineral Corporation (Petrobangla), for the construction of a gas pipeline in Bangladesh.[200] The contract was governed by Bangladeshi law and it provided for arbitration in Bangladesh under the ICC Rules. A dispute arose between the parties that was submitted to arbitration. During the pendency of that arbitration, Petrobangla, having received several adverse procedural decisions from the tribunal, successfully applied to the Bangladeshi courts to first injunct the arbitration and then revoke the authority of the tribunal to hear the arbitration. The arbitral tribunal, the Bangladeshi courts stated with little elaboration, had

balance that must be struck between the protection of the right of property and the requirements of public interest" (ibid., para. 74). Greece had therefore breached Article 1 of Protocol 1. In *Kin-Stib and Majkic v. Serbia* (Application No. 12312/05), Judgment, April 20, 2010, the European Court of Human Rights also held that a claim arising out of an arbitral award could be a "possession" within the meaning of Article 1 of Protocol 1 "if it is sufficiently established to be enforceable" (ibid., para. 83) and that, by failing "to make use of all available legal means at its disposal in order to enforce a binding arbitration award" (ibid., para. 83), Serbia had breached that obligation.

[199] See generally Luca Radicati di Brozolo and Loretta Malintoppi, "Unlawful Interference with International Arbitration by National Courts of the Seat in the Aftermath of *Saipem v. Bangladesh*," in Miguel Angel Fernandez-Ballesteros and David Arias (eds), *Liber Amicorum Bernado Cremades* (2010), p. 993; Michael Reisman and Heide Iravani, "The Changing Relation of National Courts and International Commercial Arbitration," 21 *American Review of International Arbitration* (2010), p. 5; José Alvarez, "Crossing the 'Public/Private' Divide: Saipem v. Bangladesh and Other Crossover Cases," in Albert Jan van den Berg (ed.), *International Arbitration: The Coming of a New Age?* (2013), p. 400; Gabrielle Kaufmann-Kohler, "Commercial Arbitration Before International Courts and Tribunals – Reviewing Abusive Conduct of Domestic Courts," 29 *Arbitration International* (2013), p. 153; and Berk Demirkol, *Judicial Acts and Investment Treaty Arbitration* (2018), ch. 6.

[200] *Saipem v. Bangladesh*, Decision on Jurisdiction, *supra* note 32; ibid., Award, *supra* note 32.

acted with "manifest disregard" for the law and created the "likeli-hood of miscarriage of justice." The arbitral tribunal nevertheless proceeded and it delivered an award of damages in favor of Saipem for Petrobangla's breach of contract. Petrobangla applied to the Bangladeshi courts to set the award aside and the High Court Division of the Supreme Court of Bangladesh held that there was nothing to set aside because the award was "a nullity" – "a non-existent award can neither be set aside nor can it be enforced," the Court concluded. Saipem did not appeal that decision.

Saipem instead commenced its second attempt at international arbitration, this time under the Italy-Bangladesh bilateral invest-ment treaty and before a tribunal constituted under the ICSID Convention. According to Saipem, its claim concerned:

the expropriation by Bangladesh of (i) its right to arbitration of its dis-putes with Petrobangla; (ii) the right to payment of the amounts due under the Contract as ascertained in the ICC Award; (iii) the rights arising under the ICC Award, including the right to obtain its recognition and enforcement in Bangladesh and abroad; and therefore (iv) the residual value of its investment in Bangladesh at the time of the ICC Award, consisting of its credits under the Contract.[201]

The tribunal upheld Saipem's claim. It first held at the jurisdic-tional stage that Saipem had made an "investment" within the meaning of the ICSID Convention.[202] For this purpose, though, the tribunal explained that it was not considering either the right to arbitrate or the award as itself a protected investment; rather, the tribunal explained that what was relevant was "the entire or overall operation," of which the right to arbitrate and the award were parts.[203] Saipem had no difficulty also satisfying the broad

[201] Ibid., Award, *supra* note 32, para. 102.
[202] Article 25(1) of the Convention provides that "[t]he jurisdiction of the Centre shall extend to any legal dispute arising directly out of an investment." The *Saipem* tribunal applied (at para. 99) what it referred to as the "Salini test," according to which "the notion of investment implies the presence of the following elements: (a) a contribution of money or other assets of economic value, (b) a certain duration, (c) an element of risk, and (d) a contribution to the host State's development" (drawing from *Salini v. Morocco*, ICSID Case No. ARB/00/4, Decision on Jurisdiction, 23 July 2001, para. 52).
[203] *Saipem v. Bangladesh*, Decision on Jurisdiction, *supra* note 32, para. 110. See also the further explanation of Gabrielle Kaufmann-Kohler (who chaired the *Saipem* tribunal), *supra* note 199, pp. 166–167: "An investment is an allocation of resources made in cash, in kind, or in labour, entailing a certain duration and

definition of an "investment" under the BIT, which included "any kind of property."[204]

The tribunal then proceeded on the merits to hold that, consistent with its comprehensive view of Saipem's investment, "the allegedly expropriated property is Saipem's residual contractual rights under the investment as crystallized in the ICC Award."[205] The tribunal held that the Bangladeshi court's treatment of the award as "a nullity" was "tantamount to a taking of the residual contractual rights arising from the investments as crystallised in the ICC Award."[206] Bangladesh was therefore liable to pay compensation, which the tribunal determined to be the value of the ICC award (plus interest).

The award may be viewed as a reflection of international law's ability to develop solutions to address a State's unwarranted negation of international arbitration. State courts had exercised their supervisory jurisdiction so as to derail an arbitration involving a local State entity, and the tribunal applied international law in a way that corrected what it found to be an evident injustice. But this is not to say that the award is without difficulties. Perhaps the

participation in the risks associated with the economic operation. Even where BITs have broad definitions covering 'any kind of asset' followed by an enumerative list, it is difficult to see how an arbitration agreement or an arbitral award could be an investment. Cases have rather held that the investment comprises of the contribution made in the course of the underlying transaction that gave rise to the dispute and to the award."

[204] *Saipem v. Bangladesh*, Decision on Jurisdiction, *supra* note 32, paras. 121–122. The tribunal, in the context of determining whether the right to arbitrate was capable of constituting expropriation, had regard to the proposition made in Stephen M. Schwebel, "Anti-Suit Injunctions in International Arbitration – An Overview," in E. Gaillard (ed.), *Anti-suit Injunctions in International Arbitration* (2005), p. 5, that "[t]he contractual right of an alien to arbitration of disputes arising under a contract to which it is party is a valuable right, which often is of importance to the very conclusion of the contract," and that any "[v]itiation of that right" through court interference "attracts the international responsibility of the State of which the issuing court is an organ." The tribunal did not express a view on the correctness or otherwise of that proposition in its jurisdictional decision, but it did recall in its subsequent award that "the right to arbitrate and the rights determined by the Award are capable in theory of being expropriated" (ibid., para. 122).

[205] *Saipem v. Bangladesh*, Award, *supra* note 32, para. 128.

[206] Ibid., para. 129. The tribunal accepted that, because of the possibility of enforcing an arbitral award abroad under the New York Convention, the Bangladeshi court's declaration of the award as a nullity may not necessarily involve the substantial deprivation of the investment that is required for there to be an expropriation. In this case, though, it was not disputed that the only assets of Petrobangla against which Saipem could enforce the award were in Bangladesh (ibid., para. 130).

greatest question arises from the tribunal's explanation that whether the taking amounted to an expropriation turned on a further finding that the actions of the Bangladeshi courts were "illegal" (the tribunal itself placed this term within quotation marks).[207] That is a novel requirement, as expropriation cases in international law typically do not require proof of the taking's illegality. The tribunal acknowledged this point, but considered that "given the very peculiar circumstances of the present interference, the Tribunal agrees with the parties that the substantial deprivation of Saipem's ability to enjoy the benefits of the ICC Award is not sufficient to conclude that the Bangladeshi courts' intervention is tantamount to an expropriation."[208] "If this were true," the tribunal continued, "any setting aside of an award could then found a claim for expropriation, even if the setting aside was ordered by the competent state court upon legitimate grounds."[209]

In this case, the tribunal emphasized that it "did not find the slightest trace of error or wrongdoing" in the ICC tribunal's decisions, which the Bangladeshi courts clearly construed with "manifest disregard" for the law and created a "likelihood of miscarriage of justice."[210] The tribunal concluded that "the Bangladeshi courts abused their supervisory jurisdiction over the arbitration process."[211] This idea of "abuse of right" became the foundation for the tribunal's distinction between those takings that could or could not amount to an expropriation in this context, albeit the tribunal cited just one authority for its proposition that "[i]t is generally acknowledged in international law that a State exercising a right for a purpose that is different from that for which that right was created commits an abuse of rights."[212] The tribunal also held that

---

[207] Ibid., paras. 133–134.   [208] Ibid., para. 133.   [209] Ibid., para. 133.
[210] Ibid., para. 155.   [211] Ibid., para. 159.
[212] Ibid., para. 160, citing Alexandre Kiss, "Abuse of Rights," in R Bernhadt (ed.), *Encyclopedia of Public International Law*, vol. 1, p. 5. Abuse of rights is in truth rather more controversial. Hersch Lauterpacht, in discussing the International Court of Justice's treatment of the principle, warned that:

> These are but modest beginnings of a doctrine which is full of potentialities and which places a considerable power, not devoid of a legislative character, in the hands of a judicial tribunal. There is no legal right, however well established, which could not, in some circumstances, be refused recognition on the ground that it has been abused. The doctrine of abuse of rights is therefore an instrument which ... must be wielded with studied restraint.

(*The Development of International Law by the International Court* (1958), p. 164.)
See also, for similar caution, Crawford, *supra* note 3, pp. 562–563.

Bangladesh had, through the actions of its courts, breached its international law obligation to recognize arbitration agreements under Article II(1) of the New York Convention, although it is not clear if the tribunal considered that this alone would have amounted to the "illegality" necessary for an expropriation to arise.[213] The tribunal further held that local remedies did not have to be exhausted for an expropriation, even one committed through judicial acts. But it also held that, even if local remedies did have to be exhausted, this requirement would have been met given that all reasonable remedies, in its view, had been exhausted.[214]

The conceptual awkwardness of adding an additional "illegality" requirement to certain kinds of expropriation cases but not others, and the further challenges of determining the benchmark against which that "illegality" should be assessed, raise the question of whether this kind of case may more appropriately be determined on the basis of denial of justice, rather than expropriation. The BIT in this case, notably, did not contain an obligation to provide fair and equitable treatment, which provides some explanation for the tribunal's attempts to refashion the law of expropriation to the particular facts of this case.[215]

(B) *ATA* V. *JORDAN*

Subsequent cases have developed the ideas set down in *Saipem* in different ways. The tribunal in *ATA* v. *Jordan*[216] placed particular weight on the importance of the right to arbitrate when holding that the purported extinguishment of an arbitration agreement by Jordan's highest court breached the obligation to provide fair and equitable treatment. ATA, a Turkish company, had entered into a contract with a Jordanian State-owned company, APC, for

---

[213] *Saipem* v. *Bangladesh*, Award, *supra* note 32, para. 167 (citing Schwebel, *supra* note 204, p. 5 for the proposition that that "a decision to revoke the arbitrators' authority can amount to a violation of Article II of the New York Convention whenever it de facto 'prevents or immobilizes the arbitration that seeks to implement that [arbitration] agreement' thus completely frustrating if not the wording at least the spirit of the Convention").

[214] Ibid., paras. 181–183.

[215] As Saipem pleaded before the tribunal: "Article 9.1 of the BIT does not confer to your Tribunal jurisdiction over a claim based on denial of justice, and restricts your jurisdiction to a claim for expropriation. This is why we did not bring a claim on the ground of denial of justice before you" (ibid., para. 121).

[216] *ATA* v. *Jordan*, ICSID Case No. ARB/08/2, Award, May 18, 2010.

construction works near the Dead Sea, with any arbitration in Jordan. APC commenced arbitration against ATA after a dispute arose under that contract. ATA successfully defended the suit and obtained an award of damages by way of a counterclaim. But the Jordanian Court of Appeal set that award aside. The Court of Cassation upheld that decision and added that the arbitration agreement was itself extinguished, pursuant to a curious provision of the Jordanian Arbitration Law stating that "[t]he final decision nullifying the award results in extinguishing the arbitration agreement" (a provision that had been enacted into Jordanian law after ATA and APC had entered into their arbitration agreement). APC then brought a new suit against ATA, this time before the Jordanian courts.

ATA launched ICSID arbitration against Jordan under the Turkey-Jordan BIT. A number of ATA's claims, including those based on the Jordanian courts' annulment of the award, were held to be indistinguishable from the dispute preceding that award and which arose before the BIT entered into force. These claims were therefore outside of the tribunal's temporal jurisdiction.[217] But the tribunal did hold that the review of the extinguishment of the arbitration agreement by the Court of Cassation was within its jurisdictional ambit.[218] The tribunal considered that the right to arbitrate constituted a separate "investment" within the meaning of that term as defined in the BIT, which covered "claims to [. . .] any other rights to legitimate performance having financial value related to an investment." "The right to arbitration," the tribunal explained, "could hardly be considered as something other than a 'right [. . .] to legitimate performance having financial value related to an investment.'"[219] The *ATA* tribunal, by contrast with the *Saipem* tribunal, did not consider that the investor had to satisfy any additional definition of "investment" under the ICSID Convention.[220]

On the merits, the tribunal held that Jordan's extinguishment of the investor's right to arbitration breached the BIT. The tribunal, strangely, did not set out clearly which of the BIT's obligations it considered had been breached, nor what test it was applying in

---

[217] Ibid., paras. 94–115.   [218] Ibid., paras. 116–120.   [219] Ibid., para. 117.
[220] The tribunal instead reasoned that the BIT's definition of "investment" was conclusive on the basis that "[t]he ICSID Convention leaves the definition of the term investment open to the parties, allowing them to determine its scope and application pursuant to mutual agreement in the relevant BIT" (ibid., para. 111).

order to determine whether an obligation had been breached.[221] But the tribunal emphasized that, "in concluding the Arbitration Agreement, the parties agreed and expected to preclude the submission of potential disputes under the Contract to the Jordanian State courts, where Jordan would have been both litigant and judge." "Thus," the tribunal reasoned, "it was vital to provide for arbitration as the neutral mechanism for the settlement of disputes."[222] The tribunal added that Jordan's retrospective application of its law to extinguish the parties' arbitration agreement also breached its obligation to recognize arbitration agreements under Article II(1) of the New York Convention.[223] The tribunal declared that the appropriate remedy for Jordan's breach of the BIT was "a restoration of the Claimant's right to arbitration." The tribunal accordingly ordered that the Jordanian court proceedings be terminated and that ATA was entitled to pursue a fresh arbitration against APC under its original arbitration agreement with APC.[224]

(C) WHITE INDUSTRIES V. INDIA

The range of options that may be available to an investor when faced with a State's frustration of its arbitration rights is underscored by the award in White Industries v. India.[225] This case arose in the wake of the Indian courts' delay of more than nine years in enforcing an award obtained by an Australian company against the State-owned Coal India in a Paris-seated ICC arbitration, including in dealing with Coal India's application to the Indian courts to have the award set aside (notwithstanding that India was not the seat of arbitration). The tribunal first upheld its jurisdiction on the basis of what it described as "the developing jurisprudence on the treatment of arbitral awards to the effect that awards made by tribunals arising out of disputes

---

[221] The relevant standard may have been fair and equitable treatment, as incorporated into the Turkey-Jordan BIT by way of a most-favored nation provision in that BIT (see ibid., para. 125, fn. 16).

[222] Ibid., para. 126.

[223] Ibid., para. 128 (the tribunal noted that "[i]t is arguable (but the Tribunal takes no position on the point) that the extinguishment rule might be deemed to be prospectively compatible with Article II insofar as parties electing Jordan as the venue for an arbitration or electing Jordanian law as the law of the arbitration had notice of the rule and accepted it").

[224] Ibid., paras. 131–132.

[225] White Industries Australia Ltd v. India, UNCITRAL, Final Award, November 30, 2011.

concerning 'investments' made by 'investors' under BITs represent a continuation or transformation of the original investment."[226]

The tribunal held on the merits that the delay before the Indian courts did not amount to an expropriation of that investment given that the status of the award was still pending before the Indian courts and so there could not yet be a taking.[227] Nor was the delay enough to give rise to a denial of justice or other breach of fair and equitable treatment, including because the reality of the "seriously overstretched judiciary" in India could not be ignored and the investor should reasonably have expected some delay.[228] But the tribunal did hold that the delay in dealing with Coal India's set-aside application breached India's separate obligation to "provide effective means of asserting claims and enforcing rights" (as incorporated into the Australia-India BIT from the Kuwait-India BIT through the former's most-favored nation provision), which the tribunal considered imposed a more onerous obligation on India compared to denial of justice.[229] As a remedy for that breach, the tribunal, after rejecting India's arguments that the award was not enforceable in India, considered that the investor was entitled to recover what was owing to it under the unenforced award.[230]

(D) OTHER INVESTMENT TREATY CASES

Not all treaty claims based on domestic courts' treatment of arbitral awards have succeeded. Some tribunals have taken a more restrictive approach when considering the jurisdictional threshold of a protected investment. In *Romak* v. *Uzbekistan*,[231] a Swiss company obtained an arbitral award in a London-seated arbitration against an Uzbek State-owned company that had refused to pay under a contract for the sale and purchase of grain. The Uzbek courts refused to enforce that award. Romak commenced arbitration under the Switzerland-Uzbekistan BIT and the UNCITRAL Rules claiming that this refusal amounted to an expropriation of its investment. But the tribunal declined jurisdiction. It held that the award could not be separated from the underlying transaction and, in this case, the underlying transaction was not a qualifying investment. Although the BIT

---

[226] Ibid., para. 7.6.8. [227] Ibid., para. 12.3.6. [228] Ibid., paras. 10.3–10.4.
[229] Ibid., para. 11.4. [230] Ibid., paras. 14.1–14.3.
[231] *Romak* v. *Uzbekistan*, UNCITRAL, PCA Case No. AA280, Award, November 26, 2009.

included a "claim to money" within its definition of an "investment," the tribunal also regarded what it considered to be the intrinsic meaning of an "investment," and the object and purpose of the BIT. From that perspective, the tribunal held that a one-off commercial transaction, as opposed to the commitment of funds or assets over a period of time and entailing some risk, did not amount to an "investment."[232]

In a similar vein, the tribunal in *GEA Group Aktiengesellschaft v. Ukraine*[233] rejected, on jurisdictional grounds, a German investor's claim of expropriation based on the Ukrainian courts' refusal to enforce an ICC award obtained by the investor against a Ukrainian state-owned entity in a Vienna-seated arbitration. The tribunal first held that the award was not itself a protected investment within the meaning of the BIT and that, even if the award determined the rights and obligations arising out of an "investment," the award was still "analytically distinct."[234] That award itself provided "no contribution to, or relevant economic activity within, Ukraine," as required by the definition of investment contained in that BIT.[235] But the tribunal also held that, in any event, the Ukrainian courts' decisions could not amount to an expropriation. This was because compared to the *Saipem* case, which the *GEA* tribunal described had turned on the "particularly egregious nature of the acts of the Bangladeshi courts," there was nothing discriminatory or otherwise egregious about the Ukrainian court decisions.[236]

Other tribunals, grappling in particular with the standard of review to apply when determining whether a domestic court's treatment of an arbitral award will amount to an international wrong, have adopted a relatively deferential approach toward reviewing the treatment of arbitral awards by domestic courts. In *Frontier Petroleum v. Czech Republic*,[237] the tribunal rejected the Canadian investor's claim for a breach of the fair and equitable treatment standard under the Canada-Czech Republic BIT based on the Czech courts' failure to recognise and enforce an arbitral award made in Sweden. That award was made in favor of the Canadian investor against a privately owned Czech company in connection with a failed joint venture between the two. Although the tribunal granted the

---

[232] Ibid., paras. 157–232.
[233] *GEA Group Aktiengesselschaft v. Ukraine*, ICSID Case No. ARB/08/16, Award, March 31, 2011.
[234] Ibid., para. 162.   [235] Ibid.   [236] Ibid., paras. 234–236.
[237] *Frontier Petroleum Services v. Czech Republic*, UNCITRAL, Final Award, November 12, 2010.

Canadian investor a secured lien over the assets of the Czech entity and the joint venture company, the Czech courts had refused to recognise and enforce the award based on the public policy exception in the New York Convention, which they held was engaged by virtue of the award conflicting with certain mandatory rules of Czech bankruptcy law. The tribunal upheld jurisdiction over the claim on the basis that "by refusing to recognise and enforce the Final Award in its entirety, [the Czech Republic] could be said to have affected the management, use, enjoyment, or disposal by Claimant of what remained of its original investment."[238]

The tribunal then, echoing the approach of the *Saipem* tribunal albeit considering the issue from the perspective of the BIT's obligation of fair and equitable treatment rather than expropriation, explained that it "must ask whether the Czech courts' refusal amounts to an abuse of rights contrary to the international principle of good faith."[239] In other words, the tribunal continued, it had to determine whether "the interpretation given by the Czech courts to the public policy exception in Article V(2)(b) of the *New York Convention* [was] made in an arbitrary or discriminatory manner or did it otherwise amount to a breach of the fair and equitable treatment standard."[240] The tribunal accepted that "States enjoy a certain margin of appreciation in determining what their own conception of international public policy is."[241] The test was therefore: "was the decision by the Czech courts *reasonably tenable* and made in *good faith*?"[242] The tribunal held that it was.[243]

In *Anglia Auto Accessories* v. *Czech Republic*[244] the Czech Republic also successfully defended a claim of expropriation based on the non-enforcement of an arbitral award that the investor had obtained against its Czech business partner in the Czech Republic. The tribunal accepted that the investor's protected investment included, under the wording of the United Kingdom-Czech Republic BIT, its entitlement to money under the award.[245] But the tribunal held that there was no substantial deprivation of the value of the allegedly expropriated property because the investor had already recovered more than three-quarters of the value of the award.[246]

---

[238] Ibid., para. 231.   [239] Ibid., para. 525.   [240] Ibid.   [241] Ibid., para. 527.
[242] Ibid.   [243] Ibid., paras. 529–530.
[244] *Anglia Auto Accessories* v. *Czech Republic*, SCC Case No. V2014/181, Final Award, March 10, 2017.
[245] Ibid., paras. 149–154.   [246] Ibid., paras. 292–303.

Finally, in *Gavazzi v. Romania*[247] the Italian investors had obtained an award against a Romanian State-owned entity in a Romanian-seated arbitration, which was subsequently annulled by the Romanian courts on grounds of public policy. The investors brought ICSID arbitration against Romania under the Italy-Romania BIT alleging (alongside other claims) that the annulment of that award breached the BIT's obligation to "provide effective means of asserting claims and enforcing rights" and not to "impair the right of access to its Courts of Justice." A majority of the tribunal first held, on jurisdiction, that "an award which compensates for an investment made in the host State is a claim to money covered by the BIT" and would also more generally be part of the "overall investment" to the extent that a stricter definition of "investment" under the ICSID Convention needed to be satisfied.[248] On the merits, and citing the *Frontier Petroleum* award albeit considering the issue from the perspective of the "effective means" standard rather than fair and equitable treatment, the *Gavazzi* tribunal explained that the test for whether there was a breach of the treaty's "effective means" standard was whether the Romanian courts' annulment of the award "amounts to an abuse of rights contrary to the international principle of good faith, i.e., did they interpret and apply Article V(2)(b) of the New York Convention in a discriminatory manner?"[249] The tribunal very briefly explained that it found no such proof of any abuse in view of the discretion it considered should be afforded to a domestic court "to interpret and apply this notion [of public policy] to protect essential principles of the Romanian legal order as they perceived it."[250]

D. Conclusion

The most recent cases discussed immediately above, although arising in the context of bilateral investment treaties and engaging a range of different standards of treatment (expropriation, fair and equitable treatment, and effective means[251]), represent a modern

---

[247] *Gavazzi v. Romania*, ICSID Case No. ARB/12/25, Decision on Jurisdiction, Admissibility and Liability, April 21, 2015.

[248] Ibid., para. 120.   [249] Ibid., para. 261.   [250] Ibid., para. 263.

[251] The tribunal in *SGS v. Pakistan*, ICSID Case No. ARB/01/13, Decision on Jurisdiction, October 6, 2003, also considered the possibility that a governmental negation of arbitration could amount to a breach of an umbrella clause (para. 172):

development of the classic practice concerning denial of justice by governmental negation of arbitration.

It may indeed be that these cases would be more appropriately determined as denial of justice cases. The *Saipem* tribunal's focus on expropriation rather than denial of justice may have been guided by the fact that this case was being determined under a treaty that did not itself provide an obligation of fair and equitable treatment (and therefore protection against denial of justice). That subsequent cases have echoed the *Saipem* tribunal's focus on "abuse of right," even when determining the claims from the perspective of other standards of treatment like fair and equitable treatment and effective means, demonstrates the common links between these cases. Moreover the focus on "abuse of right," and synonymous or related considerations like "arbitrariness" or "egregiousness," are themselves of a piece with classic criteria for finding a denial of justice.

The practice since the time of the first edition of this book underscores that governmental negation of arbitration can arise in a number of forms, including not just through a State's conduct during the course of an arbitration itself, but also in the context of the important roles that State courts have when it comes to supervising local arbitrations, and recognizing and enforcing foreign arbitral awards. Arbitral tribunals have in turn demonstrated an appreciation of the need to balance truly abusive conduct on the part of a State's organs in seeking to derail an arbitration or undermine an arbitral award against the recognition of the important role performed by State courts.

> ... we do not preclude the possibility that under exceptional circumstances, a violation of certain provisions of a State contract with an investor of another State might constitute violation of a treaty provision (like Article 11 of the BIT) enjoining a Contracting Party constantly to guarantee the observance of contracts with investors of another Contracting Party. For instance, if a Contracting Party were to take action that materially impedes the ability of an investor to prosecute its claims before an international arbitration tribunal (having previously agreed to such arbitration in a contract with the investor), or were to refuse to go to such arbitration at all and leave the investor only the option of going before the ordinary courts of the Contracting Party (which actions need not amount to "denial of justice"), that Contracting Party may arguably be regarded as having failed "constantly [to] guarantee the observance of [its] commitments" within the meaning of Article 11 of the Swiss-Pakistan BIT.

III

The Authority of Truncated International Arbitral Tribunals

A. The Question

The final question that the first edition posed was this: does an international arbitral tribunal from which an arbitrator withdraws retain the power to proceed and to render a binding award? "Withdrawal" was employed to mean sustained abstention from participation in the tribunal's proceedings, whether on the initiative of the arbitrator or the appointing party, and whether or not accompanied by resignation. The discussion in the first edition also embraced the case in which a party-appointed arbitrator dies or is incapacitated, and the party takes advantage of the situation to withdraw, in effect, by failing to name a replacement.

The question posed continues to present a problem of international arbitral procedure.[1] Of course, if the arbitration

---

[1] Reference is made throughout to the process of international arbitration, characterized by the decision of a tribunal of an odd number of members, on which a third party casts the decisive vote. International joint commissions, on which States are represented equally and which lack neutral membership, are not in point. Nor does this discussion consider the case in which the arbitration clause provides that, if one party fails to appoint its arbitrator, a third party shall appoint an arbitrator and that arbitrator and the single party-appointed arbitrator shall be empowered to render the award. It was precisely such an arbitral clause that gave rise to a tribunal composed of two arbitrators (Dean Ripert and Judge Panchaud) who rendered the endlessly litigated award in *Société Européenne d'Etudes et d'Enterprises (S.E.E.E.)* v. *People's Federal Republic of Yugoslavia* (1956), 24 *International Law Reports* (1957), pp. 761, 762; Clunet, *Journal du Droit International* (1959), p. 1057. Nor, of course, are those international arbitral tribunals of relevance that are composed of a sole arbitrator, rather than of three or five or more persons.

agreement expressly provides that, in the event of the withdrawal of an arbitrator, the remaining members of the tribunal, being a majority of the tribunal originally constituted, shall have the power to render an award, the problem may be resolved, assuming the remaining arbitrators are in agreement.[2] If it is provided that, in case of withdrawal, a fresh appointment shall be made in the manner of the original appointment, the problem in principle is overcome if third-party appointment of the withdrawing party-appointed arbitrator is authorized.[3] In practice, however, the stage reached in the proceedings, and/or the time required to make a fresh, third-party appointment, may result in undue and unacceptable delay.[4] Moreover, provisions for third-party appointment of a substitute arbitrator may not be sufficient to meet the situation of a claims tribunal hearing a multiplicity of claims in which arbitrators appointed by one of the parties repeatedly withdraw at critical stages of the proceedings. In arbitrations between States and aliens, and in international commercial arbitration, there usually is provision for third-party appointment, either in the arbitration agreement or in applicable rules of arbitration.[5] But such authorization by treaty in arbitration between States is not customary:

When a conditional delegation of the task of naming arbitrators is made, it is a common assumption that difficulties may arise in connection with the naming of the chairman, umpire or neutral arbitrator but that a party can

---

[2] See for an illustration of such a situation, *Lena Goldfields Company Limited* v. *USSR*, *supra* Chapter I, note 50.

[3] See, for several examples, the arbitral rules discussed in Section E.1.(b), *infra*. See also Article XLV of the Pact of Bogota, 30 *U.N.T.S.* 100. The United Nations *Systematic Survey of Treaties for the Pacific Settlement of International Disputes 1928–1948* (1948) (hereinafter cited as "*Systematic Survey*") contains a large number of treaties lacking, and a much smaller number embodying such clauses. Cf., pp. 89–92, 97–98, 100–107. Characteristically, these clauses provide for third-party appointment of the arbitrator where the State fails to name him or her. The *Systematic Survey* also notes:
Vacancies which may occur as a result of death, resignation or any other cause, shall be filled in the manner fixed for the nominations, within the shortest possible time. Though many treaties do not contain any provisions on vacancies, it may be assumed that the above rule will be followed by the parties, in any case (p. 91).

[4] See *Colombia* v. *Cauca Company*, 190 U.S. 524 (1903) discussed below.

[5] See, e.g., 2010 UNCITRAL Arbitration Rules, Article 14.

be relied upon to appoint its own arbitrator or arbitrators. Consequently arbitration treaties frequently provide a method for the appointment of a third arbitrator, in the absence of agreement between the parties thereon, but omit to provide a subsidiary method for the appointment of an arbitrator whom one of the parties has failed to appoint in pursuance of the terms of the treaty.[6]

Nor is the question disposed of either by the established rule that an international arbitral tribunal is the judge of its competence[7] or by the generally accepted rule that all questions shall be decided by a majority of the tribunal.[8] For, in the application of both rules, the problem persists: is a tribunal from which an appointed arbitrator has withdrawn a "tribunal" at all – that is, a body that can give binding judgment on its competence, by whatever vote, or upon any other issue?

Since the publication of the first edition, the question of the authority of truncated tribunals continues to persist, but developments in arbitral rules, the practice of international tribunals, and the scholarship of commentators provide a clearer framework for answering the question. This modern approach provides for a two-step procedure to be followed in the event of a withdrawing or obstructionist arbitrator. First, and when feasible, a replacement arbitrator shall be appointed pursuant to the procedure provided for the original appointment or otherwise provided for in the applicable rules. This first step, it is hoped, should resolve the majority of cases. However, as a second possible step, if it is not possible or

---

[6] United Nations, *Commentary on the Draft Convention on Arbitral Procedure* (1955), U.N. doc. A/CN.4/92 (hereinafter referred to as "the *Commentary*"), p. 18. See also *Interpretation of Peace Treaties with Bulgaria, Hungary and Romania (Second Phase), Advisory Opinion, I.C.J. Reports 1950*, pp. 221, 229 (N.B. The spelling of Romania has varied over the years, a variation which has been retained in the present publication); D.H.N. Johnson, "The Constitution of an Arbitral Tribunal," XXX *British Year Book of International Law* (1953), pp. 152, 165; L.B. Sohn, "The Function of International Arbitration Today," 108 *Recueil des Cours* 1963, vol. 1, pp. 64–67.

[7] *Systematic Survey, supra* note 3, pp. 71, 77–78; *Commentary, supra* note 6, pp. 45–47. See the *Nottebohm Case (Liechtenstein v. Guatemala) (Preliminary Objections), Judgment of 18 November 1953, I.C.J. Reports 1953*, pp. 111, 119, quoted *supra* Chapter I, note 2; and the Court's Advisory Opinion in *Interpretation of Peace Treaties with Bulgaria, Hungary and Romania (First Phase), Advisory Opinion, I.C.J. Reports 1950*.

[8] *Commentary, supra* note 6, pp. 52–54, 89; *Systematic Survey, supra* note 3, pp. 114–115.

practical to replace the withdrawing arbitrator, a truncated tribunal has the authority to proceed and render a final award.

B. The Theory

As noted in the first edition, the principles that bear upon the resolution of the problem in the sphere of international arbitration turn in some measure upon the philosophy of international arbitration that is applied. On the one hand, international arbitration, at least as between States, may be viewed essentially as a diplomatic process, akin to conciliation – i.e., a flexible instrument that, at every stage of its employment, is responsive not merely to the will of the parties, but to the will of each party. Professor Carlston, in criticizing the Draft Convention on Arbitral Procedure of the International Law Commission, presented a case for what may be termed diplomatic arbitration – or, in his phrase, "*ad hoc* arbitration" – in these words:

While it is desirable to call attention to the various circumstances in which an agreement to arbitrate may be rendered nugatory by an obstructive attitude taken by one of the parties, as the Commission does, it may be questioned whether the larger interests of the international community will be served by transforming the existing conception of *ad hoc* arbitration into the conception of judicial arbitration as envisaged by the Commission. For it must be remembered that arbitration is but one of a number of means for pacific settlement of disputes available to parties; that the International Court of Justice is already available to parties in dispute with an established procedure of judicial settlement such as the Commission would like to create for *ad hoc* arbitration; that the strength of the existing system of international arbitration *as a means for the pacific settlement of disputes* lies in its flexibility and responsiveness to the will of the parties, even though as a procedure it is subject to the interruptions which the Commission now seeks to remedy; that these interruptions or breakdowns of arbitration have in practice been few in number as against the great number of international arbitrations which have taken place successfully; that many of these breakdowns could have perhaps been avoided by a more skilled use of technique; and, finally, that the ultimate end to be sought is to preserve all the various procedures developed through history which will conduce to the amicable settlement of international disputes. Abuse of the privileges of the process of arbitration which has upon occasion occurred does not necessarily mean that those privileges should be destroyed when their existence represents a continuing safeguard to the great number of states and a strong inducing factor leading them to adopt the process as a means for the settlement of their disputes. The theoretical perfection of the process should not be carried to the point where it loses its unique identity, merges with the system of adjudication of the International Court of Justice, and discourages resort to the arbitral process by states.[9]

In contrast with diplomatic arbitration stands judicial arbitration. The International Law Commission, in introducing its endeavor to codify and develop arbitral procedure, succinctly summarized the two in the following terms:

Two currents of opinion were represented in the Commission. The first followed the conception of arbitration according to which the agreement of the parties is the essential condition not only of the original obligation to have recourse to arbitration, but also of the continuation and the effectiveness of arbitration proceedings at every stage. The second conception, which prevailed in the draft as adopted and which may be described as judicial arbitration, was based on the necessity of provision being made for safeguarding the efficacy of the obligation to arbitrate in all cases in which, after the conclusion of the arbitration agreement, the attitude of the parties threatens to render nugatory the original undertaking.[10]

The Commission noted that, while "with regard to some aspects of arbitral law and procedure" its draft gave:

... expression to what the Commission considers to represent the preponderant practice of governments and international arbitral tribunals, with regard to other aspects ... the draft has taken into account both the lessons of experience and the requirements of international justice as a basis for provisions which are *de lege ferenda* ... in the first instance, the Commission considered that it was doing no more than codify the existing practice, dating from the end of the eighteenth century, inasmuch as it

---

[9] Kenneth S. Carlston, "Codification of International Arbitral Procedure," 47 *American Journal of International Law* (1953), p. 218 (footnote omitted). For similar criticism, see also Charles de Visscher, "Reflections on the Present Prospects of International Adjudication," 40 *American Journal of International Law* (1956), p. 467. Judge de Visscher particularly criticized the Commission's proposal to have the President of the International Court of Justice appoint an arbitrator in place of one who has withdrawn (ibid., at pp. 470–471).

[10] *Report of the International Law Commission covering the work of its fourth session June 4–August 8, 1952*, General Assembly, *Official Records: Seventh Session, Supp. No. 9* (A/2163), p. 3.

based the draft on the principle that arbitration is a method of settling disputes between States in accordance with law, as distinguished from the political and diplomatic procedures of mediation and conciliation.[11]

Arbitration treaties clearly are treaties; their interpretation is governed by the rules of treaty interpretation. Where States have undertaken by treaty to arbitrate, their obligation is binding. It is an obligation they are bound to fulfill. Arbitration treaties, like other international contractual instruments, are to be interpreted in good faith in accordance with the ordinary meaning to be given to the terms of the treaty in their context and in the light of the treaty's object and purpose.[12]

The application of these rules to the question under discussion, however, is not equally self-evident. Assuming that an arbitration agreement provides for the appointment of national arbitrators by the parties and for the filling of vacancies in the manner of initial appointment, and assuming that the agreement does not authorize withdrawal of an arbitrator (this may be taken for granted), does a party that withdraws or adopts the withdrawal of its arbitrator treat the agreement as binding, fulfill it in good faith, and implement it so as to give effect to its terms and its object and purpose?

At first sight, no; and this initial reaction may well be correct. This approach, indeed, is instinct in the various drafts on arbitral procedure prepared by the International Law Commission and its rapporteur on the subject, Professor Scelle. The Commission in

---

[11] Ibid., p. 2.

[12] See Vienna Convention on the Law of Treaties, 1155 U.N.T.S. 331, Article 31 (1). It has been argued that insofar as treaties of arbitration constitute conferrals of jurisdiction upon international authority, they are to be restrictively construed. That argument was soundly dispatched by the arbitrator, the late Foreign Minister of Sweden, Östen Undén, in the case of *Interpretation of Article 181 of the Treaty of Neuilly (The Forests of Central Rhodope), Preliminary Question* III U.N.R.I.A.A. (1931), pp. 1391, 1403:

> The defendant government maintains that, in case of doubt as to the meaning of an arbitral clause, the incompetence of the Arbitrator must be presumed, according to the general rule by which a state is not obliged to have recourse to arbitration except when a formal agreement to that effect exists. The Arbitrator cannot agree with this principle of interpretation of arbitral clauses. Such a clause should be interpreted in the same way as other contractual stipulations. If analysis of the text and examination of its purposes show that the reasons in favour of the competence of the Arbitrator are more plausible than those which can be shown to the contrary, the former must be adopted.

general, and Professor Scelle in particular, took the view that, inasmuch as they "based the draft on the principle that arbitration is a method of settling disputes between States in accordance with law,"[13] essentially they asked no more of States than that they act in accordance with the law by treating their obligations as binding, in good faith, so as to carry out the signatories' intentions about the object and purpose of the agreement.

Yet, on reflection, it appears that the matter is not so simple – for this approach may assume as the answer what in fact may be the question: *what* was the intention of the parties? If arbitration is a judicial process, then clearly the object and purpose of the parties was to achieve through that process a binding award: an achievement that cannot lawfully be frustrated by the obstruction of one of the parties, as, for example, by withdrawal. However, if inter-State arbitration is a diplomatic process, subject at each stage to the unilateral will of each party, then withdrawal, if not authorized, nonetheless is not deemed prohibited. It constitutes neither a breach of a binding obligation nor an act of bad faith nor a violation of the intention of the parties – an intention that was diplomatic rather than judicial.[14] An alternative and less rigorous statement of this view would be that withdrawal is lawful, and deprives the tribunal of the power to render a binding award, where the tribunal's actions give cause. Carlston, for example, submits that "power must exist in a party to protect itself from manifest excesses of jurisdiction by a tribunal, and it need not await the rendering of the award to make its protest effective."[15]

The obvious difficulty with Professor Carlston's view is that what is a "manifest excess" is a matter of the appreciation of the withdrawing State alone. Cause for withdrawal invariably appears manifest to the withdrawing arbitrator and the appointing party; the objective observer may be forgiven for the belief that withdrawal usually rather stems from the appraisal that the withdrawing party

---

[13] *Report of the International Law Commission, supra* note 10.
[14] The remarks in the International Law Commission of Mr. François, while not directed toward the problem of withdrawal, are germane. *Yearbook of the International Law Commission 1950*, p. 271. See also Johnson, *supra* note 6, p. 173, especially note 1.
[15] Kenneth S. Carlston, *The Process of International Arbitration* (1946), p. 44.

manifestly will lose the case if it continues to participate. The body
of practice shortly to be examined lends support to that belief.

It is not the purpose of this chapter to examine in depth contrast-
ing views of the nature of the arbitral process. It is believed that the
elements of judicial arbitration evidenced in the drafts of the International Law Commission are, on the whole, soundly based not only
on legal principle but upon the body of existing codification and
precedent. Moreover, judicial arbitration, particularly as reflected
in the Commission's later drafts, would, contrary to the charge
made, hardly equate the arbitral process with proceedings before
the International Court of Justice; such arbitration would continue
to accord the parties a degree of latitude, for example, in the
drawing of the *compromis* and the selection of arbitrators that does
not characterize the Court's procedure.

The explosion in investor-state arbitration since the publication
of the first edition may make this debate, and particularly the
opposition to judicial arbitration explored in the first edition,
appear antiquated. It is even more difficult today to credit the
contention that, once the parties have entered into a treaty or
contract to arbitrate, which they implement by the establishment
of an arbitral tribunal, and that tribunal receives and studies pleadings or actually hears part or all of a case that the parties present to
it at considerable cost to themselves, one party lawfully may render
all this nugatory by the expedient of withdrawing its arbitrator.
"Arbitration means the determination of a difference between
States [or between other parties] through a legal decision . . . of a
tribunal . . . chosen by the parties."[16] If, as no one disputes, the
decision rendered is "on the basis of respect for law,"[17] is all that
is preparatory to its rendition to be based upon a theory of definitive
auto-interpretation of an international (or contractual) obligation?
If, as the International Court of Justice held in the *Ambatielos* case[18]

---

[16] Hersch Lauterpacht, *Oppenheim's International Law* (7th edition, 1952), vol. 2, p. 22.
[17] The "definitive and obligatory character of arbitral awards" was affirmed by the
Permanent Court of International Justice in the case of *Société Commerciale de
Belgique*, Series A/B, No. 78 (1939), p. 176. See also the *Case Concerning the
Arbitral Award made by the King of Spain on 23 December 1906, Judgment, I.C.J.
Reports 1960*, pp. 192, 217.
[18] *Ambatielos Case (Merits: Obligation to Arbitrate), Judgment, I.C.J. Reports 1953*,
pp. 10, 23.

and in the first phase of the *Peace Treaties* case,[19] the parties to a treaty provision for arbitration are under an "obligation" or "are obligated" in the proper circumstances to participate in constituting the tribunal, does it not follow that such a party breaches its international obligations by withdrawing its arbitrator from the tribunal to which it was bound to make an appointment?

It is concluded that the withdrawal of an arbitrator on the initiative or with the approval of the appointing government, that is not authorized by the parties or the tribunal, constitutes an international wrong. From this it follows that the withdrawing State cannot be heard to challenge the tribunal's right to proceed and to render an award. The doctrine that no legal right may spring from a wrong is embedded alike "in the jurisprudence of international arbitration" and in municipal law.[20] On the plane of legal principle, its cogency may be argued to resolve the problem under discussion in favor of the binding character of international awards rendered by truncated tribunals.

It was shown in the first edition that the preponderance of precedent supported that conclusion. Since the publication of the first edition in 1987, an apparent consensus has emerged in institutional rules, precedent and commentary not only in support of a philosophy of judicial arbitration, but also, in regards to the particular question considered in this chapter, regarding the procedure to be followed in the event of a withdrawing or otherwise obstructionist arbitrator.

---

[19] *Interpretation of Peace Treaties with Bulgaria, Hungary and Romania (First Phase), Advisory Opinion, I.C.J. Reports 1950*, pp. 65, 77.

[20] See *Case Concerning the Factory at Chorzów, P.C.I.J.*, Series A, No. 9, p. 31:

> It is, moreover, a principle generally accepted in the jurisprudence of international arbitration as well as by municipal courts, that one Party cannot avail himself of the fact that the other has not fulfilled some obligation or has not had recourse to some means of redress, if the former Party has, by some illegal act, prevented the latter from fulfilling the obligation in question, or from having recourse to the tribunal which would have been open to him.

See also the dissenting opinion of Judge Read in *Interpretation of Peace Treaties with Bulgaria, Hungary and Romania (Second Phase), I.C.J. Reports 1950*, pp. 241, 244; Gerald Fitzmaurice, "The General Principles of International Law Considered from the Standpoint of the Rule of Law," 92 *Recueil des Cours* (1957-II), pp. 118–119; *Military and Paramilitary Activities in and against Nicaragua (Nicaragua v. United States), I.C.J. Reports 1986, Dissenting Opinion of Judge Schwebel*, pp. 380, 392–394; Charles T. Kotuby Jr. and Luke A. Sobota, *General Principles of law and International Due Process* (2017), pp. 130, 139. And see Lauterpacht's conclusion: *"Ex injuria jus non oritur* is an inescapable principle of law." (*supra* note 16, vol. 2, p. 218).

That procedure can be distilled to a sequential two-step process as follows. First, and when feasible, a replacement arbitrator shall be appointed pursuant to the procedure provided in the original appointment or otherwise provided in the applicable rules. This first step, it is hoped, should resolve the majority of cases. However, as a second possible step, if it is not possible or practical to replace the withdrawing arbitrator, a truncated tribunal enjoys the authority to proceed and render a final award.[21] A corollary to the second step is that a replacement provision cannot be used to obstruct the arbitration.[22]

The emergence of this consensus regarding the ability of a tribunal to proceed in the event of withdrawing or obstructive arbitrators parallels the move away from diplomatic to judicial arbitration over the past thirty years. Particularly, in judicial arbitration, the agreement to arbitrate is a foundational provision, without which there might well have been no treaty or contract at all. In such a situation, it is implausible to maintain that, nevertheless, the parties intended that either of them could frustrate arbitration under the treaty or contract by withdrawing the arbitrator appointed by it. This self-evident proposition is even more compelling in the cases of claims treaties between States, contracts between States and aliens, and international commercial contracts, than it is regarding treaties at large. While in some cases the parties to a treaty regard dispute settlement provisions as critical, in others they do not (a fact demonstrated by the number of optional protocols to multilateral international treaties that provide for dispute settlement). But it is a commonplace for the parties to claims agreements, concession and other long-term investment agreements, and international commercial contracts to regard arbitration clauses as essential to their agreements. This being the case, it follows that the intention about their efficacy, which must be imputed to the parties, is inconsistent with permitting a party to frustrate arbitration by withdrawal of the arbitrator that it has named. Rather, the rule of interpretation that governs is that of effectiveness: *ut res magis valeat quam pereat.* Pursuant to this principle of maximum effectiveness, legal texts are

---

[21] See, e.g., 2010 UNCITRAL Rules, Article 14. See also Gary B. Born, *International Commercial Arbitration* (2nd edition, 2014), pp. 1957–1958.

[22] See, e.g., Supplemental Opinion of Mr. Böckstiegel and Mr. Holtzmann, *Uiterwyk* v. *Iran*, 19 *Iran U.S. C.T.R.* 107 (concluding that the UNCITRAL Arbitration Rules' provision on the replacement of arbitrators "cannot be invoked to disrupt the orderly process of the Tribunal or to obstruct its functions").

presumed to have been intended to have definite force and effect, and should be interpreted so as to have such force and effect rather than so as not to have it, where that can be done without violence to their terms.

It may be added that the rule of effectiveness in the interpretation of treaties was a rule of which Lauterpacht was an outstanding exponent. A rule that made international instruments meaningful rather than meaningless was congenial to his philosophical and moral approach to international law and life. He demonstrated its cogency in a typically brilliant article in the *British Year Book of International Law*, which concluded that: "... the principle of effectiveness constitutes a general principle of law and a cogent requirement of good faith. It finds abundant support in the practice of international tribunals."[23] Accordingly, while the apparent consensus surrounding the approach to be taken in the event of an arbitrator's withdrawal is relatively recent, it is grounded in the writings of eminent jurists both past and present.

Before proceeding to an analysis of the relevant cases, as in the first edition the views of the International Law Commission and of leading commentators will be summarized. Although the state of the law has developed significantly since the debates outlined below, the discussion of the International Law Commission on the subject of the authority of truncated tribunals, which resulted in a Draft Convention and Model Rules, reflects the primary considerations on both sides of this debate, and therefore has continued salience today. Indeed, the views of the Commission constitute what remains perhaps the most extensive and searching international examination of the question.

C. The Views of the International Law Commission

At its First Session in 1949, the Chairman of the International Law Commission, Judge Manley O. Hudson, singled out the problem of truncated arbitral tribunals as the one to which the Commission's Special Rapporteur on the codification of international arbitral procedure, the eminent French jurist Professor Georges Scelle, should devote particular consideration. This Professor Scelle did.

---

[23] Hersch Lauterpacht, "Restrictive Interpretation and the Principle of Effectiveness in the Interpretation of Treaties," XXVI *British Year Book of International Law* (1949), pp. 48, 83.

At its Second Session, Professor Scelle submitted to the Commission a comprehensive draft, which, in respect of truncated tribunals, prefaced a proposal with the following analysis:

42. We have now reached the most serious case, that of the *withdrawal* of an arbitrator, spontaneously or apparently spontaneously or on the orders of the Government that has appointed a national arbitrator.

Spontaneous withdrawal is inadmissible. The arbitrator was not bound to accept the task entrusted to him; but he can no more give up his functions once they have been conferred upon him than an officially installed magistrate can insist on resigning. . . .

43. The withdrawal by a Government of a so-called national arbitrator is still less admissible, since the investiture of the arbitrator is not the act of his Government, but of the Governments parties to the dispute. It is a well-established principle in public law that a juridical act cannot be revoked or modified except by persons who were competent to perform it and in accordance with the procedure by which it was originally carried out. This is what is known as the technique of the 'contrary act.' Thus the constitution of the tribunal can only be modified in the manner in which it was established, that is to say bilaterally and not unilaterally. We shall therefore accept as an obligatory rule of a procedural code that the withdrawal of an arbitrator cannot prevent the tribunal from acting nor from rendering a binding award whenever it is materially able to do so.

These regrettably frequent incidents occur most often when the hearings take a turn that is unfavourable to one of the parties, or when questions of prestige or moral susceptibility arise among the arbitrators. Witenberg cites a number of examples . . . and concludes: 'In any case the withdrawal of a national judge is an unlawful intrusion of the State into the progress of arbitration. Once arbitration has been decided on, the established tribunal should be unaffected by the unilateral will of either of the States parties to the dispute. To withdraw a national judge is a breach of the obligation implicitly but necessarily assumed under the agreement to submit the dispute to a judicial settlement.' Full approval should therefore be given to the decisions taken by presidents of mixed arbitral tribunals or commissions in such cases not to interrupt the procedure before the diminished tribunal. . . . Provision, however, must be made for the case in which the arbitral tribunal is unable to pronounce judgment, for example because the umpire and the other national judge are at variance. Here, too, the solution might consist in replacing the absent judge at the request of the remaining members of the tribunal, either by the procedure agreed upon for his appointment, or, if this procedure proves to be inapplicable or too dilatory, by a judicial authority such as the President of the International Court of Justice. At all events, the intervention of a political personality or organ in such a case cannot be too strongly deprecated.

. . .

45. To sum up the foregoing considerations as a whole, we would propose a preliminary draft text drawn up roughly along the following lines:

Once the arbitral tribunal has been set up by agreement between the parties or by the subsidiary procedures indicated above, it shall not be open to any of the contending Governments to alter its composition.

If a vacancy occurs, the arbitrator shall be replaced by the method laid down for appointments.

. . .

A "national" arbitrator may not withdraw or be withdrawn by the Government that appointed him. Should this occur, the tribunal is authorized to continue the proceedings and to render an award which shall be binding. If the withdrawal makes it impossible to continue the proceedings, the tribunal may request that the absent arbitrator be replaced, and, if the procedure employed for his appointment fails, may request the President of the International Court of Justice to replace him.[24]

Professor Scelle's draft met with a mixed reception in the Commission. In particular, Judge Hudson inquired if the principle that a truncated tribunal "is authorized to continue the proceedings and to render an award which shall be binding" actually existed "in current law," and responded that he:

did not think so, though it ought to exist. . . . If it were now maintained that the report reflected the present state of the law, he could not agree. He was quite prepared to admit that the law should be in conformity with the principles formulated by the rapporteur. But since that was not the case, he would rather the question of replacement of an arbitrator who withdrew or was withdrawn were stipulated in the *compromis* or arbitration treaty. . . .[25]

In response, Professor Scelle:

. . . agreed that what he was advocating was not a universally recognized principle of international law. But there were precedents . . . . His concern

---

[24] *Yearbook of the International Law Commission 1950, supra* note 14, vol. II, pp. 127–128. The text printed in the *Yearbook* is in French; the quoted English translation is found in U.N. doc. A/CN.4/18, at pp. 32–35. Professor Scelle's analysis, which concerns the *Hungarian Optants* case, will be referred to in our discussion of that case.

[25] *Yearbook of the International Law Commission 1950, supra* note 14, p. 270.

was to establish a principle. He would like to go further than existing law, since he considered that the Commission was not called upon merely to record positive law on the subject.[26]

Professor Scelle added that:

...he felt he must refer to the far too frequent fact that governments resorted to withdrawal of their arbitrators so as to sabotage arbitration. That had happened during the case of the Hungarian Optants. Withdrawal in that manner should be regarded as fraudulent and inadmissible. But there were instances where there was no question of fraud – illness of the arbitrator, or his inability to attend the arbitration proceedings for reasons of *force majeure*. The sentence in question did not apply to such cases.[27]

The Chairman invited Professor Scelle to re-draft the proposal "less categorically, so that the Commission would be able to reach agreement on it the following year."[28] The following year, Professor Scelle returned with a revision, albeit one that made only modest concessions to his critics. The revision was as follows:

Once the arbitral tribunal has been set up by agreement between the parties or by the subsidiary procedures indicated above, it shall not be open to any of the outstanding Governments to alter its composition.

If a vacancy occurs, the arbitrator shall be replaced by the method laid down for appointments.

...

A "national" arbitrator may not withdraw or be withdrawn by the Government which has appointed him. Should this occur, the tribunal is authorized to continue the proceedings and to render an award which shall be binding. If the withdrawal prevents the continuation of the proceedings, the tribunal may request that the absent arbitrator be replaced and, if the procedure employed for his appointment fails, may request the President of the International Court of Justice to replace him.[29]

---

[26] Ibid.   [27] Ibid.   [28] Ibid.

[29] *Report of the International Law Commission covering its Second Session, June 5–July 29, 1950*, General Assembly, *Official Records: Fifth Session, Supp. No. 12* (A/1316), pp. 19–20 (reporting in English the proposals of Professor Scelle). The French text is as follows:

Article 7

Le Tribunal une fois institué par l'accord des Parties, ou par les procédures subsidiaires ci-dessus indiquées, il n'appartient plus à aucun des gouvernements litigants d'en modifier la composition. En cas de vacance d'un siège,

In the event, the Commission ultimately accepted the essence of Professor Scelle's draft. In the course of the consideration of the draft, however, dissenting views were expressed. Professor François sought to distinguish the position of "national" arbitrators from those appointed by common agreement, maintaining that it should be possible to withdraw or replace the former.[30] From this, Professor Scelle dissented with his customary vigor. Professor Lauterpacht substantially supported Professor Scelle, maintaining that:

... it was essential to the very nature of arbitration, and in accordance with present practice, that a contending government should not be able to withdraw the arbitrator it had appointed, either because it did not favour the particular line he was pursuing or for some other reason, once the proceedings had begun.[31]

Mr. el-Khouri agreed:

... from his experience both of international arbitration and of arbitration within a State, he could say that one of the most frequent causes of its breaking down was that one party dismissed the arbitrator it had appointed, or caused him to withdraw, if the case appeared to be going against it. He therefore considered it essential to stipulate that, once the tribunal had been constituted, none of the arbitrators could withdraw or be withdrawn until the case had been completed.[32]

Mr. Kozhevnikov was of another view; not to permit a government to modify the composition of the tribunal would "conflict with the principle of national sovereignty as a fundamental principle of

---

pour des raisons indépendantes de la volonté de ceux-ci, il est procédé au remplacement de l'arbitre selon le mode prévu pour sa nomination.
. . .

Article 9
Un arbitre ne peut se déporter ou être retiré par le gouvernement qui l'a désigné, sauf dans des cas exceptionnels et avec assentiment des autres membres du Tribunal.
Au cas où le déport ou le retrait interviendraient sans l'accord du Tribunal constitué, celui-ci serait autorisé à poursuivre la procedure et à rendre sa sentence.
Au cas où le déport ou le retrait la poursuite de la procédure inopérante, le Tribunal pourrait requérir le remplacement de l'arbitre défaillant et, si le procédé utilisé pour sa nomination échouait, demander son remplacement au Président de la Cour internationale de Justice.
Yearbook of the International Law Commission 1951, p. 117.

[30] *Yearbook of the International Law Commission 1951, supra* note 29, p. 117.
[31] Ibid., p. 23.   [32] Ibid.

international law."[33] He was joined by Mr. Zourek, who described the *Hungarian Optants* case as an example of an excess of jurisdiction. In such an instance:

> . . . the withdrawal of an arbitrator became a legitimate defensive measure by which the State victim of a manifest excess of jurisdiction attempted to repel the injustice with which it was threatened.[34]

Professor Scelle was unmoved: "Clearly an arbitrator could not withdraw or be withdrawn" without infringing the principle of the immutability of the tribunal. Where there was unauthorized withdrawal, the tribunal could continue its work.[35] This last assertion was pursued by Judge Hudson, who asked:

> . . . whether a tribunal composed of three persons could ever act unless all were present. If it could, then that should be clearly stated. He knew of very few instances in which that had occurred, although some did exist, such as the Lena Goldfields case. The decisions of the French-Mexican Claims Commission in 1927 had been taken in the absence of the Mexican member, and it would be recalled that the decisions had been impugned by the Mexican Government. Later, the Governments of France and Mexico reached a compromise without, however, solving the question of principle. The International Court of Justice in its second advisory opinion on the interpretation of peace treaties with Bulgaria, Hungary and Romania had laid stress on the importance of the presence of both the national members in a three-member tribunal.[36]

Professor Scelle reiterated that:

> He was utterly opposed to the parties being given the possibility of preventing the proceedings from taking their course and the award being made. If they were to be free to do so, the tribunal would cease to be an arbitral organ, since, as soon as the case took a turn which seemed unfavourable to one of the parties, that party would clearly make every effort to bring about a suspension of the proceedings.

---

[33] Ibid.   [34] Ibid.   [35] Ibid., pp. 28, 29.

[36] *Yearbook of the International Law Commission 1952*, vol. I, p. 35 (footnotes omitted). Insofar as Judge Hudson's reference to the *Peace Treaties* case was relevant to the subject then under discussion – the power of a truncated tribunal – his reading of the case was in error. Cf., *Interpretation of Peace Treaties with Bulgaria, Hungary and Romania (Second Phase), Advisory Opinion, I.C.J. Reports 1950*, pp. 221, 229, and the discussion of that case, *infra*.

Thus he saw no reason:

...why two members of a tribunal of three might not be able to reach unanimous agreement and make an award in the absence of their colleague .... If the whole process of arbitration, once instituted, were to be made contingent on the will of the parties it would cease to be arbitration, the purpose of which was to settle disputes in accordance with the rules of law.[37]

As noted, Professor Scelle carried the Commission with him, though the fundamental differences between those supporting "diplomatic arbitration" and those supporting "judicial arbitration" made his margin narrow. The Commission adopted his revised proposal providing that:

Once the hearing has begun, an arbitrator may not withdraw or be withdrawn by the Government which has appointed him, save in exceptional cases and with the consent of the tribunal.

...

Should the withdrawal take place, the remaining members, upon the request of one of the parties, shall have the power to continue the proceedings and render the award.[38]

The Draft on Arbitral Procedure adopted by the International Law Commission was circulated to governments for their written comment. The number of governments that commented on the draft was typically few, but nevertheless the division of opinion that characterized Commission discussion was shown. The United Kingdom declared that it "strongly supported the line taken by the Commission" in favor of "judicial arbitration,"[39] and general

---

[37] *Yearbook of the International Law Commission 1952, supra* note 36, p. 35.

[38] Ibid., pp. 34–38. See also the *Report of the International Law Commission covering the work of its Fourth Session, June 4–August 8, 1952*, General Assembly, *Official Records: Seventh Session, Supp. No. 9* (A/2163), pp. 5–6.

It should be noted that the Commission's intention in adopting this draft was to debar a party's withdrawing its arbitrator once hearings in a case had begun. It was not designed to prohibit a party from changing arbitrators if a tribunal was dealing with a multiplicity of cases and if the competence of an arbitrator embraced some types of cases but not others. *Yearbook of the International Law Commission 1952, supra* note 36, vol. I, at pp. 23, 28, 29, and 33. The governing consideration "was to prevent a recalcitrant party from frustrating the proper functioning of the tribunal" (at p. 29).

[39] *Comments by Governments on Draft on Arbitral Procedure*, U.N. doc. A/CN.4/68, p. 20, published also in the *Yearbook of the International Law Commission 1953*, vol. II, pp. 232, 237. See also *Comments received from Governments regarding the draft convention on arbitral procedure prepared by the International Law Commission at its*

expressions of support for the Commission's approach were given by Chile,[40] India,[41] Norway,[42] Sweden,[43] and Uruguay.[44] In contrast, Belgium,[45] Brazil,[46] and the Netherlands[47] expressed serious doubt about the utility of the Commission's approach. The United States, while generally supportive, saw a large measure of progressive development rather than codification of international law in the Commission's draft and asked whether it might not be more suitable for a model code of arbitral procedure than for a convention.[48] The comments of India,[49] the Netherlands,[50] and one of two Uruguayan-transmitted comments[51] suggested deletion of the provision that a truncated tribunal was empowered to render an award in favor of a proviso ensuring the replacement of a withdrawing arbitrator. In particular, the Netherlands doubted whether a great number of States would accept the draft "because in their view it might restrict too much the lenient rules of arbitral procedure."[52]

Such sparse governmental comments as there were, were given considerable weight by the Commission when it met in 1953. Professor Lauterpacht, general rapporteur at that session of the Commission, suggested that, in response to them, the draft might be amended to provide for filling any vacancy resulting from withdrawal of an arbitrator consented to by the tribunal by the method laid down for the original appointment.[53] He made it clear that he stood with Professor Scelle in the view that, when a government, regardless of the decision of the tribunal, withdrew the arbitrator it had appointed, the tribunal must continue to function.[54] He

---

fifth session in 1953, U.N. doc. A/2899 and Add. 1 and 2, published in U.N. General Assembly, *Official Records, Tenth Session, Annexes, Agenda Item 52.*

[40] *Yearbook of the International Law Commission 1953, supra* note 39, vol. II, p. 237.
[41] Ibid., p. 234.   [42] Ibid., p. 236.   [43] Ibid., p. 237.
[44] *Addendum to Comments by Governments on Draft on Arbitral Procedure,* U.N. doc. A/CN.4/68/Add.2, p. 2 ff., published also in *Yearbook of the International Law Commission 1953, supra* note 39, vol. II, p. 239.
[45] Ibid., p. 232.   [46] Ibid., p. 233.   [47] Ibid., p. 235.
[48] Ibid., p. 238. The United States supported the Commission's draft on a truncated arbitral tribunal, but suggested that it be modified to provide that a party may not replace an arbitrator after the completion of the written pleadings (rather than after the proceedings have begun), except by the agreement of the parties. Ibid. When the Commission came to consider this suggestion, it rejected it (see *Yearbook of the International Law Commission 1953,* vol. I, *supra* note 39, pp. 17–18).
[49] Ibid., vol. II, p. 234.   [50] Ibid., pp. 235–236.   [51] Ibid., p. 240.
[52] Ibid., 235.   [53] Ibid., vol. I, p. 19.   [54] Ibid., p. 20.

observed that the Commission had to avoid opening "the door to continuous sabotage on the part of a government which, having once withdrawn its arbitrator, would be free to designate another, ...and then withdraw him too. That was the very contingency that Professor Scelle wished to avoid."[55]

He therefore submitted that the Commission had a choice either of allowing the tribunal to function in the absence of one or more of its members, or stipulating that any vacancy must be filled by the procedure envisaged[56] by the draft for initial appointment – a procedure that prescribed appointment by the President of the International Court of Justice in the final eventuality. He preferred the former. But the Chairman favored the latter as less "drastic."[57] Professor Lauterpacht seemed to summarize the sense of the meeting in concluding that:

...although truncated tribunals had been known since the end of the eighteenth century, the reason why they had functioned as such was because no provision for the replacement of an arbitrator had existed. The purpose of the present draft was to make provisions for replacement, and to ensure that a tribunal should always function with a quorum.[58]

The Commission thereupon adopted Professor Lauterpacht's proposals for filling any vacancy caused by withdrawal.[59] The relevant articles of the Commission's draft thus read:

Article 5
1. Once the tribunal has been constituted, its composition shall remain unchanged until the award has been rendered.
2. A party may, however, replace an arbitrator appointed by it, provided that the tribunal has not yet begun its proceedings. An arbitrator may not be replaced during the proceedings before the tribunal except by agreement between the parties.
3. The proceedings are deemed to have begun when the President or sole arbitrator has made the first order concerning written or oral proceedings.

Article 6
Should a vacancy occur on account of death or incapacity of an arbitrator or, prior to the commencement of proceedings, the resignation of an

---

[55] Ibid.   [56] Ibid., p. 52.   [57] Ibid.   [58] Ibid., vol. I, p. 52.
[59] Ibid. The vote was 11–2.

arbitrator, the vacancy shall be filled by the method laid down for the original appointment.

Article 7

1. Once the proceedings before the tribunal have begun, an arbitrator may withdraw only with the consent of the tribunal. The resulting vacancy shall be filled by the method laid down for the original appointment.
2. Should the withdrawal take place without the consent of the tribunal, the resulting vacancy shall be filled, at the request of the tribunal in the manner provided for in paragraph 2 of article 3.[60]

Article 3 in turn referred to appointment pursuant to the provisions of the undertaking to arbitrate or, in the absence of such provisions, by the President of the International Court of Justice.

Commentary on the draft text at that point, the Report of the Commission to the General Assembly – also prepared by Lauterpacht – said the following:

32. The present draft clarifies the articles which bear on the permanency and immutability of the tribunal as an organ independent of any unilateral action of the parties initially responsible for its creation. While the draft gives full effect to the traditional principle that the parties must have the full opportunity of a free choice of arbitrators, that freedom does not extend to the right to change unilaterally the composition of the tribunal subsequent to the commencement of the proceedings. Accordingly, there is no longer in article 7 of the draft any reference to the withdrawal of an arbitrator by a party. For the same reason, the present draft, following the previous draft, does not permit an arbitrator to withdraw except with the permission of the tribunal. It must be assumed that in proper cases, such as illness or personal circumstances which make it difficult for the arbitrator to continue in his office, that permission will not be withheld. At the same time, the draft makes provision against the work of the tribunal being frustrated by the withdrawal of an arbitrator for reasons not approved by the tribunal. In such case, it is laid down, the vacancy shall be filled in the manner prescribed for the cases in which the parties have been unable to agree on the appointment of arbitrators. Thus, although illicit withdrawal on the part of an arbitrator may cause some delay in the proceedings, it can no longer bring them permanently to a standstill.

33. For the latter reason it has been found unnecessary, unlike in article 7, paragraph 3, of the previous draft, to lay down that in the case of the

---

[60] Ibid., vol. II, p. 209.

withdrawal of an arbitrator the remaining members of the tribunal shall have the power to continue the proceedings and render an award. Such a procedure would hardly be warranted in cases in which the withdrawal takes place with the consent of the tribunal. However, even in cases in which an arbitrator has withdrawn in face of the refusal of the tribunal to allow him to do so, the Commission is of the opinion that the sanction as previously proposed was both too drastic and unnecessary. Undoubtedly, cases have occurred in the past in which the tribunal, after a national arbitrator has withdrawn, continued with its work and rendered an award. This was probably unavoidable seeing that no machinery was at that time in existence for filling the vacancy created by the illicit withdrawal of an arbitrator. Once such machinery is created – as is the case in the present draft – there is no longer any reason for an incomplete tribunal to proceed with the case.[61]

In respect of whether these and other provisions of its draft were expressive of customary international law, the Commission stated:

In particular, the Commission was unable to share the view that the procedural safeguards for the effectiveness of the obligation to arbitrate are derogatory to the sovereignty of the parties. The Commission has in no way departed from the principle that no State is obliged to submit a dispute to arbitration unless it has previously agreed to do so either with regard to a particular dispute or to all or certain categories of future disputes. However, once a State has undertaken that obligation it is not inconsistent with principles of law or with the sovereignty of both parties that that obligation should be complied with and that it should not be frustrated on account of any defects in hitherto existing rules of arbitral procedure. For that reason, the Commission was unable to share the view that the draft departs from the traditional notion of arbitration in a manner inconsistent with the sovereignty of States inasmuch as it obliges the parties to abide by procedures adopted for the purpose of giving effect to the obligation to arbitrate. For that obligation is undertaken in the free and full exercise of sovereignty. While the free will of the parties is essential as a condition of the creation of the common obligation to arbitrate, the will of one party cannot, in the view of the Commission, be regarded as a condition to the continued validity and effectiveness of the obligation freely undertaken.[62]

The Commission's draft, particularly insofar as it was advanced as a basis for the conclusion of a convention, met with a lack of

---

[61] Ibid., p. 204.　　[62] Ibid.

enthusiasm in the Sixth Committee of the General Assembly. Since it became apparent that any convention that might be adopted by a conference of plenipotentiaries convened by the General Assembly[63] would reject the Commission's concept of judicial arbitration, the Commission and its rapporteur turned to the suggestion that had been put forth in the Sixth Committee's debate: that of submitting to the Assembly not a draft convention, but a "model draft on arbitral procedure" of which the Assembly would take note, and that would serve as a guide to governments in their conclusion of particular arbitral agreements.

In final discussions at the International Law Commission on the draft model code, Professor Scelle found it necessary to propose some substantive as well as formal changes to the draft convention that the Commission had earlier adopted. But initially he proposed no change with respect to the articles on the immutability of the tribunal, thus maintaining the provision for filling of vacancies by the President of the International Court of Justice.[64] Should the proposed articles fail to win acceptance, he submitted:

... the only remaining way to ensure that arbitration is really effected would be to permit the remaining members of the tribunal to render their award in the absence of any arbitrators who have withdrawn or have resigned. This was recognized in the Commission's original draft. We should have no great objection to the reintroduction of this principle. Theory and practice have varied on this point; but we have come to the conclusion that the solution provided by the draft as it stands is preferable from the standpoint of the authority of the arbitral decision.[65]

The International Law Commission was largely supportive of the substance of Professor Scelle's proposals. It was observed that the provision that the composition of an arbitral tribunal once

---

[63] *General Assembly, Eighth Session: Official Records, Sixth Committee, 382nd–389th Meetings; Tenth Session, 461st–464th, 466th–472nd Meetings.* Comment upon truncated tribunals was scarce (for a statement by the representative of Mexico in favor of the Commission's draft in this regard see *Tenth Session, 467th Meeting*, p. 117; and of Pakistan *468th meeting*, p. 121; against, by the representative of Iran, *464th Meeting*, p. 99 and Czechoslovakia, *467th Meeting*, p. 115). See also "Survey of views expressed in the Sixth Committee of the General Assembly and in the written comments of Governments on the draft Convention on Arbitral Procedure adopted by the International Law Commission at its fifth session (A/2456)," U.N. doc. A/CN.4/L.71, pp. 16–17.

[64] *Yearbook of the International Law Commission 1958*, vol. II, p. 6.   [65] Ibid., p. 7.

constituted shall remain unchanged had not given rise to any serious criticism by governments.[66] However, the proposal that, once proceedings had begun, an arbitrator might withdraw only with the consent of the tribunal gave rise to some questioning. Sir Gerald Fitzmaurice observed that in practice it would be impossible to prevent an arbitrator from resigning and that, though sometimes resignations were a result of improper pressure from the government, an arbitrator might resign for personal reasons having nothing to do with the case.[67] Professor Ago proposed to delete the draft article in point and to otherwise deal with the filling of a vacancy resulting from resignation.[68] Professor Scelle made no objection to this proposal,[69] despite the expressions of surprise and regret by a number of members of the Commission.[70] Professor Scelle stated that he had become convinced of the impossibility of preventing resignations, and added that he understood the Commission to be generally opposed to the idea that the proceedings before the tribunal should continue despite the withdrawal of an arbitrator.[71] No member commented upon that observation, which, however, was preceded by Professor Verdross' suggestion that "the best remedy in cases of withdrawal of an arbitrator under pressure from his State of nationality would be to stipulate that if an arbitrator withdrew without the consent of the tribunal, the tribunal's proceedings would continue without him."[72]

A compromise solution, providing an alternative solution to withdrawal, was ultimately adopted. The final text adopted by the Commission read:

Article 4
1. Once the tribunal has been constituted, its composition shall remain unchanged until the award has been rendered.
2. A party may, however, replace an arbitrator appointed by it, provided that the tribunal has not yet begun its proceedings. Once the proceedings have begun, an arbitrator appointed by a party may not be replaced except by mutual agreement between the parties.

---

[66] Dr. García Amador, ibid., p. 21. [67] Ibid., p. 26. [68] Ibid. [69] Ibid.
[70] Mr. François, ibid., p. 26; Mr. Bartos, ibid.; Mr. Hsu, ibid., p. 29.
[71] Ibid., pp. 26, 27. He also said that he accepted the necessity of making concessions to the views of governments.
[72] Ibid., p. 27.

3. Arbitrators appointed by mutual agreement between the parties, or by agreement between arbitrators already appointed, may not be changed after the proceedings have begun, save in exceptional circumstances. Arbitrators appointed in the manner provided for in article 3, paragraph 2 [by the President of the International Court of Justice at the request of the diligent party], may not be changed even by agreement between the parties.

4. The proceedings are deemed to have begun when the president of the tribunal or the sole arbitrator has made the first procedural order.

Article 5
If, whether before or after the proceedings have begun, a vacancy should occur on account of the death, incapacity or resignation of an arbitrator it shall be filled in accordance with the procedure prescribed for the original appointment.[73]

Notably absent was the earlier provision vesting the President of the International Court of Justice with the authority to make a replacement appointment. In adopting its model draft, the Commission restated its view that an agreement to arbitrate:

... binds the parties and obliges them to carry out the undertaking to arbitrate. From this, certain consequences follow, which are legal consequences. These consequences cannot be escaped by the parties, whether they make use of the present articles to govern their arbitration or not – for these consequences are inherent in, and spring from, the simple undertaking to arbitrate, once this has been given in binding form.[74]

The Commission continued:

The present text therefore, like that of 1953, is based on the fundamental concept that an agreement to arbitrate involves in substance an international obligation equivalent to a treaty obligation. Having once entered into it (which they were free not to do) the parties are legally bound to carry it out and, in consequence, to take all the steps necessary to enable the arbitration to take place and the dispute to be finally liquidated; and, similarly, to refrain from any action, positive or negative, which would impede or frustrate that consummation. This may be styled the principle of non-frustration. Experience having shown that there are a number of ways in which a party to a dispute, despite its undertaking to arbitrate, can in fact frustrate the process of arbitration – e.g., by failing to appoint its arbitrator, or otherwise to co-operate in setting up the arbitral tribunal; by

---

[73] Ibid., vol. II, p. 84.   [74] Ibid., p. 82.

withdrawing its arbitrator during the course of the proceedings and failing to appoint another; by failing to appear and present or defend its case before the tribunal, etc. – the present text, like that of 1953, provides automatic procedures for filling in any gaps thus created by the action or inaction of the parties, and thereby for preventing the frustration of the agreement and enabling the arbitration to take place and result in a final settlement binding on the parties.[75]

The Commission concluded:

... the party taking the frustrating action, will be acting in a manner which, even if not actually contrary to the arbitral agreement as such, will be contrary to the basic principles of general international law governing the process of arbitration.[76]

The model draft was – apart from an echoing of earlier criticism of the draft's fundamental approach by the representatives of Members such as Hungary,[77] Iran,[78] Bulgaria,[79] Brazil,[80] Iraq,[81] the USSR,[82] India,[83] and Egypt[84] – moderately well received. There remained a current of opinion in various quarters averse to the draft's "judicial" disposition, but nevertheless the draft succeeded in attracting considerable support from all but the Soviet Union and like-minded States, support which included endorsement of the draft's provisions on immutability or non-frustration by

---

[75] Ibid. (footnotes omitted). [76] Ibid., p. 83.

[77] *General Assembly, Thirteenth Session: Official Records, Sixth Committee, 554th–567th Meetings*, pp. 25–26.

[78] Ibid., p. 31. [79] Ibid., p. 37. [80] Ibid., p. 41. [81] Ibid., p. 65.

[82] Ibid., p. 56. In 1950, the United Nations Secretariat prepared for the International Law Commission a "Memorandum on the Soviet Doctrine and Practice with Respect to Arbitral Procedure," U.N. doc. A/CN.4/36. For criticism of the Soviet approach to the Commission's drafts on arbitral procedure, see Percy E. Corbett, *Law in Diplomacy* (1959), pp. 170–176.

[83] *General Assembly, Thirteenth Session: Official Records, Sixth Committee, 554th–567th Meetings, supra* note 77, p. 45. In 1955, India, in criticizing the Commission's 1953 draft, had maintained that: "It is proper that on the withdrawal or disqualification of any arbitrator, the party appointing him should be given the choice of appointing a new arbitrator in his place. The present arrangement ... implies the compulsory jurisdiction of the President of the International Court of Justice." See *Comments received from Governments regarding the draft convention on arbitral procedure prepared by the International Law Commission at its fifth session in 1953*, U.N. doc. A/2899, p. 6.

[84] *General Assembly, Thirteenth Session: Official Records, Sixth Committee, 554th–567th Meetings, supra* note 77, p. 47.

representatives of Members such as Burma,[85] Greece,[86] Canada,[87] the Netherlands,[88] and Australia.[89] The General Assembly, balancing the views of the Members that favored and those that opposed the draft with those who saw little risk in merely taking note of it, decided, after considerable debate, to bring:

> ... the draft articles on arbitral procedure ... to the attention of Member States for their consideration and use, in such cases and to such extent as they consider appropriate, in drawing up treaties of arbitration or *compromis*....[90]

What light do the extended labors of the International Law Commission and of the Sixth Committee shed on the power of truncated tribunals? In the first edition it was posited that they indicate that:

(a) practice, and, still more, opinion were sharply divided;
(b) principle depends upon whether a diplomatic or a judicial approach to arbitration is adopted (though it must be borne in mind that some of the criticism which the Commission's drafts aroused was directed not so much at the principle of non-frustration as at the supervening role to be accorded to the International Court of Justice and its President); and
(c) since frustration, as by withdrawal, is "contrary to the basic principles of general international law governing the process of arbitration,"[91] the better view of the law is that truncated tribunals do have the power to proceed and to render valid awards.

That the International Law Commission itself oscillated, and adopted an alternative solution for withdrawal, that is, enforced replacement, does not derogate from this conclusion. As will be shown below, today practice and opinion are significantly less divided than were the eminent scholars debating the subject in the International Law Commission. And indeed the "better view" identified above has become the consensus view. Nevertheless, the opposing views captured by the discussion in the Commission provide an excellent overview of the historical debate.

---

[85] Ibid., p. 33.   [86] Ibid., p. 36.   [87] Ibid., p. 43.   [88] Ibid., p. 45.
[89] Ibid., p. 71.
[90] *Resolutions adopted by the General Assembly during its Thirteenth Session*, vol. I, p. 53.
[91] *Yearbook of the International Law Commission 1958, supra* note 64, vol. II, p. 83.

D. The Views of Commentators

1. Earlier Views

The views of eminent authorities like Judge Lauterpacht, Judge Hudson, and Professor Scelle have been set forth. Those of other scholars may be summarized as follows. Phillimore submits that, where an arbitrator "maliciously" absents himself or herself, the remainder of the tribunal "might be competent" to proceed, but that the death of an arbitrator ordinarily dissolves the tribunal.[92]

Comparably, Mérignhac takes a stronger stance, affirming that the absence of an arbitrator, caused by bad faith, or negligence, cannot paralyze the action of the tribunal.[93] Fiore, for his part, maintains that:

> When the absence of an arbitrator, at the time the award is to be pronounced, is manifestly due to a predetermined conclusion or subterfuge on his part, a majority of the Tribunal present should be entitled to prescribe the proper measures for obviating the difficulty and deciding the case.[94]

Ralston, citing the *Cauca* case,[95] notes that the Supreme Court of the United States recognized the power of the majority to act for the commission.[96] Witenberg, declaring that withdrawal of an arbitrator constitutes an illegitimate intervention in the process of arbitration by the withdrawing State, concludes that the tribunal seems to be able to continue its work despite the irregular

---

[92] *Commentaries on International Law* (1857), vol. 3, p. 4.
[93] *Traité théorique et pratique de l'arbitrage international* (1895), pp. 276–277. See also Judge Mosk's Additional Comments on Judge Sani's Failure to Sign Award Nos. 74–62–3 (*Blount Bros.*), 73–67–3 (*Woodward-Clyde Consultants*), 72–124–3 (*Warnecke & Associates*), 70–185–3 (*Chas. T. Main*), 71–346–3 (*Alan Craig*), 3 *Iran-U.S. C.T.R.* 294, 294–96. Johannes Voet, an 18th-century authority on Roman and Canon law, took a similar position. See *The Selective Voet* (edited and translated by P. Gane, 1955), p. 749.
[94] E.M. Borchard, *Fiore's International Law Codified* (1918), p. 514.
[95] *Colombia* v. *Cauca Company*, *supra* note 4.
[96] *The Law and Procedure of International Tribunals* (1926), p. 110. See also Carlston, *supra* note 9, pp. 203, 210.

absence of the national judge or judges.[97] And Hyde holds that, after extended participation in the work of a tribunal, a member cannot, by retiring, deprive it of the power to decide the questions at issue.[98]

However, Calvo suggests that, where an arbitrator withdraws, he should be replaced, but that, failing replacement, the tribunal should be dissolved.[99] Balasko, while stating that, under certain conditions, a truncated tribunal may render a valid award, indicates that, as a rule, it is difficult to regard such an award as duly rendered.[100] And Carlston declares:

It does seem necessary to distinguish between a willful and personal refusal of an arbitrator to join in the deliberations of the tribunal and the absence of an arbitrator caused by the direction of his government. The former is a defect which may be waived by the parties, and if no objection be raised by either of them the remaining members of the tribunal are justified in proceeding. The latter, however, deprives the tribunal of its judicial quality and power to decide.[101]

A particularly extensive and able treatment of the subject, that of Guyomar, concludes that "la jurisprudence est en cette matière

---

[97] *L'organisation judiciaire, la procédure et la sentence internationales* (1937), pp. 48–49.

[98] *International Law* (2nd edition, 1945), vol. 2, p. 1629. See also Judge Mosk's Additional Comments on Judge Sani's Failure to Sign Award Nos. 74–62–3 (*Blount Bros.*), 73–67–3 (*Woodward-Clyde Consultants*), 72–124–3 (*Warnecke & Associates*), 70–185–3 (*Chas. T. Main*), 71–346–3 (*Alan Craig*), 3 *Iran-U.S. C.T.R.* 294, 294–96.

[99] *Le droit international* (5th edition, 1896), vol. 3, p. 482.

[100] *Causes de nullité de la sentence arbitrale en droit international public* (1938), p. 95. But see p. 117.

[101] Carlston, *supra* note 15, p. 44. See also Professor Carlston's article in the *American Journal of International Law*, *supra* note 9, pp. 216–217. However, Professor Carlston recognized the force of the indication by the International Court of Justice that the withdrawal of an arbitrator does not prevent a truncated arbitral tribunal from proceeding and rendering a valid award. See Kenneth S. Carlston, *"Interpretation of Peace Treaties with Bulgaria, Hungary and Romania, Advisory Opinions of the International Court of Justice,"* 44 *American Journal of International Law* (1950), pp. 734–735. See also Howard M. Holtzmann, Stephen M. Schwebel, et al., "Working Group I – Preventing Delay and Disruption of Arbitration – III Conduct by a Party-Appointed Arbitrator during the Arbitral Proceedings – Topic 7: Failure by a party-appointed arbitrator to participate in the arbitral proceedings," in Albert Jan van den Berg (ed.), *Preventing Delay and Disruption of Arbitration/Effective Proceedings in Construction Cases*, ICCA Congress Series, Volume 5 (1991) pp, 241, 244.

incohérente."[102] Study of the cases leads to no firm conclusion; on this subject, there is no general case but there are only particular cases. The most that may be said is to record a tendency of a doctrinal origin condemning withdrawal or resignation. But Guyomar's own preference decidedly favors authorizing the tribunal to proceed despite the defection of an arbitrator.

Reisman concludes, after a review of authorities and cases, that the International Law Commission's strategy for dealing with withdrawal of a national arbitrator reflects "the contemporary doctrinal view of its unlawfulness." He continues:

The dictum of the I.C.J. in the *Peace Treaties* case to the effect that a tribunal once validly constituted may continue to operate despite the defection of a member introduces an even more feasible strategy for continuing operation of the tribunal in such circumstances.[103]

For his part, von Mangoldt holds:

The type to which the arbitral tribunal belongs cannot fail to have implications for the consequences of a party arbitrator's withdrawal, or resignation, usually checked with his "own" party, for the competence of the tribunal to continue to deal with the matter and to reach a decision. To start with, there can be little doubt about the fact that withdrawal of an arbitrator is in violation of the treaty. In more recent treaties, especially, provision is frequently made in advance for such cases, as for the case of resignation of the arbitrator without the intention of disturbing the proceedings, through provisions either for the replacement of the arbitrator, or for handling of the case further without him, which has the advantage of saving time, because a new member of the tribunal would first have to be made acquainted with its work, and part of the proceedings might have to be repeated.

Where no provisions of this kind exist, both practice and literature are inclined to favour admission of the further handling of the case even without the missing arbitrator. However, even leaving aside the fact that practical experiences with "rump tribunals" are hardly encouraging, this solution would in any case appear to present problems for the type of tribunal conducive to "conciliatory decisions," for it can hardly be supposed that the

---

[102] Geneviève Guyomar, "Le retrait ou le déport de l'arbitre en droit international," IX *Annuaire Français de Droit International* (1963), pp. 376, 380, 409.

[103] W. Michael Reisman, *Nullity and Revision: The Review and Enforcement of International Judgments and Awards* (1971), pp. 462–473. See also Holtzmann and Schwebel et al., *supra* note 101, p. 244.

compromis or general arbitration treaty would have allowed that a dispute could be dealt with and decided without the presence of both parties' arbitrators, whose absence would essentially alter the complexion of the tribunal set up. Rather, it must be concluded that it was the will of the parties that the tribunal should function only when fully constituted.

The position is simpler in the case of arbitral tribunals composed predominantly of neutral arbitrators. For representation of the position of each party in the tribunal itself is not then of such pre-eminent significance. In this case, it is easier to defend the view that decision even by a "rump tribunal" would be in keeping with the substance of the arbitration agreement.[104]

Since arbitration is not conciliation, and since it is the proper function of an arbitral tribunal to make a decision based on law rather than to conciliate the parties' divergent arguments or interests, the thrust of von Mangoldt's conclusion that "both practice and literature are inclined to favour admission of the further handling of the case even without the missing arbitrator" is persuasive.

2. Modern Views

Since the publication of the first edition, a modern consensus has emerged in the literature and in practice reflecting the continued shift away from diplomatic to judicial arbitration over the last thirty or so years. The modern view and approach is this: withdrawing or obstructive arbitrators should be presumptively replaced, but where replacement is not possible or is impractical, a truncated tribunal has the authority to continue to hear a case and proceed to render an award.

This is the view expressed, for example, by Judge Mosk, informed by his experience on the Iran-United States Claims Tribunal, that under international law a judge cannot frustrate the work of the tribunal by willfully absenting himself or herself and refusing to sign an award.[105] Similarly, Redfern and Hunter state that in the event that a party-appointed arbitrator refuses to participate or withdraws, replacement

---

[104] Hans von Mangoldt, "Arbitration and Conciliation," in Herman Mosler and Roger Bernard (eds.) *Judicial Settlement of International Disputes* (1974), pp. 532–533 (footnotes omitted).
[105] See, e.g. Judge Mosk's Additional Comments on Judge Sani's Failure to Sign Award Nos. 74–62–3 (*Blount Bros.*), 73–67–3 (*Woodward-Clyde Consultants*), 72–124–3 (*Warnecke & Associates*), 70–185–3 (*Chas. T. Main*), 71–346–3 (*Alan Craig*), 3 Iran-U.S. C.T.R. 294, 294–96.

is the preferred solution, particularly if the withdrawal takes place early in the proceedings.[106] Where, however, appointing a new arbitrator is impractical, such as when the withdrawal occurs late in the proceedings, "the only sensible course may be for the two remaining arbitrators to continue with the proceedings and to render an award without the participation of the third arbitrator."[107]

Similarly, Waincymer observes that, in the event of an arbitrator refusing to participate in the deliberations, a majority should be able to proceed so long as the chair sets a reasonable time for deliberation, but that it is preferable in such circumstances that the parties be advised so that the arbitrator might be removed and replaced or otherwise encouraged to participate.[108]

Holtzmann also summarizes that when a tribunal is faced early on with an obstructionist party-appointed arbitrator, "the most prudent course is to remove the recalcitrant arbitrator and to appoint a replacement," but where appointing an arbitrator is not a "practical solution," perhaps due to the late stage of the proceedings, "the only effective solution is for the two remaining arbitrators to continue the proceedings and render the award."[109]

Born additionally contends that, as a principle, it is not unfair for the parties' agreement to provide that two arbitrators may continue alone if the third member of the tribunal fails to participate in the tribunal's work, arguing that the remaining arbitrators remain bound by obligations of impartiality.[110] However, Born observes that the better approach, one "more faithful to the parties' original agreement," would be to provide for the prompt replacement of a recalcitrant arbitrator by the appointing institution itself.[111] Born further argues that institutional rules that provide for truncated tribunals should be enforceable under national arbitration laws and the New York Convention.[112]

---

[106] Nigel Blackaby, Constantine Partasides et al., *Redfern and Hunter on International Arbitration* (6th edition, 2015), p. 281.
[107] Ibid.
[108] Jeffrey Waincymer, *Procedure and Evidence in International Arbitration* (2012), p. 1294.
[109] Howard M. Holtzmann, "Working Group I – Preventing Delay and Disruption of Arbitration – How to prevent delay and disruption of arbitration: Lessons of the 1990 ICCA Stockholm Congress," *supra* note 101, pp. 26–27.
[110] Born, *supra* note 21, p. 1958. [111] Ibid. [112] Ibid.

As noted above, support for this modern approach can be found in proponents of effectiveness-based treaty interpretation such as Lauterpacht, who concluded that: "...the principle of effectiveness constitutes a general principle of law and a cogent requirement of good faith. It finds abundant support in the practice of international tribunals."[113] This is picked up by more modern commentators such as Peters, writing after the publication of the first edition, who contend that the authority of truncated tribunals to continue to hear a case and render an award stems from an effectiveness-oriented (*effet utile*) reading of the parties' arbitration agreements.[114] Similarly, Lew and Mistelis argue that the lack of an obstructive arbitrator's signature cannot be allowed to frustrate the arbitration, as the appropriate way to express disagreement with the award may be to write a dissenting opinion.[115]

Other modern commentators focus their concern on the imputability of the arbitrator's obstreperous conduct to the appointing party. For instance, in considering the usefulness of various institutional rules that allow for truncated tribunals, Gaillard and Savage note that the predominant concern is:

> whether such provisions infringe on a party's rights to a fair hearing and to equal treatment and, if that is the case, whether a party is entitled to waive those rights. The response to this concern is that if a party is deprived of the participation in the deliberations of the arbitrator it appointed, that will be exclusively the result of that arbitrator's conduct. To avoid any doubt on this point, the remaining arbitrators or the arbitral institution should not accept a truncated tribunal until they have determined that it is the result of the patently dilatory behaviour of the minority arbitrator, which is not unconnected to the position of the party that appointed him or her.[116]

Berger states that the requirement that all arbitrators participate in the deliberations is satisfied if each arbitrator, including the

---

[113] Lauterpacht, *supra* note 23, p. 83.

[114] Anne Peters, "International Dispute Settlement: A Network of Cooperational Duties," 14(1) *European Journal of International Law* (2003), p. 24.

[115] Julian D. M. Lew, Loukas A. Mistelis et al., *Comparative International Commercial Arbitration* (2003), p. 323.

[116] Emmanuel Gaillard and John Savage, *Fouchard, Gaillard, Goldman on International Commercial Arbitration* (1999), p. 616.

recalcitrant or withdrawing arbitrator, had the opportunity to do so.[117] In Berger's view, "it is enough if the remaining active arbitrators keep the missing arbitrator informed of all significant stages in the making of the award and thereby offer him/her the opportunity to express him-/herself and take part in the decision-making at any time."[118]

Looking to the evolution that has occurred in international arbitration since the publication of the 1976 UNCITRAL Rules,[119] Paulsson and Petrochilos note that "article 13 of the 1976 Rules did not adequately address situations in which arbitrators were physically prevented from acting, or where they resigned for tactical reasons, or failed to act in order to advance the interests of the party that appointed them."[120] Accordingly, the drafters of the 2010 UNCITRAL Rules, taking inspiration from the practice of the Iran-United States Claims Tribunal discussed below, revised the Rules to "allow remaining arbitrators, in certain exceptional circumstances, to proceed as a 'truncated tribunal' and issue an award without the missing arbitrator."[121] As is noted below, the 2010 Rules provide the best statement of the modern approach identified above.

Although the modern approach receives widespread support in the literature, a number of skeptics remain. For instance, Horvath contends that the enforceability of awards rendered by truncated tribunals "may damage the arbitral process as a whole, jeopardize the entire profession or as some scholars put it, damage a whole 'industry.'"[122]

One of the most detailed analyses of the authority of truncated tribunals to render awards in light of the shift away from diplomatic toward judicial arbitration comes from Judge Seifi of the Iran-United States Claims Tribunal. While acknowledging that "an

---

[117] Bernhard Berger, "Rights and Obligations of Arbitrators in the Deliberations," 31(2) *ASA Bulletin* (2013), pp. 244–261, 252.

[118] Ibid., p. 252.

[119] The evolution in the practice regarding truncated tribunals as found in arbitral conventions and rules is considered in Section E, *infra*.

[120] Jan Paulsson and Georgios Petrochilos, *UNCITRAL Arbitration* (2018), p. 98.

[121] Ibid.

[122] Günther J. Horvath, "Chapter 15: The Angelic Arbitrator versus the Rogue Arbitrator: What Should an Arbitrator Strive to Be?," in Patricia Shaughnessy and Sherlin Tung (eds.), *The Powers and Duties of an Arbitrator: Liber Amicorum Pierre A. Karrer* (2017), p. 148.

unjustified withdrawal by an arbitrator undermines effectiveness of the arbitral proceedings and causes serious delay," Judge Seifi questions whether truncated tribunals should be considered an "allowable remedy" to the "problem of unjustified withdrawal by an arbitrator."[123] After reviewing the work of the International Law Commission, various institutional rules and the decisions of a number of arbitral tribunals, Judge Seifi concludes:

On the basis of the strength of the principle of non-frustration and some precedents, it may be argued that, in cases where there is no specific provision for the enforced filling of vacancies, in the event of an obstructive withdrawal an incomplete tribunal may be permitted to function, on the assumption that the parties have not excluded such a possibility.

The situation in which there is a provision for the enforced filling of vacancies is totally different. The existence of such a provision implies that the parties have necessarily excluded the possibility for the remaining members to continue the proceedings, particularly if the tribunal is a three-member one, unless an express provision authorized them to continue.

. . .

[H]owever, authorizing a truncated tribunal can in some circumstances be an appropriate response to the problem of withdrawal by an arbitrator. But to glorify the legality of truncated tribunals in an absolute and extreme manner could have the consequence of undermining the concept of party confidence as one of the main pillars of international arbitration.[124]

The trend in modern practice is for tribunals to proceed as truncated tribunals in the event that replacement is impossible or impractical. This presents an appropriate balance between, on the one hand, the viability of an arbitration, and, on the other hand, facilitating the continuing participation in the arbitral process of opposing parties.

E. The Practice

1. Arbitration Conventions and Rules

The proliferation of international arbitration since the publication of the first edition has resulted in a number of new or updated

---

[123] Jamal Seifi, "The Legality of Truncated Arbitral Tribunals (Public and Private): An Overview in the Wake of the 1998 ICC Rules of Arbitration," 17(6) *Journal of International Arbitration* (2000), pp. 3, 5.
[124] Ibid., p. 45.

institutional rules which were not in force at the time of publication in 1987. Whereas the 1976 UNCITRAL Arbitration Rules, considered with respect to the practice of the Iran-United States Claims Tribunal in the first edition, did not expressly provide for truncated tribunals, today, the institutional rules of, among others, the International Chamber of Commerce,[125] London Court of International Arbitration,[126] International Centre for Dispute Resolution,[127] and the World Intellectual Property Organization[128] expressly recognize the authority of a truncated tribunal to proceed and render an award under various circumstances, while others are silent as to truncated tribunals.[129] Moreover, the 2010 UNCITRAL Rules now provide for the possibility of truncated tribunals in exceptional circumstances.[130]

While a modern approach has emerged and is reflected in many of the institutional arbitration rules available today, the ILC Draft Convention and Model Rules, discussed at length in the first edition and above, continue to serve as the historical point of departure for the law regarding the process to be followed in the event of a withdrawing or obstructionist arbitrator.

(A) ARBITRATION CONVENTIONS

(i) ILC Draft Convention and Model Rules
Article 4 of the *ILC Draft Convention and Model Rules* provides:

1. Once the tribunal has been constituted, its composition shall remain unchanged until the award has been rendered.
2. A party may, however, replace an arbitrator appointed by it, provided that the tribunal has not yet begun its proceedings. Once the proceedings have begun, an arbitrator appointed by a party may not be replaced except by mutual agreement between the parties.
3. Arbitrators appointed by mutual agreement between the parties, or by agreement between arbitrators already appointed, may not be changed after the proceedings have begun, save in exceptional circumstances. Arbitrators appointed in the manner provided for in article 3, paragraph 2 [by the President of the International Court of Justice at the

---

[125] ICC Rules 2017, Article 15(5).   [126] LCIA Rules 2014, Article 12.
[127] ICDR Rules 2014, Article 15(3).
[128] WIPO Arbitration Rules 2014, Article 35(a). See also the PCA Rules 2012, Article 12(4), SIAC Rules, Article 32(6), the HKIAC Rules 2018, Article 12(2), the SCC Rules 2017, Article 21(2) and the CIETAC Rules 2015, Article 34.
[129] See Born, *supra* note 21, pp. 1956–1957.
[130] 2010 UNCITRAL Rules, Article 14(2).

request of the diligent party], may not be changed even by agreement between the parties.
4. The proceedings are deemed to have begun when the president of the tribunal or the sole arbitrator has made the first procedural order.[131]

Articles 5 and 7 provide:

If, whether before or after the proceedings have begun, a vacancy should occur on account of the death, incapacity or resignation of an arbitrator it shall be filled in accordance with the procedure prescribed for the original appointment.

. . .

Where a vacancy has been filled after the proceedings have begun, the proceedings shall continue from the point they had reached at the time the vacancy occurred. The newly appointed arbitrator may, however, require that the oral proceedings shall be recommenced from the beginning, if these have already been started.[132]

(ii) ICSID Convention and Rules

The ICSID Convention provides in Articles 56 and 57 for the replacement of an arbitrator because of death, incapacitation, or resignation, or at the parties' proposal due to a manifest lack of the qualities required by Article 14(1).[133] The ICSID Rules (2006) provide elaboration. Prior to the constitution of the tribunal, each party may replace its appointed arbitrator,[134] and the parties by consent may replace any arbitrator.[135]

---

[131] *Yearbook of the International Law Commission 1958, supra* note 64, vol. II, p. 84.
[132] Ibid.
[133] ICSID Convention, Articles 56(1), 57. Article 14(1) provides that "[p]ersons designated to serve on the Panels shall be persons of high moral character and recognized competence in the fields of law, commerce, industry or finance, who may be relied upon to exercise independent judgment."
[134] ICSID Rules, Rule 7. The ICSID Secretariat has proposed a number of changes to the Rules regarding the replacement of arbitrators in its August 2019 *Proposals for Amendment of the ICSID Rules*. Rule 20 of the Proposed Rules provides:

(1) At any time before the Tribunal is constituted:
 a) an arbitrator may withdraw an acceptance;
 b) a party may replace an arbitrator whom it appointed; or
 c) the parties may agree to replace any arbitrator.
(2) A replacement arbitrator shall be appointed as soon as possible, in accordance with the method by which the withdrawing or replaced arbitrator was appointed.

[135] ICSID Rules, Rule 7.

An arbitrator may resign by submitting his or her resignation to the tribunal and the Secretary-General.[136] If the arbitrator in question was party-appointed, the tribunal shall promptly consider the reasons for the resignation and decide whether it consents thereto, notifying the Secretary-General of its decision.[137]

Neither the ICSID Convention nor Rules expressly provide for a truncated tribunal. Rule 11(1) provides, subject to Rule 11(2), for the filling of a vacancy through the same method by which the original appointment was made.[138] Proceedings are to be suspended until the vacancy is filled.[139] When, however, the resignation of an arbitrator is without the consent of the tribunal, Rule 11(2) and Article 56(3) of the Convention provide that the Chairman of the Administrative Council is to appoint a person from ICSID's Panel of Arbitrators to fill the vacancy.[140]

Once a vacancy has been filled, the proceedings shall resume from the point that was reached at the time the vacancy arose.[141] A newly appointed arbitrator may, however, "require" that oral proceedings be recommenced if they had already started at the time the vacancy arose.[142]

---

[136] Ibid., Rule 8(2).   [137] Ibid.
[138] Ibid., Rule 11. Rule 26 of the August 2019 Proposed Rules provides:

(1) The Secretary-General shall notify the parties of any vacancy on the Tribunal.
(2) The proceeding shall be suspended from the date of notice of the vacancy until the vacancy is filled.
(3) A vacancy on the Tribunal shall be filled by the method used to make the original appointment, except that the Chair shall fill the following vacancies from the Panel of Arbitrators:
   (a) a vacancy caused by the resignation of a party-appointed arbitrator without the consent of the other members of the Tribunal; or
   (b) a vacancy that has not been filled within 45 days after the notice of vacancy.
(4) Once a vacancy has been filled and the Tribunal has been reconstituted, the proceeding shall continue from the point it had reached at the time the vacancy was notified. Any portion of a hearing shall be recommenced if the newly appointed arbitrator considers it necessary to decide a pending matter.

[139] Ibid., Rule 10(2).
[140] See *ConocoPhillips Petrozuata B.V.* v. *Bolivarian Republic of Venezuela*, ICSID Case No. ARB/07/30, Interim Decision, 17 January 2017, para. 10 (indicating that the Chairman of the Administrative Tribunal appointed Professor Andreas Bucher following the resignation of Professor Georges Abi-Saab).
[141] ICSID Rules, Rule 12.   [142] Ibid.

(B) ARBITRATION RULES

(i) UNCITRAL Rules

The best expression of the modern approach can be found in the 2010 UNCITRAL Arbitration Rules, which were drafted with the solutions of the Iran-United States Claims Tribunal regarding obstructionist arbitrators in mind.[143]

The 1976 Rules dealt with the replacement arbitrators in the event of death, resignation, failure or impossibility to act in Article 13.[144] Article 13 of the 1976 Rules specifically provided:

1. In the event of the death or resignation of an arbitrator during the course of the arbitral proceedings, a substitute arbitrator shall be appointed or chosen pursuant to the procedure provided for in articles 6 to 9 that was applicable to the appointment or choice of the arbitrator being replaced.

2. In the event that an arbitrator fails to act or in the event of the de jure or de facto impossibility of his performing his functions, the procedure in respect of the challenge and replacement of an arbitrator as provided in the preceding articles shall apply.

However, as noted above by Paulsson and Petrochilos, "the 1976 Rules did not adequately address situations in which arbitrators were physically prevented from acting, or where they resigned for tactical reasons, or failed to act in order to advance the interests of the party that appointed them."[145] For instance, the Iran-United States Claims Tribunal had to clearly state that the replacement provision provided for in Article 13(2) could not be "invoked to disrupt the orderly process of the Tribunal or to obstruct its functions."[146]

The 2010 Rules were accordingly drafted with modern tactics of recalcitrant respondents in mind. Under the 2010 Rules, a withdrawing or obstructive arbitrator is presumptively to be replaced, generally using the method used for the initial appointment.[147] However, in the event of exceptional circumstances in which it is justified that an arbitrator not be replaced, and the hearings have

---

[143] See Paulsson and Petrochilos, *supra* note 120, p. 98.
[144] 1976 UNCITRAL Rules, Article 13.
[145] Paulsson and Petrochilos, *supra* note 120, p. 98.
[146] Supplemental Opinion of Mr. Böckstiegel and Mr. Holtzmann, *Uiterwyk* v. *Iran, supra* note 22.
[147] 2010 UNCITRAL Rules, Article 14(1).

been closed, the Rules provide that a truncated tribunal can proceed and render an award.

Specifically, Article 14 provides:

1. Subject to paragraph 2, in any event where an arbitrator has to be replaced during the course of the arbitral proceedings, a substitute arbitrator shall be appointed or chosen pursuant to the procedure provided for in articles 8 to 11 that was applicable to the appointment or choice of the arbitrator being replaced. This procedure shall apply even if during the process of appointing the arbitrator to be replaced, a party had failed to exercise its right to appoint or to participate in the appointment.
2. If, at the request of a party, the appointing authority determines that, in view of the exceptional circumstances of the case, it would be justified for a party to be deprived of its right to appoint a substitute arbitrator, the appointing authority may, after giving an opportunity to the parties and the remaining arbitrators to express their views: (a) appoint the substitute arbitrator; or (b) after the closure of the hearings, authorize the other arbitrators to proceed with the arbitration and make any decision or award.[148]

The 2010 UNCITRAL Rules are innovative in that Article 14(2) expressly prohibits the use of a replacement mechanism for obstructing the arbitral proceedings at a late stage and, to that end, provides for the authorization of a truncated tribunal.

Article 15 provides that, "[i]f an arbitrator is replaced, the proceedings shall resume at the stage where the arbitrator who was replaced ceased to perform his or her functions, unless the arbitral tribunal decides otherwise." Further, the 2010 UNCITRAL Rules provide that, where an arbitrator fails to sign an award, the award must state the reasons for the absence of the signature.[149]

(ii) PCA Rules

The 2012 Permanent Court of Arbitration Rules, a consolidation of the four prior sets of PCA procedural rules and updated in light of the 2010 revisions to the UNCITRAL Arbitration Rules, provide the possibility of a truncated tribunal in Article 12(4) (in slightly broader terms compared to the 2010 UNCITRAL Rules):

If an arbitrator on a tribunal of three, five, or more persons fails to participate in the arbitration, the other arbitrators shall, unless the parties agree otherwise, have the power in their sole discretion to continue the

---

[148] Ibid., Article 14.   [149] Ibid., Article 34(4).

arbitration and to make any decision, ruling or award, notwithstanding the failure of one arbitrator to participate. In determining whether to continue the arbitration or to render any decision, ruling or award without the participation of an arbitrator, the other arbitrators shall take into account the stage of the arbitration, the reason, if any, expressed by the arbitrator for such non-participation, and such other matters as they consider appropriate in the circumstances of the case. In the event that the other arbitrators determine not to continue the arbitration without the non-participating arbitrator, the arbitral tribunal shall declare the office vacant, and, subject to article 14, paragraph 2, a substitute arbitrator shall be appointed pursuant to the provisions of articles 8 to 11, unless the parties agree on a different method of appointment.[150]

The PCA Rules provide for the possibility of replacing an arbitrator during the course of arbitral proceedings in Article 14:

1. Subject to paragraph 2 of this article, in any event where an arbitrator has to be replaced during the course of the arbitral proceedings, a substitute arbitrator shall be appointed or chosen pursuant to the procedure provided for in articles 8 to 11 that was applicable to the appointment or choice of the arbitrator being replaced. This procedure shall apply even if during the process of appointing the arbitrator to be replaced, a party had failed to exercise its right to appoint or to participate in the appointment.
2. If, at the request of a party, the appointing authority determines that, in view of the exceptional circumstances of the case, it would be justified for a party to be deprived of its right to appoint a substitute arbitrator, the appointing authority may, after giving an opportunity to the parties and the remaining arbitrators to express their views, appoint the substitute arbitrator.[151]

---

[150] PCA Rules, Article 12(4). Although not an example of arbitrator withdrawal or a truncated tribunal, as China famously refused to participate in the proceedings, the *South China Sea Arbitration* provides an interesting example of how an institution can safeguard a respondent's right to due process when it lacks a party-appointed arbitrator in the deliberations. As an UNCLOS Annex VII arbitration, Article 9 of the Convention acknowledges the possibility of non-participation by one of the parties and confirms that such non-participation does not constitute a bar to the proceedings. The Tribunal accordingly took a number of steps, detailed in paragraphs 119 to 128 of the award, including using the public statements and position paper of the Chinese Government as a proxy for written submissions, in order to ensure procedural fairness to both parties. *See South China Sea Arbitration (Philippines v. China)*, PCA Case No. 2013–19, Award, 12 July 2016, paras. 116–128.
[151] Ibid., Article 14.

The PCA Rules additionally provide that, if an arbitrator is replaced during the course of an arbitration, "the proceedings shall resume at the stage where the arbitrator who was replaced ceased to perform his or her functions," unless the tribunal decides otherwise.[152]

Where a tribunal is composed of more than one arbitrator and an arbitrator fails to sign the award, the PCA Rules require that the reasons for the missing signature be stated in the award.[153]

(iii) ICC Rules

The 2017 Arbitration Rules of the International Chamber of Commerce recognize the authority of truncated tribunals under certain circumstances.[154] In the event of the withdrawal of an arbitrator after the proceedings have closed, Article 15 of the 2017 Rules expressly provides that the International Court of Arbitration may decide whether the remaining arbitrators may continue the proceedings as a truncated tribunal:

> Subsequent to the closing of the proceedings, instead of replacing an arbitrator who has died or been removed by the Court pursuant to Articles 15(1) or 15(2), the Court may decide, when it considers it appropriate, that the remaining arbitrators shall continue the arbitration. In making such determination, the Court shall take into account the views of the remaining arbitrators and of the parties and such other matters that it considers appropriate in the circumstances.[155]

Alternatively, the Rules also provide for the replacement of an arbitrator upon death, resignation, challenge, or the request of the parties. The Court can also replace an arbitrator at its own initiative.[156] All decisions of the Court as to the appointment, confirmation, challenge and replacement of arbitrators are to be final and, in replacing arbitrators, the Court has discretion to decide whether or not to follow the original nominating process.[157] Once reconstituted, the tribunal may decide whether and to what extent proceedings shall be repeated.[158]

---

[152] Ibid., Article 15.   [153] Ibid., Article 34(4).
[154] ICC Rules 2017, Article 15(5). Article 15 of the 2017 ICC Arbitration Rules is nearly identical to Article 12 of the 1998 ICC Arbitration Rules on replacement of arbitrators.
[155] Ibid., Article 15(5).   [156] Ibid., Articles 15(1) and 15(2).
[157] Ibid., Articles 11(4) and 15(4).   [158] Ibid., Article 15(4).

It is worth noting in the context of potentially obstructionist conduct from a party that the ICC Rules additionally provide that, "[i]n making decisions as to costs, the arbitral tribunal may take into account such circumstances as it considers relevant, including the extent to which each party has conducted the arbitration in an expeditious and cost-effective manner."[159]

(iv) London Court of International Arbitration Rules
The 2014 LCIA Rules allow for the rendering of an award by a truncated tribunal in certain circumstances and when authorized by the LCIA Court.[160] Article 12 of the Rules, titled "Majority Power to Continue Deliberations," states:

12.1 In exceptional circumstances, where an arbitrator without good cause refuses or persistently fails to participate in the deliberations of an Arbitral Tribunal, the remaining arbitrators jointly may decide (after their written notice of such refusal or failure to the LCIA Court, the parties and the absent arbitrator) to continue the arbitration (including the making of any award) notwithstanding the absence of that other arbitrator, subject to the written approval of the LCIA Court.

12.2 In deciding whether to continue the arbitration, the remaining arbitrators shall take into account the stage of the arbitration, any explanation made by or on behalf of the absent arbitrator for his or her refusal or non-participation, the likely effect upon the legal recognition or enforceability of any award at the seat of the arbitration and such other matters as they consider appropriate in the circumstances. The reasons for such decision shall be stated in any award made by the remaining arbitrators without the participation of the absent arbitrator.

12.3 In the event that the remaining arbitrators decide at any time thereafter not to continue the arbitration without the participation of the absent arbitrator, the remaining arbitrators shall notify in writing the parties and the LCIA Court of such decision; and, in that event, the remaining arbitrators or any party may refer the matter to the LCIA Court for the revocation of the absent arbitrator's appointment and the appointment of a replacement arbitrator under Articles 10 and 11.[161]

---

[159] Ibid., Article 38(5).   [160] LCIA Rules 2014, Article 12.
[161] Ibid. The 2014 LCIA Rules introduce the requirement of "exceptional circumstances" into the Article. In contrast, Article 12 of the 1998 LCIA Rules reads only:
12.1 If any arbitrator on a three-member Arbitral Tribunal refuses or persistently fails to participate in its deliberations, the two other arbitrators shall have the power, upon their written notice of such refusal or failure to the LCIA Court, the parties and the third arbitrator, to continue the

Furthermore, in the event that an arbitrator "is to be replaced for any reason," the LCIA Court may determine whether or not to follow the process used for the initial nomination.[162]

(v) Singapore International Arbitration Centre Rules

The 2016 SIAC Arbitration Rules 2016 provide that in the event of the death, resignation, withdrawal or removal of an arbitrator, a substitute arbitrator shall be appointed in accordance with the procedure applicable to the appointment of the arbitrator being replaced.[163] The President of the Court of Arbitration of SIAC may also, as a matter of discretion, remove an arbitrator who refuses or fails to act or to perform his duties in accordance with the Rules.[164] Prior to removing the arbitrator, the President shall consult the parties and the members of the tribunal.[165]

The Court may also remove an arbitrator and appoint a substitute arbitrator in the event that a challenged arbitrator does not resign voluntarily.[166] The substitute arbitrator shall be appointed in accordance with the procedure applicable to the nomination and appointment of the arbitrator being replaced.[167]

Where a party-appointed arbitrator is replaced, any hearings held will be repeated at the discretion of the tribunal.[168] Where a sole or presiding arbitrator is replaced, any hearings held will be repeated unless otherwise agreed to by the parties.[169] In the event that the tribunal has issued an interim or partial award prior to the replacement of an arbitrator, hearings related solely to that award shall not be repeated and the award will remain in effect.[170]

The SIAC Rules do envisage some role for a truncated tribunal at a late stage of the proceedings. They accordingly provide that, if any arbitrator who has been given reasonable opportunity to do so fails to cooperate in the making of the award, the remaining arbitrators may proceed to render the award.[171] The remaining arbitrators shall explain in the award the reasons for proceeding without the absent arbitrator.[172]

---

arbitration (including the making of any decision, ruling or award), notwithstanding the absence of the third arbitrator.

[162] Ibid., Article 11(1).   [163] SIAC Rules 2016, Rule 17(1).
[164] Ibid., Rule 17(3).   [165] Ibid.   [166] Ibid., Rule 16(1) and (2).
[167] Ibid., Rule 16(2).   [168] Ibid., Rule 18.   [169] Ibid.   [170] Ibid.
[171] Ibid., Rule 32(6).   [172] Ibid.

(vi) Hong Kong International Arbitration Centre Rules

According to the 2018 HKIAC Rules, an arbitrator may be replaced upon the arbitrator's death, removal, resignation or in the event of a challenge to the arbitrator.[173] Replacement of an arbitrator is generally made in the method used for the initial appointment.[174] In exceptional cases, where HKIAC has decided the circumstances justify depriving a party of its right to appoint an arbitrator, HKIAC may appoint a replacement arbitrator or authorize the remaining arbitrators to proceed with the arbitration and make any decision or award.[175] Unless the tribunal decides otherwise, the proceedings shall resume from the point where the replaced arbitrator ceased performing his or her functions.[176]

Where an arbitrator refuses to sign an award, the award shall state the reasons for the absence of the signature.[177]

(vii) Stockholm Chamber of Commerce Rules

The 2017 Arbitration Rules of the Stockholm Chamber of Commerce state that an arbitral tribunal consisting of three or more arbitrators may, where the Board of Directors of the SCC deems it appropriate, proceed with the arbitration as a truncated tribunal.[178]

The Rules also provide that the Board of Directors shall release an arbitrator from appointment where the arbitrator resigns or is unable or fails to perform his or her functions.[179] Additionally, the Board may release an arbitrator from appointment where a challenge to the arbitrator is sustained under Article 19 of the Rules.[180]

When a party-appointed arbitrator is released from appointment under Article 20 or where a party-appointed arbitrator has died, the party who appointed the arbitrator shall appoint a new arbitrator unless the Board decides otherwise.[181] When an arbitrator has been replaced, the newly constituted tribunal shall decide whether and to what extent to repeat the proceedings.[182]

(viii) AAA-International Centre for Dispute Resolution Rules

The authority of a truncated tribunal to proceed and render an award under certain circumstances is provided for in the 2014 AAA-ICDR Rules:

---

[173] HKIAC Rules 2018, Article 12(1).   [174] Ibid.   [175] Ibid., Article 12(2).
[176] Ibid., Article 12(3).   [177] Ibid., Article 35(5).
[178] SCC Rules 2017, Article 21(2).   [179] Ibid., Article 20(1).   [180] Ibid.
[181] Ibid., Article 21(1).   [182] Ibid., Article 21(3).

If an arbitrator on a three-person arbitral tribunal fails to participate in the arbitration for reasons other than those identified in Article 15(1), the two other arbitrators shall have the power in their sole discretion to continue the arbitration and to make any decision, ruling, order, or award, notwithstanding the failure of the third arbitrator to participate. In determining whether to continue the arbitration or to render any decision, ruling, order, or award without the participation of an arbitrator, the two other arbitrators shall take into account the stage of the arbitration, the reason, if any, expressed by the third arbitrator for such non-participation and such other matters as they consider appropriate in the circumstances of the case. In the event that the two other arbitrators determine not to continue the arbitration without the participation of the third arbitrator, the Administrator on proof satisfactory to it shall declare the office vacant, and a substitute arbitrator shall be appointed pursuant to the provisions of Article 12, unless the parties otherwise agree.[183]

A substitute arbitrator shall be appointed where an arbitrator "resigns, is incapable of performing the duties of an arbitrator or is removed for any reason."[186] The substitute arbitrator shall be appointed pursuant to the procedure set down in the Rules,[184] unless the parties agree otherwise.[185] When an arbitrator fails to sign the award, the award shall state the reasons for the absence of the signature.[187]

(ix) World Intellectual Property Organization Arbitration Rules

The 2014 WIPO Arbitration Rules expressly confirm the power of a truncated tribunal to render an award in certain circumstances:

(a) If an arbitrator on a three-person Tribunal, though duly notified and without good cause, fails to participate in the work of the Tribunal, the two other arbitrators shall, unless a party has made an application under Article 32, have the power in their sole discretion to continue the arbitration and to make any award, order or other decision, notwithstanding the failure of the third arbitrator to participate. In determining whether to continue the arbitration or to render any award, order or other decision without the participation of an arbitrator, the two other arbitrators shall take into account the stage of the arbitration, the reason, if any, expressed by the

---

[183] ICDR Rules 2014, Article 15(3).

[186] Ibid. Article 15(2) provides that, "[i]If a substitute arbitrator is appointed under this Article, unless the parties otherwise agree the arbitral tribunal shall determine at its sole discretion whether all or part of the case shall be repeated."

[184] Ibid., Article 12(1).   [185] Ibid., Article 15(1).   [187] Ibid., Article 30(2).

third arbitrator for such non-participation, and such other matters as they consider appropriate in the circumstances of the case.

(b) In the event that the two other arbitrators determine not to continue the arbitration without the participation of a third arbitrator, the Center shall, on proof satisfactory to it of the failure of the arbitrator to participate in the work of the Tribunal, declare the office vacant, and a substitute arbitrator shall be appointed by the Center in the exercise of the discretion defined in Article 33, unless the parties agree otherwise.[188]

(x) China International Economic and Trade Arbitration Commission Arbitration Rules

The 2015 CIETAC Arbitration Rules provide for two options in the event that, after the conclusion of the oral hearings, an arbitrator on a three-member tribunal is unable to participate in the deliberations and/or render the award.[189] First, the two remaining arbitrators may request that the Chairman of CIETAC replace the absent arbitrator pursuant to the original procedure used for the appointment or, failing that, by having the Chairman appoint a substitute arbitrator.[190] Alternatively, the remaining arbitrators may, after consultations with the Chairman, continue the proceedings and make the award as a truncated tribunal.[191]

2. The International Cases

(A) JAY TREATY CASES

An early pair of inconclusive cases sprung from provisions of the Jay Treaty. Article 6 of that treaty provided for the constitution of a mixed arbitral commission empowered to award to British creditors of residents of the United States amounts owing by the latter to the former which such British creditors had been unable to collect because of obstruction of judicial remedies. Two commissioners were to be appointed by the President of the United States, two by His Majesty, and the fifth by the other four, or failing their agreement, by lot. Three of the commissioners were to "have power to do any act pertaining to the said commission, provided that one of the

---

[188] WIPO Arbitration Rules 2014, Article 35(a) and (b). Article 32 provides for the release of an arbitrator from his or her appointment in certain circumstances. See also Articles 33 and 34 regarding the replacement of arbitrators.
[189] CIETAC Rules 2015, Article 34.   [190] Ibid., Articles 33, 34.
[191] Ibid., Article 34.

commissioners named on each side, and the fifth commissioner shall be present."[192] Article 7 of the treaty provided that a second mixed arbitral commission be constituted to ascertain and award such sums as might be owing to American citizens because of illegal captures or condemnations by British authorities of American vessels or cargo during the then current British war with France.[193] Article 7 incorporated the procedural provisions of Article 6. The commission on obstruction of judicial remedies was to sit in Philadelphia; that concerning neutral rights and duties, in London.

The Philadelphia commission held its first session in May 1797. With its work far from completed, the two American commissioners withdrew, in February 1799, on three occasions, affirming that they did so in order to prevent a vote on resolutions concerning the duty of a Loyalist claimant, Bishop Inglis, to pursue judicial remedies. The American commissioners contended that they were entitled to withdraw by the provision of the treaty requiring the presence of "one of the commissioners on each side, and the fifth commissioner."[194] Nevertheless, the commission, despite several further interruptions, continued in session for two months longer, until, in July, the American commissioners twice withdrew and then definitively withdrew, alleging the resolutions advanced by the majority were in excess of the commission's jurisdiction.[195]

The London commission was beset with similar difficulties, but fared better. At an early stage, the commissioners disagreed about the power of the commission to determine its own jurisdiction, the American commissioners maintaining that the commission was so empowered and the British commissioners contending the contrary. To forestall an adverse majority vote, the British

---

[192] As quoted by J. B. Moore, *History and Digest of the International Arbitrations to Which the United States Has Been a Party* (1898), vol. I, p. 276. See also de la Pradelle and Politis, *Recueil des Arbitrages Internationaux* (1932), vol. 1, p. 16. For an analysis of the *Jay Treaty* cases, see Guyomar, *supra* note 102, pp. 381–383. See also the unanimous award in the *St. Croix River Arbitration*, in which the arbitrators and the British and American Governments appear to have concluded that the three member commission appointed pursuant to Article V of the Jay Treaty could take a valid decision by a majority "but in the presence of the three commissioners" (Moore, p. 11). No question of the absence or withdrawal of an arbitrator arose.

[193] Moore, *supra* note 192, pp. 309–310.

[194] As quoted by Moore, ibid., p. 290. See also de la Pradelle and Politis, *supra* note 192, p. 24.

[195] Moore, *supra* note 192, pp. 290-294; de la Pradelle and Politis, *supra* note 192, pp. 25–26.

commissioners withdrew, claiming they did so as of right because of the provision requiring the presence of a commissioner from each side. The British government initially tended to support the claim of its commissioners. However, it was agreed to seek the opinion of the Lord Chancellor, Loughborough, who held "that the doubt respecting the authority of the commissioners to settle their own jurisdiction, was absurd."[196] The British commissioners accordingly were instructed to return. The commission as reconstituted in October 1798 continued its work until July 1799. At that point, the British government withdrew its commissioners in express retaliation for the American withdrawal from the Philadelphia commission.[197]

The British government prefaced this retaliatory measure with a protest of the American withdrawal. While conceding that the British commissioners in Philadelphia may have misconstrued the jurisdiction accorded the commission, the British Foreign Secretary declared that the action of the American commissioners defeated the ends of the treaty. He pointed out that, in the London commission, the British commissioners had asserted the right to withdraw and had been overruled by the Lord Chancellor. It was never imagined, he added, that the opinions of either commission would be unanimous, and both were enabled to act by majority vote. Accordingly the US government was under a duty to appoint new commissioners.[198]

The American Secretary of State (then John Marshall) responded that the United States was justified in terminating proceedings that were beyond the commission's jurisdiction. However, he suggested a lump sum settlement of the claims of British creditors. The British government took up his proposal.[199] The resultant convention, settling claims under Article 6 of the Jay Treaty, also provided for the resumption of the sittings of the London commission constituted by Article 7. The London commission duly resumed and completed its work. In so doing, it decided to allow interest for the whole period from the time the claims in question arose until the date of the award, including the time

---

[196] As quoted by Moore, *supra* note 192, p. 327. See also pp. 324–328, and de la Pradelle and Politis, *supra* note 192, pp. 45–48, 63–69, 82, 99–105, 131–132.
[197] Moore, *supra* note 192, pp. 337–339.   [198] Ibid., pp. 294–296.
[199] Ibid., pp. 297–298.

during which the commission's work had been suspended because of withdrawal of the British commissioners.[200]

What conclusions may be drawn from these bizarre events? First, the United States commissioners in Philadelphia maintained that they had a right to withdraw and thereby suspend proceedings, and the US government supported this contention. However, the claim was expressly (if not convincingly) based upon the unusual clause of the Jay Treaty providing that at least one commissioner appointed by each party be present when the commission took action. Arbitration treaties customarily provide simply for majority vote.[201] This provision of the Jay Treaty may reasonably be viewed as ground for distinguishing the case.[202] In any event, the American view was not accepted by the British government.

Second, the British commissioners sitting in London at one stage also claimed the right to suspend the commission's sittings by withdrawal, advancing the same basis for their contention. They were overruled by the Lord Chancellor, in a decision at that time accepted both by the British and American governments, and later relied on by the British government in protesting the American withdrawal in Philadelphia.

Third, neither government gave evidence of believing, in the particular circumstances, that a truncated tribunal had the right to render a binding award. The question as such appears not to have been raised, but failure to raise it may be ascribed to the express prescription of the Jay Treaty that decisions of the

---

[200] Ibid., pp. 339–340.

[201] See, for example, Articles 78 and 87 of the Hague Convention for the Pacific Settlement of International Disputes of 1907, James Brown Scott, *The Hague Court Reports* (1916), pp. 306, 307. The provisions of the Hague Convention are incorporated by reference into many other arbitration treaties (*Systematic Survey, supra* note 3, p. 107). Still other treaties expressly provide for majority vote (ibid., pp. 114–115).

[202] In Judge Seifi's view, the quorum rule and the rule of equal representation of the arbitrators of both parties in the composition of the arbitral tribunal in the *Jay Treaty* cases were default rules from which there could be no derogation. In his view, the rule of equal representation of the arbitrators of both parties is precisely the reason why there is no rule of quorum in cases arbitrated by three-member tribunals, as the absence of one party-appointed arbitrator necessarily violates the rule of equal representation and undermines the authority of the tribunal. Accordingly, the rule of quorum is made redundant by the default rule as posited by Judge Seifi. See Seifi, *supra* note 125, pp. 8, 35–36.

commissions could be taken only in the presence of a commissioner from each side.

Last, the awarding of interest for the period of suspension of the London commission is perhaps open to the interpretation that even the retaliatory withdrawal of the British commissioners was conceded to be unjustified.

(B) REPUBLIC OF COLOMBIA V. CAUCA COMPANY

The case of *Republic of Colombia* v. *Cauca Company et al.*[203] is more decisive. The assignor of the Cauca Company had entered into a concession contract with the Republic of Colombia for the construction and operation of a railroad. The concession provided for forfeiture of all installations to the government of Colombia in certain specified contingencies, one being non-completion of construction within four years.[204]

The railroad was not completed within the designated time; the government claimed a forfeiture; the Cauca Company responded that the failure was due to the fault of the government and to *vis major*. At the request of the Company (which was incorporated in West Virginia), the US government diplomatically intervened. Apparently as a result of its intervention, the Colombian government and the Cauca Company entered into an agreement which provided for the surrender of the concession and all of the railroad's installations, in return for the payment by Colombia of "a just indemnity for all the works constructed by the company during the time in which the undertaking has been in its charge, and for...rolling stock," etc.[205] In order to determine the amount of the indemnity, the agreement prescribed the constitution of a special commission, composed of three members, one named by Colombia, another by the Cauca Company and the third to be agreed upon by the Secretary of State of the United

---

[203] 106 Fed. 524 (4th Cir. 1903), aff'd. per curiam, 113 Fed. 1020; reversed on other grounds, 190 U.S. 524 (1903). See also Ex parte *the Republic of Colombia*, 195 U.S. 604 (1904).

[204] The text of the concession contract is printed in the Record, pp. 26–37, *Colombia* v. *Cauca Company*, 190 U.S. 524 (1903).

[205] Agreement of January 4, 1897, for the submission to arbitration of the claims of the Cauca Company against Colombia. Ibid., pp. 982, 986.

States and the Minister of Colombia at Washington. The agreement further provided:

Article VI. Should any of the members of the commission decline or resign from the position, or for any reason cease to act, the proceedings of the commission shall not thereby be invalidated, but the commission shall be restored by a new appointment, which is to be made by the party who appointed the member who fails to act, within thirty days, counting from the day on which such failure to act shall occur. If such party shall not comply with such obligation, the Secretary of State of the United States of America and the Minister of Colombia at Washington shall proceed by agreement to appoint the person to fill such vacancy.[206]

The commission was given, by the terms of the agreement, a maximum of 210 days within which to render its decision.

The commission was duly constituted and took up its functions. Early in the hearings, a difference arose between the commissioner appointed by Colombia, one Pena, and his two colleagues over the definition of the "works" for which an indemnity was to be paid. The majority view was against the restrictive interpretation sought by Pena. The matter was a vital one, being dispositive of much the greater part of the sum at issue. Nevertheless, Pena continued to participate in the hearings, which extended over 203 days. When little remained to be done except to formalize the holdings at which the commission, in most cases by majority vote, already had arrived, Pena resigned from the commission, charging that the majority intended to render an award in excess of its jurisdiction. The Colombian agent in the arbitral proceedings, Cisneros, simultaneously wrote to the commission, allegedly on behalf of Colombia, stating that the resignation of Mr. Pena "has destroyed the autonomy of the commission . . . under such circumstances no further act can have any force or effect as an official act on behalf of the commission."[207] It was not established whether or not Pena's resignation and Cisneros' letter were authorized or assented to by the Colombian government.[208] Upon receipt of Pena's

---

[206] Ibid., pp. 983, 987.

[207] Pena's letter of resignation and the communication of the agent of Colombia are printed at 106 Fed. 337, 345. The nationality of the arbitrators in addition to Mr. Pena does not appear but it may be that both Lewis M. Haupt and Christian F. Schramme were US nationals.

[208] In the proceedings that later took place in the US Circuit Court and the Supreme Court, the Cauca Company substantially alleged, and the Government of Colombia denied, such authorization or assent. Record, *Colombia*

letter, the remaining commissioners resolved that the commission was entitled to make its award, and proceeded to do so at that very sitting. They assigned these reasons in justification of the right of the commission to render its award: that, prior to the "attempted resignation," the commission had completed all of its work except for formal rendition of its decision; that the resignation of Pena seven days before the expiration of the life of the commission, and the concurrence by the agent of Colombia in his resignation, indicated that it was "impracticable" to procure timely appointment of a replacement; that the commission was empowered to determine its procedure and had, with the approval of all three commissioners, determined that a majority vote would be binding; and that Pena had refused to attend the meeting.[209]

On the advice of its Minister in Washington and its agent in the arbitration, the government of Colombia decided, promptly after the rendering of the "pretended award," to institute a suit in a United States court seeking a decree that would direct cancellation of the award. The Colombian government apparently acted in the hope of forestalling diplomatic intervention by the State Department in support of the award.[210] Colombia contended that the award was invalid because it was made by only two of the three arbitrators, and because the substance of the award was in excess of the commission's jurisdiction. Circuit Judge Goff, while modifying the award in respect of certain of the items accorded to the Cauca Company, upheld the award's validity. The parties to the arbitration agreement, he held, intended that they be bound by a majority vote of the commission; the commissioners themselves so determined; the three commissioners were present at all meetings except the last; in "public" proceedings, the majority binds the minority, and this arbitration was in the nature of a public proceeding, concerning as it did a concession and originating as it had in the interposition of the State Department and the action of the Colombian Congress, with the umpire being selected by the two governments. Moreover, Pena's mere writing of a resignation, which, as far as the record showed, was not submitted

v. *Cauca Company*, 190 U.S. 524 (1903), pp. 7–8, 884–885, 1105–1108; Brief for Appellant, pp. 146–150, Brief for Appellees, pp. 24, 40–41,63–65, *Colombia v. Cauca Company*, 190 U.S. 524 (1903). See the holding of the Circuit Court quoted below.

[209] The resolution of the two commissioners asserting their competence and the award are printed at 106 Fed. 337, 345–347.

[210] Record, *supra* note 208, pp. 1249–1250.

to the party that appointed him, did not necessarily create a vacancy in the commission. The court continued:

Clearly, it was not the intention of the parties to the convention that the existence of the commission should be destroyed by a resignation of the character of that presented by Commissioner Pena. It would be an impeachment of the common honesty of the parties to the agreement, and a travesty of their evidently honorable intentions, to hold that they designed it should thus be in the power of one man – actuated by, to say the least, not commendable motives – to render worthless the work resulting from the expenditure of thousands of dollars and months of careful research, in an effort to amicably adjust an unfortunate controversy, that was rapidly reaching the point of embarrassment because of its national and diplomatic character. The testimony forces me to the conclusion that Commissioner Pena's only motive in withdrawing from the commission was to prevent, if possible, a conclusion from being reached, or to render the award invalid should one be made. This conduct – keeping in view all the circumstances surrounding him and the commission of which he was still a member – was not only reprehensible in character, but was fraudulent in its tendencies. He represented the complainant, as did Cisneros, who advised him to pursue the course he did, and, while I do not find that the complainant advised such action, still I hold that it would be unconscionable to allow the party whose agents thus deported themselves to effectuate, by the decree of a court of equity, the wrong intended to be accomplished by such improper conduct.[211]

On appeal to the Supreme Court, the amount of the indemnity accorded the Cauca Company was further modified, but, on the issue of the binding character of an award rendered by a truncated tribunal, the court, in an opinion delivered by Mr. Justice Holmes, held:

The agreement gave Colombia thirty days to appoint a new member, and on its failure the Secretary of State for the United States and the Colombian Minister were to appoint him. But the commission was allowed only one hundred and fifty days 'from its installation,' which might be extended sixty days more for justifiable grounds. It had sat two hundred and three days when the resignation was announced. Manifestly it was possible, if not certain, that its only way of saving the proceedings from coming to naught was to ignore the communication and to proceed to the

---

[211] 106 Fed. 337, 348–349.

award. This it did. Colombia by its bill and argument now lays hold of the resignation of its commissioner as a ground for declaring the award void.

Colombia thus is put in the position of seeking to defeat the award after it has received the railroad in controversy and while it is undisputed that an appreciable part of the consideration awarded ought to be paid to the company under the terms of the submission. It is fair to add that the bill offers to pay the undisputed sum, but not to rescind the submission and return the railroad. We shall spend little argument upon this part of the case. Of course, it was not expected that a commission made up as this was would be unanimous. The commission was dealt with as a unit, as a kind of court, in the submission. It was constituted after, if not as the result of, diplomatic discussion in pursuance of a public statute of Colombia. It was to decide between a sovereign State and a railroad, declared by a law of Colombia to be a work of public utility. In short, it was dealing with matters of public concern. It had itself resolved, under the powers given to it in the agreement, that a majority vote should govern. Obviously that was the only possible way, as each party appointed a representative of its side. We are satisfied that an award by a majority was sufficient and effective. We are satisfied, further, that whatever might be the technical rule for three arbitrators dealing with a private dispute, neither party could defeat the operation of the submission, after receiving a large amount of property under it, by withdrawing or adopting the withdrawal of its nominee when the discussions were closed. See *Cooley* v. *O'Connor*, 12 Wall. 391, 398; *Kingston* v. *Kincaid*, 1 Wash. C.C. 448; *Ex parte Rogers*, 7 Cowen, 526; *Carpenter* v. *Wood*, 1 Met. 409; *Maynard* v. *Frederick*, 7 Cush. 247; *Kunckle* v. *Kunckle*, 1 Dall. 364; *Cumberland* v. *North Yarmouth*, 4 Greenl. 459, 468; *Grindley* v. *Barker*, 1 Bos & P. 229, 236; *Dalling* v. *Mattchett*, Willes, 215, 217. In private matters the courts are open if arbitration fails, but in this case the alternative was a resort to diplomatic demand.[212]

It is believed that the *Cauca* case lends particular support to the conclusion that a truncated arbitral tribunal is empowered to render a binding award.[213] Article VI of the arbitration agreement envisaged the possibility of the resignation of a member, and made express and detailed provision, in that eventuality, for replacement. Colombia stoutly maintained, and its Minister swore, that it would

---

[212] 190 U.S. 524, 527–528.

[213] See, e.g., *Himpurna California Energy Ltd.* v. *Republic of Indonesia*, UNCITRAL, Final Award, October 16, 1999, XXV *Yearbook Commercial Arbitration* (2000), p. 186, para. 47. Waincymer, *supra* note 108, p. 337; David D. Caron and Lee M. Caplan, *The UNCITRAL Arbitration Rules: A Commentary* (2nd edition, 2013), p. 316. *Redfern and Hunter on International Arbitration*, *supra* note 106, pp. 282–283.

"at once" have named another arbitrator had it been given the opportunity to do so after Pena's resignation, but that the immediate rendering of an award upon his resignation denied it that opportunity. Seven days was ample time, it contended, in which to appoint a replacement; and, even if it were not, the arbitration agreement's provisions for replacement and for a time limit on the proceedings were to be read consonantly, with the result that the latter could not be construed to frustrate the former.[214] Nevertheless, the Supreme Court, which may be expected to presume the *bona fides* of the sworn statements of the representative of a friendly foreign government, held that it was "possible, if not certain," that the only way of keeping the proceedings from coming to naught was for the two commissioners to proceed to render an award. That award it held valid. It is true that the court also lent weight to the fact that Colombia's action was in equity, seeking to annul an award rendered pursuant to an agreement under which the Cauca Company had relinquished its claim to the railroad, while Colombia did not offer to return the railroad. But the case's support of the principle that a truncated international arbitral tribunal may render a binding award is enhanced by the statement of Mr. Justice Holmes that, while in private matters the courts are open if arbitration fails, in this case the alternative was a resort to diplomatic demand.

Yet is the *Cauca* case actually in point as regards international law? For it may be objected that, since the arbitration was one between a private company and a foreign government, rather than between two governments, the case is not one of public international law. The arbitration agreement was signed by the government of Colombia on the one hand and the Cauca Company, rather than the government of the United States, on the other; this was not a claims commission in which the United States appeared as the nominal – and theoretically, the real – party in interest on behalf of its national. In this regard, it is interesting to note that the International Law Commission debated the question of the applicability of its draft code of arbitral procedure to arbitrations between States and aliens. Its discussion, while brief, revealed a

---

[214] Record, *supra* note 208, pp. 8–9, 1105; Brief for Appellant, *supra* note 208, pp. 8–9, 1105. Colombia also pointed out that argument about the power of a majority to bind the tribunal was irrelevant. Ibid., pp. 129–136.

sharp divergence of opinion, more members of the Commission apparently challenging than supporting the relevance of the code to such arbitrations.[215] The Commission concluded its debate with the adoption of an equivocal comment that seemingly approved the same procedures for investment disputes.[216]

Dr. F.A. Mann has argued that awards in arbitrations between States and aliens generally "ought not to be treated or reported as if they were authorities on international law."[217] In the *Cauca* case itself, the parties disputed the "international or diplomatic character" of the arbitration agreement.[218] Judge Goff held the submission to arbitration to be "in the nature of a public contention," and, in support of that conclusion, referred to the "friendly suggestions emanating from the Secretary of State of the United States" and to the mode of appointment of the umpire.[219] Mr. Justice Holmes, noting that the arbitral commission was "constituted after, if not as a result of, diplomatic discussion . . ." held that "it was dealing with matters of public concern."[220] But there was no clear holding that the *Cauca* case was an "international arbitration." For the purposes of the decision, there was no need for such a holding, and, at the stage of development at which

---

[215] *Yearbook of the International Law Commission 1958, supra* note 64, vol. I, pp. 10–14, 219, 225–228.

[216] "[N]ow that the draft is no longer presented in the form of a potential general treaty of arbitration, it may be useful to draw attention to the fact that, if the parties so desired, its provisions would, with the necessary adaptations, also be capable of utilization for the purpose of arbitration between States and international organizations or between international organizations.

Different legal considerations arise in arbitrations between States and foreign private corporations or other juridical entities. However, some of the articles of the draft, if adapted, might also be capable of use for this purpose." Ibid., pp. 227–228.

[217] F.A. Mann, "The Proper Law of Contracts Concluded by International Persons," XXXV *British Year Book of International Law* (1959), pp. 34, 54. Dr. Mann goes so far as to deplore the inclusion of such cases in publications which are concerned with public international law – a conclusion with which the editors of the United Nations *Reports of International Arbitral Awards* (see, e.g., the cases reported in vol. II, p. 61, vol. III, pp. 1571 and 1621), and *International Law Reports* (see, e.g., the cases reported in the 1951 volume, at pp. 144 and 161, the 1953 volume, at p. 534, the 1956 volume, at p. 633) have not been in agreement.

[218] Brief for Petitioner for Certiorari, *The Republic of Colombia* v. *The Cauca Company and the Colombian Construction and Improvement Company*, 181 U.S. 638, at pp. 4, 12; Record, *supra* note 208, pp. 881–882, 1107.

[219] 106 Fed. 337, 348.   [220] 190 U.S. 524, 528.

international law had arrived in 1902, such a holding would have been in advance of its times.

Whatever the force of the view that an award in an arbitration between a State and an alien is not authority in international law (a view to which it is difficult to subscribe unreservedly), it is believed that such an award, in the least, may be authority for those general principles of law that are a source of international law.[221] Moreover, not only does Article 38 of the Statute of the International Court of Justice specify that the Court shall apply the general principles of law recognized by civilized nations; it also provides that it may apply "judicial decisions and the teachings of the most highly qualified publicists of the various nations, as subsidiary means for the determination of rules of law." While this provision has been interpreted by the Court to refer to judicial decisions by it and its predecessor, it has also relied on decisions of international arbitral tribunals; and the International Law Commission has pointed out that decisions of national courts may also comprise evidence of customary international law.[222] Why then should not decisions of arbitral tribunals sitting in disputes between a State and an alien corporation be a source of such evidence? There is indeed nothing to prevent such an arbitral tribunal from applying public international law[223] any more than a national court is prevented from applying that law.[224] The relevance to international law of an arbitration between a State and an alien – even absent an explicit

---

[221] See, among a literature that since his writing of that seminal article has burgeoned, A. McNair, "The General Principles of Law Recognized by Civilized Nations," XXXIII *British Year Book of International Law* (1957), pp. 1, 6, and the *Lena Goldfields Arbitration, supra* Chapter I, and *infra*.

[222] See the references in Shabtai Rosenne, *The Law and Practice of the International Court* (1965), vol. two, pp. 611–616.

[223] "...the Tribunal holds that public international law should be applied to the effects of the Concession, when objective reasons lead it to conclude that certain matters cannot be governed by any rule of the municipal law of any State, as is the case in all matters relating to transport by sea, to the sovereignty of the State on its territorial waters and to the responsibility of States for the violation of their international obligations." *Arbitration between Saudi Arabia and the Arabian American Oil Company* (1958), 27 *International Law Reports*, p. 172. See Suzanne Bastid, "Le Droit International Public dans la Sentence Arbitrale de l'Aramco," VII *Annuaire Français de Droit International* (1961).

[224] As noted, the pages of *International Law Reports* are replete with national decisions applying international law. See also Philip C. Jessup, *Transnational Law* (1956), pp. 102, 106–107. Dr. Mann himself was an outstanding exponent of the application of international law by municipal courts. See "The

application of international law by the tribunal – is the more plausible when the substance of the issue arbitrated, and the mode of
that issue's disposition, is one comprehended by the substance of
international law. The *Cauca* case presented precisely such an issue:
that of a just indemnity for the taking of a railroad constructed by
an alien. The *Cauca* award, as modified by US courts, is consonant
with the standards applied in international arbitral awards in the
strict sense of that latter term; numbers of international arbitral
awards have dealt with similar issues in a similar way; and there is
no reason to believe that, had the signatories to the arbitration
agreement been the governments of Colombia and the United
States, rather than the government of Colombia and the Cauca
Company, the ultimate disposition of the case would have
differed. Counsel might well have been the same, for it is not
uncommon for a government that nominally represents its
national to rely upon that national's counsel; and, in this case,
the composition of the tribunal might also have been the
same, the umpire in any event having been named by the joint
act of the Colombian and US governments. The international
force of the case may be argued to be enhanced still further by
the fact that the arbitration agreement was concluded after the
diplomatic interposition of the United States on behalf of
the Cauca Company in the latter's negotiations with the Colombian government. Furthermore, it may be noted that authoritative
sources, in discussing this subject, have not hesitated to rely on
the two relevant arbitrations between States and aliens, the *Cauca*
and *Lena Goldfields* cases.[225]

And finally, even if there is basis for questioning the pertinence
of the *Cauca* case for public international law, the judgment of the
Supreme Court of the United States stands as high authority in

Consequences of an International Wrong in International and National Law,"
XLVIII *British Year Book of International Law* (1976–1977), p. 1.

[225] See the comment of Judge Hudson quoted *supra*, and the *Commentary*, *supra*
note 6, p. 28. In pleadings before the International Court of Justice, the
Government of the United States argued: "Where, in an international arbitration, one party becoming aware of the prospect of an award against it brings
about the withdrawal of its appointed arbitrator, this default is held ineffective
to frustrate the arbitration. *Colombia* v. *Cauca Co.*, . . . *Lena Goldfields Co. Ltd.*
v. *USSR. . . .*" *Interpretation of Peace Treaties with Bulgaria, Hungary and Romania,
Pleadings, Oral Arguments, Documents*, pp. 231–233. See also ibid., pp. 356–358,
and, for a like statement by the United Kingdom, ibid., p. 377.

upholding the validity of an arbitral award rendered by a truncated tribunal which sat between a State and an alien – which for the purpose of this study is significant enough.[226]

(C) NORWEGIAN SHIPOWNERS' CLAIMS

Reference is also required to a case, which, while justly famous in other respects, never seems to have been noticed in respect of truncation: the *Norwegian Shipowners' Claims* (1922).

The Special Agreement between the United States of America and Norway provided, in Article IV, that: "The decision of the majority of the members of the Tribunal shall be the decision of the Tribunal."[227] There was no quorum provision or requirement that the award be signed by the arbitrators.

The decision, carried by the President (James Vallotton of Switzerland) and the Norwegian-appointed arbitrator, Benjamin Vogt, was challenged by the arbitrator appointed by the United States, Chandler P. Anderson, who, in letters to the Agents of the United States and Norway and to the Secretary-General of the Permanent Court of Arbitration, claimed that his colleagues:

... have disregarded the terms of submission and exceeded the authority conferred upon the United States-Norway Arbitration Tribunal by the Special Agreement of June 30, 1921, which imposes definite limits upon its jurisdiction. I have therefore refused to be present when the award is announced.[228]

Immediately after the rendering of the Award, the Agent of the United States made the following declaration:

... I deem it my duty on behalf of the United States to reserve all the rights of the United States arising out of the plain and manifest departure of the

---

[226] In assessing the impact of the *Cauca* case, Judge Seifi advocates for a more nuanced approach. Although acknowledging that the case provides some support for the notion of the legality of truncated tribunals, Judge Seifi argues that the tribunal in the *Cauca* case had effectively no choice but to proceed with the rendering of the award with the tribunal in truncated form. However, where there is choice, Judge Seifi argues, the choice should not be to have an award issued by a truncated tribunal. See Seifi, *supra* note 125, pp. 27, 29.

[227] I *U.N.R.I.A.A.*, pp. 309, 311.

[228] 17 *American Journal of International Law* (1923), p. 399.

award from the terms of submission and from the "essential error," to use the language of the authorities, by which it is invalidated.[229]

The US Agent then read out the foregoing letter of Mr. Anderson. The award was signed by the President of the tribunal and the Secretary-General of the Permanent Court of Arbitration.

The report of the case published in the *American Journal of International Law* also records the following statement by Mr. Anderson:

Under an interpretation given to the provisions of the Hague Convention of 1907 for the Pacific Settlement of International Disputes, the American arbitrator was denied the right to file a dissenting opinion, or to note his dissent, because the Special Agreement creating the Tribunal did not expressly provide therefor. After communicating this interpretation to the Government of the United States, he acquiesced in so far as the interpretation precluded a dissenting opinion on the law and the facts, but as The Hague Conventions did not contemplate a disregard of the terms of submission by the Tribunal, he refused to appear to acquiesce in the action of the Tribunal by his presence and silence when the Award was announced.[230]

Despite the claim by the American-appointed arbitrator that the tribunal disregarded its terms of reference; despite his refusal to be present when the award was delivered and duly notified to the Parties; despite the claim by the Agent of the United States that the award was invalidated by manifest departure from the terms of submission and by essential error; despite the reservation recorded by the government of the United States "that the award cannot be deemed by this Government to possess an authoritative character as a precedent";[231] the Congress of the United States authorized

---

[229] Ibid.

[230] Ibid. This statement does not appear in the official print by the Permanent Court of Arbitration of the *Proceedings of the Tribunal of Arbitration convened at The Hague under the provisions of the Special Agreement between the United States of America and Norway concluded at Washington, June 30th, 1921* (1922). However, there does appear the following statement by the President of the Tribunal, with reference to Mr. Anderson's letter as just read out by the United States' Agent: "...I regret to say that I do not think that the way in which this declaration is presented on behalf of one of the members of the Tribunal is in conformity with the general convention of The Hague nor with the special agreement governing the case. We have heard nothing of this protest until this moment, and I do not think that the dissenting vote of an Arbitrator should be presented by the Agent of one of the Parties." Ibid., p. 162.

[231] I *U.N.R.I.A.A.*, p. 346.

payment of the Award in full. The Secretary of State, Charles Evans Hughes (subsequently a judge of the Permanent Court of International Justice and Chief Justice of the Supreme Court of the United States), in making payment, wrote that the United States accordingly gave "tangible proof of its desire to respect arbitral awards." He declared:

Faithful to its traditional policy, my Government is most desirous to promote the judicial determination of international disputes of a justiciable character and in this interest to give its due support to judicial determinations.[232]

While this latter stand and statement was widely and rightly noted – it is indeed a position whose implications for more current affairs have been emphasized[233] – it is worth noticing in respect of truncated arbitral tribunals that neither the American-appointed arbitrator, nor the Agent of the United States, nor the government of the United States, drew conclusions from the absence of Mr. Anderson from the final session of the tribunal at which its award was delivered. The view of Mr. Anderson and perhaps of the United States Agent appears to have been not that the award was invalid because of his absence but that, because of the award's invalidity, his absence was appropriate. In the light of that reasoning and also of the principled position of the United States in complying fully with an award that it maintained proclaimed "certain theories of law which it cannot accept"[234] and that inadequately fulfilled "the requirements of appropriate arbitral procedure" because it failed to give "the reasons on which it is based,"[235] and in the light, moreover, of the position of the majority of the Tribunal and of the Secretary-General of the Permanent Court of Arbitration, the award in respect of the *Norwegian Shipowners' Claims* must be construed as lending a measure of further support to the authority of a truncated international arbitral tribunal to render a valid award.[236]

---

[232] Ibid., p. 344.

[233] Keith Highet, "Between a Rock and a Hard Place: The United States, the International Court, and the *Nicaragua* Case," Speech delivered on November 1, 1986 to the American Branch of the International Law Association and the American Society of International Law, p. 14 (mimeographed text).

[234] I *U.N.R.I.A.A.*, p. 344.   [235] Ibid., p. 345.

[236] Such a conclusion is not shared by Judge Seifi. In his view, the case is not an example of arbitrator withdrawal, but of refusal of an arbitrator to sign an

(D) *INTERNATIONAL FISHERIES COMPANY (U.S.A.) V. UNITED*
MEXICAN STATES, AND DICKSON CAR WHEEL COMPANY (U.S.A.)
V. UNITED MEXICAN STATES

In both of these cases before the General Claims Commission that
sat between the United States and Mexico 1923–1931, the Commissioner appointed by the United States, Fred K. Nielsen, concluded
his dissenting opinions with the following statement:[237]

I consider it to be important to mention an interesting point that has
arisen since the instant case was argued. Rule XI, 1, provides:
"The award or any other judicial decision of the Commission in respect
of each claim shall be rendered at a public sitting of the Commission."
The other two Commissioners have signed the 'Decision' in this case.
However, no meeting of the Commission was ever called by the Presiding
Commissioner to render a decision in the case, and there has never been
any compliance with the proper rule above quoted.[238]

Apparently all three arbitrators were present for the hearings. But
Commissioner Nielsen appears to maintain that deliberations did
not take place, and that the awards were signed and rendered by
the majority of two in his absence, and not at a public sitting of the
Commission.

Feller was not able to secure (or, in any event, publish) the facts
that lay behind these bare statements.[239] But apparently, despite

---

award. Accordingly, Judge Seifi sees little precedential value in the *Norwegian
Shipowners' Claims* arbitration for the authority of truncated tribunals. See Seifi,
supra note 125, pp. 28–29.
[237] IV *U.N.R.I.A.A.*, pp. 691, 669. [238] Ibid., pp. 691, 746.
[239] A. H. Feller states: "This ninth session was the last under the 1929 Convention
for Further Extension and it appears to have been a troubled one. Three cases
were argued, but the Commission did not announce any decisions while the
session was in progress. Subsequently the US Government Printing Office
published the text of the opinions in the International Fisheries Case, which
had been argued at this session and in the Dickson Car Wheel Company Case
which had been argued at the previous session. Both of these opinions bear the
date line: 'July —, 1931,' and the dissenting opinions of the American Commissioner conclude with the following remarks [quoting Nielsen as in the body
of this Chapter] . . .
The Memorial of the Mexican Secretariat of Foreign Relations hints at a
more serious disagreement: 'As a consequence of an incident provoked (*pro-
vocado*) by the American Commissioner, the ninth session of the Commission
was, at first, suspended, and then declared terminated in August 1931.' The
published sources do not reveal what the character of this 'incident' was." A. H.
Feller, *The Mexican Claims Commissions* (1935), p. 59.

Nielsen's statements, the awards were not only published by the United States but eventually accepted by it as valid (at any rate, this seems to be the thrust of Mr. Cordova's statement in the International Law Commission. Mr. Cordova states that the US Commissioner had withdrawn).[240]

The facts are too skeletal to allow a confident conclusion but, insofar as any inference may be drawn from these cases, it supports the authority of a truncated international arbitral tribunal to proceed and to render a binding award. However, it should be added that, if, *arguendo*, Nielsen's view of the facts is accepted, he confronted a case which is distinguishable from those considered in this study. A majority of an arbitral tribunal cannot refuse ever to deliberate with all members on a case and the award must be delivered in accordance with the procedure, which has been adopted for that purpose or which is otherwise governing.[241] It is one thing for an arbitrator to withdraw from a case or tribunal, at his own or his principal's initiative; it is quite another thing for an arbitrator to be excluded by the tribunal from taking part in its proceedings when he is able and willing to do so.

(E) *UPPER SILESIAN ARBITRAL TRIBUNAL CASE*

The Geneva Convention on Upper Silesia was signed on May 1, 1922 – a document unique in international history as providing for the maintenance of economic unity across a political frontier. Its 606 articles laid down in the most elaborate detail the arrangements to be followed to ensure the various safeguards, which the Council [of the League of Nations] had demanded.[242] Principal among those safeguards was the Upper Silesian Arbitral Tribunal, a tribunal composed of a Polish arbitrator, a German arbitrator, and a President of

---

[240] *Yearbook of the International Law Commission 1950, supra* note 14, vol. I, pp. 268, 269, 271.

[241] See also Richard M. Mosk and Tom Ginsburg in D.M. Kolkey, R. Chernick et al. (eds.), *Practitioner's Handbook on International Arbitration and Mediation* (2012), p. 412, referencing the *International Fisheries* and *Dickson Car Wheel Company* cases for the proposition that "[o]ne arbitrator cannot...be excluded from the deliberative process."

[242] F.P. Walters, *A History of the League of Nations* (1952), vol. I, p. 156.

a third nationality, to be chosen by the League Council.[243] The arbitrators were to act independently.[244] The Convention further provided that, if a national arbitrator were to be prevented from acting, the government, which had nominated him, would nominate a replacement.[245] The whole regime prescribed by the Geneva Convention was to last for fifteen years from the date of transfer of sovereignty over portions of Silesia to Poland. At the expiration of that period, Germany and Poland respectively were to enjoy unrestricted sovereignty over their sections of Upper Silesia whose governance was during those fifteen years to be regulated in so many respects by the terms of the Geneva Convention.

The Convention accordingly was to expire on July 15, 1937. Article 606 of the Convention provided that, as of that date, the Arbitral Tribunal shall wind up pending cases.[246] On July 14, the Tribunal accepted a draft accord on which Germany and Poland had agreed for the disposition of pending cases. However, Germany and Poland were not agreed on the meaning of that accord, Poland apparently interpreting it to mean that the Tribunal should dispose of pending cases by remitting them to national courts or diplomatic authorities, Germany apparently interpreting it to mean that the Tribunal should complete action on pending cases.[247]

Nevertheless, the Tribunal held two active sessions in September and December 1937 in which it judicially dealt with a large number of cases. Not having disposed of all such cases, the Tribunal decided in December to hold a final session from mid-January to mid-February 1938. The Polish Agent subsequently responded that Poland had reckoned on the process of winding up being terminated by December 1937. On January 24, 1938, the Polish Agent announced that the Polish arbitrator had resigned, and he accordingly maintained that the activity of the Arbitral Tribunal had come definitively to an end. For his part, the German Agent contended that the resignation of the Polish arbitrator was incompatible with the July agreement on windup of pending cases.[248]

---

[243] See Georges Kaeckenbeeck, *The International Experiment of Upper Silesia* (1942), pp. 26–30. The text of the Geneva Convention appears as Appendix III, p. 567. (See Article 563, at p. 802.)

[244] Article 564, ibid.   [245] Article 566, ibid., pp. 802, 803.

[246] "Le Tribunal arbitral liquidera les affaires encore pendantes" Article 606, paragraph 3, ibid., p. 816. See also paragraph 5, ibid.

[247] Ibid., p. 507.   [248] Ibid., p. 508.

On February 7, the President of the Arbitral Tribunal, Georges Kaeckenbeeck, wrote to the Polish Agent, noting that Poland drew from the fact of the resignation of the Polish arbitrator the conclusion that, since the Tribunal was no longer fully constituted, its work was definitively terminated. President Kaeckenbeeck stated that that conclusion was not well founded either on the Geneva Convention or on the terms of the windup accord. He observed that the German Agent took a position contrary to the Polish and that Germany maintained that the President should take steps to permit the Court to finish its pending cases. In the absence of agreement between the two governments, Kaeckenbeeck declared that he could not consider his mission as President of the Tribunal terminated until the last case duly submitted to the Tribunal had been resolved. Should Poland persist in its unilateral declaration that the work of the Tribunal had come to an end, he would have to protest against what he saw as an unjustified position that would be a dangerous precedent for international arbitration. In the circumstances that he described, it was not the fault of the Tribunal that all cases had not been wound up. He did not believe that his fifteen years of service as President of the Tribunal merited such treatment by Poland. Accordingly, he called upon the Polish government to take the requisite action which would permit him to complete his mission.[249]

President Kaeckenbeeck's letter to the German Agent requested that Germany call upon Poland to permit him to complete his mission, and suggested that Germany might wish to enter into discussions with Poland with a view toward promoting a solution.[250]

Thereafter, the Polish government sent a representative to meet with Kaeckenbeeck, and, as a result of conversations with him and German representatives, Kaeckenbeeck sent them windup proposals that were accepted and acted upon. However, three cases and a number of miscellaneous matters remained pending, Poland suggesting diplomatic recourse while Germany suggested awards by the President acting as sole arbitrator.[251]

Guyomar draws from this incident the conclusion that the President of the Upper Silesian Arbitral Tribunal "never for an instant contemplated . . . the possibility of proceeding in the absence of the

---

[249] The text of Kaeckenbeeck's letter to the Polish Agent is reprinted in French, ibid., pp. 509–510.
[250] Ibid., p. 511.   [251] Kaeckenbeeck, *supra* note 243, pp. 511–512.

Polish arbitrator"[252] and thus counts this case as cutting against the authority of a truncated arbitral tribunal to act. Judge Seifi also interprets the case in this way, concluding that the suspension of the proceedings by the President of the Tribunal indicates clearly that "neither the parties involved nor the remaining members felt that an incomplete tribunal was permitted to continue the proceedings in the absence of a withdrawing arbitrator."[253]

There is indeed no indication that Kaeckenbeeck believed that the Tribunal should proceed to render judgment on cases in the absence of the Polish arbitrator. But there is nothing to indicate that, in his view, the Tribunal as a matter of law lacked the capacity to do so. On the contrary, his criticism of the resignation of the Polish arbitrator as "unjustified" and a "unilateral action contrary to law"[254] by no means so suggests. Moreover, because of the fact that the regime prescribed by the Geneva Convention had expired six months earlier and because of the ambiguities in the windup accord, there may have been room for the Polish contention that the Tribunal could not continue its work with the 1938 resignation of the Polish arbitrator. For these reasons, it is questionable whether this case can correctly be weighed against the authority of a truncated arbitral tribunal. Indeed, the fact that President Kaeckenbeeck continued to act as President of the Tribunal after the resignation of the Polish arbitrator, and, in that capacity, made proposals that terminated the proceedings with the substantial agreement of the Parties, may suggest the contrary.

(F) THE HUNGARIAN OPTANTS CASES

The cases of the *Hungarian Optants* aroused great political and legal interest in the years 1923–1930, and are sometimes cited as bearing upon the question of the authority of truncated arbitral tribunals.[255] In fact, those cases, while of considerable importance for

---

[252] Guyomar, *supra* note 102, p. 385 (translation supplied).
[253] Seifi, *supra* note 125, pp. 37, 39.
[254] Kaeckenbeeck, *supra* note 243, pp. 509–510 (translation supplied).
[255] See, for example, *Commentary, supra* note 6, pp. 28–29; and Professor Scelle's first report on arbitral procedure in *Yearbook of the International Law Commission 1950, supra* note 14, vol. II, pp. 127–128. For an able summary and analysis of the *Hungarian Optants* cases, particularly as dealt with by the League of Nations, see Reisman, *supra* note 103, pp. 686–698. For a detailed exposition

the integrity of the international arbitral process and for other reasons as well, shed little light on the question of whether a truncated international arbitral tribunal may render a valid award. The cases will be briefly described to show why this is so.

In the wake of the First World War, and pursuant to the Treaty of Trianon,[256] Transylvania was ceded by Hungary to Rumania. The Treaty of Trianon provided that Hungarian inhabitants of the ceded territories could opt to remain Hungarian nationals.[257] In that event, the Treaty provided that the Hungarian optants, who were required to move to Hungary, "will be entitled to retain their immovable property"[258] in such territories. The Treaty also provided that such property shall not "be subject to retention or liquidation" by Rumanian authorities, but be restored to their owners.[259]

Rumania adopted measures of agrarian reform that embraced its new territories as well as the older territory of the Kingdom of Rumania. Hungary claimed that these measures – whose provisions expressly applied to "absentees" from ceded territories (and those who opted for Hungarian nationality were required to become absentees) – were implemented against the Hungarian optants so as to retain or take their lands with very little or no compensation, in contravention of the Treaty of Trianon. Rumania maintained that, while the Treaty debarred measures of retention or liquidation of the property of Hungarian optants, it did not restrict measures of expropriation taken pursuant to a general agrarian reform that affected absentee Rumanian nationals and aliens alike.

---

sympathetic to the Hungarian position, see F. Deák, *The Hungarian-Rumanian Land Dispute* (1928); for the Rumanian view, Vercaru, *La Réforme Agraire en Roumanie* (1928). The dispute gave rise to a large literature, and to a cascade of legal opinions on aspects of it. See, *inter alia, La Réforme Agraire en Roumanie* (1927), which contains opinions of twenty-nine international lawyers; a second volume of the same title published in 1928 containing a further eighteen opinions; and like numbers from another perspective in *Some Opinions, Articles, Reports bearing upon the Treaty of Trianon and the Claims of the Hungarian Nationals with regard to their Lands in Transylvania*, vol. I (1927), vol. II (1928). Further extensive bibliographical references are contained in Deák, pp. 103–104, note 232, and pp. 263–268.

[256] The Treaty of Trianon between the Allied and Associated Powers and Hungary of June 4, 1920, 113 *British and Foreign State Papers* (1920), p. 486.

[257] Article 63, ibid., p. 486.

[258] 113 *British and Foreign State Papers* (1920), p. 515.

[259] Article 250, ibid., pp. 607–608.

The Treaty of Trianon provided for the establishment of Mixed Arbitral Tribunals, and further provided that claims made by Hungarian nationals for the restoration of their property, rights and interests shall be submitted to the Rumanian-Hungarian Mixed Arbitral Tribunal.[260] The provision for constitution of the Mixed Arbitral Tribunals read as follows:

239. *(a)* Within three months from the coming into force of the present Treaty, a Mixed Arbitral Tribunal shall be established between each of the Allied and Associated Powers on the one hand and Hungary on the other hand. Each such Tribunal shall consist of three members. Each of the Governments concerned shall appoint one of these members. The President shall be chosen by agreement between the two Governments concerned.

In case of failure to reach agreement, the President of the Tribunal and two other persons, either of whom may in case of need take his place, shall be chosen by the Council of the League of Nations....

These persons shall be nationals of powers that have remained neutral during the war.

If in case there is a vacancy a Government does not proceed within a period of one month to appoint as provided above a member of the Tribunal, such member shall be chosen by the other Government from the two persons mentioned above other than the President.

The decision of the majority of the members of the Tribunal shall be the decision of the Tribunal.

. . .

(c) If the number of cases justifies it, additional members shall be appointed and each Mixed Arbitral Tribunal shall sit in divisions. Each of these divisions will be constituted as above.

(g) The High Contracting Parties agree to regard the decisions of the Mixed Arbitral Tribunal as final and conclusive, and to render them binding upon their nationals.[261]

An Annex to this provision specified:

ANNEX

1. Should one of the members of the tribunal either die, retire or be unable for any reason whatever to discharge his functions, the same procedure will be followed for filling the vacancy as was followed for appointing him.[262]

---

[260] Ibid.   [261] Ibid., pp. 599–600.   [262] Ibid., pp. 600–601.

Other attempts at settlement having proved unproductive, various of the Hungarian optants presented claims to the Rumanian-Hungarian Mixed Arbitral Tribunal. In the principal case of *Emeric Kulin père c. Etat Roumain*,[263] Rumania demurred to the tribunal's jurisdiction, maintaining, *inter alia*, that the Treaty of Trianon's restrictions only concerned measures affecting uncompensated retention of enemy property. While reserving for the merits questions such as whether Rumania had discriminated against Hungarian nationals and whether promised compensation was adequate, the tribunal found that it had jurisdiction to adjudge whether or not the Rumanian expropriatory measures fell within the range of measures covered by the Treaty.[264] The Rumanian-appointed arbitrator dissented.[265]

Rumania, which had in its pleadings on jurisdiction warned that in any event it would refuse to plead the substance of the case, then announced that it would not accept the judgment; it recalled its arbitrator, and declared that he would not participate in any cases relating to the agrarian reform.

The Council of the League of Nations, to which both Rumania and Hungary then appealed, was confronted with two conflicting claims. Rumania invoked Article 11, paragraph 2 of the Covenant, claiming that the Mixed Arbitral Tribunal had exceeded its jurisdiction; that its decision was null; and that to permit a challenge to Rumanian agrarian reform to go forward would threaten the Rumanian social fabric if not the peace of Europe. Hungary countered with the request that the Council appoint substitute arbitrators pursuant to the Treaty of Trianon. It maintained that for the Council to deal with the substance of the case would undermine the integrity of the arbitral process. But if the Council wished to examine the validity of the judgment of the Mixed Arbitral Tribunal on its jurisdiction, recourse should be had to the Permanent Court of International Justice for an advisory opinion. While there was some sympathy for the latter proposal in the Council, it was not pursued because of Rumanian opposition. The League Council

---

[263] VII *Recueil des Décisions des Tribunaux Arbitraux Mixtes* (1927–1928), p. 138. The President of the Tribunal was Mr. de Cedercrantz. (The judgment appears in French; a translation into English is found in Deák, *supra* note 255, pp. 181–189.)

[264] VII *Recueil des Décisions des Tribunaux Arbitraux Mixtes, surpa* note 263, p. 138.

[265] Ibid., p. 151.

proceeded to deal with the problem in a manner that aroused considerable criticism, a criticism that has not vanished with the years.[266] The upshot was that it proposed to appoint substitute arbitrators if Hungary would accept conditions which would gravely prejudice the merits of its case.[267] This Hungary declined to do. Finally, the Council, over the objections of Rumania, decided to appoint substitute arbitrators to a Mixed Arbitral Tribunal that would be expanded from three to five members.[268] Not long thereafter, Rumania reached a settlement with Hungary.[269]

The cases of the *Hungarian Optants* do not illumine the question of the authority of a truncated arbitral tribunal to render valid awards, because apparently that question was never confronted. Hungary did not argue that the truncated tribunal could render awards; Rumania did not argue the contrary. At most, it might be

---

[266] See Reisman, *supra* note 103 and the statements of Professor Scelle: "[T]he case also shows that it is not advisable, in order to settle a dispute and complete a tribunal, to appeal to a political organ, in this case the Council of the League of Nations. The Committee of the Council appointed to study the case tried first of all to bring about a compromise between the parties *on the substance of the dispute*, which amounted indirectly to taking the case out of the tribunal's hands. The Committee even recommended that the dispute should be brought before the Hague Court. It then consulted a committee of jurists and invited the parties to limit the powers of the mixed arbitral tribunal by mutual agreement, which constituted a violation of the principle that a tribunal decides on its own competence and cannot have a case taken out of its hands. Lastly, Sir Austen Chamberlain's report proceeded to even greater lengths of illegality by proposing a penalty in case the parties did not accept the conclusions of the Committee of the Council. This penalty was to consist in not appointing the neutral arbitrators required to complete the tribunal, although under the Treaty of Trianon the Council was strictly bound to make these appointments. The object of this abuse of power was to interfere with the course of justice. Fortunately, the rapporteur's opinions were contested by the representatives of Italy (the jurist Scialoja), Holland (the Minister Loudon), Colombia (the jurist Urrutia), and Germany (the Minister Streseman), who drew attention to 'the dangerous medley of political and legal questions.'" (U.N. doc. A/CN.4/18, pp. 34–35.) See also Seifi, *supra* note 125, pp. 36–39; Hazel Fox, "States and the Undertaking to Arbitrate," in Loukas A. Mistelis and Julian D.M. Lew (eds.), *Arbitration Insights: Twenty Years of the Annual Lecture of the School of International Arbitration* (2007), p. 13.

[267] 8 League of Nations *Official Journal* (1921), pp. 1379 ff. See Reisman, *supra* note 103, pp. 692 ff.; Deák, *supra* note 255, pp. 86–145.

[268] 9 League of Nations *Official Journal* (1928), p. 446.

[269] See "International Agreements Regarding the Financial Obligations of Hungary Resulting from the Treaty of Trianon," 25 *American Journal of International Law Supplement* (1931), pp. 19, 29, 39.

inferred that Rumania, in withdrawing its arbitrator from specified cases, acted on the assumption that the tribunal so truncated for the agrarian reform cases would not be able to act, and that Hungary, by not calling upon the truncated tribunal to proceed with the agrarian reform cases, acquiesced in that assumption.

That is a possible but not a necessary inference. It is as, if not more, plausible to infer that Hungary was of the view that the procedural and substantive rights of its nationals depended vitally upon strict implementation of the pertinent provisions of the Treaty of Trianon; that that Treaty contained express provision to meet the contingency of vacancies occurring in the membership of a Mixed Arbitral Tribunal; and that, accordingly, the required course of action was to call upon the League Council to fulfil its responsibilities under that Treaty provision and to appoint a substitute arbitrator who would fully reconstitute the tribunal. Where an arbitration agreement provides for a means to fill a vacancy, a party which invokes that means cannot reasonably be said to have acquiesced in the contention (which was not debated in the *Hungarian Optants* affair in any event) that, if it did not invoke that means, or if the means once invoked were not implemented, the truncated tribunal would lack the authority to render a valid award. It was the more reasonable for Hungary to invoke the Treaty provisions for appointment of substitute arbitrators since the League Council had applied identical provisions and appointed substitute arbitrators in earlier cases.[270]

Moreover, there was every practical reason for Hungary to seek an award rendered not by a truncated but by a fully constituted tribunal. If Rumania took part, it could the less plausibly claim that the judgment was irregularly reached. And it would be the more awkward for Rumania to refuse to carry out the tribunal's judgment which the Treaty bound it to observe. If Rumania did not restore its arbitrator but the tribunal were reconstituted by the addition of a substitute arbitrator named pursuant to processes of the League Council, then, if Rumania were to defy resultant awards, it would put itself in a position of appearing to defy the then considerable authority of the League Council as well as the terms of the Treaty of

---

[270] See the Council's appointment of substitute arbitrators to the Franco-German, Franco-Austrian, Franco-Hungarian, and Franco-Bulgarian Mixed Arbitral Tribunals, 4 League of Nations *Official Journal* (1923), p. 242.

Trianon. Furthermore, in the last analysis, Hungary had to depend on Rumania carrying out the tribunal's judgments, if not freely then under a measured international pressure. (Clearly the League was not prepared to impose sanctions on Rumania in the circumstances.) Thus Hungary at once sought an award whose validity Rumania could not plausibly impugn and an award rendered in circumstances likely to conduce to wider international support of Hungary's position. If Hungary considered the possibility of moving the truncated Tribunal to proceed, it had every strategic reason to put aside that possibility even if it had concluded that the truncated Tribunal would have been entitled to do so.

In short, speculations that may be made in the cases of the *Hungarian Optants* do not contribute to resolving the question of the authority of a truncated international arbitral tribunal.[271]

At the same time, Professor Reisman has concluded that "the League Council's recommended solution suggests that the withdrawal was unlawful...."[272] by which he appears to mean that the fact that the League Council ultimately resolved unconditionally to appoint substitute arbitrators while calling on Rumania to restore its arbitrator[273] indicates that the League Council recognized that the Rumanian withdrawal of its nationally-appointed arbitrator was unlawful. It is plain that Rumania's withdrawal of its arbitrator in response to an unimpeachable decision on jurisdiction was unlawful; and, while the League Council could have been more expeditious and forthright in so concluding, Professor Reisman's opinion that it did so conclude, however belatedly and inferentially, appears to be correct.

---

[271] Looking to the particular facts at hand, Judge Seifi notes that the Treaty of Trianon provided for the establishment of a three-member tribunal and provided for a mechanism for the replacement of a withdrawing arbitrator by a third party. Accordingly, Judge Seifi contends that the *Hungarian Optants* cases imply an exclusion of the right of an incomplete tribunal to function. See Seifi, *supra* note 125, pp. 36–39. Fox appears to view the *Hungarian Optants* cases as indicating that the unilateral withdrawal of a party-appointed arbitrator after the constitution of the tribunal terminates the arbitration and the arbitrators' powers. Fox as a consequence sees truncated tribunals as a "serious challenge to the immutability of the arbitration." See Fox, *supra* note 266, p. 13 fn. 21.
[272] Reisman, *supra* note 103, p. 473.
[273] 9 League of Nations *Official Journal* (1928), pp. 414 ff., 426 ff., 436 ff., particularly p. 446.

The *French-Mexican Claims Commission* cases are squarely in point, but what that point is, is contentious.[274] France and Mexico in 1924 concluded a claims convention, providing for the establishment of a three-member Claims Commission, one member to be named by Mexico, a second by France, and a third, the President, by the agreement of the two Governments or, failing that, by appointment of the President of the Administrative Council of the Permanent Court of Arbitration. Article 1 of the Convention provided:

En cas de décès d'un membre de la commission ainsi qu'au cas où un membre de la commission serait empêché, ou, pour une raison quelconque, s'abstiendrait de remplir ses fonctions, il serait remplacé immédiatement suivant la procédure employée pour pourvoir à sa nomination.[275]

It was specified that claims of French nationals or companies for losses suffered in the Mexican Revolution would be submitted to the Commission. Mexico undertook to meet those claims, where established, *ex gratia*, even if she would not be liable under international law, provided that they were of a stipulated origin. The Convention further provided that the Commission would establish its procedures in conformity with the Convention, and that the decision of a majority of members would be the decision of the Commission.[276] The Commission was to decide the claims presented it within two years of its first meeting, which took place on March 14, 1925,[277]

---

[274] See, e.g., Seifi, *supra* note 125, pp. 29–30, noting the conflicting interpretations of the precedent set by the cases.
[275] V *U.N.R.I.A.A.*, p. 313.   [276] Article 4, ibid., pp. 314–315.
[277] Feller, *supra* note 239, p. 69. See also A. de la Pradelle, *Recueil général périodique et critique des décisions, conventions et lois relatives au droit international public et privé* (1936), pp. 10–21. A condensed report of the Commission's essential procedural decisions contained in the *Annual Digest of Public International Law Cases 1929–1930*, pp. 424–426, is of particular interest because that report, including its statement of the facts, was prepared by Professor Verzijl, the Commission's second President. See also *La Réparation des Dommages Causés aux Etrangers par des Mouvements Révolutionnaires, Jurisprudence de la Commission Franco-Mexicaine des Réclamations (1924–1932)*, 1933, a collection of the Commission's four principal awards, which contains an introduction by Professor Verzijl which summarizes the history of the Commission and which contains Verzijl's comments about what he views as the "obstruction" of the Mexican Commissioner (p. xii) and the

under the chairmanship of Dr. Rodrigo Octavio (Brazil). During that first session, the rules of procedure were drawn up but no cases were argued or decided.[278]

On March 12, 1927, a second convention was signed,[279] which extended the life of the Commission to nine months following its first meeting after the entry into force of the second convention. If the Commission proved unable to complete its work during that period, the convention provided for its extension by an exchange of notes between the two governments. It was also provided that, as soon as possible after the exchange of ratifications, the Parties would proceed to appoint a Commission President. If they did not agree, he was to be appointed by the President of the Administrative Council of the Permanent Court of Arbitration.

The first President having resigned, the Permanent Court of Arbitration designated Professor J.H.W. Verzijl (Netherlands) as President. The Commission reassembled under his chairmanship on March 26, 1928. It had before it 251 claims. During this session, which lasted until October 19, 1928, a number of cases were argued and three awards were made, from all of which the Mexican Commissioner dissented.

At the end of the session, it was agreed among the Commissioners that they would exchange drafts of their opinions on the other cases that had been argued and on which oral proceedings had been declared terminated.[280] During the next four months, the President and the French Commissioner prepared and exchanged draft opinions, but they received no communication from the Mexican Commissioner.[281] The nine-month period provided for in the 1927 Convention expired on December 26, 1928. Owing to delays on the part of the Mexican government, the exchange of notes that was necessary to extend the Commission for another nine months did not take place until April 17, 1929.[282] That simple

---

"irregular" efforts of the Mexican Government to "intimidate" the President of the Commission (pp. viii–ix, note 1). See also Luis Miguel Díaz, *México y las comisiones internacionales de reclamación* (1983), vol. II, pp. 1171–1238.

[278] The text of the rules of procedure is published in de la Pradelle, *supra* note 277, pp. 18–21.

[279] V *U.N.R.I.A.A.*, p. 316.

[280] Feller, *supra* note 239, p. 70. Feller bases this statement on a statement by Professor Verzijl.

[281] Ibid.   [282] *Annual Digest, supra* note 277, p. 424.

exchange of notes extending the life of the Commission made no reference to the possibility of replacing the President of the Commission.[283] In the meantime, because of the provision of Article VII of the Convention of 1924 providing that the Commission must decide on each claim within six months following the termination of the hearing on that claim, and because the hearings on several claims had been declared closed on September 6, 1928 the President concluded that either decisions would have to be rendered before March 6, 1929, or the pending cases that had been declared closed would have to be reopened.[284] Consequently, the President and the French Commissioner met in Paris on March 5, 1929 and handed down a decision reopening the proceedings in those cases.[285] According to Verzijl, the Mexican Commissioner was not informed of this meeting because of lack of time.[286]

On March 23, 1929, President Verzijl, in agreement with the French Commissioner, wrote to the Mexican Commissioner proposing that a session be called in Mexico City on May 13, 1929. Receiving as before no reply, he officially convoked the Commission for May 16, having been informed by the French government on April 23 that notes extending the Commission's tenure had been exchanged between France and Mexico. Verzijl received communications from the Mexican government dated April 20 and May 2, both addressed to him in his capacity as President of the Commission, the latter requesting that the session be postponed because of the inability of the Mexican Commissioner to take part. Since only five months remained to complete the Commission's large docket, Verzijl declined a postponement and, on arriving in Mexico on May 15, requested the Mexican government to designate a substitute Commissioner in accordance with the Convention.[287] But the Mexican government had, on May 7, informed the French government that it considered that Verzijl's functions as President terminated on December 26, 1928 (the date of termination of the Convention of 1927) and proposed to the French government the appointment of a new President. Mexico made no reply to Verzijl's request. For its part, the French government refused to entertain the Mexican proposals for appointment of a new President and continued to recognize Verzijl as President.[288]

---

[283] Ibid. See also V *U.N.R.I.A.A.*, p. 511.   [284] Feller, *supra* note 239, pp. 70–71.
[285] Ibid.   [286] Ibid., note 37.   [287] Ibid., pp. 71–72.
[288] *Annual Digest, supra* note 277, p. 425.

Verzijl proceeded formally to convoke the Commission to meet on May 29, referring the controversy over his status to it. While France assented to the meeting, and declared that the French Commissioner, Secretary, and Agent would attend, Mexico did not replace the silent Mexican Commissioner, forbad the Mexican Secretary to attend, and charged the President with having abused his powers.[289] Mexico informed Verzijl that it no longer considered him to be the Commission's President. The Commission nevertheless met on June 3, in the absence of the Mexican Commissioner, Agent, and Secretary and without official Mexican facilities. Two decisions were handed down, the first affirming that Verzijl continued to be President and declaring the session competent, the second declaring the oral proceedings of pending cases that had been reopened to be closed. It was announced that the Commission would proceed to render awards in these cases, whose argument was complete.

In the former decision, the Commission held that:

...although a Government may not be denied the right to propose at any moment the replacement of an umpire in office, such a proposal cannot produce any juridical effect until it has been accepted by the other Government and has thus led to a joint decision; that, therefore, a unilateral dismissal must be considered as null and void; that, indeed, the joint appointment of an umpire is a bilateral international juridical act with the effects of an international convention and creating in particular the reciprocal engagement of the States concerned to maintain the umpire in office until the manifestation of their common will to dismiss him.[290]

Thus the Commission majority held that Verzijl remained President and that its meeting was regularly convened.

In its second decision, the Commission held that:

...neither the Mexican Commissioner's unwillingness to notify to his fellow Commissioners his opinions on the cases previously pleaded in the presence of the three Commissioners, nor the absence of representation of Mexico in the Commission after its regular resumption of business,

---

[289] Ibid.
[290] Ibid., p. 425. For full texts in French, see V *U.N.R.I.A.A.*, pp. 509, 510, 512; de la Pradelle, *supra* note 277, and Feller, *supra* note 239, pp. 72, note 39; 73, note 40; and 74, note 41.

form a juridical obstacle to the pronouncing of the award in those cases by a majority decision.[291]

Thus the Commission held that, though truncated, it was empowered to proceed to render valid awards.

The Commission then proceeded to render awards in 23 claims that earlier had been fully argued. The Mexican Commissioner was absent throughout. On June 24, the Commission decided, on a motion of the French Agent, that it should suspend meetings until it could be regularly reconstituted. In so doing, the Commission adopted a further decision in which its President held:

... notwithstanding the Mexican Government's attitude the Commission would be entitled to continue its work; that, on the one hand, the unilateral refusal of a State to recognise a regularly appointed umpire in the regular performance of his functions is contrary to international law; that it must not impede the regular functioning of the Commission; and that, on the other hand, the Mexican Government's refusal to replace its Commissioner was contrary to its formal engagement under Article I of the Convention and must not form a juridical obstacle to continuing the work of the Commission, since yielding to this illegal attitude would amount to disregarding the general principle of law according to which no one may take advantage, in his own favour, of the non-fulfilment of his engagements.[292]

Professor Verzijl resigned from the Commission on August 29, 1929.[293]

Thereafter, France and Mexico negotiated a further Convention of August 2, 1930. It provided for the establishment of a two-member Commission, one member named by each government, which was to pass upon claims; if it failed to reach agreement, any such cases would be referred to an umpire. The decisions rendered by the Commission under the Convention of 1924 apparently were to be binding; at the same time, however, the claims that were referred to the new Commission were listed in an appendix to the 1930 Convention – and every one of the claims dealt with in the awards rendered in the absence of the Mexican Commissioner by the Verzijl Commission was in fact listed in that appendix. Thus in

---

[291] *Annual Digest, supra* note 277, p. 425. [292] Ibid., pp. 425–426.
[293] Feller, *supra* note 239, p. 75. Passages of the text of his letter of resignation are reproduced in French, ibid., pp. 75–76, note 42.

effect only final decisions rendered by the Commission prior to the withdrawal of the Mexican Commissioner were treated as binding by the Parties. The new Commission met in Mexico City and completed all its work in the course of 1931, without recourse to an umpire. In Feller's book, there is a list of the sums awarded by the Verzijl Commission and by its successor on the same claims. In some cases, the reorganized Commission made the same awards; in other cases, lower – sometimes markedly lower – awards.[294]

From what Feller calls this "unfortunate"[295] history diverse conclusions have been drawn. In the *Peace Treaties* case, the United States of America argued as follows:

Where, in an international arbitration, one party becoming aware of the prospect of an award against it brings about the withdrawal of its appointed arbitrator, this default is held ineffective to frustrate the arbitration....

In the *French-Mexican Mixed Claims* case, a convention of March 1927 between France and Mexico provided for the arbitration of certain international claims. Subsequently, the Mexican Government took the position that the commission president's functions had already expired, and proposed to the French Government the appointment of a new umpire. The French Government declined to accept this proposal. Thereafter, the Mexican commissioner absented himself from the commission. The commission then proceeded, with the President and the French commissioner present, to dispose of the cases which had already been presented to the commission. They held that the absence of representation of Mexico in the commission did not form a juridical obstacle to the making of awards by majority decision.[296]

The United States thus construes the *French-Mexican Claims Commission* cases as a precedent unequivocally supporting the authority of the truncated arbitral tribunal to render a valid award.

Balasko takes a like position. After setting out the history of the French-Mexican Claims Commission in some detail, and quoting in full the Commission's decision of June 3, 1929 by which it affirmed that Verzijl remained President, that the convocation of the Commission by him was effective and that its session was regular, Balasko declares: "We are entirely in agreement with the reasoning of this

---

[294] Ibid., pp. 76–77, especially note 44a.   [295] Ibid., p. 315.
[296] *Interpretation of Peace Treaties with Bulgaria, Hungary and Romania, Pleadings, Oral Arguments, Documents*, pp. 231–232.

decision."[297] He adds: "Juridically, there was no obstacle to the Commission's rendering judgment on the cases pending before it...."[298] He further maintains that the opinion of the President of the Commission rendered when the Commission decided to suspend its sittings was "not subject to attack on the juridical plane."[299] He concluded that the Mexican complaint about the Commission's inability to act "was refuted in an impeccable manner by the Commission itself" in its decision of 3 June 1929.[300]

Professor Carlston, after summarizing the facts and noting that although the President of the Commission "continued to affirm that the two commissioners had the power to continue the sessions and that Mexico could not escape its obligations under the treaty," notes that nevertheless a new commission was established to decide, among others, the claims that the "rump commission" had purported to decide. He concludes:

The fact relied upon as evidencing consent by Mexico to extension of the life of the commission, the letter addressed by Mexico to Mr. Verzijl in his capacity of presiding commissioner after the life of the commission would otherwise have terminated according to the *compromis*, lacked that clear showing of intent to waive jurisdictional objections necessary to support a conferment of jurisdictional powers otherwise lacking.[301]

But Carlston makes clear that, in his view, the absence of the Mexican Commissioner at the direction of his government deprived the tribunal of "its judicial quality and power to decide."[302]

As noted above, Professor Scelle differs; in his capacity as Special Rapporteur of the International Law Commission, he gave "full approval" to the course of action followed by the President of the Commission in rendering 23 awards in the absence of the Mexican Commissioner.[303] Judge Hudson was more reserved. He stated:

The decisions of the French-Mexican Claims Commission in 1927 [sic] had been taken in the absence of the Mexican member, and it would be recalled that the decisions had been impugned by the Mexican

---

[297] A. Balasko, *The Process of International Arbitration* (1946), pp. 268–279. Translation supplied.

[298] Ibid., p. 280.   [299] Ibid.   [300] Ibid.   [301] Carlston, *supra* note 15, p. 47.

[302] Ibid., p. 44.

[303] *Yearbook of the International Law Commission 1950*, *supra* note 14, vol. II, p. 127.

Government. Later, the Governments of France and Mexico had reached a compromise without, however, solving the question of principle.[304]

Feller drew no conclusions about the validity of the awards rendered by Verzijl's truncated tribunal. For his part, Reisman, unlike Carlston, does construe Mexico's communications to President Verzijl as indicating that it viewed the Commission as authorized to continue its work.[305] He continues:

The central question raised by this case is not whether the commission's life has been extended validly, but whether the commission's decision to continue without Mexican participation was lawful. The 1930 convention may be understood as a controlling decision to the effect that the commission's ruling was unlawful. The wisdom of the tribunal's decision may be questioned: Verzijl, the presiding commissioner, had a valid reason for avoiding postponement, since the commission had but a short time in which to complete its work. The law's generous presumption of good faith suggests that both France and Mexico wanted the commission to finish its task, and the *compromis* did provide for the appointment of a substitute in case the original national commissioner were unable to attend the proceedings. Substitution, as Verzijl suggested, would have imposed no hardship on Mexico; furthermore, Mexico had contracted for it. On the other hand, it is clear that once Mexico abstained from the commission, it would have been quite difficult to bring about compliance with its decisions. The conflict in this case was between the limit *ratione temporis* of the tribunal and a signatory's desire to participate in the commission's decisions. The problem of temporal duration is extremely complicated, but in the case of claims commissions, where time is often *not* of the essence, it can be avoided by providing for a system of "stopping the clock" when one of the signatories requests a postponement. Verzijl's decision to proceed, though undiplomatic, was not incorrect. The fact that the commission subsequently terminated proceedings reveals the presiding commissioner's uneasiness and the failure of his strategy.[306]

Thus Reisman, on the one hand, suggests that the 1930 Convention "may be understood" as a "controlling decision" holding the

[304] *Yearbook of the International Law Commission 1952, supra* note 36, vol. I, p. 35. See also Manley O. Hudson, *International Tribunals* (1944), pp. 53–54.
[305] Reisman, *supra* note 103, pp. 467–468.
[306] Ibid., pp. 467. *Yearbook of the International Law Commission 1952, supra* note 36, vol. I, p. 468. See also Holtzmann and Schwebel, et al., *supra* note 101, p. 244, quoting Reisman on the *French-Mexican Claims Commission* cases.

rendering of awards by the truncated tribunal to have been unlawful; on the other hand, he maintains that Verzijl's decision to proceed was "not incorrect."

What conclusions may be reasonably drawn from the history of the *French-Mexican Claims Commission* cases, illuminated or clouded as they may be by the foregoing quite divergent interpretations? It is believed that they are as follows:

– The *French-Mexican Claims Commission* cases embody a clear and correct holding that a truncated international arbitral tribunal from which an arbitrator has withdrawn at the direction of the State which appointed him or her may validly proceed and hand down awards.[307]

– The Commission's President was right to render the fundamental judgment that, to yield to unlawful withdrawal by holding the Commission to be incompetent "would amount to disregarding the general principle of law according to which no one may take advantage, in his own favour, of the non-fulfilment of his engagements."[308]

– The fact that France and Mexico subsequently concluded a convention which remitted to a reconstituted tribunal reconsideration of the awards rendered by the truncated tribunal "may be understood" – but equally, may not be understood – as a "controlling decision" to the effect that a truncated arbitral tribunal lacks the authority to render valid awards. In Judge Hudson's words, the compromise embodied in the 1930 Convention did not solve "the question of principle."[309] This is so in part because that convention nowhere describes as invalid the awards delivered by the truncated tribunal; rather the 1930 Convention indicates that the reason for consideration of certain claims *de novo* is that those claims were still in issue at the time when the work of that 1924 Commission came to an end,[310] a statement which may be interpreted as referring to the established

---

[307] See also *Redfern and Hunter on International Arbitration*, *supra* note 106, pp. 281–283.

[308] *Annual Digest*, *supra* note 277, p. 426.   [309] See Hudson, *supra* note 304.

[310] V *U.N.R.I.A.A.*, p. 318. "*Cette liste comprend les réclamations qui ont été dûment présentées devant la commission mixte créée par la convention du septembre 1924 et qui étaient encore en instance lors de la fin des travaux de cette commission.*"

December 26, 1928 date when the Convention expired rather than the indeterminate time when the Mexican Commissioner withdrew (he had indeed been *incommunicado* for some time before December 26, 1928). The Parties in an exchange of notes in April, 1929, agreed to extend the life of the Commission. But that act was quickly followed by the proposal of Mexico to replace the President whose tenure it claimed had expired on December 26; in the Mexican view, that December date rather than the unspecified time of the withdrawal of the Mexican Commissioner may be seen as the critical date.

Two quite different interpretations of the facts are possible. One interpretation is that France and Mexico set up a new commission and agreed to remit to it for reconsideration awards of the truncated tribunal because they believed that those awards were not validly rendered either by reason of the absence of the Mexican Commissioner, or by reason of the presence of Verzijl over Mexican objections as President, or for both reasons. But another interpretation is that France and Mexico so agreed, with Mexico alone holding to one or both of these positions, because France – whose agent and commissioner participated in the processes of the rendering of the 23 disputed awards – so agreed solely for expedient political reasons unrelated to its perception of the validity of those awards of the truncated tribunal. After all, France was more interested in having awards rendered by a process that would result in Mexican payment of these 23 and many other claims than it was in insisting upon the validity of 23 awards Mexico would not pay while, at the same time, foregoing all possibility of awards being rendered in other outstanding claims.

Since the various inferences that plausibly may be made about the motivation and effect of the 1930 Convention are contradictory, we are left with only one clear fact: the truncated Commission itself, after delivering a reasoned, reasonable, and principled opinion upholding its authority to proceed and to render awards, did render awards. Moreover, it suspended its sittings while reaffirming the regularity of its truncated session and the authority of a truncated arbitral tribunal. The subsequent ambiguous agreement and action of the French and Mexican governments do not vitiate the importance of this precedent.

(H) *LENA GOLDFIELDS ARBITRATION*

The essential facts of the *Lena Goldfields* arbitration have been set forth in the first chapter and need not be repeated.[311] But in the context of this chapter, it may be useful to amplify what was said earlier about the arbitration clause of the concession agreement which was concluded in 1925 between the government of the Union of Soviet Socialist Republics and a British Corporation, Lena Goldfields, and what followed from it.

Article 90 of the agreement provided:

All disputes and misunderstandings in regard to the construing of fulfill-ment of this Agreement...on the declaration of either of the parties, are examined and settled by the Court of Arbitration.[312]

The agreement provided that the Court of Arbitration was to consist of three members, one selected by the government, one by Lena, and the third chosen by mutual agreement. Failing such agreement, Lena was to select the super-arbitrator from a list of candidates drawn by the government from the faculties either

---

[311] Chapter I, *supra.* An extensive report of the case is found in *The Times* (London), September 3, 1930, p. 7. That report is largely reprinted in A. Nussbaum, "The Arbitration between the Lena Goldfields, Ltd., and the Soviet Government," 36 *Cornell Law Quarterly* (1950), pp. 42 ff. See also V. V. Veeder, "The *Lena Goldfields* Arbitration: The Historical Roots of Three Ideas" 47 *International and Comparative Law Quarterly* (1998), p. 747, and see further, for another case arising out of a Soviet-era dispute that is of tangential relevance to the question of truncated arbitral tribunals, the "Soviet eggs" case as recounted by Veeder in "The Natural Limits to the Truncated Tribunal: The German Case of the Soviet Eggs and the Dutch Abduction of the Indonesian Arbitrator," in R. Briner, Y. Fortier, K.P. Berger and J. Bredow (eds.) *Law of International Business and Dispute Settlement in the 21st Century: Liber Amicorum Karl-Heinz Böckstiegel* (2001), p. 795. The relevant arbitration agreement was contained in the 1925 German-Soviet Treaty, Article VI of which contained an Agreement Concerning Commercial Courts of Arbitration, and which itself contained an early example of a process for replacing a recalcitrant arbitrator, including where an arbitrator "refuse[d] to accept or fulfill the duties of the office of the arbitrator." In the "Soviet eggs" case itself, between a German company and a Soviet entity, the president of an arbitral tribunal had replaced the German company's appointed arbitrator upon his twice being unable to travel to Moscow on short notice of a hearing, and that reconstituted tribunal proceeded to attend the hearing and deliver an award. The German courts refused to enforce the award on the basis that the replaced arbitrator had not "refuse[d] to accept or fulfill the duties of the office of the arbitrator" and he had therefore been improperly replaced (by a Soviet arbitrator, no less).

[312] *The Times, supra* note 311, p. 7.

of the Mining Academy of Freiberg or the High Technical School of Stockholm. If one of the parties or its arbitrator should default, the agreement further provided that:

> ... then, at the request of the other party, the matter in dispute is settled by the super-arbitrator and the other member of the Court, on condition that such decision is unanimous.[313]

When, by 1929, the New Economic Policy was replaced by a radically changed Soviet government policy toward private enterprise, Lena, which in its first years operated profitably, maintained that the government rendered performance of the concession agreement impossible. Citing what it viewed as manifest and grave violations of the concession agreement, it invoked arbitration. Lena submitted to arbitration its claim that the government had rendered performance impossible and prevented Lena from enjoying its rights, and claimed compensation. The government agreed without qualification to the arbitration of these claims, while raising defenses and counterclaims. Lena Goldfields appointed as its arbitrator a former Attorney General, Sir Leslie Scott; the government appointed a Soviet national, Dr. S.B. Chlenow; and both elected as super-arbitrator Dr. Otto Stutzer, professor of mining at the Mining College of Freiberg, Saxony.[314]

After the Soviet government and Lena had requested the super-arbitrator to fix a date for convening the tribunal but before it met, the Soviet government telegraphed that Lena had "dissolved the Concession Agreement" by its stating that it took no further responsibilities by refusing further financing, and withdrawing the power of attorney of its representatives.[315] Lena replied that the Arbitration Court was properly and completely constituted, but from this point the Soviet government refused to participate in the arbitration, as did its appointed arbitrator, Dr. Chlenow. Dr. Chlenow, notably, made it clear to the Soviet government at the time that his refusal to participate in the arbitration (upon the government's instructions, it was clear) was unlikely to prove an effective legal step:

> In accordance with your instructions I do not consider myself an arbitrator any more and I did not attend the session of the arbitration court.

[313] Ibid.   [314] Ibid. See Nussbaum, *supra* note 311, pp. 31, 33.
[315] *The Times, supra* note 311, p. 7.

However, I consider it my duty to warn you that the position you have taken is legally very doubtful. Both parties can ask the arbitrators to recognise the arbitration as not having taken place or as having been stopped, but I have doubts that one party has the right to declare that the arbitration did not take place. It is my opinion that a party does not have the right, once the arbitration tribunal has been constituted, to call back the arbitrator it has appointed if the calling-back is legally unjustified; and the non-appearance of one of the arbitrators does give the right to the remaining two arbitrators to continue the arbitration proceedings without him. According to the newspapers, Lena Goldfields is determined to demand the continuation of the arbitration in spite of my absence. What position will you take up in that case?[316]

As V. V. Veeder noted, "[n]o expert today on the truncated tribunal could have drafted a statement on the point in clearer terms."[317] Tragically, Dr. Chlenov was arrested in 1936 for "participating in a counter-revolutionary terrorist organisation" and executed in 1937 following a secret hearing before the Military Collegium of the USSR Supreme Court.[318]

In the absence of the Soviet-named arbitrator and a Soviet Agent, the Court of Arbitration met and ruled that it had been duly constituted.[319] It declared that it was proved to the satisfaction of the Court that:

Lena would not have entered into the Concession Agreement at all but for the presence in the contract of this arbitration clause and of the preceding clause . . . whereby it was mutually agreed that "the parties base their relations with regard to this agreement on the principle of goodwill and good faith, as well as on reasonable interpretation of the terms of the agreement."[320]

It further decided:

. . . that the Concession Agreement was still operative and that according to the plain language of Article 90, paragraph 6, the jurisdiction of the Court remained unaffected . . . .[321]

The Soviet government, however, adhered to its decision not to attend the arbitration, and wholly repudiated "the Court and all the arbitration proceedings."[322] The Court subsequently held:

---

[316] V. V. Veeder, "The *Lena Goldfields* Arbitration: The Historical Roots of Three Ideas," *supra* note 311, pp. 747, 779.
[317] Ibid., p. 779.　　[318] Ibid., p. 781.　　[319] *The Times, supra* note 311, p. 7.
[320] Ibid.　　[321] Ibid.　　[322] Ibid.

Although the Government has thus refused its assistance to the Court, it remains bound by its obligations under the Concession Agreement and in particular by the terms of Article 90, the arbitration clause of the contract.[323]

On September 2, 1930, the Court rendered judgment in favor of Lena, awarding it very large damages plus interest.[324] Eventually, after repeated and vigorous diplomatic interventions by the British government, the Soviet government entered into a settlement agreement, which it partially implemented.[325]

While the *Lena Goldfields* arbitration has been cited as authority for the entitlement of a truncated international arbitral tribunal to proceed and render an award,[326] it may be distinguished on the ground that the arbitration clause itself in *Lena* expressly authorized two of the three arbitrators to render a decision where the other party-appointed arbitrator defaulted.[327]

Yet on analysis does this provision serve to distinguish the case? If a truncated arbitral tribunal is not entitled to render a valid award, then the *Lena Goldfields* Court of Arbitration was not so entitled, for it was manifestly truncated. Of course, the arbitration clause anticipated the possibility of default by a party or its arbitrator and authorized the two remaining members of the tribunal to render an award on the condition that those members acted unanimously. But to say that the truncated tribunal in *Lena* could act because of the terms of this clause is actually to say that (a) a truncated arbitral tribunal is empowered to render a binding award (b) if the parties to the arbitration agreement intended to authorize the tribunal to act even in the absence of a member, and (c) manifested that intention, as in the *Lena* case by the terms of the arbitration agreement.

So analyzed, the question comes down to one of intention. What do the parties to a treaty providing for arbitration, or to an international contract providing for arbitration, intend? Where, as in the

---

[323] Ibid.   [324] Ibid.   [325] Nussbaum, *supra* note 311, pp. 34–36.

[326] E.g. by the US government in its pleadings in the *Peace Treaties Case*. See *Interpretation of Peace Treaties with Bulgaria, Hungary and Romania (Second Phase)*, I.C.J. *Reports 1950*, pp. 231, 233.

[327] See, e.g., Seifi, *supra* note 125, pp. 26–27; Andrea Ernst, "Lena Goldfields Arbitration," in *Max Planck Encyclopedia of Public International Law* (2014), para. 17.

Lena Goldfields case, the arbitration agreement states their intention, the question is plainly answered. Where, as is generally the situation, the arbitration agreement either says nothing about the powers of the tribunal in the absence of an arbitrator, or provides that an absent arbitrator shall be replaced (normally by the original process of appointment), then the intention of the parties should be inferred from the terms of the agreement and from the agreement's context. It is typical in the context of disputes between a State or State entity and a foreign investor that the agreement to arbitrate is so indispensable that there would have been no investment contract without it. In these cases, it can be presumed that the parties cannot have intended to allow either to frustrate unilaterally the arbitration clause by withdrawing its appointed arbitrator.

Such a conclusion was reached by the tribunal in the *Himpurna* arbitration, discussed in regards to its other conclusions in the previous chapter and in more detail in regards to truncated tribunals below.[328] There the tribunal, expressly looking to the analysis provided in the first edition, adopted the view that the truncated arbitral tribunal in the *Lena Goldfields* case rendered the award because it concluded that it could not have been the parties' intention to make the arbitration susceptible to frustration by one of the party-appointed arbitrators.[329]

(I) THE SABOTAGE CASES

The so-called *Sabotage* cases (otherwise known as the *Black Tom* and *Kingsland*, or *Lehigh Valley Railway* cases) produced a classic confrontation on the question of the authority of a truncated international arbitral tribunal. The essential facts are these:

In 1921, the United States of America and Germany concluded a Treaty on the Establishment of Friendly Relations[330] that assured to the United States certain rights, indemnities, etc., provided in the Treaty of Versailles notwithstanding the fact that the United States had not ratified that latter treaty. It was provided that property of

---

[328] *Himpurna California Energy Ltd.* v. *Republic of Indonesia*, UNCITRAL, Final Award, October 16, 1999, XXV *Yearbook Commercial Arbitration* (2000), p. 186, para 49.

[329] Ibid.

[330] Otherwise known as the Treaty of Berlin. Charles I. Bevans, *Treaties and Other International Agreements of the United States of America 1776–1949*, vol. 8, p. 145.

the Imperial German government and of German nationals seized by the United States since its entry into the First World War would be retained by the United States until Germany should have made suitable provision for satisfaction of claims against it by nationals of the United States.

In 1922, the United States and Germany concluded an Agreement establishing a Mixed Claims Commission that was charged with determining the amount to be paid by Germany in satisfaction of its financial obligations under the 1921 Treaty.[331] Among the claims defined to be within the Commission's jurisdiction were claims against Germany for loss or damage to which the United States or its nationals had been subjected as a consequence of the war. The Agreement provided with respect to the mixed commission that:

Article II
The Government of the United States and the Government of Germany shall each appoint one commissioner. The two Governments shall by agreement select an umpire to decide upon any cases concerning which the commissioners may disagree, or upon any points of difference that may arise in the course of their proceedings. Should the umpire or any of the commissioners die or retire, or be unable for any reason to discharge his functions, the same procedure shall be followed for filling the vacancy as was followed in appointing him.

Article III
The commissioners shall meet at Washington within two months after the coming into force of the present agreement. They may fix the time and place of their subsequent meetings according to convenience.[332]

Thus the Parties established not a tribunal of three members reaching decisions by a majority vote, but a joint commission, deciding in the first instance by the unanimous vote of the two national members and, failing that, by the vote of a sole arbitrator, sitting with full and final powers. In practice, however, pursuant to an agreement of the national Commissioners, the Umpire was invited to sit with them, as the presiding member of the Commission, in hearing and considering claims from the outset, and thus was in a position to cooperate with them in their deliberations, and, in case

---

[331] Ibid., p. 149.   [332] Ibid., p. 150.

of disagreement between them, to act promptly upon certification of disagreement to him by the national Commissioners.[333]

A succession of Umpires was appointed and, in each case, at the request of the German government, the Umpire was an American national, selected, and appointed by the President of the United States.[334] This unusual arrangement proved satisfactory to the Parties until the events now to be described. The Commission successfully dealt with a vast number of claims – some 20,000.[335]

In 1930, the Commission rendered a decision rejecting, for lack of evidence of the responsibility of Germany, claims for damage from sabotage: *United States of America on behalf of Lehigh Valley Railway Company, et al. v. Germany.*[336] At issue was responsibility for the Black Tom and Kingsland fires. In 1933, the American Agent filed a petition for rehearing the 1930 decision on the ground of fraud and collusion among some of the witnesses. The two national Commissioners disagreed on the power of the Commission to reopen its former decision, but the Umpire sustained the jurisdiction of the Commission to reopen a case on the ground of fraud.[337] The Parties eventually proceeded to submit exhaustive evidence and argument, running into thousands of pages, on the questions of fraud and on the merits, and the Commission heard extensive oral argument. The life of the Commission was extended for a few years solely to deal with the *Sabotage* cases. The cases were closed in January 1939 and deliberations of the Commission began in February. But on March 1, 1939, the German Commissioner "retired," charging bias on the part of the Umpire, then Supreme Court Justice Owen J. Roberts, who had been serving as Umpire since 1932.

---

[333] See *Report of the American Commissioner, Mixed Claims Commission, United States and Germany,* December 30, 1933, pp. 7–8.

[334] Ibid., p. 4. While such a procedure appears to be unusual, it was not unprecedented. See Hersch Lauterpacht, *The Function of Law in the International Community* (1933), p. 219, who speaks of "the frequent fact of the national of a disputant party being chosen as umpire with a decisive vote and of his discharging the task with admitted impartiality" (ibid., and the references contained in note 5, p. 219).

[335] See *Report of the American Commissioner, supra* note 333, pp. 5, 7.

[336] Mixed Claims Commission, United States and Germany, *Administrative Decisions of a General Nature and Opinions and Decisions in Certain Individual Claims from October 1, 1926 to December 31, 1932* (1933), p. 967.

[337] See the *Report of the American Commissioner, supra* note 333, pp. 29 ff. and 63.

The German Commissioner wrote to Justice Roberts that, "I retire from the post of German Member of the Mixed Claims Commission," alleging that the Umpire had, among other transgressions, introduced into the deliberations of the Commissions an important point not made by the claimants.[338] That fact:

...made it my duty to consider whether I could still cooperate.... My conviction that you had no longer an open mind deepened.... The result to which I have come is that it is impossible for me to cooperate in a procedure which no longer offers to both parties equally the usual guarantees of a decision arrived at in a really judicial way. Our charter allows any member of the Commission to retire and this is the consequence which I have drawn.[339]

Justice Roberts acknowledged the German Commissioner's letter advising of his retirement and characterized his charges as "unjustified" and as presenting "a wholly false picture of our deliberations...."[340] At the same time, the German Commissioner sent to the American Commissioner a copy of his letter of resignation, stating that it came at a moment when the Commission's deliberations were "absolutely preliminary" and any disagreement was still "remote."[341] To this the American Commissioner replied that there was clear disagreement in the Commission's deliberations over whether the 1930 decision had been reached upon false and fraudulent evidence.[342]

When a meeting of the Commission was called for June 7, 1939 – more than three months after the resignation of the German Commissioner, during which period no sign was given that a replacement had been or would be appointed – the German Agent wrote to the US Secretary of State at the direction of his government to call attention:

...to the fact that since the withdrawal of the German Commissioner... the Commission has been incompetent to make decisions and that consequently there is no legal basis for a meeting of the Commission at this stage... the Government of the Reich will ignore the decision to call the meeting....[343]

---

[338] Mixed Claims Commission, United States and Germany, *Opinions and Decisions in the Sabotage Claims handed down June 15, 1939, and October 30, 1939, and Appendix*, Appendix, pp. i, ii.
[339] Ibid., p. iii.   [340] Ibid., p. iv.   [341] Ibid.   [342] Ibid., pp. v–vi.
[343] Ibid., pp. ix–x.

At its June session, the American Commissioner filed a Certificate of Disagreement and Opinion in the *Sabotage* cases, stating, among other things, that:

> ...the question which is now before the Commission for its decision is, whether the Commission, acting through the Umpire and the American Commissioner, has the power to proceed with the cases and to decide whether the evidence which has been adduced has proven fraud sufficient in character to set aside the decision at Hamburg; and, second, whether upon an examination of the whole record, the American Agent has failed to prove his case.
>
> Or, to put the question in a different form, did the retirement of the German Commissioner on March 1, 1939, render the Commission *functus officio* and deprive the Commission of the power to decide the questions at issue?[344]

After setting out the pertinent provisions of the 1921 Treaty, the 1922 Agreement, and the Rules of Procedure, the American Commissioner recalled that, in 1929, the Commission had entered an Order providing for special rules to apply in the *Sabotage* cases, pursuant to which in those cases "the Commission has functioned in the sabotage cases as an arbitration body with three members."[345]

He continued:

> Thus it appears that, under the organic law by which the Commission was created, and under its own Rules of Procedure, unanimity is not required, and the concurrence of only two is necessary for a decision, and this has been the practice ever since the Commission started functioning.[346]
>
> Under the organic law governing the procedure of the Commission, that is to say, the Treaty of Berlin, the Agreement of August 10, 1922, and the Rules of Procedure adopted by the Commission, and under the practice which has obtained, since the Commission was established, is it possible, after a case has been submitted to the Commission and the two National Commissioners are in disagreement as to the direct issue before the Commission, for one National Commissioner to retire and prevent a decision by the remaining members of the Commission?
>
> If it be possible for one National Commissioner, whether under the express order or with the tacit consent of his Government, thus to bring to naught and render worthless the work resulting from the expenditure of thousands of dollars and years of careful research, and thus to defeat the very purpose for which the Commission was constituted under the Treaty

---

[344] Ibid., p. 6.   [345] Ibid., p. 9.   [346] Ibid.

of Berlin, such a result would make a mockery of international arbitration.[347]

The American Commissioner then proceeded to expound *Republic of Colombia* v. *Cauca*,[348] as well as supportive municipal authority and the writings of scholars which have been cited above.[349] After reciting the enormity of the pleadings in the *Sabotage* cases, and the clear disagreement between the national Commissioners which had manifested itself on the questions of fraud and the merits, he concluded:

Under the circumstances set out above, to hold that one National Commissioner could, by his voluntary retirement, whether authorized by his Government or not, prevent the Commission from further proceeding with the cases, and especially from deciding the questions at issue when the German Commissioner announced his retirement, would defeat the purpose of the two Governments in establishing this Commission, would deprive the American Nationals in these cases of the remedy provided by the Treaty of Berlin and the Agreement of August 10, 1922, for American Nationals with claims against the German Government recognized by that treaty, and would raise many questions difficult of solution, as to the disposition of the funds now remaining in the Treasury of the United States, pursuant to the Settlement of War Claims Act.

Accordingly, I am of the opinion that the retirement of the German Commissioner on March 1, 1939, did not render the Commission *functus officio* and did not deprive the Commission of the power to decide the questions at issue at the time of his retirement.[350]

A lengthy opinion on the question of fraud and on the merits followed, in which the American Commissioner ruled in favor of annulling the 1930 decision and of establishing the liability of Germany in the *Black Tom* and *Kingsland* cases.

On the same day, the Umpire wrote that:

I concur in the views expressed by the American Commissioner to the effect that the withdrawal of the German Commissioner, after submission by the parties, and after the tribunal, having taken the cases under advisement, pursuant to its rules, was engaged in the task of deciding the issues presented, did not oust the jurisdiction of the Commission.

---

[347] Ibid., pp. 9–10.   [348] Chapter III, *supra.*
[349] See Mixed Claims Commission, *supra* note 338, pp. 34–35.   [350] Ibid., p. 20.

The full discussion of this matter by the American Commissioner renders it unnecessary for me to do more than to express my agreement with his reasoning and his conclusions. I hold that the Commission as now constituted has jurisdiction to decide the pending motions.[351]

He found that there was a disagreement between the national Commissioners, that there was material fraud in the proofs presented by Germany that led to the 1930 decision and indicated his readiness to sign awards if approved by the Commission "as to form."[352]

These proceedings were formally protested by Germany in the most emphatic and extensive terms. It protested what it saw as multiple, capital violations of the rules of procedure and of judicial propriety in the foregoing proceedings before "the rump Commission."[353] The German Chargé d'Affaires maintained, *inter alia*, that:

I again consider myself compelled now to call attention to the fact that during the vacancy in the position of the German Commissioner the Commission was incompetent to make a decision and therefore could not assemble for meetings either. The Commission is a *mixed* Commission; consequently decisions as to the holding of sessions and all other decisions can be made only by collaboration of the two National Commissioners. This self-evident principle has, in addition, been confirmed explicitly in the Agreement of August 10, 1922, between the German Government and the United States Government, Article III of which reads as follows:

"They (the National Commissioners) may fix the time and place of their subsequent meetings according to convenience."

According to this the American Commissioner and the American Umpire have no power and no right to call meetings of the Commission without the collaboration of the German Commissioner or to hold sessions at which measures concerning Germany are discussed, ordered or promulgated. The Agreement of August 10, 1922 is the charter established for the Commission by the *two* governments, which is unalterable for the Commission. Under it, the Commission is composed of the *two* ... National Commissioners, and the Agreement of August 10, 1922, gives them the right to adjust the procedure and determine its course.

In order that no doubt may arise as to the view of the German Government, it is emphasized that in none of its communications has it taken the stand that by the withdrawal of the German Commissioner the Commission has become 'functus officio' and has thereby lost its competence. The withdrawal of the German Commissioner has, in the opinion of the

---

[351] Ibid., pp. 310–311.   [352] Ibid., p. 313.   [353] Ibid., p. xi.

244

German Government, not produced such an effect; the matters covered by the Agreement of August 10, 1922, which were brought before the Commission in the proper way, within the framework of the agreements of the two Governments, belong, just as before, under its competence. The sole conclusive question here is whether during the vacancy in the position of the German Commissioner the American Commissioner, whether alone or jointly with the American Umpire, can exercise functions which the governmental agreement has entrusted to the two National Commissioners for joint exercise. Under the Agreement of August 10, 1922, no such authority of the American Commissioner exists.

By direction of my Government I therefore protest most emphatically against the holding of the further 'session of the Commission' announced by the Umpire.[354]

Among his further detailed charges was that, "at the time of the withdrawal of the German Commissioner" no disagreement between him and the American Commissioner on the issues before the Commission had crystallized.[355] The two national Commissioners had never both prepared certificates of disagreement, as was required. Furthermore:

The German Commissioner made use of the right of withdrawal which is open to the Members of international commissions at any time, and moreover is also expressly provided in Article II of the Agreement of August 10, 1922, when during the course of the deliberations it became more and more evident to him that the American Umpire was most strongly biased in favour of the American private parties concerned and against Germany.[356]

The German Chargé protested all further measures aimed at securing awards in the *Black Tom* and *Kingsland cases*, requested that the US Treasury be informed of the terms of his note, and called upon the US government to quash the violations of which he complained.[357]

The Secretary of State replied:

I must refrain from engaging in a discussion of the various complaints and protests set out in your communication and content myself by stating that since the Department is without jurisdiction over the Commission I consider that it would be highly inappropriate for it to intervene directly

---

[354] Ibid., pp. xiii–xiv.   [355] Ibid., p. xvii.   [356] Ibid., pp. xvii–xviii.
[357] Ibid., p. xxix.

or indirectly in the work of the Commission or to endeavour, in the slightest manner, to determine the course of its proceedings.

I have entire confidence in the ability and integrity of the Umpire and the Commissioner appointed by the United States despite your severe and, I believe, entirely unwarranted criticisms, and I am constrained to invite your attention to the fact that the remarkable action of the Commissioner appointed by Germany was apparently designed to frustrate or postpone indefinitely the work of the Commission at a time when, after years of labour on the particular cases involved, it was expected that its functions would be brought to a conclusion.[358]

Eight months after the withdrawal of the German Commissioner, on October 30, 1939, the Commission handed down 153 awards in the *Sabotage* cases, which, with interest, totaled $31,400,000.[359] A subsequent challenge in US courts by other holders of awards who maintained that payment on their outstanding awards would be reduced if the sabotage awards were paid – in which argument was made to the effect that the truncated Commission lacked the authority to render valid awards – failed, for unrelated reasons.[360]

In 1953, the United States and the Federal Republic of Germany concluded an Agreement for the Settlement of Indebtedness of Germany for awards Made by the Mixed Claims Commission, pursuant to which Germany undertook to pay to the United States the total amount of $97,500,000, in order to satisfy awards of the Mixed Claims Commission heretofore entered, which had not been fully satisfied. The Agreement clearly treats the awards of the Commission as valid awards.[361] There is no reason to believe that among these awards were not the partially paid awards rendered in the *Sabotage* cases.

The *Sabotage* cases give rise to the following conclusions:

– While the structure and composition of this Mixed Claims Commission was unusual, most notably in the fact that the succession of Umpires who served in the course of almost two decades were, with German agreement, nationals of the United States, the Commission was, and in the *Sabotage* cases acted as, an international arbitral tribunal in which the classic question of the authority of a truncated tribunal could be, and was, confronted.

---

[358] Ibid., p. xxx.   [359] Ibid., p. 324.
[360] *Z. & F. Assets Realization Corporation* v. *Cordell Hull*, 311 U.S. 470 (1940).
[361] *Treaties and Other International Acts Series 2796*, entered into force September 16, 1953.

– That question was answered in opposite terms by, on the one hand, the national Commissioner, Agent and the Government of Germany, and, on the other, the national Commissioner and Government of the United States, the former maintaining that the "rump Commission" from which the German national Commissioner had as of right withdrawn could not meet or act, still less render valid awards in his absence; the latter maintaining that the purposeful and indefinite withdrawal of a Commissioner who was not replaced could not frustrate the authority of the Commission to proceed and to render valid awards in cases which had been fully argued and awaited judgment. This position was maintained despite the fact that the governing treaty contained provision for filling a vacancy which procedure, however, was not followed.

– The Umpire ruled that the jurisdiction of the Commission could not be ousted by the withdrawal of the German Commissioner in the circumstances which obtained.

– While the German Government of 1939 contested the Umpire's decision on this question in the most vigorous terms, another German Government, of a very different political character, subsequently entered into an international agreement with the United States for the payment of the very awards, among others, whose rendering had been challenged by Germany in 1939. Thus Germany inferentially appears to have accepted the position that a truncated international arbitral tribunal from which a nationally-appointed member had withdrawn was entitled to proceed and to render valid awards.

Accordingly, the *Sabotage* cases in their entirety furnish pertinent and persuasive authority for concluding that a truncated international arbitral tribunal is empowered to act and to give judgment.[362]

---

[362] Carlston reserved judgment on the *Sabotage* cases, saying that "[t]he full facts concerning the circumstances leading to the German commissioner's retirement are not known." (*supra* note 15, p. 50.) Writing in 1946, Carlston, while he had the benefit of the published documentation of the Commission which has been referred to in this lecture, could not have known that, in 1953, the Federal Republic of Germany would enter into an international agreement which in effect recognized the validity of the controverted awards. Judge Seifi also approaches the *Sabotage* cases with more skepticism. He argues that the award was only given effect because money had already been set aside for the settlement of awards from the Commission. As a result, he contends that the cases do not provide persuasive support for the authority of truncated tribunals. See Seifi, *supra* note 125, pp. 28, 39.

(J) *THE PEACE TREATIES CASE*

The Advisory Opinion of the International Court of Justice in the *Interpretation of Peace Treaties with Bulgaria, Hungary and Romania* is of exceptional interest even though the authority of a truncated arbitral tribunal was not the immediate issue addressed by the Court in either phase of that case.

The Treaties of Peace between Bulgaria, Hungary, and Romania on the one hand, and the Allied and Associated Powers on the other, contain provisions obliging Bulgaria, Hungary, and Romania to take "all measures necessary to secure to all persons" under their jurisdiction the enjoyment of human rights and fundamental freedoms, "including freedom of expression, of press and publication, of religious worship, of political opinion and of political meeting."[363]

The Treaties provide that any dispute concerning the interpretation or execution of the Treaties not settled by direct diplomatic negotiations shall be referred to the Three Heads of Mission of the United States, the United Kingdom and the Soviet Union in the capital of the State concerned. Any such dispute not resolved by them "shall," unless the parties to the dispute mutually agree upon another means of settlement, be referred "at the request of either party to the dispute"[364] to a Commission composed of one representative of each party and a third member selected by mutual agreement from nationals of a third country. They further provide:

... Should the two parties fail to agree within a period of one month upon the appointment of the third member, the Secretary-General of the United Nations may be requested by either party to make the appointment.

2. The decision of the majority of the members of the Commission shall be the decision of the Commission, and shall be accepted by the parties as definitive and binding.[365]

Differences arose between Bulgaria, Hungary, and Romania, on the one hand, and the United States and the United Kingdom on the other, about the formers' implementation of the human rights provisions of the Treaties, the United Kingdom and the United States charging violation and the Governments so charged denying

---

[363] *Interpretation of Peace Treaties with Bulgaria, Hungary and Romania (First Phase)*, *I.C.J. Reports 1950*, pp. 5, 73.
[364] Ibid.   [365] Ibid.

violation of those provisions. Not otherwise having succeeded in settling those differences, the United States and the United Kingdom invoked arbitration. The Governments of Bulgaria, Hungary, and Romania refused to appoint their representatives to the arbitral commissions, maintaining that they were under no obligation to do so. The question was debated in the General Assembly, which requested the International Court of Justice to render an advisory opinion on the following questions:

"I. Do the diplomatic exchanges between Bulgaria, Hungary and Romania, on the one hand, and certain Allied and Associated Powers signatories to the Treaties of Peace, on the other, concerning the implementation of Article 2 of the Treaties with Bulgaria and Hungary and Article 3 of the Treaty with Romania, disclose disputes subject to the provisions for the settlement of disputes contained in Article 36 of the Treaty of Peace with Bulgaria, Article 40 of the Treaty of Peace with Hungary, and Article 38 of the Treaty of Peace with Romania?"

In the event of an affirmative reply to question I:
"II. Are the Governments of Bulgaria, Hungary and Romania obligated to carry out the provisions of the articles referred to in question I, including the provisions for the appointment of their representatives to the Treaty Commissions?"

In the event of an affirmative reply to question II and if within thirty days from the date when the Court delivers its opinion the Governments concerned have not notified the Secretary-General that they have appointed their representatives to the Treaty Commissions, and the Secretary-General has so advised the International Court of Justice:
"III. If one party fails to appoint a representative to a Treaty Commission under the Treaties of Peace with Bulgaria, Hungary and Romania where the party is obligated to appoint a representative to the Treaty Commission, is the Secretary-General of the United Nations authorized to appoint the third member of the Commission upon the request of the other party to a dispute according to the provisions of the respective Treaties?"

In the event of an affirmative reply to question III:
"IV. Would a Treaty Commission composed of a representative of one party and a third member appointed by the Secretary-General of the United Nations constitute a Commission, within the meaning to the relevant Treaty articles, competent to make a definitive and binding decision in settlement of a dispute?"[366]

---

[366] Ibid., pp. 67–68.

As to Question I, the Court held that international disputes object-ively had arisen over the charges and denials of violation of the human rights clauses of the Treaties: the "mere denial of the existence of a dispute does not prove its non-existence."[367] As to Question II, it concluded that, since the Treaties provide that any dispute "shall" be referred to a Commission "at the request of either party" it follows that "either party is obligated, at the request of the other party, to co-operate in constituting the Commission, in par-ticular by appointing its representative. Otherwise the method of settlement by Commissions provided for in the Treaties would completely fail in its purpose."[368] This completed the first phase of the Court's consideration of the case.

Despite the Court's opinion, the Governments of Bulgaria, Hun-gary, and Romania failed to fulfil their obligation to appoint their respective representatives to the arbitral Commissions. Thus some three months after rendering its opinion on the first two questions put to it, the Court took up the third. The question at issue was whether the provision empowering the Secretary-General of the United Nations to appoint the third member of each Commission applied to the case in which one of the parties had refused to appoint its own representative to the Commission.

The Court observed that:

It has been contended that the term 'third member' is used here simply to distinguish the neutral member from the two Commissioners appointed by the parties without implying that the third member can be appointed only when the two national Commissioners have already been appointed, and that therefore the mere fact of the failure of the parties, within the stipulated period, to select the third member by mutual agreement satis-fies the condition required for the appointment of the latter by the Secretary-General.[369]

The Court held that the text of the Treaties did not admit of this interpretation. The natural and ordinary meaning of the terms of the Treaties imported that the appointment of both national Com-missioners should precede that of the third member. The Secretary-General's power to appoint a third member was derived solely from the agreement of the Parties as expressed in the disputes clause of the Treaties; by its very nature such a clause must be strictly

---

[367] Ibid., p. 74.   [368] Ibid., p. 77.   [369] Ibid., p. 227.

construed and can be applied only in the case expressly provided for. The refusal of Bulgaria, Hungary, and Romania to fulfil their obligation to appoint their representatives to the Treaty Commissions cannot alter the conditions contemplated in the Treaties for the exercise by the Secretary-General of his power of appointment. The rule of effectiveness in the interpretation of treaties cannot justify the Court in attributing to the dispute settlement provisions of the Treaties a meaning which would be contrary to their letter and spirit. The Court continued:

> It has been pointed out that an arbitration commission may make a valid decision although the original number of its members, as fixed by the arbitration agreement, is later reduced by such circumstances as the withdrawal of one of the commissioners. These cases presuppose the initial validity of a commission, constituted in conformity with the will of the parties as expressed in the arbitration agreement, whereas the appointment of the third member by the Secretary-General in circumstances other than those contemplated in the Treaties raises precisely the question of the initial validity of the constitution of the Commission. In law, the two situations are clearly distinct and it is impossible to argue from one to the other.[370]

The Court finally observed that, while it had been claimed that a negative answer to Question III would jeopardize the future of the large number of arbitration clauses drafted in similar terms, the ineffectiveness of the clauses in the case before it did not sustain such a generalization. Normally each party to an arbitration agreement has a direct interest in the appointment of its arbitrator and "must in any case be presumed to observe its treaty obligations."[371] That this was not so in the case before the Court did not justify the Court in exceeding its judicial function "on the pretext of remedying a default for the occurrence of which the Treaties have made no provision."[372] Consequently, the Court, by a vote of eleven to two, answered Question III in the negative, with the result that it did not take up question IV.

Judge Read wrote a powerful dissent, arguing, *inter alia*, that the rule of effectiveness in the interpretation of treaties, and the weight which the Permanent Court of International Justice had given that

---

[370] Ibid., p. 229.   [371] Ibid.
[372] *Interpretation of Peace Treaties with Bulgaria, Hungary and Romania (Second Phase),* I.C.J. Reports 1950, pp. 229–230.

rule in cases of interpreting other arbitral clauses, indicated that these arbitral clauses should, in their context, be interpreted so as not to nullify dispute settlement under the Treaties. These clauses were designed to provide for compulsory arbitration, which could not be evaded by the expedient of a party violating its obligation to appoint its arbitrator. Judge Read also maintained that:

...the attention of the Court has been directed to a long line of precedents in which it has been established that a party to a dispute, under an arbitration clause, cannot prevent the completion of the arbitration and the rendering of a binding decision by the device of withdrawing its national representative from the tribunal.

I am of the opinion that the principle established by these precedents is equally applicable to the case where a party to a dispute acts in bad faith from the outset, and attempts to use the device of defaulting on its treaty obligation to appoint its national representative on the tribunal in order to prevent the provisions of the arbitration clause from taking effect.

There are three phases in the life of an arbitral tribunal. The first phase may be referred to as the constitution of the tribunal. At this stage the tribunal may deal with matters of some import, such as procedure. However, it consists largely of administrative and protocol matters: emoluments; forum; enrolment on the local diplomatic list; exchange of calling cards; and even less weighty matters. The second phase is that in which the tribunal hears the evidence and arguments. The third phase includes deliberation and judgment. I do not need to emphasize the relative importance of the second and third phases, as compared with the first. I have suggested that the principle is equally applicable to default at the outset. As a matter of fact, the case for applying the principle to default at the outset is much stronger. It is much more difficult to construe an arbitration clause as indicating the intention of the parties that a tribunal consisting of the third member and the representative of one party can hear the evidence and give a decision, than it is to construe it as indicating their intention that a decision to invite the local mayor to give an address of welcome at the opening session could be made in the absence of a national representative.

If a Treaty Commission – which, as the result of the withdrawal of a national representative, consists of the third member and the representative of the party which is not in default – is competent to hear the evidence and render a decision, it means that a Commission of two members is a "commission" within the meaning of paragraph 2 of the Disputes Article. It follows that such a Treaty Commission consisting of two members must also be a "commission" within the meaning of paragraph I of the Disputes Article. The whole foundation of the contention that only a so-called three member Commission can be a "commission" within the meaning of the Disputes Article falls to the ground.[373]

The other dissenting member of the Court, Judge Azevedo, similarly pointed out that:

One finds in the records of international law a series of cases in which an arbitration organ saw its initial composition disturbed by the disappearance of one member, either by accidental circumstances or because of the action of that member or of the State which has appointed him, action taken either openly or indirectly.

The practice of keeping in function such a tribunal is justified by the desire not to put wrongful conduct at an advantage. The same solution must prevail, therefore, in the case of absence of a member *ab initio*, particularly if his absence is not due to circumstances beyond the control of the party which should have appointed him.

In the first case, the majority is also formed by the remaining members. There is no opposition left, as the organ comprises three members. One is not confronted either by a situation different from the one envisaged by the parties, or even by a revision of the treaty with a view to obtain an abstention from the remaining judges and thereby the closure of the tribunal. In fact, it is only the natural consequence of a specific sanction required by the nature of the obligation disregarded by one of the parties.

There is no essential difference between the two cases. If one does not wish to see form overrule substance, one is compelled to adopt the same solution *ubi eadem ratio, ibi idem jus*.

An excessive respect for mere formulae should not result in the extension of a mere concept such as, for instance, the one of the 'fundamental procedural order' which has sometimes been put forward to give exceptional importance to the time of the constitution of an organ, to the detriment of social exigencies and for the exclusive benefit of those who are forgetful of their promises, whether they be individuals or States.

12. – The most critical moment for a deliberative organ is not the time of its organization, but the time when, fulfilling its purpose, it makes a decision which alone will carry legal effect *in casu*.

The organ which loses a member without being able to replace him remains, from another angle, in a more serious position than the one which started its work with an incomplete bench, but in the hope or, at least, with the possibility that a change in the attitude of the defaulting State before the end of its work would permit its completion. It is

---

[373] Ibid., pp. 241–243.

impossible ever to foresee with certainty the maintenance or the abandonment of a diplomatic position.

Excessive liking for abstractions should therefore not lead to the rejection of the extension of a reasonable solution accepted without reservations in international law, such as that of the functioning of an incomplete tribunal, not only in an analogous case, but also in a case where this application would be justified for major reasons.[374]

These references of the Court to what "has been pointed out,"[375] and of Judges Read and Azevedo to "a long line of precedents"[376] and to "the records of international law"[377] – all indicating that a truncated international arbitral tribunal retains the authority to act and to render a valid award – were not lightly made. On the contrary, as Judge Read expressly stated, the United Kingdom and the United States had, in their Written Observations and in oral argument presented to the Court, directed the attention of the Court to the precedents which establish that a party to a dispute cannot prevent the completion of the arbitration and the rendering of a binding decision by the device of withdrawing its national representative from the tribunal.[378] Thus, the United States argued that: "Where, in an international arbitration, one party becoming aware of the prospect of an award against it brings about the withdrawal of its appointed arbitrator, this default is ineffective to frustrate the arbitration."[379] In support of this proposition, it cited and quoted substantially from *Colombia* v. *Cauca Co.*, the *French-Mexican Mixed Claims* cases, the *United States-German Mixed Claims* (the *Sabotage* cases), and the *Lena Goldfields* case, as well as four authorities in international law and ten municipal cases.[380] The United Kingdom advanced a similar argument, citing the proceedings of the French-Mexican Claims Commission of 1929, the United States-German Mixed Claims Commission of 1939, and the *Lena Goldfields* Court of Arbitration.[381]

---

[374] Ibid., pp. 252–253.   [375] Ibid., p. 229.   [376] Ibid., p. 242.
[377] Ibid., p. 252.   [378] Ibid., p. 242.
[379] *Interpretation of Peace Treaties with Bulgaria, Hungary and Romania, Pleadings, Oral Arguments, Documents*, Written Statement of the United States of America, pp. 231 ff.
[380] Ibid.
[381] Ibid. Written Statement of the United Kingdom, pp. 188–190, note 1. See also pp. 369–379.

Whatever view one takes of the opinion of the International Court of Justice holding that the Secretary-General was not entitled to appoint a third member of the arbitral tribunal in the absence of prior appointment of a national commissioner – and this element of the Court's opinion is controversial[382] – it is accordingly clear that both the majority and minority of the Court, in the light of extensive argument on this precise question which was presented to the Court, concluded that ". . . an arbitration commission may make a valid decision although the original number of its members, as fixed by the arbitration agreement, is later reduced by such circumstances as the withdrawal of one of the commissioners."[383]

The significance of this conclusion of the Court for the issue under discussion may be profound. On a question of undoubted controversy – and a question, which, as the dissenting opinions of Judges Read and Azevedo indicate, was not treated by the Court in passing – the world's highest international judicial authority appears to have manifested its support of the position that a truncated international arbitral tribunal is empowered to make a valid decision. The Court's majority did not say: "It has been contended – and this is a contention on which the Court takes no position, for it concerns a situation which is not before the Court – that an

---

[382] Judge Lauterpacht suggests in *The Development of International Law by the International Court* (1958), pp. 284–291 that the majority opinion can be reconciled with the rule of effectiveness essentially on the ground that the Court believed that the Parties did not wish to conclude a fully effective arbitration agreement. See also M.S. McDougal, H.D. Lasswell and J.C. Miller, *The Interpretation of Agreements and World Public Order* (1967), pp. 168 ff. For criticism of the Court's opinion, see Professor E. Jiménez de Aréchaga, as quoted in *Yearbook of the International Law Commission 1953, supra* note 39, vol. II, p. 239 and M.O. Hudson, "The Twenty-Ninth Year of the World Court," 45 *American Journal of International Law* (1951), pp. 3–10. For support, see Charles de Visscher, *Theory and Reality in Public International Law* (third revised edition, translated by Percy E. Corbett, 1968), p. 363; Kenneth S. Carlston, "*Interpretation of Peace Treaties with Bulgaria, Hungary and Rumania, Advisory Opinions of the International Court of Justice*," *supra* note 101, pp. 728–737, especially pp. 732–735 (where Carlston appears to accept the cogency of the Court's position on withdrawal of an arbitrator); and Corbett, *Theory and Reality in Public International Law*, pp. 173–177. See also Johnson, *supra* note 6, pp. 158–161; G.G. Fitzmaurice, "The Law and Procedure of the International Court of Justice: International Organizations and Tribunals," XXIX *British Year Book of International Law* (1952), pp. 1, 55–57 and M. Whiteman, *Digest of International Law*, vol. 12, pp. 1060–1068.

[383] *Interpretation of Peace Treaties with Bulgaria, Hungary and Romania (Second Phase)*, *I.C.J. Reports 1950*, p. 229.

arbitration commission may make a valid decision although the original number of its members ... is later reduced...." Rather, indicating that it accepted this conclusion as the law, the majority stated that: "It has been pointed out that an arbitration commission may make a valid decision although the original number of its members ... is later reduced ...." Moreover, the Court proceeded to distinguish the situation of a truncated arbitral tribunal whose constitution is initially valid from that of forming a tribunal in circumstances that raise precisely the question of the initial validity of the constitution of the Commission, and it continued: "In law, the two situations are clearly distinct and it is impossible to argue from one to the other." Whether it is impossible is a question that Judge Read's dissent most cogently raised.[384] But what is pertinent for our purposes is that the Court's majority (as well as minority) quite clearly treated the authority of an arbitral tribunal initially fully constituted and subsequently truncated to make a valid decision not merely as an argument but as an accepted statement of the law.

It is true that this element of the Court's reasoning was not necessary to its holding in the case and, accordingly, it may be termed, in the usage of the common lawyer, as *obiter dictum*. But the Court's view of the law relating to the authority of a truncated international arbitral tribunal cannot be wholly discounted as *dictum* by application of a technique of the common law. As Judge Lauterpacht put it in *The Development of International Law by the International Court*:

Undoubtedly, so long as the Court itself had not overruled its former pronouncement or so long as States have not, by a treaty of a general character, adopted a different formulation of the law, the ruling formally given by the Court on any question of international law must be considered as having settled, for the time being, the particular question at issue. Yet this result, and the settlement of a particular dispute, are not the only outcome of a decision by the Court. What is almost equally important is that the reasoning of the Court, often as illuminated by the separate – concurring or dissenting – Opinions of individual Judges, sheds an instructive ray of light on the legal problem involved and, often, on some fundamental issues of international law....[385]

---

[384] Ibid., pp. 242–243.   [385] Lauterpacht, *supra* note 382, p. 62.

Just such an instructive ray of light was shed on the issue of the authority of a truncated tribunal by the Court in its Opinion in the second phase of the *Peace Treaties* case.

Judge Seifi, however, disagrees with such an interpretation of the *Peace Treaties* case.[386] In his view, the Court's opinion in the second phase of the case "rejected the idea that the Arbitral Commission could be constituted in the absence of the arbitrator of the defaulting party" in "clear and unambiguous" language.[387] Moreover, the *dictum* discussed in the first edition was, according to Judge Seifi, irrelevant:

> ... if the dictum of the court's Opinion were to be interpreted as a positive answer to the authority of an arbitral tribunal becoming truncated after its constitution, this should be rationalized because of the absence of a provision for the third-party appointment of a national member. On the other hand, in a situation where a provision has been made for the third-party appointment of the national arbitrator the facts and the circumstances are totally different. This may make the applicability of the dictum of the court's Opinion totally irrelevant.
>
> ...
>
> [M]ost views which have been expressed in support of the legality of an incomplete tribunal, including an interpretation which may be derived from the dictum of the Opinion of the court in the Peace Treaties case, have in mind a situation where no alternative method guarantees the appointment of the national arbitrator, or filling the vacancy arising from his withdrawal. As a consequence, where there exists a mechanism for the enforced filling of a vacancy arising from the withdrawal of a party-appointed arbitrator the circumstances are totally different from those assumed under the dictum of the Opinion of the court in the Peace Treaties case.[388]

Judge Seifi accordingly sees little useful support in the *Peace Treaties* case for the authority of truncated tribunals because there was no mechanism there to make a substitute appointment. However, the Court's *dictum* was subsequently endorsed by the tribunal in the *Himpurna* arbitration:

> The Arbitral Tribunal thus has no hesitation in finding that, in the circumstances of this arbitration, it has the power to proceed to fulfil its

---

[386] See Seifi, *supra* note 125, p. 10–13.   [387] Ibid., p. 10.   [388] Ibid., pp. 12–13.

mandate and render an award, since [the Indonesian party-appointed arbitrator's] non-participation is without valid excuse.

In reaching this finding, the Arbitral Tribunal notes that it was initially constituted in precise conformity with the will of the Parties as reflected in the Terms of Appointment, and that [the Indonesian party-appointed arbitrator's] withdrawal prejudices not the constitution but the continued effective composition of the Arbitral Tribunal. As the International Court of Justice observed in its Advisory Opinion in *Interpretation of Peace Treaties with Bulgaria, Hungary and Romania*, and as highlighted by Judge Schwebel... the distinction is fundamental. Having found [the Indonesian party-appointed arbitrator's] withdrawal to be without valid excuse, the Arbitral Tribunal retains the authority to render this award.[389]

(K) THE BURAIMI CASE

On 30 July 1954, an Arbitration Agreement was concluded between the government of the United Kingdom (acting on behalf of Muscat and Abu Dhabi) and the government of Saudi Arabia to arbitrate territorial disputes concerning the location of the common frontier between Saudi Arabia and Abu Dhabi and sovereignty in the Buraimi oasis.[390] It was decided "to submit the dispute to an independent and impartial Tribunal for arbitration."[391] Article I of the Agreement in part provided:

The Tribunal shall consist of five members selected as follows:

(a) Each of the two Parties to the present Agreement shall nominate one Member, provided that, if either Party fails to nominate its Member within 60 days from the date on which this Agreement comes into force, the other Party may ask the President of the International Court of Justice to make the nomination.

---

[389] See *Himpurna California Energy Ltd.* v. *Republic of Indonesia*, UNCITRAL, Final Award, October 16, 1999, XXV *Yearbook Commercial Arbitration* (2000), p. 186, paras. 46, 51, 60–61. See also Lew, Mistelis et al., *supra* note 115, pp. 324–325; *Redfern and Hunter on International Arbitration*, *supra* note 106, pp. 282–283.

[390] *Arbitration Agreement between the Government of the United Kingdom (acting on behalf of the Ruler of Abu Dhabi and His Highness the Sultan Said bin Taimur) and the Government of Saudi Arabia*, Cmd. 9272, Treaty Series No. 65 (1954). The Agreement and its accompanying exchange of notes are reprinted in J. Gillis Wetter, *The International Arbitral Process*, vol. III, pp. 357–367. Citations are to Wetter.

[391] Preamble, Wetter, *supra* note 390, p. 357.

(b) The three remaining Members, none of whom shall be a national of either Party, shall be chosen by agreement between the two Members nominated under paragraph (a) of this Article; of the three, one shall be designated by the selecting Members as President of the Tribunal. If within a period of 90 days from the date on which the appointment of the last-named Member under paragraph (a) is notified to the other Party, the membership of the Tribunal is still incomplete or the President has not been designated, either Party may request the President of the International Court of Justice to make the appointments or designation required.

(c) If any Member of the Tribunal should die, resign, or become unable to act before the Award has been given, the vacancy shall be filled by the method laid down in this Article for the original appointment....[392]

It was further provided that the tribunal, which was authorized on its own initiative to call witnesses, to conduct enquiries, and to visit particular localities in the area in dispute, "shall have the power to determine all questions of procedure not regulated in the present Agreement....";[393] that its award and all decisions on questions of procedure "shall be given by majority vote"[394] and that the award shall be final, binding and without appeal. The Tribunal was empowered to decide any question that might arise as to the interpretation of the Agreement. An accompanying exchange of notes specified conditions under which the Parties agreed to submit their territorial disputes to arbitration, including mutual withdrawal of specified forces and officials from the disputed territory, limitations on the number of police in the territory, and restriction of the area of interim oil operations. Both Parties undertook "to refrain from action which would prejudice the holding of a just and impartial arbitration."[395]

The United Kingdom named to the tribunal its former Minister to Saudi Arabia in the years 1936–1939, a retired member of the Foreign Service, Sir Reader Bullard. Saudi Arabia named its Deputy Foreign Minister, Sheikh Yusuf Yasin. The Parties agreed upon the appointment of Charles de Visscher, former Judge of the

---

[392] Ibid., p. 358.   [393] Articles VII, XII, ibid., pp. 360, 362.
[394] Article XIII, ibid., p. 362.   [395] Exchange of Notes, ibid., p. 366.

International Court of Justice, as President, and Dr. Ernesto Dihigo, former Foreign Minister of Cuba, and Dr. Mahmud Hassan of Dacca University, as Tribunal Members.

At its organizational meeting in Nice in January 1955, Sheikh Yusuf Yasin is reported to have brought forth certain complaints against the British Government, among them that his government did not enjoy equal access to Buraimi.[396] The Tribunal called upon the Parties to effect an arrangement that would accord each the same number of visits to Buraimi.[397] For its part, in succeeding months, the British Government directed to Saudi Arabia a number of complaints about what it saw as Saudi Arabian non-observance of the terms of the Arbitration Agreement and Exchange of Notes. The British Government referred those and other complaints to the tribunal, which considered them at hearings in Geneva, September 11–16, 1955. The Saudi Arabian Government at that time submitted a list of counter-complaints to the Tribunal.

The British Agent presented the following charges against Saudi Arabia:

(a) That the Saudi police contingent in the area exceeded the maximum number of 15, agreed upon by the Arbitration Agreement;
(b) That attempts were made to send arms to disputed areas;
(c) That passengers and supplies were flown to the area;
(d) That Saudi bribery on a wide scale was offered to Buraimi Sheikhs to win them over to the Saudi side.[398]

The British Leading Counsel, Sir Hartley Shawcross, contended that the Saudi Government "has been engaged in a deliberate, a systematic and persistent policy of large-scale bribery, and other improper practices which are calculated...to destroy the *status quo* as it existed at the time of the Arbitration Agreement...."[399] He introduced witnesses who testified in support of the British

---

[396] See J.B. Kelly, *Eastern Arabian Frontiers* (1964), p. 184. For a briefer treatment more sympathetic to the Saudi Arabian position, see H.M. Al-Baharna, *The Arabian Gulf States* (1975), pp. 196–238.
[397] Kelly, *supra* note 396, p. 184.   [398] Al-Baharna, *supra* note 396, p. 204.
[399] As quoted from the Minutes of Sittings, ibid., p. 2.

complaints. Counsel for Saudi Arabia (Richard Young) presented evidence to refute these charges.

Before the tribunal ruled upon the British complaints – some sources allege, minutes before –[400] Sir Reader Bullard resigned from the tribunal. His resignation was submitted in the following terms:

I have been shown by the President a copy of the letter which the United Kingdom delegation sent to him today, and I have in the meantime given very serious consideration to my own personal position as a member of this tribunal. I have always felt uneasy about the position of Sheikh Yusuf Yasin in connexion [sic] with these proceedings, but I had not realized until yesterday, when Sheikh Yusuf Yasin openly asserted the fact, that he himself was the Saudi Arabian official in charge of affairs at Buraimi, and that he accepted full responsibility for the conduct of Qureishi [a member of the Saudi Arabian security service]. Moreover, in the last few days it has become abundantly clear that Sheikh Yusuf Yasin is, in fact, in effective control of the conduct of the proceedings on behalf of the Saudi Arabian Government, and is representing that Government on this tribunal rather than acting as an impartial arbitrator.

It has been established that the first thing Qureishi did on reaching Geneva was to see Sheikh Yusuf Yasin, and the subsequent course of events leaves no doubt in my mind that the Sheikh saw fit to brief him as to his evidence and conduct before the tribunal. This I regard as completely vitiating the whole proceedings.

I have always regarded my own position as one of complete independence of the British Government, and this I know is the position which the British Government desires me to occupy. Indeed, I regard it as essential to any system of arbitration that each member of the arbitration tribunal should feel completely at liberty to give any decision he thinks right, including one against his own Government. I am afraid the position of

---

[400] See Permanent Delegation of the Kingdom of Saudi Arabia to the United Nations, "The Buraimi Dispute," p. 10 and see Wetter, *supra* note 390, p. 369, quoting an official Saudi Arabian statement; and see the full text of that statement of Saudi Arabia in reply to the British statement of October 4, which appears in 11 *Revue Egyptienne de Droit International* (1955), pp. 231–232. It is there stated that "the resignation of the British member took place at the very last moment, after the hearings had been concluded and the decision of the Tribunal had been drafted by the three neutral members. This resignation alone prevented the Tribunal from issuing its decision with respect to these fantastic charges. If the Government of the United Kingdom had been truly persuaded of the validity of its accusations, it might have induced its member to remain for another half hour to enable the Tribunal to record its judgment." And see Al-Baharna, *supra* note 396, pp. 204–206.

the tribunal has been hopelessly compromised by the conduct of Sheikh Yusuf Yasin and by other distasteful matters which have come to notice. I do not think that the tribunal is any longer in a position to reach a unanimous or judicial conclusion on the matters before it, and I feel the only step I can take which is consistent with my own independence and honour is to tender my resignation. I shall inform the United Kingdom representative of my resignation and my reasons for it.

I much regret to have to take this decision, the more so because of the very high regard I have for our distinguished president personally and for the manner in which he has conducted the proceedings in the most difficult circumstances. He will recollect, however, that on more than one occasion I spoke to him about the position of Sheikh Yusuf Yasin and expressed to him my deep personal disquiet.[401]

The Tribunal thereupon suspended its proceedings *sine die*.[402]

The Saudi Arabian Government promptly issued a statement that deplored that the tribunal should have been "paralyzed" by Sir Reader Bullard's resignation and expressed its "firm determination to press for an early appointment by the British Government of a new member of the tribunal."[403] British sources were quoted as indicating that Sir Reader's resignation did not mean an end to the arbitration proceedings, as the agreement provided for filling vacancies.[404]

Sheikh Yasin then issued a statement deploring Sir Reader Bullard's resignation which had "forced the suspension" of the tribunal when it was about to take decisions on the complaints laid down before it by both sides. The Tribunal had thus been "frustrated in expressing its views on the charges." Sheikh Yasin declared that he had known Sir Reader since 1937. There was:

... certainly nothing new to him in my position as Deputy Foreign Minister. Throughout the history of the present boundary dispute I have been in charge of the negotiations on behalf of my Government

The whole tribunal has always been aware that, in addition to my duties as a member, I have continued to discharge my duties as Deputy Foreign Minister and head of the political department of the Royal Government, in the course of which I have dealt regularly with the British Government on problems relating to Buraimi. In accordance with powers invested in

---

[401] The statement of Sir Reader Bullard is printed in full in *The Times*, September 17, 1955. It is reprinted in Wetter, *supra* note 390, pp. 369–372.

[402] *The Times*, September 17, 1955. See also Al-Baharna, *supra* note 396, p. 204.

[403] *The Times*, September 17, 1955.   [404] Ibid.

me by His Royal Highness, the Foreign Minister, and sanctioned by the Government, I have also been responsible for issuing instructions about the application of the arbitration agreement in the disputed area. My position has never been a cause for objection on the part of the neutral members, although the tribunal has been in existence for nine months and has held two full sessions.[405]

A week later, the tribunal's President, Judge de Visscher, resigned. Press reports indicate no more than that his letter of resignation stated that, following the resignation of Sir Reader Bullard, he had decided to give up his position as Member and President of the tribunal.[406]

On October 4, 1955, the Foreign Office issued a statement that set out in detail what it described as breaches of the conditions of arbitration by Saudi Arabia – notably, an attempt to overthrow the Ruler of Abu Dhabi by force and large-scale bribery. It concluded:

Possessing as they did the strongest evidence (which has still not been refuted) that Saudi Arabia was engaged in a campaign of systematic corruption designed to pervert the arbitration, Her Majesty's Government had their case before the tribunal at Geneva. Unfortunately it soon became apparent that Saudi methods, which are now well known in the Middle East, were to be extended to the tribunal itself. Not only had Sheikh Yusuf Yasin to be called to order by the president for sending a note to the Saudi Agent during a sitting of the tribunal, but Quraishi admitted under cross-examination that his first act on arriving in Geneva was to get in touch with Sheikh Yusuf Yasin, the Saudi member of the tribunal. There can be little doubt that the evidence he subsequently gave was carefully rehearsed with the Saudi arbitrator.

As appears from the statement which Sir Reader Bullard made on his resignation from the tribunal, Sheikh Yusuf Yasin made it abundantly clear that it was he who was conducting the proceedings on behalf of the Saudi Arabian Government and was representing that Government on the tribunal rather than acting as an impartial arbitrator. He was in fact the judge of his own cause.

Moreover, he asserted that Quraishi was his official, for whose acts in Buraimi he accepted responsibility. In spite of this he claimed that during the period of the Quraishi Zaid interviews mentioned above he had forgotten to take action on three British protests against the presence of

---

[405] *The Times*, September 19, 1955, reprinted in Wetter, *supra* note 390, pp. 369, 374.
[406] *The Times*, September 24, 1955.

Quraishi in the Buraimi Zone. Finally, confirmation was secured of Her Majesty's Government's suspicion that attempts had been made by the Saudis to tamper with the impartiality of the tribunal behind the president's back.

In these circumstances, Sir Reader Bullard had no choice but to declare that he could not continue as a member of the arbitration tribunal. Her Majesty's Government are in full agreement with the motives that led to Sir Reader Bullard's action.[407]

On October 26, 1955, Prime Minister Eden made the following statement to the House of Commons:

The House may recall that on 28th July, 1954, I reported that agreement had been reached with the Saudi Arabian Government to submit the Buraimi frontier dispute to arbitration. I expressed the hope that this agreement would enable us to resume the traditionally friendly relations between Her Majesty's Government and the Saudi Arabian Government....

I am sorry to have to tell the House that these hopes have been disappointed. The proceedings before the Arbitration Tribunal at Geneva have broken down and the British Member of the tribunal and its Belgian President have resigned. The reasons for these events were explained in detail in a statement issued by the Foreign Office on 4th October. I have just learned that Dr. Dihigo, one of the two remaining members of the tribunal appointed as a neutral, has also resigned.

The Saudi Arabian authorities have systematically disregarded the conditions of arbitration which were ... agreed upon. The police group which they were permitted to keep in the Buraimi Oasis for the sole purpose of maintaining law and order was, in fact, led by political officers who persistently exceeded their functions. Bribery and intimidation on a wide scale have taken place in the disputed areas, with the result that it is no longer possible, I regret to say, to estimate where the loyalties of the inhabitants lay before Turki's armed incursion. The Ruler of Abu Dhabi and the Sultan of Muscat have scrupulously observed the conditions of arbitration which Her Majesty's Government, in good faith, recommended to them. They have had to stand by and watch their subjects being suborned, and the outcome of the arbitration itself being gravely prejudiced in advance. A fair and impartial arbitration is not possible in such circumstances.

---

[407] *The Times*, October 5, 1955, reprinted in Wetter, *supra* note 390, pp. 375–377.

These facts, combined with the conduct of the Saudi Government in relation to the tribunal itself, have led Her Majesty's Government to conclude that the Saudi Arabian Government are no more willing now to reach an equitable solution by arbitration than they were previously by negotiation. Their actions and conduct amount to a repudiation of the Arbitration Agreement, and have made a continuation of the arbitration impossible.

Her Majesty's Government have, therefore, felt obliged in the exercise of their duty, to protect the legitimate interests of the Ruler of Abu Dhabi and the Sultan of Muscat, to advise them that the attempt to reach a just compromise by means of arbitration has failed. The forces of these Rulers, supported by the Trucial Oman levies, have accordingly this morning taken steps to resume their previous control of the Buraimi Oasis, and areas to the west of it.[408]

The view of these events of the Government of Saudi Arabia was quite the opposite. Commenting in detail on Prime Minister Eden's statement, an official publication of Saudi Arabia issued at the United Nations in part declared:

The British Agent had asked the tribunal to condemn Saudi Arabia on 5 counts. The Tribunal had listened to British accusations and Saudi replies, examined witnesses and considered claims. The neutral members had decided that the British charges were either unsupported by proof or irrelevant and trivial.

The British member, Sir Reader Bullard, knew that the tribunal would hand down an adverse ruling on the British demands for Saudi censure when it met September 16th. He hastily resigned at this meeting before the decision could be voted and announced.

The Belgian president did not resign *with* him, but instead tried to dissuade the British member from resigning and urged him at least to wait "ten minutes" until the tribunal rendered its decision on the pending complaints.

The record shows that the proceedings did not "break down"; they were scuttled by the British member who walked out.

After Britain had disrupted the arbitration proceedings and did not name a substitute member of the tribunal, the Belgian president resigned. But he stated that he would reconsider if both parties were "genuinely anxious to carry on the arbitration." The Cuban member later followed his lead to allow full freedom to the parties in taking next steps.

---

[408] *Hansard Parliamentary Debates, 5th Series, House of Commons,* vol. 545 (1955–56), pp. 198–199.

The record shows that the neutral members did not act *with* the British member, but only after his withdrawal terminated the arbitration proceedings.[409]

The British charges about bribery and other alleged violations of the Arbitration Agreement were vigorously contested by Saudi Arabia.[410] Saudi Arabia repeatedly called on the United Kingdom to take steps to resume arbitration, but it refused. The British Government also indicated that it would not be prepared to agree to have the case referred to the International Court of Justice[411] and revised its submission to the compulsory jurisdiction of the Court apparently in order to forestall any unilateral Saudi Arabian recourse to the Court on the matter.[412]

It would be neither necessary nor appropriate for the purposes of this study to venture an opinion on the merits of the respective positions of the United Kingdom and Saudi Arabia on the break-down of the *Buraimi* arbitration, or on the propriety of Sir Reader Bullard's resignation or subsequent resignations. The question that is relevant is: what light does the *Buraimi* arbitration shed on the authority of a truncated international arbitral tribunal to proceed and to render a binding award?

The answer must be, very little. The fact that the tribunal apparently suspended its sitting *sine die* upon the resignation of Sir Reader Bullard does not necessarily show that it regarded itself as stripped

---

[409] See Permanent Delegation of the Kingdom of Saudi Arabia to the United Nations, *supra* note 400, pp. 9–10. In this same publication, it is claimed that: "The bribery complaint was the main British charge on which the Tribunal was about to rule when the British member suddenly resigned and walked out. The neutral members had unanimously decided that the bribery charge was unsubstantiated" (ibid., p. 12).

[410] See ibid., pp. 8–12, and the proceedings of the Tribunal as reported by Al-Baharna, *supra* note 396, pp. 204–205.

[411] *Hansard Parliamentary Debates, 5th Series, House of Commons, supra* note 408, vol. 605 (1958–59), pp. 846–847. The Minister of State for Foreign Affairs said that he was certain that the Sultan of Muscat and Oman and the Ruler of Abu Dhabi would not consent to recourse to the Court. See Kelly, *supra* note 396, p. 266.

[412] See C.H.M. Waldock, "Decline of the Optional Clause," XXXII *British Year Book of International Law* (1955–56), pp. 244, 268. See also Corbett, *Theory and Reality in Public International Law, supra* note 382, pp. 181–182.

of authority to proceed; on the contrary, that decision may be taken as an indication of the authority to take decisions, in that case expressive of the judgment that the tribunal should suspend its hearings to await developments. The Tribunal might have anticipated that the United Kingdom would, pursuant to its obligation under Article I of the Arbitration Agreement, appoint another arbitrator; or that Sheikh Yusuf Yasin might resign, partially in order to facilitate such a British appointment;[413] or the Members of the tribunal may have wished to consider their own positions in the light of the British allegations, particularly the charge of attempts "by the Saudis to tamper with the impartiality of the tribunal behind the president's back."[414] (Saudi Arabia characterized that last charge as "utterly untrue and unworthy of the Government of the United Kingdom."[415])

In the event, the resignations of Judge de Visscher and Dr. Dihigo deprived the tribunal of a majority; out of five members, only Sheikh Yusuf Yasin and Professor Hassan remained. By the terms of the Arbitration Agreement, two of five Members could not act as a majority capable of proceeding and rendering an award. Thus any question of the authority of the truncated Buraimi Tribunal to act was disposed of by the resignations of three Members, that is, of a majority of the tribunal.

Presumably, by following the letter of the Arbitration Agreement, Saudi Arabia could not only have pressed, as it did, the United Kingdom to appoint a replacement and, when appointed, sought his agreement to the appointment of successors to Judge de Visscher and Dr. Dihigo; failing such appointment by the United Kingdom, Saudi Arabia might have asked the President of the International Court of Justice to name the Member that the United Kingdom failed to appoint, as well as two remaining Members. Saudi Arabia maintained steadily that it wished the arbitration to resume, but it did not, as far as is known, have such recourse to the President of the Court, perhaps because it believed that an arbitration proceeding that lacked the participation of the British

---

[413] British sources appear to have expressed the hope that Sheikh Yasin would resign: *The Times*, September 17, 1955.

[414] *The Times*, October 5, 1955.

[415] As quoted in Wetter, *supra* note 390, p. 370. See also *Revue Egyptienne de Droit International*, *supra* note 400, p. 232.

Government would not result in an award that the United Kingdom and the protected States would implement. Moreover, British-led troops had occupied Buraimi and expelled the Saudis, while making it clear that reestablishment of the previous regime would not be permitted. In these circumstances that to Saudi Arabia appeared unfavorable to effective arbitration, Saudi Arabia may have decided that it should not force the issue by resort to the President of the Court. But in any event, Saudi Arabia's not seeking the filling of vacancies on the tribunal by appointment of the President of the Court does not, in the circumstances of the *Buraimi* case, bear upon the authority of a truncated arbitral tribunal.[416]

(L) THE FRANCO-TUNISIAN ARBITRAL TRIBUNAL CASE

Another inconclusive case, which in a few respects resembles the *Buraimi* and *Sabotage* cases, is that of a judgment of a

---

[416] The conclusion that the *Buraimi* case does not shed light on the authority of a truncated arbitral tribunal was shared by Judge de Visscher, who, in response to an inquiry of one of the authors, replied by letter of July 16, 1960 as follows:

Je reçois votre lettre du 12 juillet. Je crois pouvoir vous dire que la tentative avortée d'arbitrage dans l'affaire du Buraimi ne me paraît pas rentrer dans le cadre de votre étude. Comme vous le pressentez, la question de ma démission et celle du Dr. Dihigo dans cette instance est extrêmement délicate et doit conserver un caractère confidentiel. Je puis cependant vous dire – en me limitant à cela – que cette démission a été déterminée par d'autres raisons que la démission du Sir Reader Bullard. La vrai raison est et doit demeurer secrète.

For comment on the *Buraimi* arbitration in addition to the sources cited, see R. Goy, "L'Affaire de l'Oasis de Buraimi," III *Annuaire Français de Droit International* (1957), pp. 188–205.

In Judge Seifi's view, however, the *Buraimi* case offers persuasive authority *against* the power of a truncated tribunal to continue and render an award. For him, where the withdrawal of a party-appointed arbitrator disrupts or essentially terminates the work of the tribunal, one should assume – in the absence of an indication to the contrary – that the remaining arbitrators did not believe that they could lawfully proceed as a truncated tribunal. Accordingly, applying that principle to the *Buraimi* case, Judge Seifi considers the resignation of the neutral members of the tribunal, after the resignation of the British arbitrator, to have been in recognition of their inability to continue the proceedings in the absence of a party-appointed arbitrator. See Seifi, *supra* note 125, pp. 34–36. Similarly, Fox contends that the case supports the proposition that "[t]he unilateral withdrawal of a State from continued participation in arbitration after consenting to the setting up of the arbitration tribunal ... terminates the arbitration and the arbitrator's powers." Fox, *supra* note 266, p. 20, fn. 21.

Franco-Tunisian Arbitral Tribunal in regard to two applications submitted to it by the French Government.

On June 3, 1955, France and Tunisia concluded a number of Conventions providing for the internal autonomy of Tunisia. One of these Conventions provided for a mixed arbitral tribunal to settle disputes between France and Tunisia. The Tribunal was composed of three Tunisian and three French arbitrators, each named for six-year terms; the presidency of the tribunal was to alternate, every two years, between a French and a Tunisian arbitrator. A neutral member of the tribunal, chosen without consideration of national-ity by common accord of the two governments, was to decide any dispute by a casting vote in case the tribunal were to prove equally divided. The Convention provided that: "In the event of the resig-nation or death of the President, the Vice President, or any other member of the tribunal, before the expiration of his term of office, his substitute shall be appointed in accordance with the same conditions as his predecessor..."[417] Pursuant to these provisions, the two governments each nominated their arbitrators (and nom-inated alternates as well); Professor Georges Vedel of the University of Paris was designated President; and the two governments chose as the neutral member Eelco N. van Kleffens, former Minister of Foreign Affairs of the Netherlands.[418]

On March 20, 1956, France and Tunisia signed a Protocol pro-viding for the complete independence of Tunisia. It contained a clause to the effect that the Conventions of June 3, 1955 would remain in force except for provisions incompatible with Tunisia's independence. In October 1956, France requested the tribunal to annul a Tunisian decree. When the President of the tribunal made contact with his colleagues with a view toward convening the tribu-nal, the Tunisian-appointed arbitrators took the personal view that the Convention providing for the jurisdiction of the tribunal had become inapplicable by reason of the Protocol of March 20, 1956. They and their alternates did not attend a meeting of the tribunal

---

[417] The case is reported in 24 *International Law Reports*, pp. 767–770; see p. 770. A report of the case in French appears in XII *U.N.R.I.A.A.*, p. 273.

[418] See Simone Dreyfus, "Le Conseil Arbitral Franco-Tunisien," III *Annuaire Fran-çais de Droit International* (1957), pp. 181, 182; 24 *International Law Reports 1957*, pp. 767–768. See also M. Whiteman, *Digest of International Law*, vol. 12, *supra* note 382, pp. 1071–1072 and S. Bastid in 47 *Annuaire de l'Institut de Droit International* (1957), pp. 228–230.

of November 5, 1956, which nevertheless the President regarded as duly constituted, despite the fact that only the French arbitrators were present.[419] Published sources make no reference to any action that may have been taken at that meeting.

In December 1956, the French government filed a second request for annulment of a Tunisian governmental decree. The Tunisian-appointed arbitrators and alternates persisted in refusing to attend a meeting that the President convened for March 18, 1957, remaining "silent and absent."[420]

In the meantime, in January 1957, Dr. van Kleffens, having been named the representative of the Netherlands to NATO, requested the French and Tunisian governments to relieve him of his functions as the neutral member of the tribunal.[421] Steps apparently had not been taken by the contracting governments to replace him by the time the tribunal met in April 1957. In those circumstances, President Vedel issued an order holding that, in the absence of a formal notification by the Tunisian government that it regarded the Convention as no longer valid, the abstention of the Tunisian arbitrators must be treated as a resignation and dealt with in accordance with the pertinent provision of the Convention that, in the event of the resignation of a Tribunal member, his successor must be appointed in the same way as his predecessor. Accordingly, both Governments were requested to apply that procedure. Meanwhile, proceedings were suspended, pending such appointments. President Vedel held:

As matters stand, the Arbitral Tribunal is unable to sit or adjudicate. According to the wording of Article 21 of the Convention:

> "the presence of at least four members is required for the validity of the deliberations of the Tribunal; of these, two must be Frenchmen and two Tunisians."

In order to resolve the difficulty, it is not possible to have recourse to the member of the tribunal "who is chosen without regard to nationality," as provided in Article 16 (I) (b) of the Convention. In fact, according to para. 3 (I) of this Article, this member "shall be called upon to take part in the deliberations of the Tribunal when, after the first deliberation, the Tribunal is equally divided." In the present case there has as yet been no deliberation of the tribunal, and the member of the tribunal referred to in Article 16, para. I (b), cannot be asked to intervene in the proceedings as they now stand. On

---

[419] Dreyfus, *supra* note 418, p. 183.   [420] Ibid.   [421] Ibid.

the other hand, the Arbitral Tribunal is a permanently constituted tribunal and cannot therefore be regarded as no longer seised of the matter. Nor can the office of its President be regarded as at an end, in particular as far as concerns the application submitted by the French Government on December 4, 1956. The Convention of June 3, 1955, has not been terminated by the High Contracting Parties, and the French Government, by making two applications to the tribunal, has indicated in the clearest possible manner that it regards the Convention as being still operative. As far as the Tunisian Government is concerned, to whom the applications of the French Government were transmitted by the President in accordance with Article 18 of the Convention, there has been no reservation of any kind. The fact that M. Ahmed Mestiri (one of the Tunisian Arbitrators) became Minister of Justice after his appointment as arbitrator does not give him the authority to acquaint the tribunal with the view of the Tunisian Government on the validity of the Convention of June 3, 1955. Moreover, M. Mestiri has made it clear that he was speaking in his own name and in the names of the other Tunisian Arbitrators, and not in the name of the Tunisian Government. It follows from what has been said that the legal difficulty resulting from the state of affairs which has been described is not the extent to which an arbitral tribunal remains the judge of its own competence where a defendant State denies the legal validity of the Treaty which provides for the jurisdiction of the tribunal, but the result which must follow the refusal of some of the members of a permanent arbitral tribunal to take their seats because in their opinion the treaty providing for the tribunal is invalid or no longer operative. Such refusal, in the absence of the termination of the Convention by one of the Contracting Parties, must be regarded as a resignation from the tribunal. If every member of an arbitral tribunal has the right and the duty to put forward any argument which in his view tends to show that the tribunal lacks jurisdiction, then the refusal of a member of a permanent arbitral tribunal to comply with a request to sit cannot, whatever the reasons given and even if his refusal to sit paralyses the tribunal, result in dissolving the tribunal or putting an end to its mission. The resignation of arbitrators produces its effect irrespective of its acceptance by any other authority. Such resignation must therefore simply be recorded, and the duty so to record it rests with the President. This is all the more necessary in the present case because, according to Article 18(3) of the Convention of June 3, 1955, the tribunal must, as a rule, deal with the merits of the case within four months of its being seised of the proceedings. This time-limit must be observed where the tribunal is concerned with a legislative enactment or an administrative act of general importance, which is the case here, seeing that the French Government has asked for the invalidation of certain provisions of the Decree of November 7, 1956. The fact that the tribunal is unable to adjudicate upon the merits within this time-limit must be recorded before its expiration, in order to preserve the rights of the parties. It is for the President of the tribunal to function, because this is a permanent tribunal which must at all times be in a position to operate. The replacement of arbitrators who have resigned is provided for in Article 16(2)(iii) of the Convention of June 3, 1955, which is in the following terms:

> "In the event of the resignation or death of the President, the Vice President or any other member of the tribunal, before the expiration of his term of office, his substitute shall be appointed in accordance with the same conditions as his predecessor and the substitute shall serve until the end of his predecessor's term of office. The substitute, except in the case of paragraph I (b), shall have the same nationality as his predecessor."

It follows that the Tunisian and French Governments must be requested to set this procedure in motion. Until such time as the appointment of new members permits of sittings of the tribunal, the case brought by the French Government is suspended, and the rights of the parties are reserved.

"For the reasons stated, I the President, hold as follows:

(1) The resignations of... [the Tunisian members of the tribunal] are hereby recorded.

(2) The replacement of the members who have resigned shall take place in accordance with Article 16 of the General Convention of June 3, 1955, and devolves upon the Governments of France and Tunisia.

(3) The proceedings instituted by an application of the French Government, dated December 3 and filed on December 4, 1956, are suspended until after the appointment of members of the Arbitral Tribunal who will replace the members who have resigned. The rights of the parties are reserved...."[422]

While the case is a singular one, it does not shed light on the authority of a truncated arbitral tribunal for these reasons: first, the tribunal was not an arbitral tribunal composed at all stages of three elements – party-named arbitrators from each party, and a third, neutral arbitrator; rather, the umpire was to intervene only at the stage when a difference had been established after deliberation between the French- and Tunisian-appointed arbitrators, which deliberation, as Vedel points out, had not taken place since

---

[422] The quotation is from the translation contained in 24 *International Law Reports*, pp. 768–770.

the Tunisian arbitrators had not appeared at all. Second, the governing Convention expressly provided that the presence of at least four members of the tribunal was required for the validity of its deliberations, of which two must be Frenchmen and two Tunisians; no Tunisians were present and no deliberations took place. Third, the neutral member of the tribunal had resigned before the tribunal met, so there was in any event no possibility of an umpire's deciding vote being validly cast in that state of the tribunal's composition. In the circumstances, it was not possible for the truncated tribunal to proceed and render a valid award, for it could do so neither with the expressly prescribed presence and agreement of both sets of party-appointed arbitrators nor with the alternative, residual casting vote of the neutral arbitrator after deliberation between the party-appointed arbitrators. Thus it was plausible for the President to call upon the Governments of France and Tunisia to replace the Tunisian arbitrators and (apparently by the terms of paragraph 2 of Vedel's final holding, which otherwise would have been solely directed to Tunisia), the neutral arbitrator as well.

The case has traces of the Buraimi episode in that the tribunal in both cases was left without a "majority" that could act for it. The position of the neutral arbitrator in this case resembles that initially contemplated for the umpire in the Mixed Claims Commission that sat between Germany and the United States.

(M) *TURRIFF CONSTRUCTION (SUDAN) LIMITED V. THE SUDAN*

As recounted in the second chapter, the Permanent Court of Arbitration in 1970 rendered an award in an arbitration between *Turriff Construction (Sudan) Limited and the Government of the Republic of the Sudan*,[423] from whose proceedings the Sudanese Government withdrew after pleadings had been filed and before hearings took place. At two stages in the proceedings, vacancies in the Tribunal occurred or were held to have occurred.

---

[423] An extensive and virtually verbatim report of the award by Professor Erades appears as "The Sudan Arbitration," 17 *Nederlands Tijdschrift voor International Recht* (1970), p. 200.

First, the President of the Tribunal (who had been appointed by the President of the International Court of Justice), Charles A. Cameron, resigned, and Dr. Lambertus Erades was appointed in his place.[424] No question of the Tribunal proceeding in the absence of its President arose. Second, when the Sudanese Government withdrew from the arbitration a few weeks before oral hearings were scheduled to begin, the arbitrator named by it, Judge S.M.Y. Mudawi, cabled that, owing to personal reasons, he was unable to attend the scheduled hearing and requested postponement.[425]

Thereafter, repeated efforts were made by the Secretary-General and the President of the Tribunal to obtain further information from Judge Mudawi as to the length of the postponement required. No further information having been obtained by the date when the hearing was scheduled to begin, "one arbitrator then being absent, the hearing could not then commence."[426] The reason assigned for this conclusion was the express provision of the Parties' Submission to Arbitration, which, in clause 1, paragraph 7, provided:

If a vacancy occurs no further step shall be taken in the Arbitration until it has been filled. When a vacancy is filled, the remaining Arbitrators shall be deemed automatically to have been re-appointed.[427]

Despite this provision, the Tribunal's President deemed that he was empowered to make certain procedural orders, subject to action by the Sudanese Government to set aside such orders; he made those orders, no motion to set aside ensued, and, in due course, the Tribunal confirmed those orders. Pursuant to them, the two-man Tribunal took evidence from plaintiffs' counsel, who were assembled in The Hague.

On July 4, 1969, no information still having been received from Judge Mudawi as to when and whether he would be available, the Secretary-General concluded (and the Tribunal later concurred) that a vacancy had occurred within the meaning of the Submission to Arbitration. Pursuant to that Submission, it then became the duty of the Sudanese government to name a new arbitrator forthwith to fill the vacancy. It did not and, after sixty days, pursuant to the terms of the Submission to Arbitration, the President of the International

---

[424] Ibid., p. 205.   [425] Ibid., p. 212.   [426] Ibid.
[427] Submission to Arbitration of October 21, 1966, Appendix A to the Award.

Court of Justice was requested to fill the vacancy. He did so. Meanwhile, the Tribunal had become aware of the fact that the Government earlier had purported to revoke the appointment of Judge Mudawi. The Tribunal declared that the Government had no power to revoke his appointment.[428]

In view of the provision that, where a vacancy occurs, no step shall be taken in the arbitration until it has been filled,[429] the fact that the Tribunal for that reason held that hearings could not commence in the absence of an arbitrator sheds no light on the authority of a truncated international arbitral tribunal to proceed.[430] Such a precise provision is as dispositive as a clause to the opposite effect was in the *Lena Goldfields* arbitration which authorized the truncated tribunal to act in the absence of a party-named arbitrator. But it is of interest that, despite this clause, the President of the Tribunal issued certain procedural orders and that the two-man tribunal took evidence both of which, however, were subject to scrutiny and confirmation by the three-man, reconstituted tribunal.

(N) IRAN-UNITED STATES CLAIMS TRIBUNAL CASES

We turn now to a number of cases that have been passed upon by the full Tribunal or Chambers of the Iran-United States Claims Tribunal. Article III of the Algiers Declarations provides:

1. The Tribunal shall consist of nine members or such larger multiple of three as Iran and the United States may agree are necessary to conduct its business expeditiously. Within ninety days after the entry into force of this agreement, each government shall appoint one-third of the members. Within thirty days after their appointment, the members so appointed shall by mutual agreement select the remaining third of the members and

---

[428] Erades, *supra* note 423, p. 215.
[429] But see *Redfern and Hunter on International Arbitration, supra* note 106, p. 109, emphasizing the wording of the submission agreement and indicating that the tribunal would have been able to proceed with the arbitration in its truncated form.
[430] Judge Seifi again takes a contradictory view. Noting in particular that "neither Turriff nor their arbitrator argued that the two remaining members had the authority to proceed in the absence of [Judge] Mudawi," he concludes that the conduct of the parties in response to Judge Mudawi's unavailability indicates that both the parties and the arbitrators felt that a truncated tribunal was not permitted to continue the proceedings and render an award. See Seifi, *supra* note 125, pp. 37–39.

appoint one of the remaining third President of the tribunal. Claims may be decided by the full Tribunal or by a panel of three members of the tribunal as the President shall determine. Each such panel shall be composed by the President and shall consist of one member appointed by each of the three methods set forth above.

2. Members of the Tribunal shall be appointed and the Tribunal shall conduct its business in accordance with the arbitration rules of the United Nations Commission on International Trade Law (UNCITRAL) except to the extent modified by the parties or by the Tribunal to ensure that this agreement can be carried out. The UNCITRAL rules for appointing members of three-member Tribunals shall apply *mutatis mutandis* to the appointment of the Tribunal.[431]

Article VI, paragraph 4 of the Declaration provides:

Any question concerning the interpretation or application of this agreement shall be decided by the Tribunal upon the request of either Iran or the United States.[432]

The Tribunal adopted Tribunal Rules, which incorporate the 1976 UNCITRAL Rules and, in certain cases, modify them for the tribunal's purposes. Article 13 of the 1976 UNCITRAL Rules provides:

REPLACEMENT OF AN ARBITRATOR

Article 13

1 In the event of the death or resignation of an arbitrator during the course of the arbitral proceedings, a substitute arbitrator shall be appointed or chosen pursuant to the procedure provided for in articles 6-9 that was applicable to the appointment or choice of the arbitrator being replaced....

2 In the event that an arbitrator fails to act or in the event of the *de jure* or *de facto* impossibility of his performing his functions, the procedure in respect of the challenge and replacement of an arbitrator as provided in the preceding articles shall apply.[433]

---

[431] As quoted in XX *International Legal Materials* (1981), p. 231. The text is also published at 1 *Iran-U.S. C.T.R.* 10.

[432] 1 *Iran-U.S. C.T.R.* 11.

[433] United Nations, *UNCITRAL Arbitration Rules* (1977), pp. 13–14. In the case of a three-member tribunal, Article 7 of the 1976 UNCITRAL Rules provides that each party appoints an arbitrator, who agree on the third. If one party fails to appoint its arbitrator, the other may have recourse to an appointing authority (who, absent agreement by the parties on another course, is designated by the

The Tribunal's Rules add:

Note to Article 13

Iran may, in advance, appoint up to three persons, to be available to act as a substitute member for a temporary period for a specified member, or members of the Tribunal appointed by Iran; and the United States may, in advance, appoint up to three persons, to be available to act as a substitute member for a temporary period for a specified member, or members, of the Tribunal appointed by the United States. The members of the Tribunal appointed by Iran and the United States may select, in advance, by mutual agreement, a person to act as substitute for a temporary period for any of the remaining one third of the members of the Tribunal.[434]

Article 32, paragraph 4 of the 1976 UNCITRAL Rules, which the Tribunal has not modified, provides:

An award shall be signed by the arbitrators and it shall contain the date on which and the place where the award was made. Where there are three arbitrators and one of them fails to sign, the award shall state the reason for the absence of the signature.[435]

In the course of its work, the full Tribunal and Chambers of the Tribunal at times have been confronted with the purposeful absence of one or another of the arbitrators appointed by Iran. While on occasion this fact has resulted in postponement of the Tribunal's proceedings, without any ruling as to whether in law the tribunal or its Chambers could proceed in the absence of one or more nationally-appointed arbitrators, on other occasions the Tribunal and Chambers of it have been of the view that decisions on their authority to proceed in the face of such absence had to be taken. Those decisions have uniformly sustained that authority. However, those decisions have been the subject of vigorous dissent by the arbitrators appointed by Iran. The Government of Iran initially sought to challenge certain awards reflecting those decisions in the courts of the Netherlands. Subsequently, Iran

---

Secretary-General of the Permanent Court of Arbitration) to make the appointment. If the two arbitrators fail to agree on a third, that presiding arbitrator also is appointed by the appointing authority. 1976 Rules, Articles 7-9. Where, under the 1976 UNCITRAL Rules, an arbitrator is challenged and replaced, the foregoing procedure is used to replace the arbitrator.

[434] Iran-United States Claims Tribunal, Final Tribunal Rules of May 3, 1983, 2 *Iran-U.S. C.T.R.* 405, 417–418.

[435] 1976 UNCITRAL Rules.

discontinued those cases. In view of Iran's discontinuance of its challenge to their validity in Dutch courts, it may be concluded that Iran has acquiesced in the validity of those awards. The principal Tribunal cases that have so far come to light will now be set forth.

(i) Earlier Authorities from the Iran-United States Claims Tribunal

(a) Chamber Three Decisions in Case Numbers 17, 30, and 132 Involving the Absence of Judge Sani:
On December 15, 1982, Chamber Three of the tribunal (composed of Nils Mangard, Chairman, Richard M. Mosk, and M. Jahangir Sani) handed down a decision in Case No. 17, *Raygo RJS Wagner Equipment Company* v. *Star Line Iran Company*[436] in the claimant's favor for a certain sum plus interest at 12 percent. The signatures of Judge Mangard and Judge Mosk appear above lines below which their names are typed; there is no signature above the line on which Judge Sani's name is typed. Below their names appears the following: "Judge Jahangir Sani took part in the hearing and deliberations in this case. The tribunal was informed that he in effect would not sign the award, and he was not present or available at the signing."[437]

On February 3, 1983, Judge Sani caused to be circulated as a Tribunal document his "Reasons for not signing the decision made by Mr. Mangard and Mr. Mosk in Case No. 17."[438] Judge Sani declared that:

I was not notified of the deliberative session which resulted in the issuance of an Award in the present case; nor did I happen to be present on the Tribunal premises and, consequently, at the meeting itself, when it was held.

The fact that the said Award was rendered without consultation with, and in the absence of, one arbitrator – together with the deficiencies which I shall elaborate upon below – constitute in my view so serious a violation of recognized legal principles as to necessitate that I not take part in the signing of the issued Award.

1. *The Award Is Rendered without Deliberation and in my Absence*
On Wednesday 13 December 1982, at the same time that I had been requested to return to Tehran to further discuss my resignation tendered

---

[436] Case No. 17, 1 *Iran-U.S. C.T.R.* 411.   [437] Ibid., p. 415.
[438] Ibid., pp. 415–417.

in relation to case No. 30, I was confronted by the unanticipated and surprising news that Mr. Mangard and Mr. Mosk had proceeded to issue Awards in cases Nos. 17 and 132

...I expressed my utter repudiation of what had transpired in the preceding few days, and stated unequivocally that my colleagues' issuance of awards in the cases mentioned above without my presence and participation were legally unsupportable. I sensed there that my colleagues had formed a wrong impression of my resignation. Supposing that I had tendered my resignation, so closely following that of Mr. Bellet, to further delay the issuance of award in case No. 30, they had considered themselves bound to also take actions in relation to cases Nos. 17 and 132, for which Hearing sessions had been held but no deliberations had taken place.[439]

Judge Sani proceeds to set out in detail his understanding of the facts that support the foregoing claims.

On March 3, 1983, Judge Mosk filed his "Comments" with respect to the foregoing statement of Judge Sani. He protested what he saw as that statement's disclosure of deliberations of the Chamber. He declared that Judge Sani "refused to participate in some of the deliberations in Case No. 17 and did not sign the Award," and maintained that it is "for the signing members to provide the reasons for the absence of Judge Sani's signature, not Judge Sani," citing the *travaux préparatoires* of the UNCITRAL Rules to this effect. Judge Mosk contended:

...under international law, Judge Sani cannot frustrate the work of the Chamber or the Tribunal by wilfully absenting himself and refusing to sign an award.[440]

In support of that conclusion, Judge Mosk cited the *Sabotage* cases, the *French-Mexican Mixed Claims Tribunal* cases, *Colombia* v. *Cauca Co.* and various commentators. He observed that the Code of Civil Procedure of Iran provides:

Where one of the arbiters after he has been informed, does not appear in the session held for proceedings or consultations, or he appears but refuses to give award, the award given by the majority of votes shall be valid even if unanimity of votes has been a condition in the agreement for arbitration.[441]

---

[439] Ibid., p. 416.   [440] Ibid., p. 425.   [441] Ibid.

He continued:

> ...Judge Sani's statement of facts is inaccurate. This case was heard on September 1 and 2, 1982. During the four months subsequent to the hearing there were numerous deliberations in the case....
>
> Following deliberations, Judge Mangard, late in the week of December 5, 1982, distributed to all members of the Chamber the proposed award and invited all members, including Judge Sani, to comment on the proposed award. After the distribution of the proposed opinion, Judge Sani agreed to be present at a meeting scheduled for the following week (December 13, 1982) to discuss the case.[4] [n. 4 With thousands of cases pending and few of them decided, one could not reasonably complain that the Tribunal has proceeded in haste.] The date selected for such a meeting was based on Judge Sani's request. Subsequently, however, Judge Sani refused to appear at the scheduled meeting even though he was on the premises of the Tribunal during that same week. Judge Sani sent word that he had communicated to his Government his resignation as a member of the Tribunal.[5] [n. 5 Of course one's resignation must be tendered to and accepted by the Tribunal. President Lagergren has stated, when a Member of the Tribunal resigns, it is for the Full Tribunal to accept the resignation and to decide from which date the resignation shall take effect...] Chairman Mangard then requested Judge Sani to attend a meeting of the Chamber on December 14, 1982. Again he refused. Judge Sani sent word that he would not appear and would not participate in any further deliberations because of the above mentioned communications concerning his resignation. No document or other notification concerning any such purported resignation was ever received by the Tribunal. Judge Sani's representatives then stated that Judge Sani might reconsider his purported resignation if the substance of this and the other awards was changed. On December 15, 1982 Judge Sani's representative reported that he had spoken to Judge Sani and that Judge Sani would not sign any awards. After Judge Sani's refusal to participate in further discussions, the award was signed and filed. The same basic events transpired with respect to two other awards (Case Nos. 30 and 132).[442]

Judge Mosk proceeded to set out further detail, which, in his view, demonstrated that Judge Sani used "his purported or threatened resignation" (which he noted would cause delay in Tribunal proceedings and jeopardize awards) to attempt to extract changes in awards and delays in proceedings.[443]

---

[442] Ibid. pp. 425–426.   [443] Ibid., p. 427.

Judge Sani replied to Judge Mosk's comments in a statement of April 7, 1983. After denying that he violated the secrecy of deliberations rule, Judge Sani contended that the provisions governing the establishment and operation of the tribunal demonstrate that a valid decision could not be taken in the absence of an arbitrator. Judge Sani maintained:

... we might examine the rules of this very complex phenomenon of an Iran-United States Arbitral Tribunal – which is established to determine not only a great number of extremely large claims but many issues highly sensitive to both Governments – so as to find out whether the possibility of determining the issues of such magnitude in the absence of one arbitrator is provided for. I am absolutely convinced that given the special composition of the Tribunal, such provision would have been contrary to anyone with the least foresight. The issue deserves further explanation, albeit a brief one:

Paragraph (b) of Article 3 of the "Introduction to the Tribunal's Provisionally Adopted Rules" specifies that "Arbitral Tribunal means either the Full Tribunal or a chamber . . . ." Paragraph (d) of the same Article further states that "(c)hamber" means a panel of three members composed by the President of the Tribunal from among the nine members of the Full Tribunal, pursuant to his powers under Article III, Paragraph 1 of the Claims Settlement Declaration. Paragraph 1 of Article III of the Claims Settlement Declaration, which overrides all other relevant rules, declares that "(t)he" Tribunal shall consist of nine members or such larger multiple of three as Iran and the United States may agree are necessary to conduct its business expeditiously. Within ninety days after the entry into force of this agreement, each government shall appoint one-third of the members. Within thirty days after their appointment, the members so appointed shall by mutual agreement select the remaining third of the members and appoint one of the remaining third President of the Tribunal. *"Claims may be decided by the Full Tribunal or by a panel of three members of the Tribunal as the President shall determine . . . ."* (emphasis added).

Turning now to Paragraph 1 of Article 31 [of the UNCITRAL Rules] which stipulates that 'when there are three arbitrators, any award or other decision of the Arbitral Tribunal shall be made by a majority of arbitrators,' we will realize that, at least until such time as the final deliberation is concluded and appropriate decision is made, the presence of all the three members is absolutely necessary.[444]

---

[444] Ibid., pp. 428, 431–432.

Judge Sani stated that reference to Iranian arbitration law was not relevant in international proceedings. He also contended that, in view of the circumstances surrounding his resignation, he had not willfully absented himself. Judge Sani then recounted his view of the facts in support of his claim that final deliberations had not taken place in respect of Case No. 17. Among the various attachments to his statement is a memorandum of December 10, 1982 from Judge Mangard to Judges Mosk and Sani, stating:

> I attach my draft opinion in Case No. 17. We have discussed this case on several occasions, and it is my intention to have the Award signed before we leave for Christmas. I therefore suggest that we deal with Case No. 17 again on Monday 13 December 1982 at the Chamber Meeting.
>
> My draft opinion in Case No. 132 was circulated yesterday. It should also be discussed on Monday so that an Award can be signed later in the week.[445]

On April 7, 1983, Judge Sani also filed "Mr. Jahangir Sani's Reasons for Not Signing the Decisions Made by Mr. Mangard and Mr. Mosk in Case No. 132," where he takes a position similar to that respecting Case No. 17:

> The fact that the Award was rendered without consultation with, and in the absence of, one arbitrator, constitutes so serious a breach of recognized legal principles that I am compelled to refrain from signing such an award.[446]

Judge Sani contended that "there had not been the slightest discussion" of Cases Nos. 17 and 132;[447] he also contended that "final deliberations had not yet taken place"[448] in respect of Cases Nos. 17 and 132. He recounts that, when he met with Judges Mangard and Mosk on January 4, 1983 for deliberation on those cases, discussions at once broke down over what he regarded as an effort "to lend a semblance of legality to a decision which had been issued without regard for the Rules of the Tribunal."[449]

On January 14, 1983, "The Opinion' of Judge Jahangir Sani in Case No. 30" was filed; it is not clear whether or not it was circulated then or in April. It begins:

---

[445] Ibid., pp. 439–440.   [446] 2 *Iran-U.S. C.T.R.* 14.   [447] Ibid.
[448] Ibid., p. 15.   [449] Ibid., p. 16.

Pursuant to Article 32 of the Provisionally Adopted Tribunal Rules, which provides that if an Arbitrator 'fails to sign, the award shall state the reason for the absence of the signature,' I hereby cite the reasons for my refusal to sign Award No. 30 (on damages and costs), and I request that, in accordance with the express terms of said Article, the same be reflected in the text of that Award.[450]

The "opinion" proceeds to recount interplay between Chamber Three and the full Tribunal on questions of damages and costs, and, especially, rate of interest on an award. Judge Sani maintains that a compromise was reached among the members of Chamber Three to provide for an 8½ per cent interest rate, but its execution was made contingent on his consent to issuing awards in the two other contested cases, which he rejected. Thus he refused to sign the alternative award containing provision for 12 percent interest. He charged that the parties to the case had been given no opportunity to address the Chamber on the complex issue of damages; that the members of Chamber Three had had no opportunity to discuss the subject; that the compromise rate of 8½ percent had been set aside because of his stand in unrelated cases and, finally, that there was not adequate deliberation on these issues. He concluded:

If it be assumed that my non-participation in the scheduled meeting of Monday 13 December 1982 was justified – and subsequent events indicate that my two colleagues did at any rate consider it to be justified – then the decision by my two colleagues to meet alone, possibly continue deliberation, and issue the Award was incompatible not only with our own Provisionally Adopted Rules but with all other judicial and arbitral principles. It is precisely for this reason that in Paragraph 4 of Article 32 of said Tribunal Rules no reference will be found to the absence of an arbitrator from the deliberation or adjudication sessions, but merely to the failure of an arbitrator to sign, which attest to the assumption that the arbitrator must have attended the deliberation and adjudication meetings, but then simply refused to sign.[451]

The statement of Judge Sani on Case No. 17 was answered by "Further Comments" of Judge Mosk of April 13, 1983,[452] as well as

---

[450] *Granite State Machine Co.* v. *The Islamic Republic of Iran*, 1 *Iran-U.S. C.T.R.* 452.
[451] Ibid., p. 454.
[452] *Raygo RJS Wagner Equipment Company* v. *Star Line Iran Company*, 1 *Iran-U.S. C.T.R.* 441.

by related comments in a concurring opinion filed on April 13, 1983 in Case No. 132 in which Judge Mosk declared:

Judge Sani's complaint seems to be that after the draft opinion was prepared, he wanted more deliberations, despite the fact that he would not attend them and would not sign the award in any event.

Apparently under Judge Sani's theory, an award is invalid unless he has been able to deliberate not once, not twice, but as many times as he desires and only at the times which suit his preference. Under this theory, few of the thousands of cases before this Tribunal could be decided.

Even if such a frivolous notion could be advanced, in the two months following the hearing in the instant case, there were adequate deliberations, and each of the members of the Chamber was given every opportunity to meet to deliberate further.[453]

Judge Mosk maintained:

Judge Sani's assertion that there was no discussion concerning this case is not correct. There were deliberations in which Judge Sani participated subsequent to the hearing on October 22, 1982, just as there were deliberations in which Judge Sani participated in Case Nos. 17 and 30. After such deliberations, proposed drafts of the awards and opinions were circulated among all members, including Judge Sani, and he was invited to attend further deliberations. As discussed in my comments with respect to Award No. 20-17-3, Judge Sani chose to absent himself and refused to sign any award.[454]

A footnote to Judge Mosk's opinion adds:

This is the third award of the chamber that Judge Sani has refused to sign. He even refused to sign a Full Tribunal decision: *Decision on Disposition of Interest Earned on the Security Account* – Case A-1, 3 August 1982 [1 *Iran-U.S. C.T.R.* 189]. Also, it should be noted that recently in two awards in another chamber – Nos. 31-157-2 *(Nasser Esphahanian)* and 32-211-2 *(Ataollah Golpira)* – another arbitrator appointed by the Government of Iran refused to sign the awards on the grounds that they were "tainted with improper

---

[453] *Rexnord, Inc.* v. *The Islamic Republic of Iran et al.*, 2 *Iran-U.S. C.T.R.* 6, 28–29. Judge Sani's "Reasons for Not Signing the Decision made by Mr. Mangard and Mr. Mosk in Case No. 132" appears at p. 14. The Chairman of Chamber Three, Judge Nils Mangard (a former Swedish judge of extensive arbitral experience) issued, on June 13, 1983, "Notes on Judge Jahangir Sani's refusal to sign the Awards issued in Cases Nos. 30, 17 and 132" (filed with the Tribunal on 4 July 1983). They affirm that the Award ultimately issued as No. 30 was the subject of extended deliberation and negotiation among the members of the Chamber.

[454] Ibid., p. 28.

motives." From all of Judge Sani's writings it appears that his idea of a compromise is an award that includes provisions he desires in return for his signature on the award as a dissenting arbitrator.[455]

(b) Chamber Three's Issuance of Five Awards without Judge Sani's Signature:

The Tribunal voted to accept Judge Sani's resignation on September 5, 1983, to take effect when his successor arrived. On September 2, 1983, Chamber Three filed awards in Case Nos. 185,[456] 346,[457] 124,[458] 67,[459] and 62,[460] all of which were rendered in the absence of Judge Sani. Each of these awards is signed by Judges Mangard and Mosk. While Judge Sani's name is also typed, no signature appears above his name while the signatures of Judges Mangard and Mosk do appear. Attached to each award is an "Explanation for Failure of Judge Sani to Sign Awards."

That explanation of the Chamber recounts that deliberations in these cases were held, with Judges Mangard, Sani and Mosk present, after hearings in each case took place and before summer recess. During the Chamber's final meeting prior to recess, it was determined that the Chamber would reconvene in early August 1983 for deliberations. On August 6, Chairman Mangard issued a schedule of meetings under which the awards in these and other cases were to be completed during that period. By letter of August 10, 1983, the Agent of Iran stated to the tribunal:

... that Judge Mostafa Jahangir Sani the Iranian Arbitrator of Chamber Three of the Tribunal has submitted his resignation to the Government of the Islamic Republic of Iran. His resignation has been accepted by the Government and will be effective as of 10 August 1983. His successor will be introduced to the Tribunal in due course.[461]

---

[455] Ibid.
[456] *Chas. T. Main International, Inc.* v. *Mahab Consulting Engineers, Inc. et al.*, 3 Iran-U.S. C.T.R. 270.
[457] *Alan Craig* v. *Ministry of Energy of Iran et al.*, ibid., p. 280.
[458] *John Carl Warnecke & Associates* v. *Bank Mellat*, ibid., p. 256.
[459] *Woodward Clyde Consultants* v. *the Government of the Islamic Republic of Iran et al.*, ibid., p. 239.
[460] *Blount Brothers Corporation* v. *Ministry of Housing and Urban Development, et al.*, ibid., p. 225.
[461] See, e.g., *Chas. T. Main International, Inc.* v. *Mahab Consulting Engineers, Inc. et al.*, 3 Iran-U.S. C.T.R. 276.

The explanation continues:

No reasons were cited for the purported resignation. The President of the tribunal ordered that certain Hearings before the Full Tribunal, which were scheduled to take place during its 15-17 August 1983 Meetings, be postponed. In addition, the Chairman of Chamber Three cancelled the meetings set for the finalization of awards and further deliberations during the week of 8 August 1983.

Judge Jahangir Sani did not appear at the Full Tribunal meeting held on 15 August 1983. At the 17 August 1983 Full Tribunal meeting, the President stated that the tribunal had as yet received no valid reasons for Judge Jahangir Sani's absence and had not authorized that absence. The President also declared that it would be for Chamber Three and the Full Tribunal to determine the legal consequences of that absence in the individual cases pending before them. Thereafter, the Chairman of Chamber Three ordered that the Hearings scheduled for 18, 19, and 25 August and the Pre-Hearing Conference scheduled for 1 September be postponed.

By a letter dated 18 August 1983 and conveyed by post and telex, the Chairman of Chamber Three informed Judge Jahangir Sani of the President's declarations and notified him that a new schedule had been set under which, *inter alia*, the finalization and signing of the award in this case would take place on 2 September 1983.

In a telex dated 24 August 1983 to the Chairman of Chamber Three, Judge Jahangir Sani acknowledged receipt of the letter of 18 August 1983 and informed the Chairman that he considered his resignation to the Islamic Republic of Iran to be effective upon the tribunal and that he was no longer legally authorized or empowered to participate in the taking of decisions or the issuance of awards except for "the preparing and drafting, or drawing up and elaborating, of a judicial opinion or award which has previously been communicated or announced."

Judge Jahangir Sani was not present for the signing of the Award in this case at the 2 September Chamber meeting.

Under the above circumstances, the tribunal has determined that it may proceed with the signing of the Award in the absence of Judge Jahangir Sani pursuant to Article 32, paragraph 4, of the tribunal Rules.[462]

The position that it is understood that Judge Sani took in response to Judge Mangard's requests to attend sessions of Chamber Three is that neither the tribunal nor its President is legally competent to accept the resignation of a governmentally appointed arbitrator;

---

[462] Ibid., pp. 276–277.

rather, the authority that appointed the arbitrator is the authority that accepts his resignation. An arbitrator has an unquestionable right to resign. As of the date when his government accepts his resignation, the arbitrator is no longer legally authorized or empowered to take part in the issuance of an award. Since the Government of Iran had accepted his resignation as of August 10, Judge Sani believed that he could not take part in meetings or actions of the tribunal subsequent to that date.

For its part, the government of the United States maintained:

> ... this matter fundamentally concerns the question of whether the Government of Iran or an arbitrator appointed by it has the power to frustrate the work of this Tribunal. We submit that, pursuant to the Claims Settlement Declaration, the answer must be no. This Tribunal has been established as an independent institution for the adjudication of claims, which is designed and intended to fulfill its task despite any lack of cooperation by either party.

> Within this general context, the matter of Judge Jahangir Sani raises, as the Tribunal has recognized, a number of separate questions. As to these, we set forth the following views:

A. There can be no legally effective resignation by any member of this Tribunal without submission of such resignation to, and its acceptance by, this Tribunal.

B. An arbitrator cannot resign without notice and without disposition of pending cases, absent compelling justification.

C. The Government of Iran has violated its obligations under the Claims Settlement Declaration by purporting to 'accept' Judge Jahangir Sani's resignation.

D. The Tribunal is not only empowered but required to continue both administrative and judicial functions despite such purported resignation.[463]

The US letter noted that, in prior instances, the Tribunal had taken the position that resignations must be submitted to and accepted by the tribunal. It continued:

> Under the Claims Settlement Declaration, no other principle could apply. Neither Government has control over the composition of this Tribunal. The Government of Iran has argued that, because it is

---

[463] Letter of the US Agent, John R. Crook, to the President of the Tribunal, Judge Gunnar K.A. Lagergren, of August 16, 1983, pp. 1–4.

empowered to appoint arbitrators, it must be empowered to effectuate their withdrawal. However, the Government of Iran does not have unfettered authority concerning the appointment of Iranian arbitrators. It has a threshold duty to appoint such arbitrators, but it has no power to delay or withhold such appointments. If either Government fails to appoint its respective arbitrators, the appointing authority shall do so. Article 7, Tribunal Rules.

Moreover, even if the Governments had complete control over the appointment of arbitrators, they could not control withdrawal. The party-appointed arbitrators, once appointed, are independent. Article 10(1), Tribunal Rules. An arbitrator who is controlled by his respective Government is not independent. The Government may not determine, as the Government of Iran purports to do, whether and when an arbitrator is to resign.

Moreover, the principle that a party may not unilaterally withdraw an arbitrator once proceedings have commenced is recognized in any effective system of arbitral procedure.[464]

It further argued:

This Tribunal has also confirmed in past practice the principle that, once an arbitrator has accepted his responsibilities, he is not entitled to resign at will. "Spontaneous withdrawal is inadmissible". G Scelle .... Absent compelling reasons, the Tribunal must have adequate notice of resignation and arrangement must be made for the disposition of pending cases ....

This principle rests in theory upon the contractual relation between the arbitrator and the parties. Statutory law frequently contains express provision that an arbitrator may not resign at all once proceedings have commenced, absent acceptable justification. Thus, under the Dutch Code of Civil Procedure, (which Iran elsewhere alleges to govern this Tribunal,)

> Arbitrators who have accepted their mandate cannot withdraw except for reasons to be approved by the Court. They are liable to compensate the damages of the parties should they, without any justifiable reasons, fail to make their award within the period of time fixed for it. Article 628.

> The comparable statutory provision of Iranian Law, Art. 649, has already been cited. Indeed, this appears to be a generally accepted principle of law. See, e.g., Article 1014 of the French Code of Procedure; Article 813 of the Italian Code of Civil Procedure; Article 245 of the Zurich Code of Civil Procedure; Section 13.3 of the English Arbitration Act; Article 1689 of the Belgian Code of Civil Procedure (Arbitration Articles of 1972.)

---

[464] Ibid., pp. 4–6.

This principle is also implicit in the UNCITRAL Rules. In his commentary on UNCITRAL Rule 13, Pieter Sanders states:

"The Rules do not give any indication as to the circumstances in which a resignation may be justified, and, indeed, they could hardly be expected to do so. Once the arbitrator has agreed to function he should fulfil his task. Exceptionally there may be good reasons for not continuing, such as a heart attack. II *Yearbook Commercial Arbitration* (1977), p. 191."[465]

The US letter further contends that Iran violated its obligations under the Algiers Declaration by purporting to accept the resignation of Judge Sani and that the tribunal is not only empowered to act but directed to act despite the purported resignation of Judge Sani:

...the Government of Iran does not have the right to control the withdrawal of its party-appointed arbitrators. Even if it had such right, however, it would not be entitled to withdraw an arbitrator in the disruptive fashion attempted here. The Government of Iran, having contemplated Judge Jahangir Sani's retirement for a period of some eight months, announced it to the Tribunal on August 10, 1983, only a few days in advance of resumed sessions. Not only has the Government of Iran made no arrangement whatsoever for appointment of a replacement, it cannot even say when a replacement might be appointed. No acceptable or convincing excuse is possible for this outrageous disruption of Tribunal operations. This is clear additional evidence of Iran's intention to frustrate Tribunal operations and, in particular, to disrupt proceedings in Chamber 3.

The Government of Iran is not entitled to obstruct the operations of this Tribunal. The Government of Iran has agreed in the Algiers Declarations to the establishment of this Tribunal "for the purpose of deciding claims.". . . This treaty obligation is binding, and must be performed by the parties in good faith . . . Here, the Government of Iran has not merely failed to lend its cooperation to operations of the Tribunal, it has deliberately disrupted them.[466]

Finally, the United States maintained that the Tribunal is not only empowered to act but directed to act despite the purported resignation of Judge Sani:

The unjustified and unsanctioned withdrawal of an arbitrator, whether by his own actions or by the actions of one of the Governments, cannot be permitted to disrupt the work of this Tribunal. In the past, the Tribunal

---

[465] Ibid.   [466] Ibid., p. 4.

has adhered to this principle. Over the past year, arbitrators appointed by the Government of Iran have, repeatedly and increasingly, refused to participate in the Tribunal in the attempt to block actions deemed undesirable by the Government of Iran. The Iranian arbitrators refused to attend the 59th, 69th and 81st Full Tribunal meetings over small claims matters, the resignation of Judge Bellet, and the budget. . . . The Iranian arbitrators in both Chamber 2 and Chamber 3 have refused to attend scheduled deliberations in order to prevent the issuance of awards. To the great credit of the Tribunal, it has uniformly shown wisdom and strength in response to such tactics, and has in each instance acted on whatever matter has triggered the boycott.

We submit that this is the only possible result. It is evident from the UNCITRAL Rules which, under Article III(2) of the Claims Settlement Declaration govern the conduct of this Tribunal except as modified, that this Tribunal is designed and intended to operate despite the default or non-cooperation of either an arbitrator or a party . . . Moreover, should the express provisions of the rules prove insufficient to accomplish this end, the Tribunal is empowered to take such steps as are necessary. By the express agreement of the parties in Article III(2) of the Claims Settlement Agreement, the Tribunal is directed to regulate the conduct of its business "to ensure that this agreement can be carried out."

It is evident that the agreement of the parties cannot be carried out if the only remedy for the willful and unjustified absence of arbitrators is challenge and replacement. This mechanism by itself cannot prevent disruption of Tribunal operations for months at a time. Under Article 7 of the Tribunal Rules, a party has 30 days to appoint a replacement party arbitrator. If the party fails to do so, the appointing authority is allowed in principle another 30 days to make such appointment. If an appointment is named, but does not act, some time must be allowed for the process of challenge. If such challenge is successful, the process of appointment begins anew. Thus, the Tribunal must be empowered to act in the interim, and cannot simply wait for a replacement to be named . . . .

International precedent further supports the power of this Tribunal to continue despite the unjustified absence of an arbitrator . . . First, it appears that Tribunals which have actually been confronted with the question have upheld almost uniformly their power to continue proceedings. Second, although there has been some academic debate among commentators, the weight of authority, especially authorities of this century, strongly supports the Tribunal's power to continue. Indeed, where the Tribunal is clearly designed to operate on a majority basis notwithstanding party default, it is debatable whether there is any contrary authority at all.

Accordingly, the Tribunal can and must continue to operate despite Judge Jahangir Sani's purported withdrawal, and not permit the resignation and replacement of arbitrators to impede the disposition of pending cases.[467]

(c) Issuance of Awards by Chamber Two Where Judge Shafeiei Was Absent without Leave:

On December 1, 1982, the Chairman of Chamber Two, Judge Pierre Bellet, submitted a letter requesting the President of the tribunal to accept his resignation. The President stated in response that, when a Member of the tribunal resigns, it is for the Full Tribunal to accept the resignation and to decide from which date the resignation shall take effect. It was in due course determined that Judge Bellet's resignation would take effect as of August 1, 1983; in the meantime, efforts were made to agree upon a successor, which task, failing agreement of the Parties, was finally remitted to the designation of the appointing authority.

On July 27, 1983, Chamber Two (Bellet, Chairman, Shafei Shafeiei, and George H. Aldrich, arbitrators) issued four awards[468] at the end of which the names of Judges Bellet, Aldrich, and Shafeiei appear in typescript, but only the signatures of Judges Bellet and Aldrich are above the lines below which their names are typed. To these awards is appended a statement of the same date, signed by Judges Bellet and Aldrich, as follows:

Deliberations in this case began soon after the Hearing on 19 April 1983. All three arbitrators participated fully in these deliberations, which continued until the end of May. Throughout the period from February to late June the three arbitrators had been in agreement that July would be fully dedicated to the final deliberations in this and the other pending cases, in view of the 1 August effective date of Chairman Bellet's resignation from the tribunal.

On 23 June 1983, however, Mr. Shafeiei sent Chairman Bellet a note informing him that he intended to be absent from the tribunal on vacation until the end of July. The Chairman responded by a note dated 29 June saying that, while a brief vacation was acceptable, Mr. Shafeiei was expected after 5 July. Nevertheless, after a further exchange of notes,

---

[467] Ibid., pp. 4–6.

[468] *Intrend International, Inc.* v. *Imperial Iranian Air Force, et al.*, 3 Iran-U.S. C.T.R. 110; *Gruen Associates, Inc.* v. *Iran Housing Company, et al.*, ibid., p. 97; *Reynolds Metal Company* v. *Islamic Republic of Iran et al.*, ibid., p. 119; and *National Airmotive Corporation* v. *the Islamic Republic of Iran et al.*, ibid., p. 91.

Mr. Shafeiei has absented himself until the present and has given no address or telephone number where he could be reached. . . . The Chairman has had all the successive drafts of this award since Mr. Shafeiei's departure deposited in his office in due time so that, if he had been present, he could have read and commented upon them, but no comments have been received. The Chairman also deposited in Mr. Shafeiei's office on 20 July 1983 a letter informing him of the place and time of signature. Mr. Shafeiei failed to attend the signing. In these circumstances, an arbitral tribunal cannot permit its work to be frustrated. This statement is made pursuant to Article 32, paragraph 4 of the Tribunal Rules of Procedure.[469]

Judge Shafeiei on August 9, 1983 filed three memoranda, which, in essentially identical terms, condemn the issuance of the foregoing awards in these terms:

The recording of the name of an arbitrator at the bottom of an award signifies that he participated in the making of that award – that is, that he participated in the Chamber hearings and in completely democratic discussions and deliberations, in taking a decision, in preparing the draft award, in studying it and, finally, in preparing the final award and signing it. I have had absolutely no part or role in the formulation of the present Awards, nor have I been present therein. Everything has been carried out in my absence and even without my knowledge. . . .

Pursuant to the terms of the Claims Settlement Declaration signed on 19 January 1981 by the two Governments of Iran and the United States, meetings of the Tribunal's Chambers must be attended by both of the two arbitrators appointed by their respective Governments and by the jointly-appointed arbitrator. Under no circumstances may a Chamber meeting be convened in the absence of either of the two arbitrators appointed by their respective Governments, even with respect to urgent administrative matters. The action by Mr. Bellet and Mr. Aldrich constitutes a flagrant and intentional violation of the Algiers Declarations and other regulations governing the Tribunal.

Today, it is clearer than ever before that the Government of Iran has become a victim of breach of trust because of the existence of the Security Account, which has induced this Chamber to engage in blatant, intentional violations of the Algiers Declarations and the Tribunal Rules.

[469] Identical statements are attached to the *Intrend*, *Gruen* and *Reynolds* awards; a shorter statement of like content appears in the *National Airmotive* Award on Agreed Terms.

At any event, nothing can justify, or diminish the odiousness of, these illegal acts by the above-mentioned gentlemen – particularly in light of the fact that this illegal behaviour has been engaged in by someone who was for years a guardian of the law as Chief Justice of the Supreme Court of France. In addition, the lies, hypocrisy and duplicity involved here further heighten the responsibility of these arbitrators with whom I was, and am, condemned to work.[470]

Judge Shafeiei attached to these memoranda a sheaf of correspondence and memoranda. In a letter to Judge Lagergren of August 5, 1983, he maintains that, even if he was wrong in taking leave during July (which he denies), "clear provision has been made for such exigencies in Article 13, paragraph 2 of the Tribunal Rules."[471] He contends that the awards were prepared by Judges Bellet and Aldrich even though they knew that he was on leave and unable to take part. This was, he maintains, "an abuse of authority . . .". The Islamic Republic of Iran was "the victim of a betrayal of trust"[472] because monies in satisfaction of the awards were paid out of the Security Account. Judge Lagergren is criticized for authorizing payment of the awards. Judge Shafeiei continues:

Now it is, after all, the duty and prerogative of the Agent of the Islamic Republic of Iran to study the issues relating to betrayal of trust, *ultra vires*, and illegal withdrawal from the Security Account. Perhaps these acts also have ramifications in penal law. It is also the duty of the Agent of the Islamic Republic of Iran to study the subject of criminal prosecution of arbitrators who have violated the law, and to take appropriate action.

Once more, I draw your attention to the awards in Case Nos. 188 and 220. I played no role in those cases, and I was neither present nor involved therein. Everything was carried out on a two-member basis. These awards are not 'Tribunal awards' but rather arbitrary decisions by two arbitrators violating the law.[473]

In a second memorandum dated August 8, 1983, Judge Shafeiei expands at length upon these themes, maintaining that he had a right to take leave when he chose despite the schedule of Chamber

---

[470] "The Reasons Why My Signature Does not Appear at the end of the So-Called 'Awards' Nos. 58-449-3, 59-220-2, 60-83-2, and 61-188-2, Which Have Been Illegally Rendered by Mr. George Aldrich and Mr. Bellet," filed August 9, 1983, 3 *Iran-U.S. C.T.R.* 124.

[471] Judge Shafeiei appears to refer to Article 13, paragraph 2 of the UNCITRAL Rules.

[472] 3 *Iran-U.S. C.T.R.* 125, 127.   [473] Ibid., p. 128.

Two and its Chairman's purported denial of his leave. He states that he refused to accept any date for meetings in July. Judge Shafeiei maintains that Chamber Two was "under no obligation whatever to subject all of the cases in whose final hearings Mr. Bellet had taken part to final examination and deliberations prior to the expiration of his term of office."[474] He continued:

It is also a certain and decisive fact that, pursuant to Article III, Paragraph 1 of the Claims Settlement Declaration, each of the Chambers of this Tribunal must be made up of three members, in the manner set forth in this Article.

The Chambers of this Tribunal are not able, under any circumstances, to hold meetings except in the presence of both of the two arbitrators appointed by the two Governments, respectively. Therefore, it was completely illegal for Chamber Two to hold judicial meetings, deliberate, render decisions, and sign awards in my absence. The actions by Mr. Bellet and Mr. Aldrich constitute blatant and conscious violations of the Algiers Declarations and the Tribunal Rules.[475]

Among the attachments to Judge Shafeiei's memoranda is a memorandum from him to Judge Bellet of June 23, 1983 in which Judge Shafeiei states that: "I need to take advantage of the few holiday weeks that are left between now and the end of July. I request you kindly not to hold any Chamber Meetings in my absence."[476] Judge Bellet replied:

You had informed me of your desire to take some rest during the week of 27 June to 3 July, and although that did cause problems for me, I accepted it.

However, it has never been mentioned that you would leave until the end of July, and I am very much astonished that you have not informed me of this before.

You are aware of the Presidential Order of 15 June 1983, pursuant to which Chamber Two is "in function" until 31 July.

You are aware of the fact, since several months, that I must leave this Tribunal by 31 July 1983, and that several cases are being deliberated by us, which must be decided before that date.

You cannot be irregularly absent, and therefore I invite you to be present here again as of the 5th of July, after the days of rest you will have taken.[477]

---

[474] Ibid., p. 137.   [475] Ibid., pp. 139–140.   [476] Ibid., p. 132.   [477] Ibid.

Judge Shafeiei replied on July 1, stating, among other things:

Naturally I am aware since a long time that your mission will end on 31 July, but that circumstance cannot deprive me of my annual holidays. On the other hand, nothing obligates us to decide, through accelerated and abnormal deliberations, all these cases, of which some are extremely voluminous and complicated.

It has often happened in the past that you have made decisions by yourself, but in the name of the Tribunal, on administrative matters, which conduct is not permitted under the Tribunal Rules. I therefore find it necessary to point out to you that you may not irregularly hold a Chamber Meeting during the Tribunal's annual recess and during my absence.[478]

Judge Bellet responded on July 13 as follows:

I have consulted the Full Tribunal Minutes. It shows on the record of the 72nd Meeting that the annual recess extends only until 17 July, and not after that date . . . .

. . . it was understood between the three of us, that we would discuss the cases that are still pending as soon as he [Judge Aldrich] had returned, and you yourself have insisted, on that occasion, that the deliberations in the ITT Case, since resolved, be deferred to July 1983.

Therefore, I was very surprised: first when, suddenly, you asked for a first week of rest, from 27 June to 4 July, and then when you informed me by your letter of 23 June, that you would leave for a longer period, during an indefinite amount of days.

You should have advised us of this in advance, so that I, as the Chairman of the Second Chamber, could have taken the appropriate measures for the solution of the pending cases, before my leaving the Tribunal.

Moreover, the President of this Tribunal has signed on 15 June 1983 an Order which implies that we should be available at any time during July 1983.

Therefore, amiably but firmly, I ask you to be present, until the end of July, at all our meetings, to deliberate with us, especially on the cases of INTREND, GRUEN, HOFFMAN, and CHAS T. MAIN, and then to proceed to the signing of the awards.

In case you do not come, Mr. Aldrich and I will have to proceed without you.[479]

Judge Bellet was informed by Judge Shafeiei's associate that he was on vacation and that there was no way to reach him. Drafts of

---

[478] Ibid., p. 134.   [479] Ibid., p. 136.

awards delivered to Judge Shafeiei's office were returned unopened.

On October 13, 1983, Judge Aldrich released his "Comments... on Judge Shafeiei's Reasons for non-Signature" of the four disputed awards. He declared:

Judge Shafeiei says his absence for the month of July was permissible and justified and was for the purposes of rest and completing some backlogged Chamber work. The facts, however, force me to the conclusion that his absence was impermissible and that it was intended: (a) to avoid any further deliberations with Judge Bellet; (b) to attempt thereby to prevent Chamber 2 from rendering awards in the pending cases prior to the 31 July effective date of Judge Bellet's resignation; and (c) to provide grounds for attacks on any awards issued during that absence.

The Chamber had structured its entire hearing schedule for the spring of 1983 with a view to the time available to it before the August 1 effective date of Judge Bellet's resignation to deliberate on and decide the cases it heard. This was discussed at innumerable Chamber meetings from at least January 1983. Those discussions indicated that all three members of the Chamber clearly understood that... the month of July was the time during which we would have to work intensively to conclude deliberations and issue awards. In early January at the 72nd meeting of the Full Tribunal when the Tribunal vacation period from 10 June to 17 July was decided upon, I made it clear to our colleagues in the other chambers that Chamber 2 could not follow that schedule because of Judge Bellet's resignation and would have to meet throughout July. Judge Bellet concurred, and Judge Shafeiei did not disagree.

Until late June Judge Shafeiei never indicated to me or, so far as I know, to Judge Bellet any disagreement with our plan to work through July to finish the pending cases. In fact, in late May, just before my departure for the United States, he urged strongly that the Chamber not issue its awards in the Kimberly-Clark and ITT cases (awards numbered 46 and 47) saying we should discuss them further during July. See Judge Shafeiei's reasons for not signing award number 46 (filed on 27 May 1983) in which he quotes a letter he wrote Judge Bellet as follows:

"I am of the opinion that this issue and other issues should be studied and discussed with greater care. I am preparing myself for this study and shall have completed this work in the coming weeks. The Award will certainly have been signed prior to the termination of your incumbency."

Since it was well understood that I was leaving The Hague two days after the day that award was signed and would not return until 25 June, Judge

Shafeiei's argument can only be understood as meaning that he wanted the further deliberations to occur during July.

Upon my return to the offices of the Tribunal on 27 June, I was understandably quite surprised to see Judge Shafeiei's letter to Judge Bellet dated 23 June stating that he would be on vacation until the end of July. I spoke to Judge Shafeiei at the earliest opportunity and urged him to reconsider that decision. He told me how unhappy he was with Judge Bellet and said he did not wish to meet further with him, but I was left with the impression that he would remain in The Hague at least part of the time and would be prepared to discuss directly with me certain draft awards and might participate in further Chamber meetings if that could be done amicably. In the event, however, he left the city soon thereafter and apparently did not return until August.

To what extent Judge Shafeiei's absence was motivated by dislike of continued work with Judge Bellet and to what extent it was motivated by a desire to prevent the pending cases from being decided before Bellet's resignation took effect, I cannot know. In the light of the above summarized facts, however, I could not escape the conclusion that his absence during July was unauthorized, was contrary to what the Chamber (and apparently he) had previously planned and assumed, and was designed to prevent, if possible, the Tribunal from dealing with the cases then under deliberation while Judge Bellet remained Chairman of the Chamber and, in any event, to provide an argument for attacks on any awards issued during that absence. I note in this connection that Judge Shafeiei's letter of 23 June requested that no Chamber meetings be held in his absence, although he knew that both deliberations and urgent administrative decisions were pending.

I made informal efforts through Judge Kashani and the Iranian Agent, Mr. Kashan, to urge Judge Shafeiei to return before the end of July, but these efforts proved unavailing. In light of this situation, Judge Bellet and I decided that the Chamber was justified, and in fact obligated, by international law and precedent to proceed with the awards on which we could agree, explaining therein the reasons for the absence of Judge Shafeiei's signature. Any other conclusion, in a continuing tribunal of this type with many cases on its docket, would permit the Tribunal's work to be sabotaged. In this connection, we were aware that the Full Tribunal on a number of occasions had met and taken decisions, even judicial decisions, in the absence of one or more arbitrators.[480]

---

[480] Comments of George H. Aldrich on Judge Shafeiei's Reasons for Non-Signature of Awards Numbered 58-449-3, 59-220-2, 60-83-2, and 61-188-2 of 13 October 13, 1983, ibid., pp. 145–146.

(ii) Subsequent Authorities From the Iran-United States Claims Tribunal
It is notable that the problem of the absence of Iranian-appointed arbitrators has persisted since the publication of the first edition, but similar results have followed.

(a) Issuance of Award by Chamber Two without Judge Bahrami-Ahmadi's Signature:

In Case No. 298, *Saghi* v. *Iran*, Chamber Two rendered an interlocutory award as a truncated tribunal. The award reads simply:

> Mr. Bahrami-Ahmadi did not participate in the deliberation of this Case, stating that in his view such cases are not admissible and he refused to sign the present Award.[481]

In his Declaration, Judge Bahrami-Ahmadi writes:

> I have neither participated in the deliberations in that case, nor signed the legal opinion relating thereto....
>
> 2. The Tribunal Rules do not grant any authority for two members of a Chamber to issue an Award without the third member's having participated in the deliberations thereon. The Chambers of this Tribunal are three-member arbitral panels, and a necessary precondition of the validity of their Awards is that all three arbitrators have been effectively present at the deliberative sessions thereon. Therefore, I regard the present "Interlocutory Award" as constituting a "legal opinion" by my colleagues, for which the instant Declaration cannot be construed as a separate or dissenting Opinion by this writer. My purpose here is merely to note that the document which has been issued cannot be taken as constituting an Award by Chamber Two of the Tribunal....[482]

When the case was subsequently argued on the merits, Iran maintained that the interlocutory award was invalid because it was signed by only two arbitrators.[483] The Chamber held that it could not accept that argument, observing that Article 32(4) of the Tribunal's rules make a

---

[481] *Saghi* v. *Iran*, 14 *Iran-U.S. C.T.R.* 3.

[482] Declaration of Hamid Bahrami-Ahmadi with Respect to the Legal Opinion Issued by Two Members of Chamber Two, in Connection with Case No. 298, 14 *Iran-U.S. C.T.R.* 3.

[483] See Stephen M. Schwebel, "The Validity of an Arbitral Award Rendered by a Truncated Tribunal," *Justice in International Law: Further Selected Writings* (2011), pp. 182, 186.

provision for that occurrence.[484] The majority additionally added, in its Comments on the Declaration of Judge Bahrami-Ahmadi, that:

While we understood the reasons why Judge Bahrami-Ahmadi felt it necessary to refuse to participate in the deliberation and signature of the Interlocutory Award...it was clear to us that he understood the reasons why we felt obliged to proceed without him. As this Tribunal has previously held, a continuing international tribunal with many cases on the docket cannot permit its work to be frustrated by the refusal of one of its members to deliberate a claim or to sign an award.[485]

The Iranian-appointed arbitrator did sign this award on the merits, albeit while dissenting.[486]

(b) Issuance of Award by Chamber Three without Judge Ansari Moin's Signature:

In Case No. 129, *Sedco, Inc., et al.* v. *National Iranian Oil Company et al.*, Chamber Three of the Iran-United States Claims Tribunal issued an Order of May 17, 1985 which recounted that the Iran-appointed Member, Judge Parviz Ansari Moin, was absent from hearings held on May 14 and 15, 1985 "without notification and without any expressly official explanation to date."[487]

Hearings in the case had been postponed several times, with hearings finally agreed to be set for May 14 and 15, 1985.[488] Iran then requested a further postponement by three months, stating that its representatives were unable to participate on the May dates.[489] The Chamber rejected the request, and Judge Ansari Moin, without notice or explanation, failed to be present at the start of the hearing on May 14, 1985.[490] The representatives of the Iranian Respondents also failed to appear.[491]

It appeared that the Iranian Members of the tribunal "had been recalled...to Iran by the Iranian Government...," a report that prompted the claimant to argue that the absence of Judge Ansari Moin was unjustified and contrary to the required independence of a Tribunal member.[492] The claimant requested that the scheduled hearing proceed "before the two remaining Members of the

---

[484] Ibid.
[485] *Saghi* v. *Iran*, Comments on the Declaration of Judge Bahrami-Ahmadi, Case No. 298, 14 *Iran-U.S. C.T.R.* 3.
[486] Ibid.   [487] Caron and Caplan, *supra* note 213, pp. 623, 686, 772.   [488] Ibid.
[489] Ibid.   [490] Ibid.   [491] Ibid.   [492] Ibid.

Chamber . . . ," particularly since its expert witness was present in The Hague on that day and would not be available at a later stage.[493]

Chamber Three accordingly proceeded to hear the witness without the presence of Judge Ansari Moin. The Chamber made a tape recording of the testimony, which would be made available to all the members of the Chamber and the parties.[494]

The Chamber ultimately rendered an award, which Judge Ansari Moin refused to sign. The award rendered by the Chairman and Judge Brower states:

> The Chairman in a memorandum to the Chamber Members of 11 June 1987 declared that the Award in this Case would be signed during the week of 29 June 1987. On Thursday, 2 July 1987, the last working day of that week, the Arbitrators met on the tribunal's premises at which time the completed Award was presented for signature. The Chairman and Judge Brower signed the Award at that time, and it was agreed that Judge Ansari would sign an explanatory statement to be appended to the Award so that it might be filed no later than 5 p.m. on Monday, 6 July 1987, thereby satisfying the requirement of Article 32, paragraph 4, of the Tribunal Rules that the Award be signed by all three Arbitrators.
>
> The Tribunal notes with regret that by the agreed deadline on 6 July Judge Ansari had not presented the statement and consequently, although Judge Ansari participated fully in the deliberations, the Award does not bear his signature.[495]

Judge Ansari Moin argued that the award was made improper by incorrect premises, substantive and fundamental errors, and blatant bias on the part of the Chairman.[496]

(c) Issuance of Award by Chamber One without Judge Ameli's Signature:

The award rendered by Chamber One in the *Starrett Housing Corp. v. Iran* case was done without the signature of Judge Ameli. The award states that, "[h]aving fully participated in the deliberation of the Case and in the drafting of the Final Award and having been informed of the time when the Final Award would be signed, Mr. Ameli failed to sign."[497] Judge Holtzmann further noted:

---

[493] Ibid.   [494] Ibid.
[495] *Sedco, Inc., et al. v. National Iranian Oil Company et al.*, 15 *Iran-U.S. C.T.R.* 23.
[496] Statement by Judge Parviz Ansari Concerning His Reasons for Not Signing the Award in Case No. 129, ibid.
[497] *Starrett Housing Corp. v. Iran*, 16 *Iran-U.S. C.T.R.* 112.

After the Hearing in this Case on 16-24 January 1987, all three arbitrators met for deliberations at the following times: 24 January, 9-13 March, 29 June-3 July, 20-23 July and 11-14 August 1987. Copies of successive drafts of the Final Award were circulated among all of the arbitrators, and were discussed in detail. The changes in the last draft that resulted in the text of the Final Award, as signed, were also reviewed and discussed by all of the arbitrators.

During the deliberation meetings held on 20-24 July 1987, the time for signing the Final Award was scheduled for 5 p.m. 13 August 1987. The last week of deliberations began on 11 August 1987. During these meetings the time for signing the Final Award was rescheduled to 4 p.m. on 14 August 1987 in order to permit further time for deliberations. All arbitrators were invited to attend and sign at that time. On the afternoon of 14 August all three arbitrators met and reviewed a few final proposed changes in the last draft. At the conclusion of that meeting, Judge Ameli stated that he refused to sign the Final Award.[498]

Judge Ameli wrote that he did not sign the award because, among other reasons:

1. The Award did not decide many disputed issues critical to the outcome of the Case, although those issues were reflected in the Facts and Contentions of the Award itself.
2. As to the issues the Award has decided it has given no reasons for many of them, without agreement or authorization of the Parties to do so and contrary to the clear requirements of Articles 32(3) and 33(2) of the Tribunal Rules.
3. As to the issues the Award has decided and given reasons, many of them are contrary to the facts of the record, provisions of governing law, rules of logic or common sense and are supported by no relevant authority.[499]

(d) Issuance of Award by Chamber One without Judge Mostafavi's Signature:

In the *Uiterwyk* case, Chamber One had to deal with a slightly different situation.[500] The majority view may best be presented by citing the first part of paragraph 30 of the Award:

---

[498] Additional Statement by Judge Holtzmann Concerning Judge Ameli's Refusal to Sign the Final Award, ibid.

[499] Statement of Mr. Ameli, ibid.

[500] See Holtzmann, Schwebel, et al., *supra* note 101. See also Schwebel, *supra* note 483, p. 185.

30. Mr. MOSTAFAVI took part in the Hearing and in three sessions of oral deliberations on various procedural issues in the Case. However, at the third session, he announced that, in view of his dissent from decisions reached by a majority of the Chamber on procedural issues, he did not wish to take part in further deliberations. The Chairman then informed Mr. MOSTAFAVI that, in accordance with the Tribunal Rules and Tribunal practice, the Chamber could and would nevertheless continue the deliberations and prepare an Award notwithstanding his absence. Mr. MOSTAFAVI then withdrew from further participation in the arbitration of this Case. The other two Members of the Chamber continued the deliberations and prepared the Award. This is in accordance with the established practice of the Tribunal to continue its work and make awards despite the failure of one arbitrator to participate. The practice of the Tribunal in this respect is necessary to prevent disruption and frustration by one Member of the Tribunal's performance of its functions and is fully in accordance with recognized principles of international law. As Judge Stephen SCHWEBEL has observed, "the weight of international authority, to which the International Court of Justice has given its support, clearly favors the authority of an international tribunal from which an arbitrator has withdrawn to render a valid award."...[501]

The views of Judge Mostafavi are contained in his letter of 3 June 1988 to Judge Böckstiegel as Chairman of Chamber One and President of the Tribunal, to which an answer was filed in the supplemental opinion of the majority of the Chamber, both of which are reprinted with the partial award.[502]

The supplemental opinion of the two other arbitrators describes in detail the procedures that were followed when Judge Mostafavi declined to rejoin the deliberation.[503]

The supplemental opinion also contains an analysis of Article 13 (2) of the 1976 UNCITRAL Arbitration Rules, which permits replacement of an arbitrator who fails to act, and points out that the provision "is not the exclusive procedure for dealing with failure of an arbitrator to act," and that it "cannot be invoked to disrupt the orderly process of the Tribunal or to obstruct its functions."[504] The supplemental opinion adds that "[m]oreover, the Tribunal is aware of no reason why it has been *de jure* or *de facto* impossible for Mr. MOSTAFAVI to perform his functions in this case."[505]

Thus, in the *Uiterwyk* case, Chamber One reaffirmed the Tribunal's by then well-established principle that a truncated tribunal has

---

[501] *Uiterwyk* v. *Iran*, 19 *Iran-U.S. C.T.R.* 107.
[502] Supplemental Opinion of Mr. Böckstiegel and Mr. Holtzmann, ibid.
[503] Ibid.   [504] Ibid.   [505] Ibid.

the power to render an award when faced with an absent or obstructive arbitrator, expressly observing that the presence of a provision for replacement of an arbitrator does not provide the "exclusive" procedure for addressing the situation.[506]

(e) Issuance of Award by Chamber Two without Judge Khalilian's Signature:

Chamber Two was faced with the situation of an arbitrator refusing to sign the final award in Case No. 39, *Phillips Petroleum Co. v. Iran*. Here, the truncated tribunal noted in its award that:

Having fully participated in the deliberation of the Case and having been informed of the time when the Final Award would be signed at the Tribunal, Mr. Khalilian was present but declined to sign. In these circumstances we conclude that the Tribunal is justified, and in fact obligated, by international law and precedent to proceed with the signature of the award. Any other conclusion, in a continuing tribunal of this type with many cases on its docket would permit the Tribunal's work to be sabotaged. This statement is made pursuant to Article 32, paragraph 4, of the Tribunal Rules.[507]

For his part, Judge Khalilian noted in his supplemental statement that he had requested additional meetings in order to continue deliberation but was rejected by the other arbitrators.[508]

(f) Decision by the Tribunal on Case Nos. A3, A8, A9, A14, and B61:

A more recent decision of the full Tribunal is deserving of closer analysis. The issue before the Tribunal concerned the resignation of Judge Noori, which became effective the day after the completion of the hearing in Cases Nos. A3, A8, A9, A14, and B61 (referred to summarily as Case No. B61).[509] The question was whether Judge Hamid Reza Oloumi Yazdi, who had replaced Judge Noori as a regular Member of the Tribunal, would be able to participate in further proceedings.[510] The United States opposed replacement, arguing that the Tribunal was obligated to deliberate and decide the cases as a truncated tribunal of eight judges.[511]

---

[506] See Holtzmann, Schwebel, et al., *supra* note 101. See also Lew, Mistelis et al., *supra* note 115, pp. 326–327.
[507] *Phillips Petroleum Co. v. Iran*, 21 Iran-U.S. C.T.R. 79.
[508] Statement by Judge Khalilian as to Why It Would Have Been Premature to Sign the Award, ibid., para. 4.
[509] *Iran v. United States* (Case No. B61), Decision by the Tribunal, May 7, 2007.
[510] Ibid. [511] Ibid., para. 12.

This implicated Article 13(5) of the Tribunal Rules, referred to as the Mosk Rule, which provides:

After the effective date of a member's resignation he shall continue to serve as a member of the Tribunal with respect to all cases in which he had participated in a hearing on the merits, and for that purpose shall be considered a member of the Tribunal instead of the person who replaces him.[512]

In its decision on the matter, the Tribunal held:

The Tribunal finds that it has applied the Mosk Rule to Mr. Noori's participation in Case No. B61 by its decisions of 6 November 2006 and 7 March 2007. In light of Mr. Noori's communications to the President of 13, 18, and 22 April 2007, however, the Tribunal decides that he has clearly failed to accept the financial terms fixed by the Tribunal for his participation under the Mosk Rule. The Tribunal notes that Mr. Noori has repeatedly refused to indicate his willingness to serve under the Mosk Rule on the financial terms set by the Tribunal [. . .]. Mr. Noori's refusal to comply already has forced the postponement of deliberations in Case No. B61. It would be contrary to an important interest underlying the Mosk Rule – the facilitation of efficient proceedings – to continue to apply the Mosk Rule to Mr. Noori. Article 13, paragraph 5, of the Tribunal Rules of Procedure does not compel the Tribunal or the Member who has resigned to continue his or her services so long as the Tribunal is satisfied, as it is here, that such continuation does not advance the conduct of the proceedings and that the replacement of such Member does not result in undue delay in the proceedings. Accordingly, the Tribunal decides that, under the present circumstances, Mr. Noori has removed himself from application of the Mosk Rule as regards Case No. B61.

The Tribunal wishes to add that, when it took its 6 November 2007 decision, both it and the States Parties had every reason to believe that Mr. Noori would serve fully under the Mosk Rule until the final disposition of Case No. B61. Subsequently, however, as a consequence of Mr. Noori's conduct, both the Tribunal and the States Parties were confronted by a situation they thought had been excluded. The Tribunal would note in that regard that it has no power to compel compliance with the Mosk Rule, that it fixed reasonable financial terms for Mr. Noori's Mosk Rule service in Case No. B61, and that the subsequent actions of Mr. Noori himself have made unavoidable the non-application of that Rule to him in that Case. The Tribunal has acted throughout this matter entirely consistently with the Tribunal Rules of Procedure, its precedents, and practices.

In view of its decision with respect to the Mosk Rule as regards Case No. B61, the Tribunal must decide the effect of that decision on the

---

[512] Iran-United States Claims Tribunal, Final Tribunal Rules of May 3, 1983.

composition of the Tribunal for the remaining proceedings in that Case. While the United States asserts that the appropriate composition should be a truncated Tribunal of eight Members, so that all will be persons who participated in the many hearing sessions, the Tribunal decides that such a result would be both unnecessary and inconsistent with its past practice and inconsistent with the structure of the Tribunal as provided in the Algiers Declarations. In that connection, the Tribunal notes that the substantial pleadings and evidence are all available to its new Member and that all hearings, which took place over a period of some fifteen months, were transcribed and are also available to him.

. . .

To avoid proceeding with deliberations in a truncated fashion, whatever the reason for a Member not acting, the Tribunal always has taken all appropriate measures so that another regular Member, a Substitute Member or, in *Arco Exploration, Inc.* and *Sun Company, Inc.*, a complete stranger to the Tribunal, is appointed or assigned to fill the gap. This is as it should be in a Tribunal whose very structure rests on equal three-Member elements, one each appointed by the States Parties and a third by one of the methods prescribed in the Claims Settlement Declaration. It would be inconsistent with the entire scheme of the Tribunal for the result to be otherwise.

. . .

Viewing the Claims Settlement Declaration on the basis of the Vienna Convention, in light of all of the foregoing, it cannot reasonably be doubted that a Tribunal Member who declines or is unable to participate in deliberations under the Mosk Rule following his resignation can, indeed must, be replaced by his successor in a case heard only by the resigning Member. To do otherwise would leave a States Party to the Claims Settlement Declaration divested of the right to consideration of cases by a Tribunal constituted as is enshrined in that Declaration. This would be particularly egregious in a case where a States Party's appointees would be reduced from three to two, leaving it in an "unequal" position. This, the Tribunal respectfully submits, would do violence to the carefully negotiated Algiers Declarations, a result the Tribunal cannot accept.[513]

Accordingly, the Tribunal held that in the particular situation of Judge Noori's resignation, in which the arbitrator failed to act in respect of the Mosk Rule and where the arbitrator could be replaced without undue delay to the proceedings, replacement should be the default. Nevertheless, the Tribunal did not reject *per se* the continuation of the proceedings by a truncated tribunal and thus it did not go against the relatively consistent jurisprudence of earlier cases on the authority of a truncated tribunal to render an award. It rather

---

[513] *Iran* v. *United States*, Decision by the Tribunal, May 7, 2007, paras. 10–12, 23, 26.

held that a truncated tribunal was not required by the unique circumstances arising from Judge Noori's resignation.

(iii) Conclusions From the Iran-United States Claims Tribunal Cases

The foregoing exposition, lengthy as it is, only partially reflects the positions taken by those concerned in the episodes which have been recounted. But it is believed that the exposition is adequate to convey the essential facts and legal issues in dispute.

There are numerous questions of fact in controversy.[514] No comment need be offered beyond the observation that a majority of a judicial body, composed of persons of established ability and integrity, has set forth factual conclusions within its own knowledge, concerning its own procedures, exchanges and actions.

As to the law of the matter, the two primary contentions of the various Iranian arbitrators essentially appear to be these:[515]

(a) The Algiers Declaration specifies a Tribunal composed of three elements. "Claims may be decided by the full Tribunal or by a panel of three members of the Tribunal.... Each such panel shall...consist of one member appointed by each of the three methods...," namely, one by each Party and a chairman not of the nationality of the Parties who is jointly appointed or appointed by an appointing authority.[516] Thus neither the full Tribunal[517] nor any of its Chambers is validly composed in the absence of any of its nationally-appointed arbitrators.[518]

---

[514] See also Seifi, *supra* note 125, p. 33, noting the persistent confusion as to the facts of these cases.

[515] See also Schwebel, *supra* note 483, p. 185.

[516] Article III, paragraph 1, 1 *Iran-U.S. C.T.R.* 10.

[517] As indicated in Judge Aldrich's Comments of October 13, 1983, there have been a number of meetings of the full Tribunal at which decisions have been taken in the absence of one or more Iranian arbitrators. These appear to embrace a variety of subjects, including the resignation of arbitrators, adoption of Tribunal Rules, the interpretation and application of the Algiers Declarations and the UNCITRAL Rules, and certain administrative and procedural decisions. It is further understood that the full Tribunal has decided that, if it found it necessary to vote on an administrative issue in the absence of an arbitrator appointed by a Party, one of the arbitrators appointed by the other Party would not take part in the vote, although he would retain the right to take part in deliberations. The President of the full Tribunal, Judge Lagergren, issued Orders postponing certain long-scheduled hearings in view of the absence of an Iranian-appointed arbitrator. (Case Nos. a-16, 582, 591, and 111).

[518] See also Seifi, *supra* note 125, p. 31, noting the requirement that panels be constituted as three-member panels.

(b) In the event – if actually there is such an event, which the Iranian arbitrators deny that there has been – that an arbitrator fails to act, the sole recourse of others concerned, pursuant to Article 13 paragraph 2 of the 1976 UNCITRAL Rules which governs, is to invoke the procedure of challenge and replacement of an arbitrator. There is no warrant, when the Rules expressly provide for the governing procedure, for the Tribunal or a Chamber proceeding otherwise in the absence of an arbitrator and purporting to render final awards.

The reasoning of the majority of the Tribunal and its Chambers that has led to the rendering of awards in the absence of Iranian-appointed arbitrators may, in the light of the passages that have been quoted from opinions of Chambers and of arbitrators, and of the arguments advanced by the Government of the United States, be summarized as follows:

(a) The specification of the Algiers Declaration about the three elements which compose the Tribunal and its Chambers is descriptive of the constitution of the Tribunal and its Chambers. It is not a quorum requirement. If a nationally-appointed arbitrator absents himself or herself from the Tribunal or Chamber which has been properly composed, that of itself does not prohibit the Tribunal or Chamber from acting.
(b) The challenge and replacement procedure set out in Article 13, paragraph 2 of the 1976 UNCITRAL Rules cannot be interpreted to permit a Party to frustrate the continued proceedings of the Tribunal or its Chambers.[519] Where a case has been pleaded and heard, and deliberation among all the arbitrators of the Tribunal or Chamber has begun, unauthorized absence of an arbitrator will not require the invocation of the challenge and replacement procedure, which by its nature will take extended time and which might require fresh hearings. By the terms of the Algiers Declaration, the Tribunal is directed to conduct its business so as "to ensure that this agreement can be carried out."[520] To permit unauthorized absences necessarily to set in motion the

---

[519] See also *Himpurna California Energy Ltd.* v. *Republic of Indonesia*, UNCITRAL, Final Award, October 16, 1999, XXV *Yearbook Commercial Arbitration* (2000), p. 186, para. 59; M. Scott Donahey, "Defending the Arbitration against Sabotage," 13(1) *Journal of International Arbitration* (1996), pp. 93, 109.
[520] Article III, paragraph 2, 1 *Iran-U.S. C.T.R.* 10.

challenge-and-replacement procedure could be to enable one side to ensure that the agreement could not be carried out, for a succession of unauthorized absences could lead to an unending succession of challenge and replacement actions, during which periods the work of the Tribunal and its Chambers would be stultified. Under Article 7 of the 1976 UNCITRAL Rules which the Tribunal Rules incorporate, a party has thirty days to appoint a replacement of a party arbitrator. If the party fails to do so, then the appointing authority (if he has been designated) has thirty days to appoint a replacement. If that arbitrator, after appointment, also were to fail to act for the reasons which motivated his predecessor to withhold participation, or other reasons, the process of challenge would have to begin again.

Moreover, while the Tribunal has adopted a provision permitting the President to assign a substitute arbitrator to replace an arbitrator who is unable to act due to a circumstance "expected to be of relatively short duration,"[521] Iran (unlike the United States) has not appointed any substitute arbitrators, so this recourse also has not been open. In these circumstances, and in view of the body of supportive international precedent, the Tribunal and its Chambers are entitled to proceed and to render awards in the unauthorized absence of a nationally-appointed arbitrator.[522]

With respect to the differences over point (a), it may be noted that there are precedents in international arbitration, which have been set forth in this chapter, which treat provisions for the composition of a tribunal as not being a quorum rule (this was the position in the *Cauca* case, the *Hungarian Optants* cases, the *French-Mexican Claims Commission* cases, the *Sabotage* cases and the *Peace Treaties* case.) Where the parties intend that provisions for the composition of a tribunal shall constitute a quorum rule, or that there will be express provision for a quorum, they can so specify. This was the case in the *Jay Treaty* cases, where it was provided that "one of the commissioners named on each side" must be present

---

[521] 2 *Iran-U.S. C.T.R.* 417–418.

[522] See also M.A. Solhchi, "The Validity of Truncated Tribunal Proceedings and Awards," 9(3) *Arbitration International* (1993), pp. 303, 313; Donahey, *supra* note 519, p. 109; *Himpurna California Energy Ltd.* v. *Republic of Indonesia*, UNCITRAL, Final Award, October 16, 1999, XXV *Yearbook Commercial Arbitration* (2000), p. 186, para. 59; Caron and Caplan, *supra* note 213, p. 284.

for the commission to act, and in the *Franco-Tunisian Arbitral Tribunal* cases, where the governing treaty prescribed that "the presence of at least four members is required for the validity of the deliberations of the Tribunal; of these, two must be Frenchmen and two Tunisians." In the absence of specifications such as these, provisions for the constitution of an arbitral tribunal cannot reasonably be interpreted as imposing a quorum requirement.

With respect to differences over point (b), the Tribunal and its Chambers can sustain the validity of having taken decisions and adopted awards in the absence of Iranian arbitrators not only by reliance upon the reasoning just set forth, but also by invoking the rule of effectiveness in the interpretation of treaties. They may rely as well on the substantial body of international precedent which has been analyzed in this chapter.

This is not to say that there is not room for argument over whether in the case of the failure of an arbitrator to act, recourse must, at any rate in the first place, be had to the provision of Article 13, paragraph 2 of the 1976 UNCITRAL Rules for challenge and replacement.[523] But it is believed that, in the particular circumstances of a Tribunal charged with the continuing disposition of thousands of claims, the approach taken by the tribunal since the publication of the first edition – a standard of "appropriate measures" to be taken to avoid the tribunal proceeding in a truncated manner – balances the provisions of the Tribunal's Rules with the need to prevent arbitrator replacement from obstructing the proceedings.[524] As noted in the first edition, the fact that the governing Rules provide a procedure for replacement (which was not followed) is not dispositive in the case of the Iran-United States Claims Tribunal any more than it was dispositive in other international arbitral cases, among them, the *Cauca* case, the *French-Mexican Claims Commission* cases, and the *Sabotage* cases. In those cases, the procedures for replacement of absent arbitrators for which the governing treaties provided were not followed, but the

---

[523] Judge Seifi, for his part, contends that "[t]he existence of [a provision for the enforced filling of vacancies] clearly implies that the parties have necessarily excluded the possibility for the remaining members to continue the proceedings, particularly if the tribunal is a three-member one, unless an express provision authorized them to continue." See Seifi, *supra* note 125, p. 45.
[524] See *Iran* v. *United States*, Decision by the Tribunal, May 7, 2007, paras. 10–26.

tribunals in question held that they remained competent to proceed and to render final awards despite the unauthorized absence of a nationally-appointed arbitrator.

(O) *IVAN MILUTINOVIC V. DEUTSCHE BABCOCK*

Moving away from the jurisprudence of the Iran-United States Claims Tribunal, the *Ivan Milutinovic* arbitration, despite providing little clear guidance on the authority of truncated tribunals, is nonetheless an important illustration of the controversy that continues to surround the authority of a truncated tribunal.

The initial arbitration was an ICC commercial arbitration in Zurich concerning a monetary dispute between members of a construction consortium that had contracted to build a power station in Homs, Libya.[525] At a late stage in the hearings, and after the tribunal had taken a decision to reject the claimant's request to allow the introduction of additional evidence, the claimant's appointed arbitrator, Professor Jovanovic, withdrew.[526] Professor Jovanovic announced his resignation because "he disagreed with the decision of the Arbitral Tribunal."[527] The claimant's counsel thereupon refused to present the claimant's final pleadings.[528]

The remaining members of the tribunal expressed their intention to continue the proceedings, following which the claimant moved in the ICC Court of Arbitration to replace the chair and other remaining arbitrator.[529] The ICC Court of Arbitration "refused to accept the resignation" and held that the withdrawing arbitrator "was obliged to continue to act as arbitrator."[530] The absent arbitrator did not attend a further internal meeting of the tribunal, however, and instead reaffirmed his resignation.[531] The remaining arbitrators rendered an award that the absent arbitrator

---

[525] See Schwebel, *supra* note 483, p. 182; Stephen M. Schwebel, "The Authority of a Truncated Tribunal," in Albert Jan van den Berg (ed.), *Improving the Efficiency of Arbitration Agreements and Awards: 40 Years of Application of the New York Convention*, ICCA Congress Series, Volume 9 (1999) p. 314, pp. 314–318.
[526] Schwebel, "The Authority," *supra* note 525, p. 315.
[527] Schwebel, *supra* note 483, p. 188.   [528] Ibid.
[529] Schwebel, "The Authority," *supra* note 525, p. 315. See also Schwebel, *supra* note 483, p. 188.
[530] Schwebel, "The Authority," *supra* note 525, p. 315.   [531] Ibid., p. 315.

did not sign, and that was submitted to and accepted by the ICC Court.[532]

The course of subsequent proceedings in Swiss courts was complex and contradictory.[533] A challenge to the position of the two remaining arbitrators was first rejected, then upheld on appeal and again rejected on appeal to the Swiss Federal Tribunal. But then a request for nullification of the award that was initially dismissed by the Zurich Court of Appeal was sustained by the Swiss Federal Tribunal. The consequence was that the award was quashed and a new tribunal was then established by the ICC.[534]

That result, after ten years of arbitration and litigation, was unfortunate. The judgment of the Swiss Federal Tribunal was inconsistent with the principle that a party may not invoke its own wrong – or a wrong that it adopts as its own – to deprive another party of its rights.[535] It ran counter to the predominant practice of international arbitration and it placed the Swiss Federal Tribunal in conflict with the ICC Court of Arbitration. It appears likely, however, that the decision would have been different under the new Swiss Law on Private International Law.[536]

(P) *HIMPURNA V. INDONESIA*

The underlying facts of the dispute in the *Himpurna* arbitration and the tribunal's conclusions regarding denial of justice have been described in the previous chapter. What remains to be explored here is the particularly intriguing complication presented in the case: an

---

[532] Schwebel, *supra* note 483, p. 188.
[533] Schwebel, "The Authority," *supra* note 525, pp. 315–316.
[534] Schwebel, *supra* note 483, p. 188.   [535] Ibid.
[536] See ibid., pp. 199–200; Tobias Zuberbühler, Klaus Muller et al., *Swiss Rules of International Arbitration: Commentary* (2005), p. 135; Trevor Cook and Alejandro I. García, *International Intellectual Property Arbitration*, Arbitration in Context Series, vol. 2 (2010) p. 164. In a more recent case, the Swiss Federal Tribunal refused to set aside an ICC award rendered in Geneva in which an arbitrator had refused to participate in deliberations without formally stepping down. There, the Swiss court distinguished the situation in the *Ivan Milutinovic* arbitration – where an arbitrator had purported to resign – and the circumstances of an arbitrator refusing to participate in the deliberations without resigning. In the latter case, the Swiss court concluded the proper outcome was for the remaining arbitrators to proceed as a truncated tribunal and render the award. See Eric A. Schwartz and Yves Derains, *Guide to the ICC Rules of Arbitration* (2nd edition, 2005), p. 205.

arbitrator in the case was effectively kidnapped by the State party that appointed him.[537] This forced the remaining arbitrators to consider their authority to render an award under such circumstances.

As discussed in the previous chapter, the arbitration arose after Himpurna California Energy and Patuha Power Ltd. entered into energy sales contracts with the Indonesian state electricity corporation, PT. Perusahaan Listruik Negara, to explore and develop geothermal resources in Indonesia.[538] Following the economic crisis of 1997, however, the state electricity company failed to purchase the energy supplied. Accordingly, Himpurna requested arbitration under the arbitration clause in the contract, which called for arbitration under the 1976 UNCITRAL Rules.[539]

An award was rendered against the state electricity company in May 1999.[540] However, following the refusal of the company to pay damages, Himpurna and Patuha revived arbitral proceedings it had earlier commenced against Indonesia, relying on the State's pledge to ensure the state electricity company's performance in a 1996 letter from the Minister of Foreign Affairs of Indonesia.[541]

Hearings were originally scheduled for August 1999 in Jakarta; however, following the aggressive conduct of the lawyers representing PLN in the related arbitration between Himpurna and PLN, it was agreed by the arbitrators to move the hearings between Himpurna and Indonesia overseas, to Paris (two sessions) and then to The Hague.[542]

The hearings in The Hague were scheduled for September 22–23, 1999. On September 17, Indonesia sought an injunction in the District Court of The Hague, forbidding the claimant and the arbitrators from participating in a hearing, or

"at least" to forbid them from doing so within the Kingdom of The Netherlands, and to forbid them "from entering the Peace Palace and the area

---

[537] See Pierre Lalive, "On the Transfer of Seat in International Arbitration," in James A.R. Nafziger and Symeon C. Symeonides (eds.), *Law and Justice in a Multistate World: Essays in Honor of Arthur T. von Mehren* (2002) 515; Veeder, *supra* note 311, p. 795.

[538] See *Himpurna California Energy Ltd. v. Republic of Indonesia*, UNCITRAL, Interim Award and Final Award, September 26, 1999 and October 16, 1999, XXV *Yearbook Commercial Arbitration* (2000), p. 109.

[539] Ibid., p. 110.   [540] Ibid.   [541] Ibid.

[542] H. Priyatna Abdurrasyid, "They Said I Was Going to Be Kidnapped," 18–6 *Mealey's International Arbitration Report* 29 (2003), p. 30.

surrounding the Peace Palace at The Hague at the Carnegieplein 2 in order to hold such a hearing," all subject to a penalty of US$ one million per day.[543]

At the same time the law firm representing Indonesia issued summons for the claimant and the individual arbitrators, who were in transit to the Netherlands,[544] to appear on September 20 before the President of the District Court.

The hearing on Indonesia's injunction was held on September 20 and the following day the District Court announced that Indonesia's application for an injunction had been denied.[545] However, the hearings in the arbitration at the Peace Palace were ultimately aborted due to the non-appearance of the Indonesian-appointed arbitrator, Professor Priyatna.

Professor Priyatna had made it to the Netherlands, arriving in Amsterdam shortly before 8 a.m. on September 20. Prior to departing Washington on the 20th, however, an individual, apparently from the Indonesian Embassy in Washington, intercepted Professor Priyatna at the airport, handing him a letter from the Indonesian Minister of Finance instructing him not to attend the hearing in The Hague.[546] Professor Priyatna proceeded to fly to Amsterdam but at Schiphol airport was again intercepted by a group of Indonesian individuals, who took him to the Ibis hotel at Schiphol airport.[547] At the hotel, Professor Priyatna recounts, two officials from Jakarta were waiting for him, one of whom told him: "If Mr. Priyatna is not prepared to be absent voluntarily, we shall be forced to carry out a kidnap."[548]

Professor Priyatna was ultimately kept in the hotel room for one night and two days before being accompanied back to Schiphol airport by the group of Indonesian officials.[549] At the

---

[543] *Himpurna California Energy Ltd.* v. *Republic of Indonesia*, UNCITRAL, Interim Award, September 26, 1999, para. 88.

[544] Professor Priyatna notes in his article about the ordeal that he was concerned about the Indonesian government preventing him from attending the hearing prior to leaving for The Hague. The presiding arbitrator, Mr. Jan Paulsson, suggested he leave from Jakarta several weeks earlier and go to Australia or Paris first as a means of avoiding such efforts by Indonesia. He ultimately went to Washington, D.C. in order to visit his son at the same time, but while in the United States was visited by people from the Indonesian Embassy several times. Priyatna, *supra* note 542, p. 30.

[545] *Himpurna California Energy Ltd.* v. *Republic of Indonesia*, UNCITRAL, Interim Award, September 26, 1999, para. 22.

[546] Priyatna, *supra* note 542, p. 30.   [547] Priyatna, *supra* note 542, p. 31.

[548] Ibid.   [549] Ibid.

airport the group encountered Mr. de Fina, his co-arbitrator on the tribunal, and Professor Albert Jan van den Berg, who had been asked by the presiding arbitrator Mr. Paulsson to attend the hearing in the District Court of The Hague, and who had gone to look for him at the airport.[550] Professor Priyatna spoke briefly to Mr. de Fina and Professor van den Berg, and then was accompanied onto the plane by the individuals from the Indonesian Embassy.[551] The events from Professor van den Berg's perspective are detailed at length in the Interim Award of September 26, 1999:

Mr. de Fina told me that he had tried to contact Professor Priyatna at the Carlton Ambassador Hotel at The Hague on Monday, 20 September 1999, but was advised by the hotel that another gentleman had cancelled the reservation of Professor Priyatna and that a message was left for him at the hotel in which it was said that Professor Priyatna would not come. We arrived at the Carlton Ambassador Hotel [on 21 September 1999] at approximately 15.15 hours. Mr. de Fina wanted to know what had actually happened with the cancellation of Professor Priyatna's reservation and wanted also to have more information about the messages. Both of us then spoke with Ms. Arjanne van Beelen, the front office manager, and thereafter with Ms. Karen de Hey, a trainee who had both received the telephone calls and messages. Ms. van Beelen told us two telephone calls had been received with respect to Professor Priyatna, one in the morning between 11.45 and 12.15 hours, which she had taken, and one in the afternoon at around 14.30 hours which had been taken by Ms. de Hey. Ms. van Beelen told me that the person who had called her was Mr. R [ossidi] M. "Hosen" (her phonetic spelling for "Husein") from the Embassy of the Republic of Indonesia. She recognised his voice as she had spoken with him before at other occasions in relation to other reservations for the Embassy of the Republic of Indonesia. During that conversation, Mr. Husein said, according to Ms. van Beelen, that he wanted to leave a message for Mr. de Fina and Mr. Paulsson that "Mr. Priyatna cannot come to the hotel to meet you" and that he cancelled the reservation. According to Ms. de Hey, Mr. Husein called at 14.30 hours, informing her that "Mr. Abdurrasyid" would not come to the hotel and that his reservation could be cancelled. According to Ms. De Hey, after she had found out that "Mr. Abdurrasyid" was the same as Professor Pryatna, when she asked whether the reservation should be cancelled for

---

[550] Ibid.   [551] Ibid.

the other three days, Mr. Husein answered that these days should be cancelled as well. According to Ms. de Hey, Mr. Husein asked her to give a message to Mr. de Fina and Mr. Paulsson that "Mr. Abdurrasyid does not come." ... Thereupon, Mr. de Fina and I went to the Embassy of the Republic of Indonesia at the Tobias Asserlaan 8, at The Hague (at five minutes distance from the hotel) in order to deliver a copy of the pleading notes and exhibits submitted in the aforementioned court proceedings at The Hague. ... We arrived at the Embassy at approximately 15.45 hours. I asked the guard to see Mr. Husein. The guard answered that he had gone to Schiphol Airport. I then asked whether he knew where Professor Priyatna was. The guard answered that he did not know of Professor Priyatna. I said that I had an urgent message for Mr. Husein and would like to have his mobile telephone number. The guard wrote down for me the mobile telephone number of Mr. Husein .... Back in the car, I tried to call Mr. Husein on my mobile but there was no answer. Two minutes later I received a call from Mr. Husein who wanted to know who had called and why (this is possible of caller identification in the Netherlands). I asked Mr. Husein whether Professor Priyatna was with him since I wanted to give him documents. Mr. Husein answered that Professor Priyatna was not with him. I asked him then whether he knew where he was. Mr. Husein answered that he did not know but that he would call me if he knew where he was. I then asked him whether he was in the airport. He answered that he was bringing other people to the airport. I then asked whether he had seen Professor Abdurrasyid before. Mr. Husein answered that he had seen him yesterday morning (Monday 20 September 1999) when he was waiting for another guest at the airport Schiphol. He further said that he knew and recognised him and was asked to cancel his hotel reservation. Mr. Husein further told me that he had cancelled the hotel on Monday. I asked Mr. Husein whether he knew where Professor Priyatna had gone. Mr. Husein answered that he did not know. Mr. Husein repeatedly said to me that when he would know where Professor Priyatna was, he could call me back and, upon his request, I gave him my mobile number. After this telephone conversation, I obtained information by phone through the airlines booking system that Professor Priyatna was booked on a flight from Amsterdam to Jakarta the same evening (Tuesday 21 September 1999): KL 837, departure time 20.20 hours. Mr. de Fina and I then proceeded to Schiphol Airport, where we arrived at 17.15 hours. Together with my driver (Jan-Hein Dissel), we waited at the KLM check in counter in the departure hall. At around 17.50 hours we noticed two people of possible Indonesian nationality, but not Professor Priyatna. We followed them from the check in counter and saw them going to a group of approximately 8 Indonesian looking persons, one of whom was Professor Priyatna. Professor Priyatna immediately shook hands with Mr. de Fina and myself and both went some 10 meters aside for a conversation. In the meantime, I shook hands with the Indonesian looking persons, one of whom introduced himself as Mr. Husein with whom I had the aforementioned telephone conversation. A number persons of the group thereafter spread out through the departure hall, watching us closely. My driver took position in the middle. After having been with what was left of the group of Indonesian looking persons, I walked over to Professor Priyatna and Mr. de Fina. That part of the conversion was to the following effect. I informed Professor Priyatna that the injunctions sought by the Republic of Indonesia had been rejected by the District Court. When I told him that these injunctions meant that the Dutch Court does not prevent him from attending the hearing on 22 September in the Peace Palace, Professor Priyatna said that a person had travelled from Jakarta to Washington to read him a letter that the person said was from a Minister, asking him not to take part in the arbitration, and that he felt obliged to return to Jakarta. He told me also that another person had travelled from Jakarta to Amsterdam who waited for him when he arrived from Washington in Amsterdam on Monday morning, 20 September 1999, and that that person read him the same (or similar) letter. When Mr. de Fina asked him for a copy of the letter, Professor Priyatna answered that the letter had not been handed over to him but that he would fax a copy when he will have gotten the letter. I told Professor Priyatna that I had a copy of the pleadings and the documents submitted in the aforementioned District Court proceedings with me for him, but he declined to accept them. Professor Priyatna also said that he considered Mr. de Fina and Mr. Paulsson as his friends and did not want to lose friendship but that he could not continue the case. When I inquired about the hotel where he stayed, he answered the Ibis hotel at the airport. During the conversation, which lasted approximately 10 minutes, Professor Priyatna appeared to be quite shaken and at certain moments I noticed that he was on the verge of crying. After this conversation, Professor Priyatna rejoined the group of Indonesian looking persons and when my driver left his position to follow us, the other persons of apparent Indonesian origin also rejoined the group. Mr. de Fina and I were then driven by my driver to my office where we immediately recorded our respective statements.[552]

In the absence of the Indonesian arbitrator, the remaining arbitrators proceeded to render an interim award, detailing the events and the circumstances of the arbitrator's absence.[553] In their final award, the tribunal addressed the question of the power of a truncated

---

[552] *Himpurna California Energy Ltd.* v. *Republic of Indonesia*, UNCITRAL, Interim Award, September 26, 1999, para 97.
[553] Ibid.

tribunal to continue proceedings and render an award.[554] Relying extensively on the analysis found in the first edition, and a review of the relevant cases,[555] the tribunal concluded that the appropriate solution in the circumstances of the case was for the truncated tribunal to continue in the Indonesian-appointed arbitrator's absence, rather than to remove and replace him:

[T]he authority supporting a truncated tribunal's ability to proceed and render an award is plentiful. Its pertinence in this arbitration is beyond question.

. . .

A possible course may be to remove and replace an arbitrator who has withdrawn, if the withdrawal takes place at a sufficiently early stage that his replacement would cause only limited disruption. Such a solution is, however, manifestly inappropriate when an arbitrator withdraws at an advanced stage in the proceedings and that withdrawal is found by the Arbitral Tribunal to be without valid excuse.

. . .

The Arbitral Tribunal thus has no hesitation in finding that, in the circumstances of this arbitration, it has the power to proceed to fulfil its mandate and render an award, since [the Indonesian-appointed arbitrator's] non-participation is without valid excuse.[556]

Accordingly, recording that "[t]he weight of well-established international authority makes clear that an arbitral tribunal has not only the right, but the obligation, to proceed when, without valid excuse, one of it's members fails to act, withdraws or . . . purports to resign,"[557] the tribunal rendered the award in the tribunal's truncated form.

What conclusions can be extracted from the dramatic events of the *Himpurna* arbitration? In the first place, they demonstrate the great

---

[554] *Himpurna California Energy Ltd.* v. *Republic of Indonesia*, UNCITRAL, Final Award, 16 October 1999, paras. 40–68.

[555] Ibid., paras. 45–54. See also *Redfern and Hunter on International Arbitration, supra* note 106, para 4.160.

[556] Ibid., paras. 55–60. The tribunal also cited the *Uiterwyk* case, *supra* note 501, for the propositions that Article 13(2) of the 1976 UNCITRAL Rules, which permits replacement of an arbitrator who fails to act, "is not the exclusive procedure for dealing with failure of an arbitrator to act," and that it "cannot be invoked to disrupt the orderly process of the Tribunal or to obstruct its functions." (Para 58.) Note, however, that Article 14(2) of the 2010 UNCITRAL Rules, while unlike the 1976 Rules expressly contemplating the possibility of a truncated tribunal, only contemplates a tribunal proceeding on a truncated basis from a time after the closure of proceedings.

[557] Ibid., para. 43.

and innovative lengths that a disruptive party may go to in order to avoid arbitral proceedings or an unfavorable award. More critically, however, the tribunal's decision in the *Himpurna* arbitration to proceed in the absence of the party-appointed arbitrator – a decision indeed supported by that absent arbitrator[558] – demonstrates in practice the soundness of the conclusions of the first edition and the extent to which the authority of a truncated tribunal to proceed and render an award has been recognized since publication in 1987.

(Q) *CME V. CZECH REPUBLIC*

Another case in point is a 2001 investment arbitration under the Dutch-Czech BIT and 1976 UNCITRAL Rules. The subject of the dispute was CME's investments in a joint venture for the acquisition and use of licenses for broadcasting throughout the Czech Republic.[559] CME claimed that ČNTS, a Czech television services company in which CME held a 99 percent equity interest, had been commercially destroyed by the actions taken by the Czech Media Council in 1999.[560]

Arbitration was initiated in February 2000 and the tribunal was composed on July 21, 2000 with Judge Schwebel and Dr. Jaroslav Hándl as party-appointed arbitrators and Dr. Wolfgang Kühn as chairman of the tribunal.[561] Hearings were held in Stockholm in April and May 2001, after which the three members of the tribunal exchanged a number of faxes on the questions before the tribunal, which were to serve as the basis for oral deliberations in Düsseldorf in June 2001.[562] Those deliberations were attended by all three arbitrators and involved a discussion of all significant issues before the tribunal.[563]

---

[558] Priyatna, *supra* note 542, p. 30. Professor Priyatna recalls his thinking at the time in his article on his ordeal: "The assumption of the Indonesian party was that if I were not present (a wrong assumption), the session could not proceed. Such notion represented a misunderstanding about arbitration, because the absence of an arbitrator would thereby delegate full authority to the Chairman to make an award on a dispute without argumentation input from the arbitrator who was absent. Therefore, this assumption constituted a stupidity on the party of the Indonesian party. (According to information obtained, such attitude was adopted by the Indonesian party based on suggestion/advice from a foreign lawyer engaged by the Government of Indonesia.)"

[559] *CME* v. *Czech Republic,* UNCITRAL, Final Award of March 14, 2003, para. 8.

[560] Ibid., para. 19.

[561] *CME* v. *Czech Republic,* Judgment of the Svea Court of Appeal, May 15, 2003, p. 5.

[562] Ibid., p. 87.   [563] Ibid.

After the Düsseldorf deliberations it became clear that the tribunal was not going to adopt Dr. Hándl's view and Dr. Hándl made it clear that he did not wish to participate in the production of the draft award, and did not wish to receive the introduction or parts of the draft award.[564] On July 30, 2001, Dr. Kühn completed the draft award and distributed it to the co-arbitrators, and Dr. Hándl made a number of comments "largely constituting a repetition of his reply to the list of questions and what he stated at the deliberations in Düsseldorf."[565] A number of exchanges continued between the members of the tribunal regarding the text of the draft award during the rest of the summer, however, Dr. Kühn was left with the impression that Dr. Hándl was attempting to delay the award.[566]

On September 13, 2001 the tribunal rendered a partial award, which Dr. Hándl refused to sign in protest but from which he did issue a dissenting opinion.[567] On September 19, 2001 Dr. Hándl resigned.[568] In his dissenting opinion, Dr. Handl accused the other two arbitrators of excluding him from deliberations, not giving him sufficient time to prepare his dissent and being biased against the State party.[569] The partial award was signed by the remaining two arbitrators and included the following note:[570] "The Chairman of the Tribunal, on his behalf and that of Judge Schwebel, pointed out to Dr Hándl that his failure to sign would be in breach of his obligations as arbitrator.... The UNCITRAL Rules that govern this arbitration provide, in Article 32(4), that: "An award *shall* be signed by the arbitrators...." (emphasis supplied). The Tribunal is confirmed in the conclusion that an arbitrator's failure to sign the award is a violation of the arbitrator's professional responsibilities by its examination of the rules and practice of the principal arbitral institutions as well as the papers and proceedings of the Stockholm and Paris Congresses of the International Council on Commercial Arbitration."[571]

---

[564] Ibid., p. 88.   [565] Ibid.   [566] Ibid., p. 89.
[567] *CME* v. *Czech Republic*, UNCITRAL, Partial Award, September 13, 2001, Judgement of the Svea Court of Appeal, p. 6.
[568] Ibid., para. 34; *CME* v. *Czech Republic*, Judgment of the Svea Court of Appeal, May 15, 2003, p. 6.
[569] *CME* v. *Czech Republic*, UNCITRAL, Dissenting Opinion of Dr. Jaroslav Hándl, September 11, 2001, pp. 1–3.
[570] *CME* v. *Czech Republic*, UNCITRAL, Partial Award, September 13, 2001, p. 179.
[571] Ibid., para. 625.

The Czech Republic initiated annulment proceedings in 2003 in Sweden. In its claim for annulment, the Czech Republic argued that Dr. Hándl was excluded from crucial parts of the deliberations.[572] However, the Svea Court of Appeal refused to annul or set aside the award. In so doing, the Court of Appeal noted that the case required it to balance claims of due process against the requirement of promptness. Particularly, the Court of Appeal held that:

> when two arbitrators have agreed upon the outcome of the dispute, the third arbitrator cannot prolong the deliberations by demanding continued discussions in an attempt to persuade the others as to the correctness of his opinion.[573]

Furthermore, the Court held that the Czech Republic failed to prove that the other two arbitrators excluded Dr. Hándl from the deliberations or failed to give him sufficient time to prepare his dissent.[574] In particular, the Court of Appeal concluded that Dr. Hándl "received all essential communications between the arbitrators" and that Dr. Kühn:

> appears the whole time to have treated [Dr.] Hándl correctly and [Dr.] Hándl appears to have been afforded an opportunity to submit his comments to the extent which reasonably may be dictated by considerations of courtesy between colleagues. [Dr.] Hándl's feeling of having been excluded is probably, in all essential regards, connected to the fact that he did not meet with support for his opinion in the case.[575]

The CME Arbitration does not truly serve as an example of a truncated tribunal, as the Svea Court of Appeal rightly concluded that Dr. Hándl was never absent from the deliberations in the underlying arbitration, he issued a dissenting opinion from the tribunal's partial award, he resigned after that partial award was issued, and the Czech Republic also soon after replaced him with Sir Ian Brownlie. However, it is nonetheless a useful example for this chapter: first, as an example of the creative, if ultimately unsuccessful, ways in which an obstructive arbitrator or respondent may attempt to construct a post hoc narrative to impugn an award; and second, as recognition of the need for an arbitral tribunal to balance claims of due process against procedural promptness, even if that balance results in the proceedings continuing as a truncated tribunal.

---

[572] CME v. Czech Republic, Judgment of the Svea Court of Appeal, May 15, 2003, p. 13.
[573] Ibid., p. 87.   [574] Ibid.   [575] Ibid., p. 89.

(R) *CROATIA V. SLOVENIA*

The *Croatia* v. *Slovenia* maritime dispute also provides useful insight into the authority of a truncated tribunal to render an award, albeit under particularly convoluted circumstances.

The maritime delimitation arbitration between Croatia and Slovenia arose under a 2009 arbitration agreement to determine the maritime and land boundary between the two States, Slovenia's junction to the High Seas, and the regime for the use of the relevant maritime areas.[576] The arbitration occurred pursuant to the PCA Optional Rules, and was to be heard by a five-member tribunal.[577] Article 2 of the Arbitration Agreement provided:

(1) Both parties shall appoint by common agreement the President of the Arbitral Tribunal and two members recognized for their competence in international law within fifteen days drawn from a list of candidates established by the President of the European Commission and the Member responsible for the enlargement of the European Commission. In case that they cannot agree within this delay, the President and the two members of the Arbitral Tribunal shall be appointed by the President of the International Court of Justice from the list.

(2) Each Party shall appoint a further member of the Arbitral Tribunal within fifteen days after the appointments referred to in paragraph 1 have been finalized. In case that no appointment has been made within this delay, the respective member shall be appointed by the President of the Arbitral Tribunal.

(3) If, whether before or after the proceedings have begun, a vacancy should occur on account of the death, incapacity or resignation of a member, it shall be filled in accordance with the procedure prescribed for the original appointment.[578]

Pursuant to the Arbitration Agreement, on January 17, 2012 the parties agreed to appoint Judge Gilbert Guillaume as the presiding arbitrator and to appoint Professor Vaughan Lowe and Judge Bruno Simma as arbitrators. On January 26, 2012 Slovenia appointed Dr. Jernej Sekolec as arbitrator and on January 31, 2012 Croatia appointed Professor Budislav Vukas as arbitrator.[579]

---

[576] *Croatia* v. *Slovenia*, PCA Case No. 2012-04, Final Award, June 29, 2017, para. 1.
[577] See *Croatia* v. *Slovenia*, PCA Case No. 2012-04, Partial Award of June 30, 2016 and Final Award of June 29, 2017.
[578] *Croatia* v. *Slovenia*, Final Award, para. 145.   [579] Ibid., paras. 146–147.

Hearings in the arbitration took place in the Peace Palace in The Hague from June 2 to 13, 2014.[580] On April 30, 2015 Croatia forwarded to the tribunal a letter addressed to Slovenia, which questioned why the Slovenian Minister of Foreign Affairs appeared on television in Slovenia on January 7, 2015 and April 22, 2015 making statements about the possible outcome of the arbitration.[581] Slovenia responded on May 1, 2015 that it had "no information whatsoever concerning the outcome of the arbitration, nor any 'informal channel of communication with the Tribunal.'"[582] Nevertheless, on June 19, 2015, the tribunal informed the parties that deliberations had progressed sufficiently to allow the tribunal to render an award in the fourth quarter of 2015.[583]

By letter dated July 9, 2015, the tribunal determined that the award would be rendered on December 17, 2015.[584] However, on July 22, 2015, Serbian and Croatian newspapers published transcripts and audio files of two telephone conversations reportedly involving the arbitrator appointed by Slovenia and one of the two agents designated by Slovenia.[585]

On July 23, 2015, the tribunal notified the Parties that the Slovenian-appointed arbitrator in question, Dr. Sekolec, had resigned from the tribunal and it invited Slovenia to appoint an arbitrator to replace him.[586] On July 28, 2015, Slovenia appointed H.E. Mr. Ronny Abraham, President of the International Court of Justice.[587]

On July 30, 2015, Croatia notified Slovenia by Note Verbale that it "considers that the Republic of Slovenia has engaged in one or more material breaches of the Arbitration Agreement," entitling Croatia to terminate the Agreement "in accordance with Article 60, paragraph 1 of the Vienna Convention on the Law of Treaties."[588] The tribunal notified the parties on the same day that the Croatian-appointed arbitrator, Professor Vukas resigned.[589] Professor Vukas cited the conduct of Dr. Sekolec and the agent of Slovenia as having "violated the basic principles of a fair arbitration proceeding."[590]

---

[580] Ibid., para. 171.   [581] Ibid., para. 174.   [582] Ibid., para. 175.

[583] *Croatia v. Slovenia*, Partial Award of June 30, 2016, para. 31.

[584] Ibid., para. 36.   [585] Ibid., para. 6.

[586] *Croatia v. Slovenia*, Partial Award of June 30, 2016, para. 38.

[587] Ibid., para. 42.   [588] Ibid., para. 44.   [589] Ibid., para. 43.

[590] Resignation Letter of Professor Budislav Vukas, July 30, 2015.

Judge Abraham subsequently resigned from the tribunal.[591] On September 25, 2015, the tribunal informed the parties that the president, in accordance with the procedure for the replacement of party-appointed arbitrators provided for in Article 2 of the Arbitration Agreement, had appointed Mr. Rolf Einar Fife to succeed Judge Abraham, and Professor Nicolas Michel to succeed Professor Vukas.[592] The tribunal was then considered to have been properly reconstituted.[593]

Despite the effort the tribunal went through to replace both party-appointed arbitrators, the tribunal made a point of noting in its final award that "it was a well-established principle of international procedural law that a unilateral decision to withdraw from dispute settlement proceedings cannot of itself bring such proceedings to a halt."[594]

The *Croatia* v. *Slovenia* arbitration provides an illustration of the practical and flexible approach that may be taken in response to a State party's unilateral withdrawal of an arbitrator. The decision in this case not to proceed as a truncated tribunal, despite the late stage of the proceedings, was an understandable one in light of the extraordinary circumstances before it and the threat that these circumstances posed to the parties' compliance with the award.

3. Miscellaneous Cases

Several lesser-known cases issued since the publication of the first edition merit treatment.

(A) AGENCE TRANSCONGOLAISE DES COMMUNICATIONS CASE

The *Agence Transcongolaise des Communications* arbitration appears to be an example of an outlying case from the increasingly consistent recognition of the authority of truncated tribunals to render awards over the last thirty years. The case is also an example of a surprising judgment of the Paris Court of Appeal.

---

[591] Ibid., para. 46.   [592] Ibid., para. 49.
[593] *Croatia* v. *Slovenia*, Final Award of June 29, 2017, para. 199.
[594] Ibid., para. 197 (referring to the earlier Partial Award, para. 142).

The arbitration arose out of a later agreement entered into within the framework of a 1957 contract between the Congolese authorities and the Gabonese mining company Compagnie Minière de l'Ogooue Comilog S. A. (Comilog), concerning the right to transport manganese from a Gabon mine through the Congo by way of the public railway Congo Océan.[595] The agreement that was the subject of the arbitration was a traction agreement concluded in 1991 and provided that disputes that could not be amicably settled between the parties were to be referred to ad hoc arbitration according to the arbitration clause in the original 1957 contract.[596]

The events leading to the arbitration were these: in September 1991 a train composed of a Comilog engine and driven by a Comilog employee with wagons owned by the Agence Transcongolaise des Communications – Chemin de fer Congo Océan (ATC-CFCO) collided with a Congolese passenger train.[597] The parties could not find an amicable solution to their dispute concerning their respective responsibilities for the collision and commenced arbitration in Paris.[598] Comilog and ATC-CFCO appointed their respective arbitrators and the president of the French Railways (SNCF) appointed the chairman of the tribunal, as provided for in the 1957 contract.[599]

On September 15, 1997 the arbitrator appointed by ATC-CFCO resigned, following his receiving of a draft award from the chairman of the tribunal. In his resignation letter the arbitrator stated that his resignation was in protest of the intervention of a SNCF legal staff representative in the tribunal's deliberations.[600] At the same time, ATC-CFCO indicated its "intention to commence summary proceedings on the issue before the president of the Paris Court of First Instance and to challenge the two remaining arbitrators, affirming that the arbitral tribunal should be reconstituted entirely, and appointing a new arbitrator."[601]

Nevertheless, on September 25, 1995 the truncated tribunal of two rendered an award in which it found that ATC-CFCO was to bear 90 percent of the responsibility for the accident.[602] The award

---

[595] *Agence Transcongolaise des Communications – Chemin de fer Congo Océan* v. *Compagnie Minière de l'Ogooue – Comilog*, Paris Court of Appeal, July 1, 1997, XXIVa *Yearbook Commercial Arbitration* (2010), p. 281.
[596] Ibid.   [597] Ibid.   [598] Ibid.   [599] Ibid., p. 281.   [600] Ibid., p. 282.
[601] Ibid.   [602] Ibid.

was not signed by ATC-CFCO's appointed arbitrator, but the award stated he was "notified but absent."[603] ATC-CFCO sought annulment of the award before the Paris Court of Appeal for violations of due process, irregularity of the arbitral procedure, and violation of international public policy.[604]

In reviewing the award, the Paris Court of Appeal held that the arbitral tribunal which rendered the award was not duly constituted at the time that the award was rendered.[605] Particularly, the Court of Appeal concluded that the parties' arbitration agreement only provided for an award made by a three-person tribunal, and thus the award made by the truncated two-person tribunal was invalid, regardless of the conduct of the absent arbitrator.

Thus, the Paris Court of Appeal ignored the possibly dilatory and wrongful nature of the arbitrators' resignation and instead confined itself to the question of whether the award was made in a manner compatible with the arbitration agreement and the tribunal's jurisdiction thereunder.[606] Finding that it was not, the judgment certainly appears to be inconsistent with the predominant principles of international arbitration. If, without regard to the dilatory and wrongful nature of an arbitrator's resignation, and after arbitral proceedings have resulted in a draft award, those proceedings can be stultified by that resignation, that would seem to considerably undermine the effectiveness of the arbitral process in a way that the parties to an arbitration agreement cannot reasonably have intended.

(B) THE MALECKI CASE

The *Malecki* v. *Long* arbitration[607] adds an interesting dimension to the question of the authority of a truncated tribunal: the notice to be given to parties in the event of an arbitrator's withdrawal.

The contract underlying the dispute concerned the division of property between the Longs (US nationals and residents) and the Maleckis (French nationals and at the time US residents) following

---

[603] Ibid.   [604] Ibid.   [605] Ibid.   [606] Ibid.
[607] *Louis, Philippe and Rachel Malecki* v. *Adena Inc. and David, Donna and Carolyn Long*, Paris Court of Appeal, April 21, 2005, 3 *Revue de l'Arbitrage* (2006), p. 673.

the divorce of Philippe Malecki and Carolyn Long.[608] The contract contained an arbitration clause and on September 28, 1999 the Maleckis filed a request for arbitration against the Longs with the American Arbitration Association (AAA) in Philadelphia, under its then existing Commercial Rules of Arbitration.[609] Each party appointed an arbitrator and the AAA appointed the chairman of the tribunal.[610] In January 2001, the Maleckis dismissed their counsel and notified the AAA that they were moving to France.[611] The AAA subsequently notified the parties that the arbitration would from that point forward be administered by the ICDR.[612]

The Maleckis then informed the tribunal in February and March 2001 that they would not attend the hearings and would not take part in the proceedings.[613] Then, prior to the first hearing in April 2001, the arbitrator appointed by the Maleckis wrote to their former counsel, the other members of the tribunal, and the AAA to notify them that he would not be participating in the arbitration.[614] The Maleckis were not notified of the arbitrator's letter or his withdrawal.[615] The now truncated tribunal rendered an award against the Maleckis in June 2001, noting in a footnote that the arbitrator appointed by the Maleckis did not participate in the proceedings.[616] The Maleckis then contested the award before the Paris Court of Appeal.[617]

In considering the award, the Paris Court of Appeal first concluded that the arbitration had been conducted in accordance with the International Rules of the ICDR.[618] However, the Paris Court of Appeal then noted that

the possibility offered under the International Rules to continue the procedure with only two arbitrators in certain circumstances, can in no event amount to an anticipated and automatic agreement of the parties in this respect, without the parties having been heard.[619]

Accordingly, seeing that the Maleckis were not notified of the party-appointed arbitrator's withdrawal and thus not given an opportunity to be heard on the issue, the Paris Court of Appeal concluded that the award had been "rendered in breach of collegiality by an irregularly constituted tribunal."[620] The Court additionally

---

[608] The basic facts are summarized in both the Paris Court of Appeal's decision and in Denis Bensaude, "Malecki v. Long: Truncated Tribunals and Waivers of Dutco Rights," 23 *Journal of International Arbitration* (2006), pp. 81, 82, fn. 7.
[609] Ibid., p. 82.   [610] Ibid.   [611] Ibid.   [612] Ibid.   [613] Ibid.
[614] Ibid., p. 83.   [615] Ibid.   [616] Ibid.   [617] Ibid.   [618] Ibid., p. 85.
[619] Ibid., p. 86.   [620] Ibid., pp. 85–86.

remarked that the failure of the Maleckis to participate in the proceedings was not sufficient justification for the failure of the tribunal to keep them informed of the tribunal's constitution.[621]

The *Malecki* case can thus be distinguished from those cases rejecting the authority of a truncated tribunal, as the Paris Court of Appeal refused to recognize the award only due to absence of notice to the Maleckis, not due to the truncated nature of the tribunal. Indeed, the Paris Court of Appeal clearly recognized "the power offered under the International Rules [of the ICDR] to continue the procedure with only two arbitrators in certain circumstances."[622] Those circumstances, however, were not satisfied by the facts of the *Malecki* case.

(c) SUPPLIER (US) V. STATE ENTERPRISE (BELARUS) (GERMANY NO. 118/E20)

A case with a more uncertain view on the power of a truncated tribunal to proceed and render an award is a case that ended up before the German Federal Supreme Court.

In an arbitration conducted under the auspices of the International Arbitration Court at the Belarusian Chamber of Commerce and Industry between an American supplier and a Belarusian state enterprise, the resulting award in favor of the American supplier was signed by the president of the tribunal and the arbitrator appointed by the American party.[623] In the award of July 12, 2005, in place of the signature of the third arbitrator, appointed by the Belarusian respondent, the president inserted a statement to the effect that the concerned arbitrator was on vacation.[624]

In reviewing the award on the Belarusian respondent's application for annulment, the Supreme Commercial Court of Belarus held that the tribunal violated the IAC Rules, which provided that the same tribunal that hears the case must render the award.[625] The Court found that the third arbitrator did not sign the award because he did not participate in the decision-making and that he disagreed with the reasoning of the others. In the Court's view, under such circumstances the president should have requested the appointment of a substitute arbitrator.[626] The Court accordingly annulled the award.[627]

---

[621] Ibid., p. 86.   [622] Ibid.

[623] *Germany No. 118 / E20, Supplier (US)* v. *State Enterprise (Belarus)*, Bundesgerichtshof [Federal Supreme Court], III ZB 14/07, May 21, 2007, XXXIV *Yearbook Commercial Arbitration* (2009), p. 504.

[624] Ibid.   [625] Ibid., pp. 504–505.   [626] Ibid., p. 505.   [627] Ibid.

Similarly, in the German enforcement proceedings, the Dresden Court of Appeal denied enforcement based on Article V(1)(e) of the New York Convention, which provides for the refusal of recognition or enforcement of an arbitral award where it has been set aside at the seat.[628] On appeal, the German Supreme Court further concluded that since the award was rendered by only two of the three arbitrators in violation of the IAC Rules, recognition should be refused under Article V(1)(d) of the New York Convention, finding an irregularity in the arbitral procedure.[629]

Thus it cannot be said that either the Belarusian or German courts pronounced clearly on the authority of a truncated tribunal. The holdings in the case were instead limited to the circumstances of the case, where it appears that the remaining arbitrators failed to follow the procedure provided for in the relevant arbitration rules, although the precise circumstances in which they failed to do so are unclear. The German Federal Supreme Court also noted that aspects of the US claimant's new argument on appeal, regarding the previously missing arbitrator's supposed presence during deliberations, were "generic and unsubstantiated."[630] The annulment of the award in Belarus and the failure of the American supplier to have the award recognized in Germany accordingly provide little insight into the potential authority of a truncated tribunal to render an award in the absence of such procedural irregularities – but they do provide a cautionary reminder that the authority of a truncated tribunal, and particularly the circumstances in which a tribunal may proceed on a truncated basis, can remain controversial.

(D) *PUMA CASE*

In a 2017 case, the Supreme Court of Spain considered when a tribunal might be considered "truncated," thus invoking the principles established regarding the authority of such tribunals to render awards.

The Supreme Court's decision arose out of an arbitration commenced by Puma AG RD Sport (Puma) against Estudio 2000 in Madrid.[631] Puma appointed Mr. Calixto as arbitrator, Estudio

---

[628] Ibid.   [629] Ibid.   [630] Ibid.
[631] (1) *Mr. Marcos*, (2) *Mr. Obdulio* v. *Puma S.E.*, Supreme Court of Spain, First Civil Law Chamber, February 15, 2017, XLII *Yearbook Commercial Arbitration* (2017), p. 784.

2000 appointed Mr. Marcos and the two arbitrators appointed Mr. Obdulio as president.[632] The tribunal held several meetings to discuss the award but the tribunal diverged in its views as to the amount of indemnification to be awarded to Estudio 2000.[633] Two of the arbitrators, Mr. Obdulio and Mr. Marcos, had reached an agreement on the amount of indemnification by May 28, 2010, and, as of May 31, 2010, Mr. Calixto was not in agreement and asked for a reduction in the amount agreed by his co-arbitrators.[634] On June 2, 2010, Mr. Obdulio and Mr. Marcos met, deliberated, and issued a final award to the parties (and to Mr. Calixto) that granted Estudio 2000 the amount of indemnification upon which they had agreed.[635] They did not inform Mr. Calixto of this meeting, and they knew that he was traveling outside of Madrid on that date and was therefore unavailable.[636] The final award noted that it was signed by the majority only, as is permitted under the Spanish Arbitration Law.[637]

The award was subsequently annulled by the Court of Appeal of Madrid, which found that there had been a violation of the principle of arbitral collegiality in the rendition of the award, due to the two arbitrators' exclusion of the third.[638] Puma then filed a civil responsibility claim against the two arbitrators for the fees they received as arbitrators, which was granted by the lower court and affirmed on appeal by the Court of Appeal of Madrid.[639]

The two arbitrators then appealed to the Supreme Court of Spain, arguing that they were protected by the Spanish Arbitration Law, which, as noted, allows awards to be rendered by a majority.[640]

Looking at these peculiar facts, the Supreme Court of Spain concluded that this was not a case of a truncated tribunal rendering an award, which the Court defined as arising when an arbitrator strategically resigns as part of an agreement with the appointing party.[641] As that was not the case in the relevant arbitration, the Court upheld the decision of the Court of Appeal of Madrid that the third arbitrator was unduly excluded from the deliberations of the award.[642]

The facts of the case demonstrate how the principle of the authority of a truncated tribunal to proceed and render an award must still be seen in the light of, and does not eradicate, the basic principle of tribunal collegiality. The Supreme Court of Spain had

---

[632] Ibid. [633] Ibid. [634] Ibid. [635] Ibid. [636] Ibid. [637] Ibid.
[638] Ibid. [639] Ibid. [640] Ibid. [641] Ibid., p. 785. [642] Ibid., para. 4.

some justification in preventing two members of a tribunal, knowing that a truncated tribunal could have the authority to render an award, from succeeding with an attempt to artificially truncate itself by excluding one of its members from the deliberations.

(e) CASES OF REPLACEMENT OF ARBITRATORS

There are of course a number of cases in which arbitrators have died, become incapacitated, resigned or for various reasons become unable to act, where they have been routinely replaced. The issue of the authority of the arbitral tribunal to act pending replacement did not arise; given the particular circumstances, all concerned were content to await replacement in accordance with the governing provisions.[643] Such cases equally shed no light on the question of the authority of a truncated international arbitral tribunal to proceed and to render a valid award.

(f) MUNICIPAL AUTHORITIES

It is not proposed to set out separately the relevant municipal authorities, which have been adverted to in passages reproduced from proceedings of the Iran-United States Claims Tribunal and elsewhere in this chapter. It may be noted that a substantial number of municipal authorities in support of the conclusion that an arbitral tribunal from which an arbitrator withdraws may proceed and render a valid decision in matters of public concern were cited in the pleadings which have been referred to in the *Peace Treaties* case.[644]

F. Conclusions

The conclusions from the first edition were summarized as follows:

– Withdrawal of an arbitrator from an international arbitral tribunal which is not authorized or approved by the tribunal is a wrong

---

[643] The *Arbitration between Saudi Arabia and the Arabian American Oil Company, supra* note 223, p. 117, provides one such illustration. Another is *Holiday Inns/ Occidental Petroleum* v. *Government of Morocco*, ICSID *Eleventh Annual Report*, 1976/1977, p. 4.

[644] *Interpretation of Peace Treaties with Bulgaria, Hungary and Romania, Pleadings, Oral Arguments, Documents*, pp. 192, 233, 357, 360.

under customary international law and the general principles of law recognized and applied in the practice of international arbitration. It generally will constitute a violation of the treaty or contract constituting the tribunal, if not in terms then because the intention of the parties normally cannot be deemed to have authorized such withdrawal.[645]

– Such a wrongful withdrawal may not, as a matter of international legal principle, debar an international arbitral tribunal from proceeding and rendering a final award.[646]

– While the precedents are not uniform, and the commentators are divided, the weight of international authority, to which the International Court of Justice has given its support, clearly favors the authority of an international arbitral tribunal from which an arbitrator has withdrawn to proceed and to render a valid award.[647]

To this we add:

– A modern approach has developed over the past thirty years, along with the continued shift away from diplomatic arbitration and toward judicial arbitration.

– This modern approach provides for a two-step procedure to be followed in the event of a withdrawing or obstructionist arbitrator. First, and when feasible, a replacement arbitrator shall be appointed pursuant to the procedure provided for the original appointment or otherwise provided for in the applicable rules. This first step, it is hoped, should resolve the majority of cases. However, as a second possible step, if it is not possible or practical to replace the withdrawing arbitrator, a truncated tribunal has the authority to proceed and render a final award.

We further note that, in addition to revealing a modern approach, case law since the first edition indicates that the use of withdrawal as a tactic to frustrate arbitral proceedings has somewhat declined. But this positive development must be viewed next to the reality that numerous other obstructionist tactics have arisen in international arbitration over the past thirty years. Even if international arbitral proceedings today may be less likely to be frustrated by a withdrawing arbitrator, they may just as well be frustrated by, among other

---

[645] See also Schwebel, *supra* note 483, p. 188.   [646] Ibid.   [647] Ibid.

tactics, repeat interlocutory challenges to arbitrators,[648] extensive delays by arbitrators,[649] or spurious but time-consuming procedural motions.[650] This indicates that recalcitrant respondents will continue to search for ways by which to delay unwanted arbitral proceedings.

The theory and practice identified in the first edition on the authority of a truncated tribunal to proceed and render an award and the conclusions listed above therefore continue to be relevant to informing how contemporary arbitral tribunals face both old and increasingly innovative impediments to the timely rendering of a final award.

---

[648] See, e.g., *ConocoPhillips Petrozuata B.V.* v. *Bolivarian Republic of Venezuela*, ICSID Case No. ARB/07/30, Interim Decision, January 17, 2017, para. 15. See also *Redfern and Hunter on International Arbitration, supra* note 106, p. 259; Born, *supra* note 21, pp. 1932–1933.

[649] See, e.g., *ConocoPhillips Petrozuata B.V.* v. *Bolivarian Republic of Venezuela*, ICSID Case No. ARB/07/30, Decision on Jurisdiction and the Merits, Dissenting Opinion of Georges Abi-Saab, February 19, 2015 (published a year and a half after's the majority's September 2013 decision).

[650] Revisions to arbitral rules have accordingly sought to address the prevalence of such tactics, with the 2017 ICC Rules for instance expressly allowing cost awards to take into account a party's conduct during the arbitration. 2017 ICC Rules, Article 38(6). See also *Agent* v. *Principal and Managing Director of principal*, Final Award, ICC Case No. 7453, XXII *Yearbook Commercial Arbitration* (1994), p. 124, holding that one of the defendants in the arbitration "must bear and pay the entire costs of this arbitration . . . and also the entire legal costs of claimant and out of pocket expenses of counsel to claimant" due to its obstructive and dilatory conduct during the arbitration. See also *Proposals for Amendment of the ICSID Rules*, ICSID Secretariat, August 2019, Rule 51.

Index

333

Index

Index

Index

Index

Index